FRANCHISING &

LICENSING

FRANCHISING &

LICENSING

TWO POWERFUL WAYS TO
GROW YOUR BUSINESS IN ANY ECONOMY

FOURTH EDITION

ANDREW J. SHERMAN

American Management Association

New York • Atlanta • Brussels • Chicago • Mexico City • San Francisco
Shanghai • Tokyo • Toronto • Washington, D. C.

This publication is designed to provide accurate and authoritative information in regard to the subject matter covered. It is sold with the understanding that the publisher is not engaged in rendering legal, accounting, or other professional service. If legal advice or other expert assistance is required, the services of a competent professional person should be sought.

Library of Congress Cataloging-in-Publication Data

Sherman, Andrew J.
    Franchising & licensing : two powerful ways to grow your business in any economy / Andrew J. Sherman.—4th ed.
        p.   cm.
    Includes bibliographical references and index.
    ISBN-13: 978-0-8144-1556-6
    ISBN-10: 0-8144-1556-3
    1. Franchises (Retail trade)—United States.   2. License agreements—United States.
I. Title.   II. Title: Franchising and licensing.

    HF5429.235.U5S54   2011
    658.8'708—dc22

                                                                    2010021379

About AMA
American Management Association (www.amanet.org) is a world leader in talent development, advancing the skills of individuals to drive business success. Our mission is to support the goals of individuals and organizations through a complete range of products and services, including classroom and virtual seminars, webcasts, webinars, podcasts, conferences, corporate and government solutions, business books and research. AMA's approach to improving performance combines experiential learning—learning through doing—with opportunities for ongoing professional growth at every step of one's career journey.

Printing number
10   9   8   7   6   5

This book is dedicated with love
to my first franchisee,
Matthew Harris Sherman,
and to my wife, Judy Joffe Sherman
and daughter, Jennifer Rachel Sherman.

I thank them for their
never-ending support and patience.

CONTENTS

PREFACE TO THE FOURTH EDITION

It is hard to believe that 20 years have passed since the publication of the first edition of *Franchising & Licensing* in 1991. The impact of technology and globalization has had a permanent effect on the dynamics of the franchise relationship. When the manuscript was being written for the first edition in the late 1980s, I could not have envisioned the many changes in today's franchise relationships or the diversity in the number of industries and companies that would pursue franchising as their primary growth strategy. It has been my honor to work with companies launching franchising programs in dozens of different industries and at various stages of growth—ranging from start-up to Fortune 500 companies—all over the globe.

A wide variety of recent events and trends are affecting the growth and development of domestic and international franchising:

❒ From the franchisor's perspective, the weak capital markets have limited access to the resources needed for more organic or traditional growth strategies, thereby making franchising the strategy of choice to accomplish such objectives and brand building, provided that the prospective franchisee can access the capital *they* need to develop the territory.

❒ From the franchisee's perspective, more families in a recessionary environment (and with job losses averaging 300,000 per month) want to have greater control over their own destiny and are pursuing many different types of franchised opportunities as a way of owning their own businesses.

❒ The very weak residential real estate market has fueled the growth of many different types of home improvement and home services franchisors, as Americans invest less resources into the pursuit of making their homes more comfortable.

❒ Trust building, proper governance, and leadership have become hyper-critical in this post-Madoff era. Franchisors must have integrity when interacting with franchisees, or their systems will fail.

❐ The ease of access to technology, as well as a desire to avoid the hassles (and fears) of going to a shopping mall, have fueled an increase in online sales of products and services. Franchising systems are forced to offer sites that facilitate e-commerce and that create a balance for sharing these new sales and customers with the franchisees in their systems.

❐ The improvements in Internet technology and smartphones, as well as travel/logistics concerns, have changed how franchisees are recruited, meetings are held, and data is gathered.

❐ The impact of the Internet on franchise sales (as well as related legal implications) are discussed in new sections in Chapters 6 and 10 of this fourth edition.

Yet, as volatile as the global and domestic economies have been since the publication of the third edition, franchising has remained relatively stable. Each year, hundreds of new companies launch new franchising programs, and tens of thousands of families invest in franchised businesses as the first step in their journey toward achieving the American dream. Even with all of the new technology and all of the new developments, franchising is, and always will be, about mutual commitment, trust, fairness, and communication in a uniquely interdependent relationship that has helped fuel our economy for nearly 100 years.

History has shown that the leveraging of intellectual capital can be an effective and capital-efficient way to perpetrate business growth whether economic conditions are weak or strong. Companies of all sizes and in many different industries are realizing that their intangible assets can be a source of new revenue and profit centers and that they can thereby bring greater control, predictability, and loyalty to their distribution channels. The critical importance of adopting this more strategic perspective to the management and leveraging of intellectual capital is discussed in greater detail in the first chapter.

Andrew J. Sherman
Bethesda, Maryland
Spring 2010

ACKNOWLEDGMENTS

The strategies, concepts, issues, and best practices discussed in this book are the result of over 30 years' experience in franchising, from both a legal and business perspective. Thanking all the people with whom I have had the pleasure of working along the way would be impossible. For their support and loyalty, my many domestic and international clients, as well as my esteemed colleagues at Jones Day, including Steve Brogan, Mary Ellen Powers, Andrew Kramer, John Majoras, Michael Shumaker, Greg Shumaker, and Noel Francisco, all deserve special mention.

Certain individuals deserve special mention for their time, hard work, support, and updates to this fourth edition. I wish to thank my colleagues Alan Schaeffer for his input and additions to Chapters 5 and 6, Ilene Tannen for her assistance on Chapter 8, Jeff Jones and Todd Kennard for their updates to Chapter 9. and law student Kevin Bale for his research assistance on Chapter 21. We have a dynamic and talented group of global lawyers at Jones Day focused in the areas of franchising and licensing, and I am honored to be part of the team. I owe special thanks to my assistant, Jo Lynch, who often serves as my right arm, for her organizational skills and patience.

Also, certain well-recognized individuals in the franchising and emerging business communities have been friends and mentors over the years. For their support, advice, and general friendship, I want to especially thank Bob Gappa at Management 2000, Jerry Darnell, John Rogers at Davis & Company, John Reynolds at the International Franchise Association, Tom Portesy and Richard Macaluso at MFV Expos, Verne Harnish of Gazelles, Amit Pamecha at FranConnect, John May at New Vantage Partners, and Bill Keating at the Dickinson School of Law.

Robert Nirkind of AMACOM Books was there, as always, to provide moral and logistical support in pulling this project together. He is an excellent orchestrator and sounding board. I also want to thank Mike Sivilli and Fred Dahl at AMACOM for their skillful editing.

Last, but certainly not least, I am grateful to my wife Judy, to my son Matthew, and to my daughter Jennifer, all of whom once again sacrificed time with me so that I could complete this manuscript. I couldn't ask for a more supportive family.

PART ONE

THE FOUNDATION FOR FRANCHISING

CHAPTER 1

Leveraging Intellectual Capital to Create Growth Opportunities and Profitable New Income Streams

ntellectual capital consists of human capital, intellectual property (IP), and relationship capital, and these are the key assets for driving growth and maximizing shareholder value in all types of economic conditions.

The biggest challenge that many companies face is how to keep growing in a slowing economy. The primary but not exclusive focus of this book is on two key strategies, franchising and licensing, as methods for leveraging the intellectual capital of a company into new revenue streams, market opportunities, and profit centers. For many years, companies of all sizes and in many different industries did not understand how to harvest their intangible assets; traditionally, they viewed these assets relatively passively as a way to defend market share instead of proactively as a source of new opportunity.

The strategic views toward the use of intellectual capital has evolved in the boardroom over the past three decades, as described in Figure 1-1.

CEOs and business leaders of companies of all sizes are often guilty of committing a very serious strategic sin: the failure to properly protect, mine, and harvest the company's intellectual property. This is especially true at many technology-driven and consumer-driven companies. From 1997 to 2001, billions of dollars went into the venture capital and private equity markets, and the primary use of these proceeds by entrepreneurs was the creation of intellectual property and other intangible assets. Eight years later, however, emerging growth and middle market companies, in many cases, have failed to leverage this intellectual capital into new revenue streams, profit centers, and market opportunities because of a singular focus on the company's core business or a lack of strategic vision or expertise to uncover or identify other applications or distribution channels.

Entrepreneurs and growing company leaders may also lack the proper tools to understand and analyze the value of the company's intellectual assets. In a recent study by Professor Baruch Lev at NYU, only 15 percent of the "true value" of the S&P 500 was found to be captured in their financial statements. Given the resources of an S&P 500 company, it is likely that smaller companies have their intangible assets even more deeply embedded

Figure 1-1. Strategic views on intellectual capital: past, present, future.

Traditional View	*Reactive and passive approach:* IP assets enhance the company's competitive advantage and strengthen its ability to defend its competitive position in the marketplace (IP as a barrier to entry and as a shield to protect market share)
Current View	*Proactive/systemic approach:* IP assets should not be used merely for defensive purposes but should also be viewed as an important asset and profit center that is capable of being monetized and generating value through licensing fees and other channels and strategies, *provided* that time and resources are devoted to uncovering these opportunities, especially dormant IP assets, which do not currently serve at the heart of the company's current core competencies or focus.
Future View	*Core focus/strategic approach:* IP assets are *the* premiere drivers of business strategy within the company and encompass human capital, structural/organizational capital, and customer/relationship capital. Intellectual asset management systems need to be built and continuously improved to ensure that IP assets are used to protect and defend the company's strategic position in domestic and global markets and to create new markets, distribution channels, and revenue streams in a capital-efficient manner to maximize shareholder value.

and that the number for privately held companies may be as low as 5 percent. Imagine the consequences and opportunity cost if you were preparing to eventually sell your business (or even structure an investment with a venture capitalist or strategic investor) and 95 percent of your inherent value gets left on the table! This gap in capturing and reflecting this hidden value points out the critical need for a legal and strategic analysis of an emerging company's intellectual property portfolio.

Intellectual asset management (IAM) is a system intended to create, organize, prioritize, and extract value from a set of intellectual property assets. The intellectual capital and technical know-how of a growing company are among its most valuable assets, provide its greatest competitive advantages, and are the principal drivers of shareholder value. Yet rarely do companies have adequate personnel, resources, and systems in place to properly manage and leverage these assets. *IAM helps growing companies ensure that strategic growth opportunities are recognized, captured, and harvested into new revenue streams and markets.*

As demonstrated in Figure 1-2, the harvesting of intellectual capital is a *strategic process* that must begin with an inventory taken by the company's management team and by qualified outside advisors in order to get a comprehensive handle on the scope, breadth, and depth of the company's intangible assets. In these times of shareholder distrust of and disappointment in the management teams and boards of publicly held companies, corporate leaders owe it to shareholders to uncover hidden value and to make the most of the assets that have been developed with corporate resources. The leadership of the company will never know whether it has a "Picasso in the basement" unless it *both* (1) makes the time to take inventory of what's hiding in the basement and (2) has a qualified intellectual capital inventory team that is capable of distinguishing between a Picasso and a child's art project. Once these assets are properly identified, an intellectual asset management system

Figure 1-2. Harvesting IP.

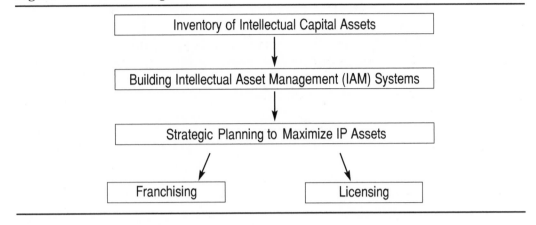

should be developed to ensure open communication and strategic management of these assets. At that point, the company is ready to engage in the strategic planning process to determine how to convert these assets into profitable revenue streams and new opportunities, thereby enhancing and protecting shareholder value.

A review of your current IAM practices includes an analysis of the following:

❑ What IAM systems, procedures, and teams are in place now?
❑ How and when were these systems developed?
❑ Who is responsible/accountable for managing these systems within the company?
❑ To what degree are adequate systems for internal and external communication and collaboration currently in place?
❑ What idea/technology harvesting filters are in place, as well as procedures for innovation decisional analysis (as to whether to move forward, prepare a budget, allocate resources, create a timetable, etc.)?
❑ Are the strategy and process for harvesting and leveraging intellectual assets reactive or proactive?
❑ What are the real or perceived internal hurdles (politics, red tape, budgeting processes, organizational structure) and/or external hurdles (market conditions, state of the art moving quickly, competitor's strategies, etc.) that stand in the way of improving IAM practices and procedures?
❑ What can be done to remove or lower those barriers?

The first step in developing an effective IAM system is to conduct an intellectual property audit. The IP audit is a multidisciplinary process to gather data and take inventory on all of the franchisor's intellectual property assets so that it can then be managed and leveraged properly and profitably. An IP audit can also include a competitive assessment of the strength and depth of the franchisor's inventory of intellectual assets relative to other franchisors and to competing nonfranchisors. This competitive assessment may be especially critical in anticipation of either a capital formation or merger/

acquisition transaction. It can also be a useful tool to determine where future research and development dollars or branding budgets should be directed, to the extent that the franchisor is losing competitive position to others or has noticeable holes or dangerous weaknesses in its IP portfolio. As the company matures, its inventory of intellectual assets should be getting stronger and deeper, not shallower, in order to protect its market position as well as to continue to deliver and maintain its value proposition in the management of its relationship with customers, suppliers, and channel partners.

A strategic planning process, coupled with IAM systems, will help you and your team uncover opportunities for growth. (See Figures 1-3 through 1-5.) Key questions include:

❏ What patents, systems, and technologies have noncompeting applications that could be licensed to third parties to create new revenue streams, joint ventures, or partnering opportunities, distribution channels, or profit centers?

❏ What brands lend themselves to extension licensing or co-branding opportunities?

❏ What distribution channels or partnering opportunities can be strengthened if the company has greater control of them or provides additional support and services to them?

❏ What types of different growth and expansion strategies are being used by the company's competitors? Why?

❏ Where are the strategic/operational gaps in the company's current licensing and alliance relationships?

Figure 1-3. Leveraging intellectual capital.

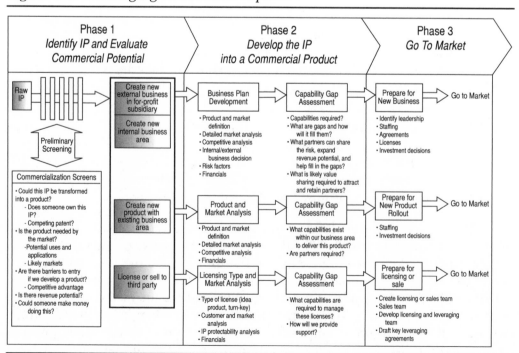

Figure 1-4. IP harvesting analytical process.

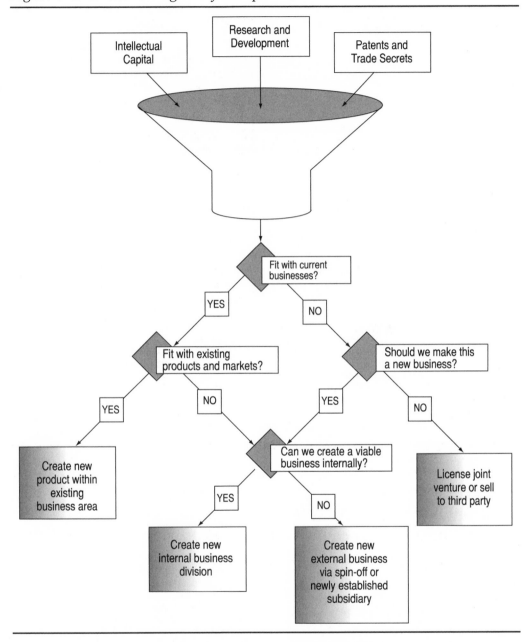

☐ As shown in Figure 1-6, the strategic planning process will help identify the different *types* of protectable intellectual property and the ways in which it can be leveraged into new opportunities.

The balance of this book is devoted to the various types of intellectual capital leveraging strategies, with a focus on business-format franchising in Chapters 2 through 17, licensing in Chapter 19, and joint ventures and strategic alliances in Chapter 20.

Figure 1-5. Phase 2 strategic options.

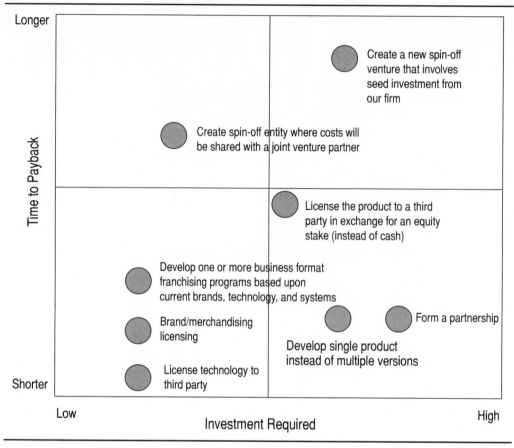

Figure 1-6. Strategic planning and IAM.

Protectable Types of Intellectual Property

- Patents
- Trademarks (including brands and slogans)
- Copyrights
- Trade dress
- Trade secrets
- Distribution channels
- Show-how and know-how
- Web site design and content
- Customer and strategic partner relationships
- Proprietary processes and systems
- Knowledge and technical workers

Possible New Opportunities and Revenue Sources

- New independent ventures
- Joint ventures
- Licensing
- Outright sale
- Co-branding
- Franchising
- Enter new domestic markets
- Develop new ancillary products
- Licenses
- Strategic partnerships,
- Cooperatives, consortiums
- Outsourcing
- International expansion
- Government contracts

PART TWO

BUILDING A FRANCHISING PROGRAM

CHAPTER 2

The Foundation of Franchising

ver the last seven decades, franchising has emerged as a leading IP-leveraging strategy for a variety of product and service companies at different stages of development. Recent International Franchise Association (IFA) Educational Foundation statistics demonstrate that retail sales from franchised outlets comprise over 50 percent of all retail sales in the United States, with total economic output (including gross sales) estimated at over $2.3 trillion and employing over 21 million people at over 900,000 establishments in 2008. In an era when unemployment is running in excess of 10 percent and underemployment is nearly 20 percent, franchised businesses provided jobs to 21 million Americans, nearly one out of every seven citizens in the private sector.

Notwithstanding these impressive figures, franchising as a method of marketing and distributing products and services is really appropriate only for certain kinds of companies. Despite the favorable media attention that franchising has received over the past few years as a method of business growth, it is not for everyone. A host of legal and business prerequisites must be satisfied before any company can seriously consider franchising as an alternative for rapid expansion.

Many companies prematurely select franchising as a growth alternative and then haphazardly assemble and launch the program with an approach toward franchise development that parallels the sale of used cars. Other companies are urged to franchise by unqualified consultants or advisors who may be more interested in professional fees than in the long-term success of the franchising program. And still others move too quickly in the development of their franchising program without devoting the time and resources needed for the development of an effective and viable business and economic model.[1] This oversight has caused financial distress and failure at both the franchisor and franchisee level and usually results in litigation. Current and future members of the franchising community have a duty to take a re-

---

1. The model should include a pro forma for both the franchisor and the typical operating franchisee to ensure fairness and economic viability for both parties to the relationship.

sponsible view toward the creation and development of their franchising programs and to embrace the notion that this is a *get-what-you-give,* relationship-driven business model and expansion industry.

Responsible franchising starts with an understanding of the strategic essence of the business structure. As Bob Gappa of M2000 has been preaching for many years, the franchise system has three critical components: the brand, the operating system, and the ongoing support provided by the franchisor to the franchisee.

❑ The brand creates the demand, allowing the franchisee to *obtain* customers. The brand includes the franchisor's trademarks and service marks, its trade dress and décor, and all the intangible factors that create customer loyalty and build brand equity.

❑ The operating system essentially delivers the promise, thereby allowing the franchisee to *maintain* customer relationships and build loyalty.

❑ The ongoing support and training provide the impetus for growth, providing the franchisee with the tools and tips to *expand* its customer base and build its market share. The responsibly built franchise system provides value to its franchisees by teaching them how to get and keep as many customers as possible, who consume as many products and services as possible and as often as possible. *Early-stage and emerging franchisors must embrace the notion that there is no greater calling than helping others get into business for themselves and supporting the transformation of their lives and the wealth of their families.*

In fact, most litigation in franchising revolves around the gap between the *actual* needs of the franchisees to remain competitive in the marketplace and the *reality* of what kind of support the franchisor is capable of providing. The seed of the disappointment is in the recruitment phase of the relationship, and it continues beyond the start-up, as the franchisee struggles to remain competitive *unless* the franchisor delivers on its promises and is committed to providing excellent initial and ongoing training and support. Franchisors can significantly reduce the risk of these disputes by emphasizing ethics and integrity as the strategic essence of the franchising program, by insisting on these standards, and by following a code of conduct that ensures the adoption of these norms at all levels of the organization.

Reasons for Franchising

A wide variety of reasons are cited by successful franchisors as to why franchising has been selected as a method of growth and distribution. Through franchising, they are able to:

❑ Obtain operating efficiencies and economies of scale.

❑ Increase market share and build brand equity.

❑ Use the power of franchising as a system to get and keep more and more customers—building customer loyalty.

❒ Achieve more rapid market penetration at a relatively low capital cost.

❒ Reach the targeted consumer more effectively through cooperative advertising and promotion.

❒ Sell products and services through a dedicated distributor network.

❒ Replace the need for internal personnel with motivated owner/operators.

❒ Shift the primary responsibility for site selection, employee training and personnel management, local advertising, and other administrative concerns to the franchisee, licensee, or joint venture partner with the guidance or assistance of the franchisor.

In the typical franchising relationship (see the different types in Figure 2-1), the franchisee shares the risk of expanding the market share of the franchisor by committing its capital and resources to the development of satellite locations modeled after the proprietary business format of the franchisor. The risk of business failure of the franchisor is further reduced by the improvement in competitive position, reduced vulnerability to cyclical fluctuations, the existence of a captive market for the franchisor's proprietary products and services (due to the network of franchisees), and the reduced administrative and overhead costs enjoyed by a franchisor.

The Foundation of Franchising

Responsible franchising is the *only* way that franchisors and franchisees will be able to harmoniously coexist in the twenty-first century. Responsible franchising requires not only a secure foundation for launching the program, but also a genuine commitment to the success of franchisees throughout the life of the relationship, from recruitment and through growth, maturity, renewal or termination, and thereafter. Any company considering franchising as a method of growth and distribution or any individual considering franchising

Figure 2-1. Types of franchise relationships.

TYPES OF FRANCHISEES

Buy A Job (home-based; low investment)	Sales and distributorships (product-driven) & routes	Retail store (business format emphasis)	Management-driven (multiunit) large territory or region; managing or leading a team of managers on a permit or district basis as well as satellite carts, kiosks, etc.	Financial investment (large-scale projects, such as hotels)

Scale of resources needed, business acumen required, and other requirements.

Lowest ⟵――――――――――――――――――――――――――――⟶ Highest

as a method of getting into business must understand the key components of this foundation:

- A *proven prototype* location (or chain of stores) that will serve as a basis for the franchising program. The store or stores must have been tested, refined, and operated successfully and consistently profitable. The best practices and lessons learned from the prototype should be relevant and applicable to the target markets that domestic and overseas franchisees will operate. The success of the prototype should not be too dependent on the physical presence or specific expertise of the system's founders.

- A *strong management team* made up of internal officers and directors (as well as qualified consultants) who understand both the industry in which the company operates and the legal and business aspects of franchising as a method of expansion.

- *Sufficient capitalization* to launch and sustain the franchising program to ensure that capital is available for the franchisor to provide both initial as well as ongoing support and assistance to franchisees. (The lack of a well-written business plan and adequate capital structure are often the principal causes of the demise of many franchisors.)

- A *distinctive and protected trade identity* that includes federal and state registered trademarks, as well as a uniform trade appearance, signage, slogans, trade dress, and overall image.

- *Proprietary and proven methods of operation and management* that can be reduced to writing in a comprehensive operations manual, that are not too easily duplicated by competitors, that maintain their value to the franchisees over an extended period of time, and that are enforced through clearly drafted and objective quality control standards.

- *Comprehensive training programs for franchisees* that integrate all of the latest education and training technologies and that take place both at the company's headquarters and at the franchisee's proposed location at the outset of the relationship and on an ongoing basis.

- *Field support staff* who are skilled trainers and communicators and who are available to visit and periodically assist franchisees as well as to monitor quality control standards.

- *A set of comprehensive legal documents* that reflect the company's business strategies and operating policies. Offering documents must be prepared in accordance with applicable federal and state disclosure laws, and franchise agreements should strike a delicate balance between the rights and obligations of franchisor and franchisee.

- A *demonstrated market* demand for the products and services, as developed by the franchisor and distributed through the franchisees. The franchisor's products and services should meet minimum quality standards, not be subject to rapid shifts in consumer preferences (e.g., fads), and be proprietary in nature. Market research and analysis should be sensitive to trends in the economy and specific industry, the plans of direct and indirect competitors, and shifts in consumer preferences.

Also, understanding what business you are *really* in is important. For example, many of the major oil company franchisors *thought* that they were in the gasoline business until they realized that they were in the *convenience* business and quickly jumped into minimarts or fast-food and quick-service restaurants, either directly or via co-branding.

❑ *A set of carefully developed uniform site selection criteria and architectural standards* that can be readily and affordably secured in today's competitive real estate market.

❑ *A genuine understanding of the competition* (both direct and indirect) that the franchisor will face in marketing and selling franchises, as well as of the competition the franchisee will face when marketing its products and services.

❑ *Relationships* with suppliers, lenders, real estate developers, and related key resources as part of the operations manual and system.

❑ *A franchisee profile and screening system* to identify the minimum financial qualifications, business acumen, and understanding of the industry that a successful franchisee requires.

❑ *An effective system of reporting and record keeping* to maintain the performance of the franchisees and to ensure that royalties are reported accurately and paid promptly.

❑ *Research and development capabilities* for the introduction to consumers of new products and services on an ongoing basis through the franchised network.

❑ *A communication system* that facilitates a continuing and open dialogue with the franchisees and as a result reduces the chances for conflict and litigation within the franchise network.

❑ *National, regional, and local advertising, marketing, and public relations programs* designed to recruit prospective franchisees as well as consumers to the sites operated by franchisees.

Strategic Prerequisites to Launching a Franchising Program

Typically, the most important strategic prerequisites for the success of any business-format franchise system are the operation and management of a successful prototype and a business and financial model that makes sense for both franchisor and franchisee. This prototype location is where virtually all operating problems are to be resolved, recipes and new products tested, equipment and design decisions made, management and marketing techniques tested, a trade identity and goodwill established, and financial viability proven. The franchisor is in theory offering a tried and tested package to a franchisee, and the contents of that package must be clearly identified prior to sale. It is irresponsible and potentially unlawful to ask people to part with their life savings to invest in a system that is not ready for replication. The financial aspects of the business model should be analyzed and tested to ensure that both parties can do well and are fairly rewarded for their efforts.

The concept of a system or prescribed business format that is operated according to a uniform and consistent trade identity and image is at the heart of a successful franchising program. Therefore, a prospective franchisor must be able to reduce all aspects of running the business to be franchised into an operations and training manual for use by franchisees in the day-to-day operation of their business. These systems must be adequately and clearly communicated in the initial and ongoing training program. If a company offers services that are highly personalized or a product that is difficult to reproduce, then franchising may not be the most viable alternative for growth because of the difficulty in replicating these systems or products in the operator's manual or in the training program. Similarly, if all the kinks in the system have not yet been worked out, considering franchising is probably premature.

A number of other important business and strategic factors must be considered before franchising. First, franchising should not be viewed as a solution to undercapitalization or as a get-rich-quick scheme. Although franchising is less capital-intensive than the construction of additional company-owned sites, the initial start-up costs for legal, accounting, and consulting fees can be high. Second, franchisors must view franchising as the establishment of a series of long-term relationships because the ongoing success of the company as a franchisor will depend on the harmony of these relationships. A field support staff must be built to provide ongoing services to the existing franchisees, as well as to maintain quality control and uniformity throughout the system. New products and services must be developed so that franchisees can continue to compete with others in their local markets. Innovative sales and marketing strategies must be continually developed to attract new customers and to retain existing patrons of the franchised outlet. If the franchisor expects the franchisee to continue to make its royalty payment on gross sales each week, then an array of valuable support services must be provided on an ongoing basis to meet the franchisee's changing needs.

Franchising as a Strategic Relationship

Prospective and current franchisors must always bear in mind that, first and foremost, franchising is about *relationships*. The franchisor and franchisee knowingly and voluntarily enter into a long-term interdependent relationship, each relying on the other for its success. The exact nature of the franchisor-franchisee relationship has been compared to, among other things, the relationship between a parent and child, between a football coach and the team, between a conductor and the orchestra, and between a landlord and the tenants. The award of the franchise has been compared to the state that grants a driver's license: You may use and renew the privilege of driving but only subject to the rules of the road and the payment of ongoing fees. Like the relationship between franchisor and franchisee, you have the freedom to drive but not necessarily however or wherever you want. Much emphasis in recent years has been placed on avoiding the them-versus-us mentality and organizational culture, with a new focus on we-and-they. The focus has been on how can *we* work together for each other's benefit, where the enemy is not each other but rather the competition.

The financial output of these parties, working together, can be very powerful in a competitive marketplace. In fact, some say that franchising truly arrived when Warren Buffett, arguably one of the most financial savvy men on the planet, announced that his holding company, Berkshire Hathaway, Inc., agreed to acquire Dairy Queen with 5,800 franchised outlets worldwide. For years, Buffett had also been one of the largest shareholders of McDonald's and has hinted that other franchisor acquisitions may occur in the near future. Franchising continues to be an alternative growth and acquisition strategy for sophisticated international conglomerates. Visionary multibrand franchisors, such as Yum! Brands (owner of Pizza Hut, Taco Bell, KFC, A&W, and Long John Silver's), have broken new ground in multibranding and co-branding establishments around the globe. In 2005 through 2008, a host of general-purpose and specialized private equity funds began investing in and acquiring franchisors at a much more frantic pace (as discussed in Chapters 13 and 16). Even very large established companies began exploring the via-

---

Box 2-1. Reconnecting to your strategic roots.

During especially challenging economic times, some already established smaller and midsized franchisors have lost their way, questioning why they adopted franchising as a method for growth in the first place. As discussed in Chapter 12, periodic strategic planning meetings should be conducted to help the leadership of the company *reconnect to its core strategic roots* as a way of reminding itself as to why franchising is still a sensible approach and/or what may need to change. The core strategic roots may include such developments as these:

- The company has built respected brands and replicable systems and is now seeking to harvest its intellectual capital.
- The leadership of the company has always taken metaphysical pleasure in helping others get into business for themselves (teaching others to fish).
- The company has developed a mutually beneficial business mode that established a balance between the franchisor's upside and the franchisee's upside.
- The leadership of the company are masters in the art of handholding and support and of networking with its franchisees.
- Strong and sustainable demand trends for the products and services offered and developed by the franchisor could be successfully marketed in the franchisee's marketplace.

bility of domestic and overseas growth through franchising, such as Proc-
ter & Gamble's rollout of Mr. Clean® branded and franchised car washes and
Tide® branded and franchised laundromats. This trend is likely to continue
as companies of all sizes and in all industries search for strategies to drive
shareholder value without significant new investments of capital and other
resources.

Yes, franchising is about *relationships*. And like marriage, the most sa-
cred of relationships, if the parties are to stay committed to each other for
the long term, both parties must respect one another, stay loyal to one another, and each day search for ways to strengthen their bond.

A recent survey seems to indicate that this new focus on the strategic
aspects of the relationship seems to be working. Whereas over one-half of
our nation's marriages wind up in divorce, nearly 92 percent of the nation's
franchisees said they would get "married" to their franchisor again. In a 2008
survey conducted by the Gallup Organization and published by the International Franchise Association (IFA) Educational Foundation, more than 9 of
10 (92%) of the franchise owners surveyed said they were either very or
somewhat successful. Of those who had been in business 11 years or more,
96 percent indicated that they were very or somewhat successful. Gallup
surveyed 1,001 U.S. franchisees, nearly 8 out of 10 of whom own only one
franchised small business. Women accounted for 28 percent, and nearly half
of those who responded had a professional or managerial position before
purchasing a franchise, while nearly 2 of 10 were involved in either services/
labor or retail sales. Given the high satisfaction ratings, it is not surprising
that nearly two-thirds (65%) of franchise owners said they would purchase
the same franchise again if given the opportunity. Of those who wouldn't
buy the same franchise again, nearly half (43%) said they would consider
buying a different one. Nearly two-thirds (64%) said they would be less successful if they had tried to open the same type of business on their own. On
average, franchise owners reported annual gross incomes of over $100,000.
Nearly one of four (24%) earned over $125,000 or more in 2009.

The franchisor whose goals are to build a system and to achieve franchisee satisfaction ratings to meet or exceed these levels of satisfaction must
establish a culture of honesty, trust, passion, and genuine commitment to
long-term success. This process often begins during recruitment by carefully
screening and educating qualified candidates to ensure that the long-term
objectives are truly shared and that both parties' best interests are truly
aligned. This type of strategy will lead to mutually beneficial relationships
and significantly decrease the chances of litigation. Some degree of franchisee failure will be inevitable, and typically two factors are at play: one
that you can control and one that you often cannot. You *can* control the
quality of your systems, training, and support tools and the innovation of
your marketing to increase the chances of success. Other than through careful screening and continuous monitoring, you *cannot* usually control local
market conditions or changes in the franchisees' personal lives that may affect their performance.

Curbing the Failure Rate of Early-Stage Franchisors

One of the underlying premises of this book is that successful franchising requires a commitment to building a proper foundation and platform from which to launch and build the franchising program. My mission is to ensure that readers avoid the mistakes made by the hundreds—yes, hundreds—of failed franchisors over the years. Each year since the early 1990s, between 75 and 100 franchisors *went out of business*. This figure represents between 3 and 5 percent of all franchisors operating during those years. Figure 2-2 presents 40 common reasons why franchisors fail. *Read them carefully, and read them often* if you intend to mitigate the risk of your company's meeting the same fate in launching and building its franchising program.

Understanding the New Sophisticated Franchisee

One way to avoid failure is to genuinely understand the profile of today's prospective franchisee. Once certain basic premises are understood, the growing franchisor can make wide variety of marketing, planning, operational, and strategic decisions. As a general rule, franchisees in today's competitive markets are getting smarter, *not* dumber. The better educated, better capitalized franchisee is here to stay. As franchising has matured, prospective franchisees have more resources (seminars, media articles, trade shows, International Franchise Association programs, etc.) than ever before to turn to for information and due diligence. These new, sophisticated franchisees are very different from their mom-and-pop predecessors of the 1970s and 1980s, and they may be displaced executives with advanced business degrees, Gen Y candidates from wealthy families and top universities, back-to-work moms with impressive career accomplishments, and even gray Americans coming out of retirement whose health far exceeds their current wealth.

These prospects are better trained to ask all the right questions and to hire the right advisors in the investigation and franchise agreement negotiation process. These new franchisees are also better heeled and more likely to organize themselves into associations and take action if they are not receiving the required levels of support and assistance. They are also more likely to suggest valuable improvements to the system, which the franchisor should carefully consider and take seriously. As discussed in Chapter 10, franchisors that fail to mold their sales and support systems around currently available technologies, social networking tools, and the expectations of these new age franchisees and that continue to conduct business the old-fashioned way are headed down the road toward disaster and litigation.

A Commitment to Being (and Staying) Creative and Competitive

Today's franchisor must have an initial and ongoing commitment to being creative and competitive. Market conditions and technology that affect

Figure 2-2. Forty common reasons for franchisor failure.

- Lack of leadership by the franchisor
- Choice of the wrong professional advisory team
- Failure to provide adequate support or controls
- Lack of franchise communications systems
- Complex and inadequate operations manuals
- Inability to compete against larger franchisors
- Disregard for franchise registration and disclosure laws
- Not joining the International Franchise Association (IFA)
- Franchise system failure to reflect the mission, core values, and vision of the company
- Breakaway franchisees
- Unworkable economic relationship with franchisees
- Royalty underpayments/nonpayments by franchisees
- Lack of effective financial controls
- Unprotected trademarks
- Inadequate training program
- Decentralized advertising
- Choice of the wrong subfranchisors or areas developed
- Lack of an effective public relations strategy
- Inadequate relationships with key vendors
- Premature termination of franchisees on high turnover rates

- Difficulty attracting qualified franchisees
- Lack of proper disclosure documents
- An unproven and unprofitable prototype
- Premature launch into international markets
- Inadequate site selection criteria
- Lack of proper screening system for prospective franchisees
- Lack of effective business and strategic planning
- Entering oversaturated markets
- Failure to develop and enforce recruitment selection and criteria
- A capital structure that creates unreasonable pressure to sell franchises
- Lack of effective compliance systems
- Operational systems that can be easily duplicated
- Lack of experienced management
- Excessive litigation with franchisees
- Lack of ongoing research and development
- Unbridled geographic expansion
- Unprofitable and unhappy franchisees
- Unwillingness to enforce franchise agreement
- Improper earnings claims
- Lack of market research

franchising are changing constantly, and today's franchisee expects you to change at the same pace. For example, the ability to adopt your franchising system to allow for growth and market penetration into alternative and nontraditional venues is critical. The more creative and aggressive franchisors in the retail and hospitality industries are always searching for new locations with captive markets, such as airports, hotels, hospitals, highway roadside travel plazas, universities, sports arenas, or military bases. In such locations, trends toward outsourcing, the demand for branded products and services, and the desire to enhance the captive customer's experience have all opened up new doors and opportunities for franchising. In other cases, franchisors have pursued co-branding strategies to penetrate these new markets, again taking advantage of the trend toward convenience stores, grocery store chains, and gas stations all wanting to provide their patrons with an enhanced customer experience and to offer more comprehensive and integrated solutions to their consuming needs. And, again, the trend toward branding and the ability to share costs, positioning for differentiation, and the penetration of new market segments at a relative low cost have opened up many doors for the creative and aggressive franchisor who is committed to capturing more market share and serving more and more customers. (See Figure 2-3.)

Figure 2-3. Franchising trends and survival practices.

- Understanding the profile/needs of today's prospective franchisee

- Adjusting multiunit development strategies and schedules based on the reality of capital market access

- Engaging the flow of current consumer trends (e.g., are you a retail coffee store or selling coffee makers?) (People do more for themselves in recessionary times.)

- Redefining franchise recruitment and selection system and criteria

- Updating operations manuals and training programs

- Retraining field support teams in times of crisis

- Embracing technology for franchisee training and support (e.g., the death of the superconference)

- Alternative formats and sites (miniunits, express stores, carts, kiosks, satellites, co-branded units/ shared costs, etc.)

- Pricing and company/discounting model

- Hosting educational events and seminars (e.g., pre- and after-market and after-purchase support)

- Contests and frequent buyer points systems (e.g., affinity/loyalty/referral programs)

- Charitable fund-raisers and cause-related marketing

- Redefining product and services lines (e.g., the return of oatmeal)

- Enhancing the customer experience and personalized customer

- Fresh (and realistic) looks at global markets and trends

- Not fighting Web 2.0, engaging in social networking

- Mind games—that is, understanding *how* the brain buys and *how* consumer purchasing decisions are influenced (taking a deeper dive into understanding consumer behavior, as well as current and prospective franchisees as consumers)

- Sharing the risk and wealth (creating opportunities and efficiencies via federations, cooperatives, consortiums, associations, buying groups, etc.)

CHAPTER 3

Developing the Operations and
Training Programs

 t the heart of any successful franchising program is a prescribed *system* that ensures quality control and consistency throughout the franchise network. In most franchised businesses, the key elements of this system have been developed and fine-tuned in the operation of the franchisor's prototype location. The administration of the system requires effective and comprehensive *documentation* that must be provided to each franchise, both at the inception of the relationship and on an ongoing basis.

The documentation required to properly administer the franchise system includes:

❐ Statement of corporate philosophy, policies, and general rules of operations.

❐ Confidential operations and procedures manual.

❐ Local sales, marketing, and public relations kit.

❐ Site selection, architectural, interior design, signage, equipment, and inventory specifications.

❐ Guidelines for financial record keeping and reporting.

❐ Quality control and inspection reports.

❐ Special manuals for subfranchisors and area developers (where applicable).

Depending on the nature of the franchisor's business, many of these required items may be combined into a single confidential operations manual ("The Manual"). *The manual is the heart and soul of the franchising program, designed to be a resource for the franchisee when the franchisor cannot be there.* Despite the importance of the manual to the long-term success of the franchising program, many early-stage franchisors experience great difficulty in their attempts to prepare a proper manual. Yet a franchisor unable to properly document and communicate the critical steps of successfully operating the business (often in painstaking detail) is doomed to failure and really has no business getting into franchising in the first place. Franchisors should also take steps to use available computer and communications technologies to support the franchisees. For example, a growing number of franchisors are making their manuals available to franchisees on a password-encrypted intranet system and sending manual updates and system bulletins via e-mail. Sophisticated franchisees are demanding access to key operational data using this technology.

Preparing the Manual

Before sitting down to prepare your operations manual, keep in mind the following basic principles and guidelines:

1. The operations manual is a living, breathing document. Its contents will develop and change as your franchise system develops and changes, but it must remain stable at the core by being consistent with the franchisor's root mission, values, and vision. Be sure to preserve this level of flexibility in your franchise agreement.

2. Because your franchise system will inevitably evolve, prepare the manual in a format that is user-friendly and easy to update. For example, a series of three-ring notebooks with tabs for each major heading will make section or page replacements and additions quick and easy, although current best practices are to ensure that the manual can also be accessed on a secure intranet and updated electronically.

3. Assume nothing about the skills and experience of your typical franchise. The manual should be understandable by all types of learning personalities and skill sets. The text of the manual should be written at a high school reading level of comprehension and should anticipate that your franchisee is likely to be a complete novice in your industry. Franchisees *will* ignore dry, technical, and difficult-to-use manuals, causing a breakdown of quality control throughout the system. Be creative in your use of charts and diagrams that may be effective teaching tools and help avoid quality control breakdowns. The more user-friendly the manual is, the more it will actually be used.

4. No detail should remain unaddressed in the manual. Do not leave any operating discretion in the hands of the franchisee. Everything ranging from preopening procedures to the preparation of products to employee discipline must be included. Remember that comprehensiveness in the preparation of your manual provides a certain level of legal protection. Franchisees will not be able to claim, "They never told me how to _____ " in any subsequent litigation if all details are addressed.

5. The manual must be comprehensive (yet generic) enough to be followed by all franchisees that must run their businesses in a range of different markets and operating conditions. It should be prepared with a cus-

tomer-centric philosophy that ought to be applicable to all types of markets and that seeks to maximize the customer's experience. For example, if procedures are different lone stand-alone facilities (as opposed to kiosks in a regional mall), then these expected differences must be included and discussed. If advertising strategies differ in a rural area (as opposed to an inner-city location), then these differences must be anticipated and included in the manual.

6. The manual should anticipate and answer some of the questions most commonly asked by your franchisees. The more often they need to call you for assistance, the larger the administrative staff (and thus overhead) you need to maintain.

7. Remember that the manual is confidential and proprietary. As such, it should be treated as a trade secret under the law of intellectual property. Each franchisee and its employees must develop procedures for the protection and care of the manual. Access should be restricted to those on a need-to-know basis. Remember that the manual is *licensed, not sold* to a franchisee. It remains the property of the franchisor at all times. Special receipts should be developed for providing the manual to franchisees, as well as special forms for ordering replacement manuals.

8. The manual should at all times be consistent with the representations made in the franchise disclosure document (FDD), the disclosure document that must be delivered to prospective franchisees under federal and state law, as well as with the specific obligations contained in the franchise agreement. One easy way to find yourself in litigation with your franchisees is through inconsistencies between promises made in the FDD and actual obligations contained in the manual.

9. Avoid the temptation to turn your operations manual into a strategic business plan. Naturally, one *section* should address the franchisor's overall goals, mission, and values; however, the bulk of the manual should teach the franchisee on a step-by-step basis exactly how to perform key tasks, not just be a high-level strategy dissertation.

10. If the end goal of the manual is not to create delighted repeat customers who become passionate advocates for the brand, then tear it up and start over!

Suggested Outline for the Operations Manual of a Franchisor

An operations manual should encompass virtually every aspect of the business to be operated by the franchisee, from before the grand opening to the ongoing, day-to-day operating procedures and techniques. The manual should reinforce and, where applicable, cross-reference the obligations of the franchisee under the franchise agreement. The following outline has been designed for a typical franchisor in the services business.

Section A: Introduction

1. Foreword/notice of proprietary and confidential information
2. Acknowledgments and disclaimers

> ## Box 3-1. The relationship between the franchise offering circular and the manual.
>
> Many franchise lawyers tend to be rather vague in the preparation of franchise disclosure documents and franchise agreements, with common references to information contained in the manual. Their rationale is that amending a manual is far less complicated than amending a registered disclosure document or binding legal agreement. Although I generally advocate this practice, be careful. If the document is too vague, it will be challenged by the examiners in the registration states. Similarly, if the franchisor attempts to introduce a significant new program, operating procedure, or policy, it may trigger a so-called material change that *will* require amendment of the offering circular and perhaps even the franchise agreement itself. See Chapter 6 for a more detailed discussion of material change regulations.

3. The strategic essence of franchising 101
4. History of the franchisor
5. The franchisor's management team
6. The franchisor's obligations to the franchisees (an overview)
7. The franchisee's obligations to the franchisor and the system (an overview) and to protect and promote the franchisor's brands

Section B: Timetables for Opening the Franchised Business

This is a comprehensive timetable that the franchisee is to follow, beginning on the date that the franchise agreement is signed to the first date that business will be conducted and beyond.

Section C: Preopening Obligations and Procedures

1. Architectural, engineering, interior design, and site construction specifications
2. Minimum requirements for utilities, ventilation, etc.
3. Signage
   a. General information
   b. Description and explanation of signs to be used, interior and exterior
   c. Dimensions, specifications, etc.
4. Ordering and receiving fixtures, supplies, equipment, and inventory
5. Building the management team: managers, employees, and professional advisors
6. Application for licenses, permits, utilities, insurance, and bonding

7. Lease review and negotiations
8. Community involvement, trade groups, charities, chambers of commerce, etc. (pre- and postopening)
9. Recommended reference books on small business management and business
10. Territorial rights and responsibilities for growth and market penetration/ market share
11. National, regional and local advertising cooperatives and commitments

Section D: Office Policies

1. Image, decor, and theme
2. Quality standards of services
3. Pricing policies and fee structure
4. Service and courtesy to clients
5. Handling typical complaints and problems
6. Employee appearance (uniforms) and hygiene
7. Hours of operation

Section E: Office Operation and Maintenance

1. General housekeeping
2. Basic duties of personnel: office manager, sales staff, employees, etc.
3. Daily office: opening procedure, checklists
4. Daily office: closing procedure
5. Daily, weekly, and monthly reports
6. Self-inspection
7. Health and safety standards
8. Rest rooms
9. Pest control
10. Parking lot care and management (where applicable)
11. Alarms, locks, and keys
12. Emergency procedures

Section F: Equipment, Computer System, Inventory, and Supplies

1. Equipment, inventory, and supply list for a typical franchised office
   a. Specifications
   b. Approved vendors
   c. Repair and maintenance (equipment only)
2. Operation and management of the franchisor's proprietary database

3. Approved vendors for equipment, inventory, and supplies
4. Procedures and protocols for purchasing equipment and supplies

Section G: Administration

1. Personnel: job chart, position descriptions, hiring, qualifications and interviewing, application form; checking references, hours, shifts, timekeep-
   ing, vacancies, sick pay, time off, training, payroll taxes, law concerning
   employees, rules of conduct for employees, bulletin boards, and required notices
2. Record keeping and accounting
3. Collections and accounts receivable management
4. Managing accounts payable
5. Recruitment and training
6. Quality control
7. Group insurance policies
8. Other types of insurance (liability, worker's comp, health, life, business
   interruption, etc.)

Section H: Sales Promotion

1. Grand opening promotion plans (with timetable)
2. General ongoing promotion: newspaper, radio, direct mail, advertising
   cooperatives, community groups
3. Special promotions: franchisee referral programs, customer referral
   premiums, etc.
4. Public relations
5. Use of public figures
6. Use of coupons and direct-marketing mailers
7. Group discounts and promotions
8. Maintaining high visibility in the community
9. Understanding and analyzing local demographic statistics and trends

Section I: Protection of Trademarks and Trade Secrets

1. Trademark usage and guidelines
2. Examples of trademark misuse
3. Care and protection of trade secrets
4. Use and care of the operations manual
5. Key employee nondisclosure agreements
6. Protection of proprietary computer software and manuals

Section J: Payment and Preparation of Reports to the Franchisor

1. Guidelines and requirements for payments and reporting to the franchisor
2. Examples of forms

Section K: Guidelines for Transfer of a Franchise

1. Requirements
2. Sample forms and notices

Section L: Financing and Corporate Structure

1. Required corporate structure
2. The franchisor and franchisee as independent parties
3. Financing and loan applications
4. Financing alternatives

Section M: Miscellaneous

1. Participation in franchise advisory councils
2. Procedures for opening additional units

Drafting the Operations Manual: Selected Topics

The preparation of a comprehensive operations manual is truly an art. No level of attention or detail may be ignored. For example, most franchisors might (and for good reason) assume that a typical franchisee would know how to prepare a peanut butter and jelly sandwich. Yet many levels of details need to be addressed if the old-fashioned PB&J sandwich is a staple on the franchisor's menu, such as:

- ❐ What type of peanut butter? Chunky or smooth? Any particular brand?
- ❐ What flavor jelly? Grape? Apricot? Strawberry? May a customer choose?
- ❐ How many ounces of peanut butter per sandwich? Of jelly?
- ❐ What type of bread should be used? White? Wheat? Rye? May a customer choose?
- ❐ Is the bread served toasted or untoasted? Toasted using what type of oven? How long should the bread be in the oven?
- ❐ Is the sandwich served with condiments? Pickles? Potato chips? Coleslaw? How much of each condiment?
- ❐ How is the sandwich to be served? What type of packaging?
- ❐ What are the suggested price ranges for the sandwich? Does the condiment selected affect the price? What other products should be recommended to the customer when the sandwich is ordered?

Now multiply the answers to these questions by the number of issues that must be addressed for the franchisee to properly operate the specific franchised business, and you begin to get a feel for the level of detail required.

For example, the operations manual of a temporary services franchisor will emphasize hiring and recruiting techniques, sales training, interviewing and screening methods, development of referrals, fee structure, use and protection of the proprietary computer system and database, public relations, and administrative management.

The specific organization and content of each manual will vary from franchisor to franchisor and from industry to industry. Naturally, the manual of a fast-food operation may have a more detailed section on sewage, plumbing, food preparation, inventory controls, and lavatory facilities than that of a services-driven business.

Consider the level of detail contained in the sample provisions in Figure 3-1 dealing with garbage, refuse, and rodent control for a fast-food franchisor.

Another critical area for a fast-food operation, which must be addressed in a detailed manner, is the management of relationships with vendors. Franchisees in the fast-food business are likely to have daily contact with food suppliers and sundry vendors; weekly contact with uniform and linen supply companies, equipment maintenance and service companies, trash collectors, vending machine dealers, and pest control companies; and periodic contact with insurance agents, sign makers, security system installers, locksmiths, plumbers, and cash register equipment companies. The franchisor must develop quality-control criteria and specifications for the selection and approval of these vendors. Legal counsel should review the mechanics of the vendor approval process to consider all applicable principles of antitrust law. Qualification standards must be carefully developed, clearly communicated, and reasonably enforced throughout the franchise system. Nepotism, greed, and the failure to approve qualified suppliers are a cause of constant conflict between franchisors and franchisees, as discussed in Chapter 9.

Who Should Prepare the Manual?

Among early-stage franchisors, there is often an issue as to *who* should prepare the manual. Perhaps the best solution is for the franchisor's management team to work closely with an experienced consulting firm. This approach creates a balance between the substance of the manual being reflective of the franchisor's operational polices and the quality of the technical and explanatory writing that an experienced consultant can bring to the table. If the manual is written *only* by the franchisor's management team, then critical areas are likely to be omitted or, without the technical skills needed to write such a document, may not properly convey useful information at a level that all users of the manual can grasp. On the other hand, if the manual is prepared only by the consultant, without proper input from the franchisor, then the end product is likely to be generic and not truly reflective of the operational success factors that drive the franchisor's system.

Figure 3-1. Sample operations manual provisions for garbage and refuse.

Containers

(1) Garbage and refuse shall be kept in durable, easily cleanable, insect-proof and rodent-proof containers that do not leak and do not absorb liquids. Plastic bags and wet-strength paper bags may be used to line these containers, and they may be used for storage inside the food service establishment.

(2) Containers used in food preparation and utensil washing areas shall be kept covered after they are filled.

(3) Containers stored outside the establishment, and dumpsters, compactors, and compactor systems, shall be easily cleanable; provided with tight-fitting lids, doors, or covers; and kept covered when not in actual use. In containers designed with drains, drain plugs shall be in place at all times, except during cleaning.

(4) There shall be a sufficient number of containers to hold all the garbage and refuse that accumulates.

(5) Soiled containers shall be cleaned at a frequency to prevent insect and rodent attraction. Each container shall be thoroughly cleaned on the inside and outside in a way that does not contaminate food, equipment, or utensils, and detergent or steam shall be provided and used for washing containers. Liquid waste from compacting or cleaning operations shall be disposed of as sewage.

Storage

(1) Garbage and refuse in the premises shall be stored in a manner to make them inaccessible to insects and rodents. Outside storage of unprotected plastic bags or wet-strength paper bags or baled units containing garbage or refuse is prohibited. Cardboard or other packaging material not containing garbage or food wastes need not be stored in covered containers.

(2) Garbage refuse storage rooms, if used, shall be constructed of easily cleanable, nonabsorbent, washable materials; shall be kept clean; shall be insect-proof and rodent-proof; and shall be large enough to store the garbage and refuse containers that accumulate.

(3) Outside storage areas or enclosures shall be large enough to store the garbage and refuse containers that accumulate and shall be kept clean. Garbage and refuse containers, dumpsters, and compactor systems located outside shall be stored on or above a smooth surface of nonabsorbent material such as concrete or machine-laid asphalt that is kept clean and maintained in good repair.

Disposal

(1) Garbage and refuse shall be disposed of often enough to prevent the development of odor and the attraction of insects and rodents.

(2) Where garbage or refuse is burned on the premises, the burning shall be done by controlled incineration that prevents the escape of particulate matter in accordance with law. Areas around incineration facilities shall be clean and orderly.

Reasoning

Proper storage and disposal of garbage and refuse is necessary to minimize the development of odors, to prevent such waste from becoming an attraction and harborage or breeding place for insects and rodents, and to prevent the soiling of food preparation and food service areas. Improperly handled garbage creates nuisance conditions, makes housekeeping difficult, and may be a possible source of contamination of food, equipment, and utensils.

(continues)

Figure 3-1. (Continued).

Examples of violations

- Garbage stored in unprotected plastic bags outside of building

- Lid on outside garbage storage container left open

- Refuse containers not cleaned frequently

- Drain plugs missing on dumpster-type storage units

- Outside refuse area not kept clean and neat

- Outside garbage cans and dumpster-type storage unit set on unpaved area

Discussion

Complying with each section of the manual makes compliance with other sections much less a task. An excellent example of this interrelationship is in the requirements of this section easing compliance with the following sections on insect and rodent control.

- Note some of the specific requirements of these paragraphs:

- Storage of garbage and refuse in plastic bags is approved for inside the restaurant building, but not outside.

- Hot water, detergent, or steam is provided for washing containers.

- Dumpsters or containers must be located on a nonabsorbent slab of concrete or blacktop, preferably some distance away from the establishment doors so as not to entice vermin into the establishment.

- Indoor garbage and refuse storage rooms must be insect and rodent proof.

- Cardboard or other packaging material not containing garbage or food wastes need not be stored in covered containers.

Insect and Rodent Control

General Requirements

Effective measures intended to minimize the presence of rodents, flies, cockroaches, and other insects on the premises shall be utilized. The premises shall be kept in such condition as to prevent the harborage or feeding of insects or rodents.

Openings

Openings to the outside shall be effectively protected against the entrance of rodents. Outside openings shall be protected against the entrance of insects by tight-fitting, self-closing doors; closed windows; screening; controlled air currents; or other means. Screen doors shall be self-closing, and screens for windows, doors, skylights, transoms, intake and exhaust air ducts, and other openings to the outside shall be tight-fitting and free of breaks. Screening material shall not be less than sixteen mesh to the inch.

Reasoning

Insects and rodents are capable of transmitting diseases to humans by contamination of food and food-contact surfaces. Because insects require food, water, and shelter, action must be taken to deprive them of these necessities.

Examples of violations

- Front/back door of restaurant propped open for prolonged period

- Screening on doors and windows in poor repair

- Evidence of recent rodent activity

- Outside doors not self-closing or tight-fitting

Discussion

A restaurant cannot keep both pests and customers. One or the other must go, and there can be no doubt as to which is more expendable. There is no place for pests in the facility. Your pest control measures may include:

- Mechanical means such as the use of screen and screening materials, traps, electric screens, and even "air curtains."

- Chemical means such as the use of sprays, repellents, baits, and other insecticides.

- Preventive measures such as cleanup campaigns, proper storage techniques, and other measures related to sanitation and good housekeeping.

A proper warning: Prevent contamination by pests without introducing contamination by pesticide. A number of federal regulations cover the handling, use, storage, and disposal of pesticide. Be aware of these regulations if you are conducting your own control program.

If you select a pest control company, be certain it is knowledgeable and competent. The following guidelines are offered in choosing a reliable pest control company and ensuring quality service:

- Reach a complete understanding with a company before work starts or a contract is signed. Find out what the pests are, what will be done, over how long a period of time, and what results can be expected at what cost.

- Be sure you know what is and isn't guaranteed. Be sure the company will back up its work.

- Ask whether the technician who will serve your food service operation has been trained. There are numerous home study courses, as well as frequent seminars and training courses run by associations and universities.

- Ask your fellow operators for the name of the company they are currently using or may have used in the past. Find out if they were happy and satisfied with the service.

- Seek value from the pest control company you hire. Don't just look at the price.

- Pests of concern to the food service operation may generally be placed in three classes:

  1. Insect pests, including roaches, ants, flies, and pantry pests

  2. Rodent pests, including mice and rats

  3. Pest birds, including pigeons, starlings, and sparrows

Designing Effective Training Programs

A properly designed training program does an effective job on an initial and ongoing basis for preparing the franchisee for the real world. This world includes the preopening steps and challenges, the logistics of grand opening, the steps necessary to manage and motivate your employees, the procedures for dealing with an angry customer, the tips for negotiating with a difficult vendor, and the strategies for handling a fierce competitor. This is the world that the franchisee must face day in and day out, and this is the world that your operations manual, as well as initial and ongoing training programs, must address. The training program must be designed to meet the expectations of the franchisee and be reflective of its typical background, skills, and training prior to signing the franchise agreement. Special programs (at a separate training fee) may be needed for candidates who lack either deep business acumen or industry knowledge. Many new franchisees are likely to have either strong general business skills or deep industry experience but are not likely to have both. The curriculum should be flexible enough to address the needs of *both* types of candidates and the operations manual may need to be augmented accordingly.

For example, in a food business, franchisees must learn how to prepare every item on the menu and not from behind a desk but inside a real training kitchen. They must understand employee hiring, promotion and termination techniques, purchasing, product handling, key financial management ratios, cost controls, store design and construction, and advertising and marketing. Business education skills must be coupled with technical and operational instruction in the trenches. Role playing and field training must be a critical part of the training program. The training materials must be effective, and the instructors knowledgeable both in their fields and as quality instructors and coaches. The training program should incorporate appropriate technologies, such as webcasting and webinars, interactive CD-ROM, training videos, electronic data interchange (EDI), and electronic ordering and inventory control programs (POS systems), where appropriate, and it should offer skilled scoring and evaluation techniques, with a final exam to determine eligibility to open a store.

Training and education in a franchise system can be a lot more than an instructor standing in front of a group of attendees, lecturing with viewgraphs or slides. Technology can be used to enhance the learning process, as well as to deliver the actual training materials. Technology can be used to improve your training and education programs as follows:

❐ To reduce administrative and delivery costs, including travel for instructors and students and the number of instructors needed

❐ To enhance the effectiveness and flexibility of the learning process

❐ To demonstrate your company's commitment to integrate available technology into training and support programs

❐ To reduce replication costs for the printing and distribution of training materials (For example, a CD-ROM disk or jump drive weigh a lot less than five bulky spiral notebooks.)

Interactive systems respond to the actions of the learner. According to Daniel Grunberg at ChainWave Systems in Lexington, Massachusetts, studies have shown that interactive systems greatly improve the learning process because they hold the franchisee's attention more effectively. The most widely used method for producing a training course is to put it on videotape. Although this is an easy-to-duplicate medium that people can access with just a VCR player, its drawbacks are the lack of interactivity and easy search capability.

The Internet is fast becoming a popular way to deliver instructional material. Sometimes called "distance learning" or "webcasting," it allows people, wherever they are located, to access the materials. With the speeds of most users' current Internet access, this is not a great way to deliver lengthy video sequences, but it may be perfect for your franchise system otherwise. You can quickly modify and update materials without incurring additional reproduction costs, as you would with CD-ROM or DVD. Users can access the material instantly from anywhere in the world for the cost of their local Internet access.

Once you determine the mix of appropriate technology, the traditional classroom learning, and field support that will make up the bulk of your initial training program, the next step is to plan your agenda. The actual agenda for the training program must now be disclosed as part of the franchisor's obligations in item 11 of the franchised disclosure document (FDD, see Chapter 5). See Figure 3-2.

Figure 3-2. A portion of a sample training agenda from the FDD of a restaurant franchisor.

Franchisees Training Agenda Topics to Be Covered	Instructional Material	Hours of Classroom Training	Hours of On the Job Training	Instructor
Opening	Manual	8	16	See Note 1
Closing	Manual	2	6	See Note 1
Open prep	Manual	2	6	See Note 1
Open prep/fry	Manual	2	6	See Note 1
Close fry	Manual	0	8	See Note 1
Swing dish	Manual	2	6	See Note 1
Open broiler	Manual	2	6	See Note 1
Close broiler	Manual	0	8	See Note 1
Open window	Manual	0	8	See Note 1
Swing window	Manual	0	8	See Note 1
Close window	Manual	0	8	See Note 1
Swing host/hostess	Manual	2	6	See Note 1
Open host/hostess	Manual	0	8	See Note 1
Open server	Manual	2	6	See Note 1
Close server	Manual	2	6	See Note 1
Swing server	Manual	2	6	See Note 1
Out of house/human resource	Manual	8	0	See Note 1
Managers and the law	Manual	8	0	See Note 1
Management shift/follows (5 a.m. and p.m. shifts floor supervision; standard responsibilities)	Manual	0	80	See Note 1
Final validation	Manual	4	0	See Note 1

As discussed at the outset of this chapter, training transcends the initial session provided at the outset of the relationship and must be delivered on an ongoing basis. The franchisor must be committed to using its field support staff as well as available technology, such as software applications, video conferencing, electronic bulletin boards, and satellite technology to communicate periodically its best practices, system changes and updates, operational tips, key financial data, industry trends, and other key information.

Even the megaplayers in the software industry are recognizing the need and importance of this technology. Microsoft recently introduced an update to its special application of its intranet and extranet business process automation software for the franchising community. The software was designed to meet the information and communication needs of the typical franchisor in keeping its franchisees well trained and informed on an ongoing basis.

This software application, called Microsoft Solution Providers, enables franchisors and their franchisees to increase productivity, efficiency, and cost savings by automating all information sharing and distribution processes currently delivered through conventional distribution methods. An extranet provides secure, external access to an intranet. Franchisors can even take the technology further by customizing to meet their needs as a franchise organization. The aim is to communicate smarter and faster and at a lower cost. Some of the benefits offered by this software are:

❐ Reduced costs associated with internal and external business transactions, such as paper materials, printing and postage, as well as time.

❐ Enhanced communication and information distribution capabilities, enabling franchisors and franchisees to easily search and browse large databases and bulletin boards containing the latest news and information from all parts of the company, including sales, marketing, human resources, legal, and finance. By implementing intranet applications, franchises are empowered to seek out and access the information they need most. Franchisees also receive ongoing syndicated content feeds specific to their industry.

❐ Streamlined business processes, such as report generation, order placement, fulfillment, personnel information, and database management.

❐ Secure, interactive communication between corporate headquarters and franchisees through the use of Internet technology such as chat forums. With an Intranet, franchisors and franchisees have instant access to the latest resources and information, 24 hours a day, seven days a week. Franchisees are able to increase interaction with customers and increase sales during business hours, with the option to handle administrative operations such as product ordering and sales tracking.

The solution offered by Microsoft Solution Providers addresses the issues of openness, scalability, and reliability. Microsoft, along with the software product teams, will work with franchisors to develop, implement, and support customized intranet and extranet solutions. Microsoft Solution Providers uses the Microsoft Solutions Platform of products as building blocks for customized solutions and offers various value-added services, such as integration, consulting, software customization, development of turnkey applications, and technical training and support.

Automated financial systems are another area where franchisor/franchisee communications and training can be strengthened. The most common example is a point-of-sale (POS) system. These systems have multiple advantages that originate from automating the input of financial transactions so that daily, weekly, monthly, and annual reports can be generated. These reports can then be analyzed, providing information about performance to assist the franchise system—both franchisors and franchisees—in planning, marketing, and sales strategies.

A POS system collects and stores data about transactions and sometimes controls decisions made as a part of a transaction, such as validating a credit card. (These were the first computerized information systems.) POS systems are based on detailed models of how the transaction should be processed. Most contain enough structure to enforce rules and procedures for work done by franchisees. Some systems bypass clerks entirely and totally automate transactions.

Franchising companies normally use real-time processing POS systems. Once data for the transaction has been collected and validated, the POS stores the data in a standard format for later access by others. This reliable data assists management in more effectively evaluating and assisting franchise owners. Franchisees also request comparisons with each other to understand their individual strengths and weaknesses and to compare themselves to the average and top peers.

Information generated from a POS system can also improve a franchisee's bottom line. Aside from the time savings of automated reporting, POS systems offer the potential for increased information sharing among franchisees. For instance, if one franchisee observes that another outlet is more successful than he is in selling a specific product or service, he can contact the franchise owner to find out the reasons for the success and learn how to improve his own store's performance.

CHAPTER 4

Developing System Standards and Enforcing Quality Control

any owners and executives of growing and established companies fear that the decision to franchise will result in the loss of quality control over the operations and management of their business, resulting in a dilution of their brand and damage to their goodwill. In reality, a variety of vehicles are available to franchisors for maintaining the level of quality that they and their consumers have come to expect. A well-planned franchising or licensing program will include a wide variety of system standards, training methods, operational manuals, and internal policies and procedures to establish quality control guidelines, along with a carefully assembled field support staff to educate franchisees and to enforce the franchisor's quality control guidelines.

To succeed, a franchise system demands quality control. A system that does not maintain and enforce an effective quality control strategy is not likely to survive in the competitive marketplace. The strategic principle that *a chain is only as strong as its weakest link* applies directly to this aspect of the overall franchise system. The licensor of a trademark has an obligation under federal trademark laws to control the quality of the products and services offered in connection with the trademark. Thus, by establishing and enforcing quality control standards, a franchisor not only ensures uniformity of quality but also satisfies an obligation of the federal Lanham Act that is imposed on the owner of a trademark. Failure to monitor and control the operations of a franchisee/licensee could result in a so-called statutory abandonment of the franchisor's rights in the trademark because the franchisor may no longer distinguish a particular product or service from those offered by others in the market. Therefore, the trademark laws provide a *justification* and basis for the implementation of reasonable controls over franchisees/licensees in all aspects of the business format.

Developing and Enforcing System Standards

The glue holding the typical franchise system together consists of the uniform policies, procedures, and specifications that all franchisees must follow. These rules and regulations, typically found in the operations manual, must be:

- ❏ *Carefully planned and developed by the franchisor.*
- ❏ *Clearly articulated* by the franchisor to the franchisees, both initially and on an ongoing basis.
- ❏ *Accepted* by the network of franchisees as being understood and reasonable.
- ❏ *Consistently applied.*
- ❏ *Rigidly enforced* by the franchisor, typically through its field support staff.

Obviously, the development of uniform standards is of little utility unless systems are in place for monitoring and enforcing these standards, as well as penalties for noncompliance with the standards, which are typically found in the franchise agreement.

Compliance with quality control standards requires mutual respect by and among the franchisor and all of its franchisees. The franchisor must be reasonable and resist the temptation to overdo the development and enforcement of system standards. The franchisee must understand that reasonable standards are in the best interests of all franchisees in the network. Franchisees typically have a love-hate relationship with system standards. On the one hand, they love reasonable standards that result in happy consumers and that weed out noncomplying franchisees. On the other hand, they detest standards that are unattainable, vaguely communicated, and arbitrarily or too rigidly enforced.

System standards, which are prescribed in the operations manual and other written and electronic communications from the franchisor, are deemed to be part of the franchise agreement under the contract law doctrine of incorporation by reference. System standards dictate, among other things:

- ❏ The required and authorized products and services to be offered and sold and, subject to local antitrust laws, the prices at which franchisees may sell authorized products and services.
- ❏ The manner in which the franchisee may offer and sell these products and services (including food and beverage preparation, storage, handling, and packaging procedures).
- ❏ The required image and appearance of restaurant facilities, vehicles, and employees.
- ❏ Designated and approved suppliers and supplier approval criteria and procedure, types, models, and brands of required operating assets (such as equipment, signs, furnishings, furniture, and vehicles); and supplies (such as ingredients, packaging, and ancillary items, such as utensils and napkins).
- ❏ Use and display of the trade and service marks.
- ❏ Advertising and promotional programs and the materials and media used in these programs.

- ❏ Terms and conditions of the sale and delivery of items that the franchisee acquires from the franchisor and its affiliates.
- ❏ Staffing levels and training.
- ❏ Days and hours of operation.
- ❏ Participating in market research and testing and product and service development programs.
- ❏ Payment, point-of-sale, and computer systems.
- ❏ Reporting requirements.
- ❏ Insurance requirements.
- ❏ Health and safety procedures.
- ❏ Customer interaction and satisfaction.

These standards, which a franchisor implements at the beginning and during the course of the franchisee relationship, in tandem with the franchisor's willingness and ability to enforce those standards system-wide, usually will determine the success of the franchise system. System standards must be communicated to franchisees in well-organized and understandable formats.

The obvious dilemma from the preceding list is that many of these system standards are moving targets. They can and will change as technology and market conditions change, and franchisors must be able to modify the system standards without seeking an addendum to the franchise agreement every time a modification to the system is necessary. The franchisor must build a culture—right at the start of the relationship—where the franchisee accepts that change is inevitable and expected and that it should be warmly embraced. Changes to the system must be viewed as a positive evolution of the business format, not as a burden. To accomplish this, however, there must be a culture of trust; the franchisee wants to be assured that these changes are reasonable and necessary. If the change involves new products and services, the franchisee wants to be assured that adequate market research went into their development and that they are not the whimsical or harebrained idea of the franchisor's founder. Most franchisors build a certain degree of flexibility into their franchise agreements to allow the peaceful implementation of system changes.

Over the course of the relationship, events and trends may trigger change: new competitive conditions, a change in territorial policies, technological innovations, the addition or loss of a key supplier, the introduction of alternative locations, a merger or acquisition, or a change made to rectify deficiencies in existing franchise agreements, particularly those relating to system change. These events may require the franchisor's consent and/or execution of the franchisor's then current form of franchise agreement, which may include broader change language. For example, a franchisor might condition the sale of a franchised unit or the renewal of the term of the franchise agreement on an upgrade of the refurbishment of the franchised unit to the franchisor's then current design criteria. In addition, a franchisor might condition the opening of additional units by the franchisee upon the franchisee's agreement to comply with these new policies for its existing franchised units and/or an agreement to comply with some specific element of change in the system. These opportunities may, however, be limited by existing franchise agreement language and by the scope or the required upgrade.

A sample clause providing the flexibility of the franchisor to modify the system standards from time to time is shown in Figure 4-1.

Methods for Enforcing Quality Control and System Standards

A franchisor may use many methods to maintain certain levels of quality that help distinguish the franchisor's products and services from those of its competitors. This chapter examines the use of (1) the franchise agreement, (2) operations manuals, (3) initial and ongoing training programs, (4) tying

Figure 4-1. Sample clause for modifying system standards.

You acknowledge and agree that the development and operation of your Store in accordance with the mandatory specifications, standards, operating procedures and rules we prescribe for the development and operation of [ABC] stores (the "System Standards") are the essence of this Agreement and essential to preserve the goodwill of the Marks and all [ABC] stores. Therefore, you agree that, at all times during the term of this Agreement, you will develop, maintain and operate the Store in accordance with each and every System Standard, as periodically modified and supplemented by us in our discretion during the term of this Agreement. Among the aspects of the development and operation of franchised [ABC] stores that we may regulate through the System Standards are the following:

(1) design, layout, decor, appearance and lighting; periodic maintenance and cleaning; replacement of obsolete or worn-out improvements, equipment, furniture, furnishings and signs; periodic painting, redecorating and remodeling and the frequency of such painting, redecorating and remodeling; use of signs, banners, graphics, emblems, lettering and logos; and periodic modification of the Store in accordance with our plans, specifications and directions at such time or times as we require;

(2) types, models and brands of required or authorized equipment, furniture, furnishings, signs and other products, materials and supplies;

(3) requirements for stocking, storing and rotating an inventory of products for resale of such types and formats and in such packages as we may prescribe and other specifications relating to inventory practices and product mix; and

(4) designated or approved suppliers (including us and our affiliates) of equipment, furniture, furnishings, signs, inventory, and other products, materials and supplies.

We may from time to time modify System Standards, and such modifications may obligate you to invest additional capital in the Store and/or incur higher operating costs, but such modifications will not alter your fundamental status and rights under this Agreement. System Standards may accommodate regional or local variations or other factors as we determine. Although we may require you to refurbish the Store (including changes in signage, floor covering, wall covering and other decor features except for fixtures) to conform with System Standards, we will not require such refurbishing more often than once every five (5) years. You agree that System Standards prescribed from time to time in the Confidential Operating Manual, or otherwise communicated to you in writing, will constitute provisions of this Agreement as if fully set forth in this Agreement. All references to this Agreement include all System Standards as periodically modified.

---

arrangements, (5) approved supplier programs, and (6) field support personnel to establish, ensure, and maintain quality control. The limitations imposed by law with respect to the controls that may be imposed upon a franchisee/licensee are also explored.

Field Support Staff and Quality Control

Training and the Role of the Field Support Staff

The franchisor's field support staff plays a critical role in ensuring that the operations manual guidelines are followed:

❏ As a quality control "policeman" and system standard enforcer.

❏ As a strategic consultant and problem solver.

❏ As the source and deliverer of new methods and best practices.

❏ As the protector of the consuming public's interests in health, safety, and hygiene.

Many franchisors view their field support personnel as necessary for providing franchisees the ongoing support and assistance the franchisor is obligated to provide under its franchise agreement. Although ongoing support is an important component of the role of field support personnel, franchisors may overlook their important contribution that a thoughtfully assembled field support staff can make to ensuring that franchisees maintain the franchisor's quality control and uniform system standards. These two components of the role of field support staff should be carefully considered by current and prospective franchisors.

For the early-stage franchisor, it is not difficult to make periodic visits to each franchisee for the purpose of providing support and assistance, ensuring compliance with quality control guidelines, and listening to franchisees' questions and concerns. This task becomes more of a challenge as the franchisor's network of franchisees continues to grow and spread throughout the country, making it impossible for the franchisor to offer the same level of handholding to its franchisees. Thus, growth could have an adverse impact on the quality of the products and services offered by the franchise system. The franchisor's system can succeed and prosper when it has 500 franchisees only by developing and training a field support staff that can continue to provide handholding and ensure compliance with quality control standards as well as when the franchisor had only five franchisees. Also critical is providing the field support team with the latest communication and computer technology to properly support and monitor the network of franchisees. A well-designed intranet system, cell phones and pagers, and portable computers can all play a role in making the system stronger and bringing it closer together from a quality control perspective.

Ongoing Support and Assistance

Most franchisors undertake to provide franchisees some level of ongoing support and assistance. A field support staff is generally assembled for this purpose. A franchisor's ability to duplicate the level of success and quality offered by its prototype facility is in the hands of this staff.

For this reason, field support personnel should be carefully selected and trained. To ensure consistency, each member of the field support team should receive *exactly the same types and levels of training*. They should all know the intricacies of the franchise business, be sensitive to the needs and concerns of franchisees, and be diplomatic in their dealings with franchisees. The information provided to the franchisees should be accurate and consistent. If various members of the field support staff nationwide interpret a particular standard or role differently, then the standard itself may be considered waived or even abandoned. If there is no consistency in the enforcement and communication of standards, then they will be viewed as not being standards at all, and the franchise will lose consumer goodwill, trademarks and the proprietary system will be diluted, and on occasion litigation and lowered franchisee morale will ensue.

Field support personnel must be able to recognize and satisfy the ongoing needs of franchisees, using a positive management philosophy, motivation techniques, good communication, and innovative franchisee programs. If field support personnel are successful in maintaining good relationships with franchisees, franchisees will be motivated to comply with the necessary controls established by the franchisor for the operation of the business. Maintaining a good relationship with franchisees is accomplished through conducting regular regional and national meetings, providing retraining programs and periodic seminars that focus on various areas of interest to franchisees, offering management consulting services, and maintaining routine telephone and personal contact.

Meetings and Seminars

Regional and national meetings should be used, among other things, as a forum for franchisees to voice their concerns and questions. The franchisor should take all franchisee questions, concerns, and criticisms seriously and directly address each by (1) offering immediate comfort and suggestions at the meeting, (2) addressing problems raised in printed or electronic newsletters or follow-up bulletins after the meeting, and (3) conducting interviews one-on-one with the franchisee(s) who raised the concerns. The ability of the franchisor's field support personnel to address such concerns and offer franchisees comfort and/or solutions is critical to the viability of the franchisor's system. The franchisor must, at all times, be perceptive to the needs and concerns of its franchisees and capable of providing meaningful, realistic, and practical solutions.

Seminars that focus on a particular aspect of the operation of the franchise business should be conducted on a regular basis. The franchisor's field support staff should play an important role in developing these seminars.

Through personal contacts with franchisees, they can offer insight into appropriate topics for seminars and identify essential issues that franchisees would find beneficial. Seminars can be excellent tools to both educate and motivate franchisees.

The field staff functions in many ways as the eyes and ears of the franchisor and serves as an intermediary in resolving problems and maintaining standards. See Figure 4-2 for a list of various franchisee support tools.

Training and Retraining Programs

The franchisor must carefully develop a training program that covers all the topics of concern to franchisees. The initial training program must be comprehensive and informative, covering topics such as management and operation of a business, preparation of products and/or provision of services, quality control, managing personnel, advertising and marketing, bookkeeping and reporting, use of trademarks, maintaining the confidential nature of trade secrets, legal obligations, and customer relations. In developing an initial training program, franchisors must be mindful that many franchisees have never owned or operated a business. For this reason, adequate initial training and ongoing assistance and support are crucial to the success of the franchisees and the franchisor. The most effective training programs combine old-fashioned personal hands-on support with the appropriate use of technology-driven training tools. Both components must be utilized in the training program, and one is not a substitute for the other. Marketing topics should *not necessarily* predominate the training session. Franchisees must be taught not only how to bring in the business, but also *how to deliver* the products and services once the customer is in the door.

Franchisors should also consider implementing retraining programs for franchisees who need continuous reinforcement of the franchisor's business

Figure 4-2. Various franchisee support tools.

Global advisory councils

National advisory councils

Regional advisory councils

Special-purpose advisory councils (technology, branding, communications, new products, etc.)

Peer-to-peer support

Mentoring programs

Coaching programs

One-on-one consulting

Annual business planning process

Webinars

Specialized field support or business consulting sessions

Refresher courses on key operational challenges

format, standards, and guidelines. Retraining should be recommended (or required) for franchisees who continuously fail in one or more identifiable areas of the operation of the franchise business. For example, a franchisee has continuously failed to provide the franchisor with all the required monthly, quarterly, and annual reports mandated by the franchise agreement. The franchisor's field support personnel have worked with the franchisee several times to correct the deficiency, but the problem has not been resolved. Field support personnel report to the franchisor that the franchisee is (1) unfamiliar with the reporting requirements and forms, (2) not accustomed to the computer-generated accounting system, and (3) willing to learn and comply but *slow*. This franchisee may have good intentions but may just need some additional training in and attention to the financial aspects of the business. He or she should, therefore, be allowed (or required) to attend a retraining program that focuses on accounting, reporting, record keeping, and other financial matters. If the franchisor's field support personnel continuously report the same franchisee deficiencies for a group of franchisees, then the franchisor may want to reevaluate that portion of its training program to determine its overall effectiveness. The field support visit to the franchisee's site should be viewed as a quality control enforcement check *as well as* a tutoring and assistance session for troubled franchisees.

Management Consulting Services

Some franchisees have problems that cannot be resolved with the periodic assistance of field support personnel. For this reason, some franchisors offer management consulting services to franchisees at an hourly rate. Although this is a more costly means of resolving a franchisee's problems, it may be the only way to identify and deal with them. If a consultant (usually someone who is part of the field support staff) is on-site for one to two weeks, the franchisee's deficiencies will be more quickly and accurately identified. Once problems are identified, the consultant can suggest methods and techniques for resolving them, assist in the implementation, and, to a certain extent, monitor the results. Management consulting services should be offered to franchisees only if the franchisor truly has the personnel and expertise to provide meaningful services. Additionally, the rates charged for consulting services should be reasonable so as not to be perceived by the franchisee as merely a moneymaking vehicle for the franchisor.

Personal and Telephone Contact

Field support personnel are notorious for their regular monthly visits to the franchise location, inspections, unexpected visits, and telephone calls. These are the traditional and most effective methods for providing on-site field support and quality control inspections of franchisees. If, however, a visit by the field support staff is viewed as an intrusion (or even as spying) on the franchisee's ability to operate the business independently, then the franchisor has not succeeded in establishing a good relationship with its franchisees. It is difficult to balance the franchisee's desire for independence with the franchisor's need for quality control. If an appropriate balance is not found, franchisees may become resentful and resist the franchisor's necessary controls, thus creating an unnecessarily tense and hostile relationship. The field support staff is primarily responsible for striking the appropriate balance between the interests of the franchisees and those of the franchisor. It is therefore critical that the franchisor use care in the hiring and training of its field support personnel.

The personal visit to a franchisee's operating location by a field support person offers the best opportunity for establishing the appropriate relationship and striking that balance of interests. The franchisor should put together a staff large enough to cover the entire network on a regular basis, such as once per month. If the staff is spread too thin, it will not be able to conduct timely follow-up visits to check on the franchisee's progress with certain problems. Additionally, the field support person who is responsible for visiting too many franchisees is less likely to remember each franchisee's problems and concerns, possibly making it more difficult to establish and maintain the necessary rapport between the franchisor's staff and the franchisee.

The field support representative should set aside enough time to prepare for each visit (see Figure 4-3) and time to summarize the meeting soon afterward. These details may be overlooked if the franchisor's field support staff is overloaded. A franchisee will recognize an unprepared representative and certainly won't appreciate the inconvenience and waste of time that a lack of preparedness is likely to create. Each field support person typically develops a personal style, and each franchisee has different needs, but this is no excuse for straying from the uniform system standards that must be continuously communicated to the franchisees.

The visit itself should be carefully orchestrated and always include (1) follow-up on goals set during the last meeting, (2) a walk-through inspection, (3) training (usually in an area of weakness or a newly introduced service, product, method, or technique), (4) identification of the franchisee's successes and weaknesses, (5) the establishment of goals to be met by the next visit, (6) identification of franchisee's needs and concerns, (7) a talk with employees and customers, and (8) reinforcement of quality control guidelines.

Figure 4-3. Preparing for a site visit.

- Send confirmation of visit, including an agenda of things franchisee should have prepared (unless the visit is intended to be a random "surprise" for enforcement and monitoring purposes).

- Contact franchisee to get input for developing the agenda.

- Identify staff members needed for meetings, and secure time for them during the visit.

- Evaluate franchisee's sales data and reports.

- Review report from last visit.

- Check on timeliness of royalty and other payments to franchisor.

- Develop goals for visit.

Inspections of the franchisee's facility should be conducted in accordance with a standardized checklist developed by the franchisor. A point-scoring method is typically used for such evaluations. Field support personnel should be required to report the results of these evaluations to the franchisor within a specified time frame. All reports should note both deficient and outstanding-quality performance.

Except for certain major infractions for which there is no effective means of correcting (these typically result in immediate notice of termination under the franchise agreement), franchisees should be given the opportunity to cure or correct defaults or deficiencies. The field representative should be responsible for (1) offering guidance to the franchisees on ways to correct the cited deficiencies and (2) following up with franchisees to see that deficiencies have been corrected. Typically a franchisee is given 30 days to correct deficiencies unless the deficiency cannot be corrected within this time period.

Unannounced Visits and Test Customers

Field visits and inspections should occur on a regular basis. A recent study conducted by the International Franchise Association indicates that most franchisors conduct monthly field calls and that a large number of franchisors also conduct such calls on a quarterly, bimonthly, or semiannual basis. In addition to regularly scheduled visits, field personnel should conduct periodic surprise or unannounced visits and inspections. Many franchisees may be put off by unannounced inspections, viewing them as an infringement on their independence. For this reason, the field personnel should carefully orchestrate surprise inspections. Franchisees should be informed from the start that an imminent inspection should have no effect on the standards, service, products, cleanliness, or other aspects of its business operation. The field person should be viewed as "just another customer," grading and judging the same way customers do. The difference is that the field person will go behind the scenes to check aspects of the business that create the product and service. The inspection is designed to help the franchisee improve its performance. An unsatisfied customer won't return; the field person, on the other hand, will help the franchisee identify and correct any problems.

Franchisors often discover that adjacent franchisees establish a network to inform other franchisees that the field support person is in the area. As a franchise system grows, the communication network makes it more and more difficult to conduct truly surprise visits. Nonetheless, such visits should continue to be used as part of the franchisor's quality control program.

Test customers are an alterative or supplement to surprise visits by field personnel. Generally the franchisor will hire people unfamiliar to its franchisees to act as customers for the purpose of evaluating the franchisee's performance in the areas of customer relations, product and service quality, and cleanliness. To achieve the best results, test customers should not identify themselves as such and should report to the field person with detailed observations. Later, the field support person who usually deals with the franchisee should make an announced visit for the purpose of discussing the observations of the test customer. Maintaining the anonymity of test customers (1) prevents franchisees from alerting other area franchisees that a surprise inspection is likely and (2) puts the franchisee on notice that any customer could in fact be a test customer sent by the franchisor.

Team Approaches to Field Support

Some franchisors have developed a *team* approach toward providing field support and enhancing system standards. For example, at Cost Cutters Family Hair Care, each new franchisee is assigned a service team made up of one person from four key departments: marketing, education/operations, finance, and product/distribution. Teams and franchise owners meet yearly to develop goals and action plans to meet them. Progress is tracked monthly. In addition, Cost Cutters revisits each new shop at 45 days, six months, and one year. The focus is on troubled areas during the follow-up visits. Some franchisors have also developed formal mentoring programs, designed to match new franchisees with veterans. Veteran franchisees talk at least once a week with new franchisees during their critical first 90 days in business.

Beyond formal training and support programs, many leading franchisors are also focused on being accessible, responsive, and treating their franchisees as partners. Follow-up training can also include town hall meetings, one-day sessions that are held two times a year. In addition, an operators exchange group, formed and run by franchisees with 20 or more stores, can draw together members three times a year to discuss issues geared to larger franchisees.

The Impact of Technology and Software Systems on Quality Control and Relationship Management

Today's franchisor will typically use a wide variety of technology tools and communications systems to establish standards and enforce quality control, as well as to manage overall franchise system compliance (see Chapter 6). These tools and programs can be used in virtually all aspects of franchise recruitment, support, and compliance:

- ❑ *Recruitment*: Lead generation, online application and screening, online FDDs, and closing
- ❑ *Construction*: Automated plans and blueprints, construction management
- ❑ *Training:* Web conferencing, webinars, intranet
- ❑ *Royalty and financial reporting:* Online reporting, electronic banking, POS systems
- ❑ *Franchisee-level marketing:* Contact management software, social networking tools, ad builders

❑ *Franchise support:* Help desks, ongoing training, and best practices
❑ *Franchisee-level sales:* Sales data collection and analysis, e-commerce order processing and shipping, inventory monitoring and supply management tools, etc.

Refer to the technology-readiness checklist in Figure 4-4, supplied by our friends at FranConnect Software. Consider *your* answers carefully.

The Development of Enforcement Systems

As a general rule, the franchisor has an obligation to develop reasonable and attainable system standards and procedures. Once developed, the standards and procedures should be clearly communicated and uniformly enforced. The enforcement must be neither too loose nor too rigid. If the penalties for noncompliance are too loose, the franchisor will be viewed as a toothless lion who neither intends nor has the power to insist on compliance. If the enforcement is too rigid, the standards will be resented and disregarded, resulting in litigation and poor franchisee morale throughout the network.

Many times, the enforcement strategy adopted depends on the franchisor's own stage of growth. For example, a gentle rap on the knuckles (in lieu of an actual termination) may be more prudent early on in the franchisor's own development because of the impact of a dispute at this stage. The costs of litigation, the perception of actual and prospective franchisees, and the nature of the infraction should all be considered. If the young franchisor adopts a quasi-acquiescence policy of enforcement, then issues of waiver and laches should be discussed with legal counsel. As the franchisor grows and matures, rigidly enforcing system standards and applying significant penalties for noncompliance becomes easier because the threat of termination becomes a more powerful deterrent.

The franchisor should consider the following general factors in determining how to proceed against a franchisee in noncompliance with system standards: (1) whether the franchisee in question has a high profile in the system, (2) the exact nature of the franchisee's infraction(s), (3) the current condition and stability of the franchisor's industry, (4) the availability of a replacement franchisee for the site, (5) the quality of the training program and operations manual in the area where the infractions have incurred, (6) any potential counterclaims by the franchisee, (7) the quality of the evidence gathered by the field support personnel to prove the incidents of noncompliance, (8) the reaction of the other franchisees within the system to the enforcement action, and (9) the geographic location of the franchisee in question.

The penalties that may be applied by the franchisor to the noncomplying franchisee include a formal warning, a written notice of default, a threat of termination, actual termination, damages or fines, a forced sale or transfer, or a denial of a benefit, such as eligibility for participation in a new program. Support for those penalties must be found in the franchise agreement or separately negotiated.

Figure 4-4. A technology-readiness checklist.

Franchise Development: Is the franchise company reaching out to all its leads through e-mail or phone within 30 minutes of receiving them, qualifying them and then focusing on the leads with the highest potential through a well-defined, step-by-step process?

Franchise Performance: Is the franchise organization providing continuous, real-time feedback to franchisees on their performance by providing dashboards and reports that take into account key performance indicators such as monthly and yearly sales rankings, comparison of stores open the same amount of time or in a similar region, category sales breakdowns, income and expense analysis?

Franchise Relationships: Are franchisees directed to use the intranet on a daily basis to create a continuous communication channel, effectively share ideas, and build a strong relationship with your franchisees?

Franchise Support: Has the franchisor implemented online support tools that allow franchisees to get answers to their questions 24/7 rather than calling limited-support staff members for answers to every question? Has a knowledge base been created about frequently asked questions that can be used by existing and new franchisees?

Royalty Management and Cash Flow: Are there automated POS or data-collection tools for collecting sales and royalty data? Is royalty collection enforced through electronic-funds-transfer transactions, eliminating delayed payments and improved cash flow?

Legal and Compliance Information Management: Has a database been created to track all communication with franchisees and all relevant legal information to reduce the costs associated with litigation, legal discovery processes, and franchise compliance efforts?

Marketing Automation: Is the organization leveraging tools that enable one-click print and e-mail marketing for franchisees to help them improve their sales and marketing efforts?

The courts have recognized that in some cases the franchisor is obliged to take legal action against a franchisee who fails to follow system standards in order to protect the franchisor's intellectual property. For example, in *Adcom Express, Inc. et. al. v. EPK, Inc.*, the court upheld a franchisor's termination of its California franchisee for refusing to use the franchisor's New York franchisee for deliveries in the New York territory in breach of a material provision of the franchise agreement. The court relied on the Adcom franchise agreement provision, which gave the franchisor discretion to terminate the franchise upon default and also provided that "good cause for termination means any breach of any material provision of the Franchise Agreement or any intentional, repeated or continuous breach of any provision of the Agreement, without the [franchisor's] consent." The court stated that there was "no doubt" that requiring a franchisee in the freight forwarding business to use other franchisees in the system for deliveries is a material provision of the franchise agreement. In *Great Clips, Inc. v. Levine*, a franchisee was permanently enjoined from continuing to violate its franchise agreement by departing from the franchisor's single-price, $11 haircut policy. In another case, *Novus de Quebec v. Novus Franchising, Inc.*, an auto glass repair franchisor terminated its area developer for "failure to comply with the uniformity and quality standards" in the franchise agreement and for failure to cooperate with an audit inspection as required under the agreement. The area developer also had awarded franchises to franchisees of competing franchise systems after the franchisor had already rejected them as suitable candidates. The district court rejected the area developer's request for an injunction to prevent termination of the license, citing the area developer's "total disregard for the spirit and philosophy behind the Novus System and for the goodwill associated with the Novus marks and System."

In another case, a franchisee's noncompliance with the franchisor's system was determined to cause irreparable harm to the franchise system and its marks. In *Burger King Corp. v. Stephens*, the court granted Burger King's request for an injunction to force a franchisee to cease operating where the franchisee had violated Burger King's operating standards and Burger King was thus "[unable] to insure the maintenance of high quality service that the trademarks represented, [thereby] causing irreparable injury to the franchisor's business reputation and goodwill." Other examples of courts protecting franchisors and licensors from possible damage to their marks by licensees or franchisees are *Cottman Transmission Systems, Inc. v. Melody* (continued use of marks by a terminated franchisee could cause irreparable harm by loss of consumer faith and confidence); *Jiffy Lube International, Inc. v. Weiss Brothers, Inc.* (unauthorized use of franchisor's trade dress and marks enjoined because a continuing infringement would cause irreparable harm); *Star Houston, Inc. v. Texas Dept. of Transportation and Saab Cars U.S.A., Inc.* (dealer's refusal to participate in new signage program was a material breach constituting good cause for termination). These cases affirm the right of a franchisor to apply quality control measures to ensure consistency in the licensed products and services offered under the given marks and thus to protect the value (i.e., goodwill) of its intellectual property.

Other Methods of Enforcing Quality Control Standards in a Franchise System

Operations Manuals and Training Programs

The franchisor usually provides the franchisee with a comprehensive operations manual, which is generally reviewed for the first time at the initial training session for owners and managers of the franchise business. These manuals and training programs instruct the franchisee on all aspects of operating and managing the business within the quality control standards established by the franchisor. The operations manual should set forth in a clear and concise fashion the minimum levels of quality to be maintained in all aspects of the business, from cleanliness to customer service, recipes, and employee relations. These standards should be taught and reinforced throughout the training program.

Architectural and Engineering Plans and Drawings

In most types of franchised businesses, uniformity of physical appearance is imperative. The franchisor often provides detailed architectural drawings and engineering plans, both as a service to franchisees and as a method of standardizing. These plans reinforce the importance of a consistent image in the minds of consumers, who may be looking for the "golden arches" or "orange roof" in their search for a familiar place to eat along the highway. Plans may include specifications for signage, counter design, display racks, paint colors, HVAC systems, lighting, interior decoration, or special building features.

Trade Dress

Trade dress is also a method of enforcing quality control and design standards. The leading case on the protection of a franchisor's trade dress is *Taco Cabana International, Inc. v. Two Pesos, Inc.*, affirming a jury's finding that Taco Cabana had a protectable trade dress that was inherently distinctive and that consumers might likely confuse or associate Taco Cabana with a competitor restaurant that had infringed on Taco Cabana's trade dress. The court explained that "an owner may license its trade dress and retain proprietary rights if the owner maintains adequate control over the quality of goods and services that the licensee sells with the mark or dress."

Site Selection Assistance

The top three priorities for the success of a franchisee's business have often been cited as location, location, and location. Many franchisors assist franchisees in selecting a proper site for their franchise business and even assist in lease negotiations and supervision of construction. Such efforts not only help to ensure the franchisee's success but also provide an additional basis for maintaining quality control in terms of minimum parking requirements, traffic patterns, minimum/maximum square footage, demographics of the local market, and prevention of market saturation.

Intranets and Technology

Modern franchisors are also turning to intranets, videoconferencing and related communications, and computer technologies as a way to enforce systems standards, provide support, and monitor quality control. The diverse technologies available for use in intranets include e-mail, Web browsers, groupware, Java, streaming audio and video, "push" technology, and countless other Web-based software applications.

The enforcement of quality control and system standards can be accomplished by publishing product, service, and marketing information that can be accessed easily and inexpensively by each franchisee in the system, as well as by designated, password-controlled individuals within a franchisee organization, using public telecommunications networks. Outside contractors and suppliers also can be given limited access to the intranet to facilitate their interaction with the system.

An intranet can also provide a secure central point for collecting financial information for tracking financial performance and maintaining financial controls. Intranets also can permit authorized external users, such as suppliers, shareholders, and analysts, to have limited access to certain financial data, in order to build better relationships through timely and accurate communications. Other finance and accounting applications on an intranet can be used specifically for company-owned operations, such as budgeting, payroll, expense reports, and cash management and online banking. Intranets also can be used to replace the so-called centralized cash registers and other forms of legacy systems, for greater control over franchisee operations. The addition of a secure transaction processing feature to an intranet could also be used to facilitate inventory management, as well as to enhance cash management, reporting, and other controls.

National or Uniform Advertising Programs

Advertising and the promotion of the franchise business on a local and national level is an essential part of virtually all franchise systems. If the franchisees are left on their own to develop advertising and promotional materials for local television, radio, and newspapers, the system will not be sending out a uniform message about the products and/or services offered by the franchise network. Additionally, franchisors will not have control over the quality and content of the advertising materials used by franchisees. Franchisees may not be knowledgeable of the laws prohibiting unfair or deceptive advertising and trade practices. Thus, without the franchisor's guidelines, they are likely to stumble into trouble, diminishing the goodwill the franchisor has worked hard to build. For this reason, a centralized advertising program, engineered by the franchisor's in-house staff or an outside advertising agency, develops newspaper, television, and radio advertisements for use by franchisees in their local markets, helping the franchisor maintain a certain minimum level of quality in advertising. Moreover, a centralized advertising program should include a franchisor review and approval process for advertisements developed by franchisees.

Approved Supplier Program

The franchisee will need a wide variety of raw materials, office and business supplies, equipment, foodstuffs, and services in order to operate the franchise business. The level of control that the franchisor is entitled to exercise over the acquisition of these supplies and materials will vary, depending on the nature of the franchise business and the extent to which such goods are proprietary. Franchisors may be prohibited, under certain circumstances, from forcing a franchisee to buy all equipment and supplies from them or their designated sources.

The franchisor does, however, have a right to establish objective performance standards and specifications to which alternate suppliers and their products or services must adhere. Such standards are justifiable for the purpose of ensuring a certain minimum standard of quality.

In establishing an approved supplier or vendor certification program, the franchisor should carefully develop procedures for the suggestion and evaluation of alternative suppliers proposed by the franchisee. The standards by which a prospective supplier is evaluated should be clearly defined and reasonable. This evaluation should be based on:

1. Ability to produce the products or services in accordance with the franchisor's standards and specifications for quality and uniformity.

2. Production and delivery capabilities and ability to meet supply commitments.

3. Integrity of ownership (to ensure that association with the franchisor would not be inconsistent with the franchisor's image or damage its goodwill).

4. Financial stability.

5. Familiarity of the proposed supplier with the franchise business.

6. Negotiation of a satisfactory license agreement to protect the franchisor's trademarks.

The franchisor should always reserve the right to disapprove any proposed supplier who does not meet these standards. In addition, an approved supplier should be removed from the list of suppliers if, at any time, it fails to maintain these standards. Other reasonable standards, as applicable in the franchisor's industry, may also be adopted.

Special Legal Issues Affecting Exclusive Supplier and Vendor Certification Programs

For certain highly proprietary aspects of the franchise business such as the so-called secret sauce, the franchisor typically has the authority to require the franchisee to purchase those products *exclusively* from the franchisor or from a supplier designated and approved by the franchisor. This is known as a "tying arrangement." Not all tying arrangements are permitted under applicable antitrust laws. Proposed tying programs continue to be one of the greatest sources of conflict and litigation between franchisors and franchisees. This section discusses how and when a franchisor can legally require its franchisees to purchase products solely from the franchisor (or a specific supplier, which may or may not be affiliated with the franchisor). It also examines the limitations on the franchisor's right to impose a tying arrangement and discusses other limitations on the franchisor's controls over franchisees.

Federal antitrust law identifies a *tying arrangement* as an arrangement whereby a seller refuses to sell one product (the tying product, franchise) unless the buyer also purchases another product (tied product, food products or ingredients, for example). Such arrangements are perceived as posing an unacceptable risk of stifling competition and as a general matter are not favored by the courts.

One of the critical factors examined by the courts in determining whether a transaction or set of purchase terms constitutes an unlawful tying arrangement is a tie-in between *two separate and distinct products* or services that are readily distinguishable in the eyes of the consumer whereby the availability of the tying product is conditioned on the purchase of the tied product.

For example, in a case involving Kentucky Fried Chicken Corp. (KFC), the court discussed the distinction between two separate products unlawfully tied together by a seller and two interrelated products that are justifiably tied together. In that case Marion-Kay, a manufacturer and distributor of chicken seasoning, counterclaimed against KFC, alleging unlawful tying of its KFC franchises to the purchase of its own special KFC seasoning exclusively from two designated distributors. The court found that the alleged tying product (the KFC franchise) and the alleged tied product (the chicken seasoning) were not two separate products tied together unlawfully. Rather, the court stated that the use of the KFC trademarks and service marks by franchisees is *so* interrelated with the KFC chicken seasoning that *no person could reasonably find that the franchise and the seasoning are two separate products*. In the Kentucky Fried Chicken case, the court recognized the *need* and the *right* of a franchisor to require its franchisees to purchase certain products from the franchisor directly or from *its* designated sources if those products are so intimately related to the intellectual property licensed to the franchisee as to be necessary for maintaining the quality of the product identified by the trademark. The crucial inquiry is into the relationship between the trademark and the product allegedly tied to it.

In a similar case involving Baskin-Robbins franchisees, the court found that the trademark licensed to the Baskin-Robbins franchisees was inseparable from the ice cream itself and concluded that the trademark was therefore utterly dependent on the perceived quality of the product it represented. If the trademark serves *only* to identify the tied product, there can be no illegal tie-in, because the trademark and the quality of the product it represents are so inextricably interrelated in the mind of the consumer as to preclude any finding that the trademark is a separate product.

The crucial distinction is between a *product-driven* franchise system (distribution system), where the trademark represents the end product marketed by the system, and a *business-format* system in which the connection between the trademark and the products the franchisees are compelled to purchase is remote. In a product-driven system, a tying arrangement is more likely to be upheld because the products being tied to the purchase of the franchise are an integral part of the franchisor's system and are intimately related to the trademarks being licensed to the franchisee.

A *business-format franchise* is usually created merely to implement a particular business system under a common trade name. The franchise outlet itself is generally responsible for the production and preparation of the system's end product or service. The franchisor merely provides the trademark and, in some cases, also provides the supplies used in operating the franchised outlet and producing the system's products. Under a distribution system, the franchised outlet serves merely as a conduit through which the trademarked goods of the franchisor flow to the ultimate consumer. Generally, these goods are manufactured by the franchisor or by its licensees according to detailed specifications.

In a related case involving the Chicken Delight franchise system, the tied products imposed on the franchisees were commonplace paper products and packaging goods that were neither manufactured by the franchisor nor uniquely suited to the franchised business. Under the business-format franchise system, the connection between the trademark and the products the franchisees are compelled to purchase were remote enough that the trademark, which simply reflects the goodwill and quality standards of the enterprise it identifies, *may be considered as separate* from the commonplace items used to provide the product or service.

Therefore, for tying arrangements to be looked upon favorably, the court must find that the tied products are uniquely related to the franchise system and *intimately related* to the trademarks being licensed to franchisees. Thus, the purchase of certain products, which are sold by franchisees under the franchisor's trademarks and are highly proprietary and an integral part of the system, may be restricted by designating certain suppliers (even if that supplier is the franchisor) and maintaining strict product specifications.

On the other hand, restrictions on the purchase of supplies such as forms, service contracts, business cards, and signage are unlikely to be upheld as a valid tie-in because these items, although an integral part of the system, are not uniquely suited to the system or intimately related to the trademarks licensed to the franchisees. Furthermore, as more fully discussed later in the chapter, a restriction on the purchase of these supplies could not be justified if less restrictive alternatives are available that would yield the same level of quality control. In the case of commonplace supplies, a court could find that providing strict specifications for the quality and uniformity of supplies and allowing franchisees to obtain the approval of other suppliers for these items would be less restrictive and thus the favored method of ensuring quality and uniformity.

Justification for Certain Types of Tying Arrangements

An otherwise illegal tying arrangement may, under appropriate circumstances, be justified by a franchisor and upheld by a court. One such justification recognized by the courts is a tying arrangement necessary to preserve the distinctiveness, uniformity, and quality of a franchisor's products in connection with the license of the franchisor's trademarks.

In the case of a franchisor who grants a license to its franchisees to use its trademarks, the franchisor (licensor) owes an affirmative duty to the public to ensure that, in the hands of the licensee, the trademark continues to represent what it purports to represent. If a licensor relaxes quality control standards by permitting inferior products under a licensed mark, this may well constitute a misuse or even statutory abandonment of the mark. Courts have qualified what would appear to be a level of absolute discretion being vested in the franchisor by stating that *not all* means of achieving and maintaining quality control are justified. Rather, they have held that a restraint of trade can be justified only in the absence of less restrictive alternatives.

If specifications of the type and quality of the products to be used by the franchisee are sufficient to ensure the high standards of quality and uniformity that the franchisor desires to maintain, then this less restrictive alternative must be utilized in lieu of requiring the franchisee to purchase those products only from the franchisor. If specifications for a substitute would require such detail that they could not be supplied (i.e., they would divulge trade secrets or be unreasonably burdensome), then protection of the trademarks may warrant the use of what would otherwise be an illegal tying arrangement.

Whether such a tying arrangement is unlawful will depend on whether the franchisor can successfully demonstrate that restriction of sources to approved suppliers, as opposed to the exclusion of other potential sources, is necessary and justified in order to ensure product distinctness, uniformity, and quality. For example, in *Ungar v. Dunkin' Donuts of America, Inc.*, the court denied the franchisor's motion for summary judgment of an unlawful tying claim, holding that a requirement that franchisees purchase supplies from approved sources might have constituted an unlawful tying arrangement in view of allegations that the approved supplier system was merely a vehicle for payment of kickbacks and the franchisor was unwilling to approve new suppliers, despite their ability to meet specifications. Similarly, in *Midwestern Waffles, Inc. v. Waffle House, Inc.*, the court held that a franchisor's requirement that franchisees purchase equipment and vending services from approved sources could constitute a *per se* illegal tying arrangement because, although an approved source requirement was not by itself illegal, if franchisees were coerced into purchasing equipment from companies in which the franchisor had an interest, then the illegal tie could exist.

In another case, the tying arrangement was rejected. In *Siegel v. Chicken Delight, Inc.*, the court held that a franchisor's trademark and licenses were separate and distinct items from its packaging, mixes, and equipment that purportedly were essential components of the franchise system. The court explained that, in determining whether an aggregation of separable items should be regarded as one or more items for tie-in purposes in normal cases of sales, it must analyze the function of the aggregation and address such questions as cost savings and whether items involved are normally sold or used. "In franchising, it is not what articles are used but how they are used that gives the system and its end product entitlement to trademark protection."

In *William Cohen & Son, Inc. dba Quality Foods v. All American Hero, Inc.*, the issue of whether the franchisor's requirement that its franchisees purchase all of their supplies of marinated steak sandwiches from an affiliate company amounted to a *per se* illegal tying of the sandwich meat portions to the grant of restaurant franchises and could not be decided on summary judgment. Similarly, in *Carpa, Inc. v. Ward Foods, Inc.*, a seafood restaurant franchisor unlawfully tied the purchase of design fixtures, equipment, and food products to the use of its trademark where franchisees were required to pay large surcharges to the franchisor for approved items.

More recently, several courts have again recognized the business justification standard as an appropriate defense to an allegation that a franchisor is involved in an illegal tying arrangement. In 1987, the U.S. Court of Appeals held that a United States importer of German automobiles was justified in requiring its dealers to purchase all of their replacement parts from the importer as a condition of their securing a franchise to sell the automobiles in order to secure quality control, to protect goodwill, and to combat free-riding dealers. The court was satisfied with the substantial evidence to support the importer's assertion that the tie-in was used to ensure quality control in view of the fact that the importer purchased 80 percent of its parts from German manufacturers and subjected parts purchased from other manufacturers to an elaborate and rigorous inspection procedure.

On August 27, 1997, the United States Court of Appeals for the Third Circuit affirmed a lower court ruling dismissing antitrust claims against Domino's Pizza brought by an association of Domino's Pizza franchisees. The case, *Queen City Pizza, Inc. v. Domino's Pizza, Inc.*, involved an allegation by the plaintiffs that Domino's Pizza had monopolized the sale of ingredients and supplies to its franchisees and had engaged in illegal tying and exclusive dealing arrangements in violations of Sections 1 and 2 of the Sherman Act. The lower court had ruled that all of the plaintiff's antitrust claims failed because Domino's Pizza could not as a matter of law possess market power in ingredients and supplies sold to its franchisees. In dismissing the Sherman Act claims, the lower court concluded that whatever market power Domino's Pizza might have had over its franchisees arose out of its franchise agreement. The Court of Appeals held that Domino's-approved ingredients and supplies sold to Domino's Pizza franchisees could *not* be a relevant product market for antitrust purposes. The Court stated that a relevant product market includes all reasonably interchangeable products available to consumers (i.e., pizza stores) for the same purpose. Since ingredients and supplies sold by Domino's Pizza to its franchisees were comparable to (and reasonably interchangeable with) ingredients and supplies available from other suppliers and used by other pizza companies, these items could not be a separate market for antitrust purposes.

Whether a legally recognizable justification exists to warrant a tying arrangement ultimately depends on (1) the licensor's legitimate need to ensure quality control, (2) the availability of "less restrictive means" to achieve protection of the quality control, and (3) whether the alleged tied product is truly proprietary in nature. The relationship between the trademark and the product must be sufficiently intimate to justify the tie-in on grounds of quality control, uniformity, and protection of goodwill. More importantly, a tie-in otherwise justified in the name of quality control will not be upheld if less restrictive means are available for ensuring quality and uniformity.

There is a continuous struggle between the antitrust laws that generally disfavor tying arrangements and the trademark laws that impose a duty on the owner of a trademark to monitor the use of the mark by licensees to ensure that the licensor's standards of quality are maintained and that the licensee's use of the mark is consistent with those intentions.

Quality Control and the Field Support Staff

The franchisor's quality control program, which is for the most part administered by the field support staff, is the front line of defense for the franchisor's trademarks. Field support personnel are responsible for enforcing the franchisor's quality control standards and for reporting field conditions to the franchisor. Quality control strategies developed by top management may be misguided if the information gathered and reported by field support personnel is not accurate. The franchisor should therefore closely monitor its field support personnel and replace those who are lenient, arbitrary, or inconsistent.

In a large system, the field support staff is typically the only contact the franchisee will have with the franchisor. Therefore, all members of the field support staff have to possess the qualities necessary to create and maintain a good relationship with franchisees while reinforcing the franchisor's necessary standards. A properly administered quality control program provides the franchisor with a method for policing franchisees so as to achieve positive results and uniformity throughout the franchise system. By establishing, maintaining, and enforcing high standards of quality, all parties, including the franchisee, will benefit. Thus, the importance of quality control should be properly explained to franchisees (initially at training) and reinforced on an ongoing and consistent basis by field support personnel.

The role of field support staff does not end with the enforcement of quality control standards. Often, they act as troubleshooters in helping franchisees improve their business. In emergency situations, they may even step in as operating manager. For this reason, the franchisor's field personnel should be well educated in the intricacies of operating the franchise business. They should be able to handle any situation that may arise. They will be looked to as leaders and should be comfortable in that role. Above all, field support personnel should be good listeners and communicators.

Pricing as a Quality Control Enforcement Tool

Until recently, virtually all types of vertical price restraints were viewed by the courts as *per se* illegal, thereby giving franchisors the power to *suggest* prices but not the ability to *set* them. In November 1997, the U.S. Supreme Court reversed 30 years of case law by holding that vertical *maximum* price fixing arrangements were no longer *per se* illegal under Section 1 of the Sherman Act but that, rather, such maximum price fixing arrangements were now to be evaluated under a so-called rule of reason standard. Under this standard, a maximum price-fixing agreement is illegal only if it "imposes an unreasonable restraint on competition, taking into account a variety of factors, including specific information about the relevant business, its condition before and after the restraint was imposed, and the restraint's history, nature and effect" (*State Oil v. Kahn*).

The facts in *Kahn* involved a gasoline station operator who leased the station from State Oil Company and whose agreement required Kahn to buy gasoline from State Oil at a suggested retail price less a specified margin. The agreement also required that any profit Kahn earned as a result of charging customers more than the suggested retail price be rebated to State Oil. When Kahn was being evicted after falling behind on his lease payments, he sued State Oil for preventing him from raising his prices, asserting vertical maximum price fixing in violation of Section 1 of the Sherman Act. The *Kahn* court did not change the law on minimum price fixing arrangements, however, and such arrangements are still *per se* illegal. The result of *Kahn* is that a supplier or franchisor must now determine whether the imposition of maximum prices somehow restrains trade unreasonably.

Although minimum price fixing is *per se* illegal, at least one court has held that setting price points without either a floor or ceiling may be permitted. In *Great Clips, Inc. v. Levine*, the court found that Great Clips' even-dollar, single-price restrictions did not violate the Sherman Act. The Great Clips pricing policy required franchisees to charge an even-dollar price (e.g., $7.00, $8.00, $9.00, etc.) but did not set the price. Great Clips also required franchisees to post a single price for haircuts on its price board. Great Clips did allow franchisees to offer discounts from the even-dollar price, however, but only on 21 days out of every three months. This restriction was imposed to ensure compliance with certain consumer fraud regulations, according to Great Clips. Franchisees were also permitted to offer coupons through direct mail and print media.

The *Great Clips* court explained that the even-dollar single price restriction was not anticompetitive because Great Clips franchisees were free to set the price within the restricted pricing structure. Even the imposition of the "3 weeks per 3 months" discount policy did not violate the Sherman Act, the court explained, because franchisees had many ways to set their prices without violating the franchisee agreement. The court noted Great Clips' "legitimate and important interests in how the franchise is run"; it also noted that Great Clips' marketing strategy was procompetitive because it would stimulate interbrand competition and that it must be the focus of the inquiry.

Suggested resale prices have long been recognized as a form of manufacturer/supplier price maintenance that does not violate antitrust laws. Problems sometimes do arise, however, when steps are taken to *force* dealers or retailers to observe so-called suggested prices. On the other hand, a manufacturer/supplier is free to refuse to sell to a distributor/retailer who refuses to sell at the suggested price. The inquiry typically focuses on coercion by the manufacturer.

The *Great Clips* court addressed the practice of offering discounts and coupons in the context of examining the franchisor's control over the retail prices of its franchisees. The court explained the general rule that pricing restrictions such as those imposed by Great Clips will not be *per se* illegal, even though they may affect the franchisee's prices, because such restrictions do not directly limit the franchisee's freedom to independently establish its prices. In the Great Clips system, the court noted, the franchisees were free to establish discounts and special events pricing. The court noted that even though Great Clips further limited its franchisees pricing practices with the three-week/three-month discount limitation, the franchisees remained free to offer coupons through such means as "direct mail promotions, return customer coupons, newspaper advertisements, flyer distributions, radio offers and business discounts through paycheck stuffers," among others. Thus, as long as Great Clips did not actually specify the prices to be charged, the even-dollar, single-price policy, *together with the franchisee's ability to offer discounts and coupons on a limited basis*, was not *per se* an unreasonable restraint of trade in violation of the Sherman Act and, in the court's view, did not constitute an unreasonable restraint.

If a franchisor chooses to restrict the use of coupons, discounts, and rebates, that indirect price restriction policy would not by itself be a violation of the Sherman Act. The anticoupon policy in conjunction with specified price points, however, would be problematic based on the analysis in *Great Clips*, which allows certain indirect restrictions, such as the even-dollar and/or single-price policies, so long as the franchisee retained flexibility and independence in setting prices. The combination of these pricing restrictions would appear to cross the line from reasonable to unreasonable under *Great Clips*.

Under *Kahn*, a franchisor has some flexibility in setting *maximum* resale prices of the products sold by its franchisees, provided the franchisor can justify its policy for imposing what might be argued is an anticompetitive restriction. If a franchisor wishes to impose maximum prices, it should document this policy as necessary in order to compete effectively and set forth all the reasons demonstrating that this policy does not unreasonably restrain trade. Even after *Kahn*, however, the prices set may only be a ceiling, not a floor. In other words, the franchisor may not set specific retail prices because doing so is akin to setting minimum prices, which remains *per se* illegal.

In addition, a franchisor may rely on the *Great Clips* decision for the ability to establish a pricing policy providing for even-dollar pricing or single-price requirements, as long as no minimum is set. The franchisor may also choose to restrict its franchisees from offering coupons or discounts. At the same time, however, *Great Clips* dictates that such anticouponing policies in conjunction with even-dollar-pricing restrictions would constitute an antitrust violation.

U.S. Supreme Court Changes Course on Minimum Resale Price Maintenance

On June 28, 2007, the Supreme Court issued a landmark decision expressly overruling nearly a century-old precedent holding that it was *per se* unlawful for manufacturers and wholesalers to require retailers not to sell their products below a specified price (a practice referred to as "vertical resale price maintenance," or RPM). In *Leegin Creative Leather Products, Inc. v. PSKS, Inc.*, the court held that manufacturers and wholesalers can engage in RPM practices as long as their minimum prices satisfy the rule of reason. Although this was generally seen as good news for the creators of products and as potentially bad news for small retailers and especially consumers, the effects may prove unpredictable both in the marketplace and the courtroom.

The *Leegin* case arose out of a dispute between Leegin Creative Leather Products, a designer and manufacturer of Brighton leather goods and accessories, and one of its retail distributors, PSKS. Leegin instituted a policy under which it refused to sell its products to retailers who discounted the products below Leegin's suggested retail prices. A year later, Leegin learned that PSKS was discounting Brighton products up to 20 percent below Leegin's suggested retail prices. Leegin stopped selling to PSKS, and, in response, PSKS sued Leegin, alleging violation of the federal antitrust laws.

The lower courts applied the existing *per se* prohibition on minimum price fixing, which meant that Leegin could not present any testimony about the favorable business effects of its minimum pricing policy. There was no dispute that Leegin had ceased sales to PSKS because it was violating the policy, and PSKS won a substantial jury verdict against Leegin. However, on appeal, the Supreme Court reversed, eliminating the *per se* rule against RPM, and therefore sent the case back for a new trial in which Leegin could introduce evidence of the "pro-competitive effects" of its minimum pricing policy under the rule of reason analysis.

Under the rule of reason, a minimum retail price restraint will be enforceable unless it is "an unreasonable restraint on competition." The rule of reason analyzes whether a price restraint has a harmful and anticompetitive effect on consumers or whether the restraint stimulates competition that truly is in the consumers' best interests. In other words, for the relevant product market (i.e., genuine leather pocketbooks) and the geographic location (i.e., Denton County, Texas), did the restraint provide no benefit to consumers on an interbrand basis, or did it provide them with a better choice overall when considering price, service, and product quality and variety of styles? If the effect is not yet clear, is the restraint likely to be clear in the future?

An example of a valid procompetitive reason would be instituting minimum prices to prevent bargain retailers or Internet sellers from taking customers from full-service retailers who charge higher prices because they spend time and money building up the reputation of the brand through advertising and point-of-sale service. The court has also noted that minimum retail price maintenance by new product sellers may be particularly procompetitive because minimum pricing by emerging brands is likely to increase interbrand competition in competitive markets by allowing new brands to entice well-reputed retailers to "make the kind of investment of capital [i.e., promotion] and labor [i.e., point-of-sale service] that is often required in the distribution of products unknown to the consumer."

What *Leegin* Means for Franchisors as Product Sellers

Although most franchisors are primarily in the business of providing intellectual property by licensing trademarks and business methods, as well as advisory and other services, to their franchisees, a substantial minority also sell products to their franchisees; some also directly sell products to their franchisees for resale. *Leegin* grants franchisors the right to impose minimum resale prices on the products they sell to franchisees in its system.

The court in *Leegin* stated that if a retailer challenges a minimum-pricing policy, the seller will have to affirmatively demonstrate that the policy has procompetitive effects. Thus, it will be important for franchisors instituting RPM programs to act reasonably and judiciously in formulating their minimum prices, and they should keep a record of all factors considered and decisions made with respect to their minimum pricing policies.

The franchisor should identify the procompetitive purpose it hopes to achieve by using a resale price policy. For example, the franchise system may be able to document that its franchisees (and other retail sellers, if appropriate) are not providing adequate service to the consumer, thereby either reducing the total number of sales or reducing the percentage of additional purchases by customers. By mandating a minimum price, the franchisor can guarantee that the retailer will achieve a minimum gross profit margin on each unit sold, and in exchange the franchisor will be able to require that high-quality service be provided to consumers and cease selling to retailers who don't provide it. (See Figure 4-5.)

Figure 4.5. Steps in developing a mandatory retail pricing policy.

1. Identify the procompetitive effect intended through mandating retail prices.

2. Monitor the franchisees' subsequent performance, and steps taken by competing brands, to make sure that the pricing policy is having the intended effect.

3. Within a reasonable time after implementing the policy, measure whether the intended procompetitive effect has been achieved.

What about the franchisor who does not sell finished or semifinished products to their franchisees, but nevertheless cares about pricing because of store-level advertising programs? The *State Oil v. Khan* decision (cited earlier in this chapter) eliminated the *per se* prohibition on maximum resale prices, thereby making it easier for McDonald's and other systems to effectively implement maximum price promotions (such as the $1 menu). The *Leegin* decision arguably takes the next step and allows franchise companies to specify the retail price (without exception) that their franchisees will charge, a practice that certainly will make standardized promotion of all system units much easier.

CHAPTER 5

The Regulation of Franchising

Introduction

he offer and sale of franchises are regulated under federal and state law. Federal franchise law is embodied principally in a regulation promulgated by the Federal Trade Commission (FTC) and commonly referred to by those involved in franchising as the "FTC Rule" (codified at 16 CFR §437). The FTC Rule, which became law in 1979 and was formally titled "Disclosure Requirements and Prohibitions Concerning Franchising and Business Opportunity Ventures," requires franchisors to make certain disclosures to prospective franchisees in the United States and its territories. The FTC Rule applies to product- and business-format franchises that have three elements:

❐ The franchisee sells goods or services or operates a business identified by or associated with the franchisor's trademark, service mark, trade name, advertising, or other commercial symbol designating the franchisor (a Mark) that are identified by the franchisor's Mark.

❐ The franchisor exercises significant control over or provides significant assistance in the franchisee's method of operation.

❐ The franchisee is required to make payment of $500 or more to the franchisor or a person affiliated with the franchisor at any time before to within six months after the business opens.

In addition to the FTC Rule, over a dozen states (known as "registration states") have enacted their own rules and regulations governing the offer and sale of franchises. The franchise laws of a particular registration state typically apply to the offer or sale of a franchise when the franchisee is a resident of that state or when the franchise will be operated within its borders. The registration states include most of the nation's largest commercial marketplaces, such as California, New York, and Illinois. State franchise laws typically use a three-element (or "three-legged stool") definition similar to the FTC Rule, although the "legs" may differ, as discussed later in this chapter.

In 2007, the FTC adopted amendments to the FTC Rule, now entitled "Disclosure Requirements and Prohibitions Concerning Franchising" (referred to as the "Amended FTC Rule"). These were the first changes to the FTC Rule since its adoption almost 30 years earlier. Among other things, the Amended FTC Rule dictated the use of a single disclosure document to provide the potential franchisee with the information necessary to facilitate an informed purchase. This new format is entitled (not surprisingly) the franchised disclosure document (FDD) and may be used anywhere in the United States. This change is significant because, prior to the adoption of the Amended FTC Rule, a franchisor could choose to follow one of two formats: the FTC format or the Uniform Franchise Offering Circular (UFOC) format. The FTC format was prescribed under the original FTC Rule, and the UFOC format was developed by the Midwest Securities Commissioners Association in 1975 and later monitored and revised by the successor organization, the North American Securities Administrators Association. Most franchisors used the UFOC format, however, because it was the format required in the registration states. The Amended FTC Rule simplified the disclosure process by eliminating the dual format system and prescribing one standard for the information that must be included in the FDD and its format. The Amended FTC Rule also prescribes the timing for the delivery of the FDD, which must occur at least 14 days before any binding agreement is signed or any payment to the franchisor is made.

Other key improvements in the Amended FTC Rule have made it easier both for U.S. and overseas franchisors to explore opportunities in the U.S. market. These improvements may help reduce the level of preliminary effort and expense required for franchisors to test the waters of franchise expansion in the United States. Some of these are summarized in Figure 5-1.

Under the Amended FTC Rule, foreign franchisors may prepare their financial statements with a comprehensive basis of accounting standards other than U.S. GAAP, as long as there is an audited reconciliation to U.S. GAAP. Also, foreign franchisors may now use a non-U.S. accounting firm as long as that firm (1) is registered with the Public Company Accounting Oversight Board (PCAOB), the U.S. entity charged with monitoring auditing standards for public companies, and (2) has recently audited one or more financial statements included in a filing with the U.S. Securities and Exchange Commission (SEC). Foreign accountants registered with the PCAOB are subject to the same auditing standards as their U.S. counterparts.

One other note regarding the regulation of business opportunity ventures: The original FTC Rule regulated both franchises and business opportunity ventures (as indicated by the formal title of the original FTC Rule). Business opportunity ventures are similar in some ways to franchises but are defined by a different set of three characteristics (where the company is similar to the franchisor and the buyer is similar to the franchisee):

❏ The company sells goods or services that are supplied by the company or a person affiliated with the company.

Figure 5-1. Key Improvements in the Amended FTC Rule.

1. *New Exemptions for Larger, Sophisticated or Experienced Franchisees*: Under the Amended FTC Rule, three new exemptions are available for transactions involving larger, sophisticated, or experienced franchisees. If a franchisor can take advantage of one or more exemptions, then the franchise disclosure and related compliance requirements will not apply. These new exemptions are available if:

   (a) the franchisee is a high-net-worth company or individual (at least US $5 million) and has been in business for at least 5 years;

   (b) the franchisee must make a large initial investment (more than US $1 million); or

   (c) the franchisees are insiders, such as officers, directors, general partners, managers, or owners of a franchisor.

   In addition to these new exemptions, the exemptions that were included in the original FTC Rule are still available. These include exemptions for (1) fractional franchises, (2) leased department arrangements, (3) purely verbal agreements, and (4) minimum required payments below the $500 threshold within the first six months of operations (which really is simply a method of avoiding the required payment element of the franchise definition under the Amended FTC Rule). Another important exemption related to the required payment element is the inventory exemption. Under the Amended FTC Rule (and in the original FTC Rule), a required payment under the franchise definition specifically excludes payments for the purchase of "reasonable amounts of inventory at bona fide wholesale prices for resale or lease." A "reasonable amount" is an amount that is not more than what a "reasonable businessperson" normally would purchase for a starting inventory or supply or to maintain an ongoing inventory or supply. This inventory exemption also includes goods intended to be furnished to the public through lease. Franchisees in the auto or furniture rental business, for example, can therefore take advantage of this exemption. The inventory exemption does not include goods that a franchisee must purchase for its own use in the operation of the business, such as equipment or ordinary business supplies, however.

   Finally, the Amended FTC Rule also excludes (1) relationships between employer and employees and among general partners (but not limited partners) in a business, (2) membership in retailer-owned cooperatives, (3) certification and testing services, and (4) single trademark licenses. This last exclusion includes one-on-one licensing arrangements where the license of a trademark is to a single licensee who manufactures the trademarked goods according to the licensor's specifications. This is common, for example, in the clothing industry where trademark owners license the manufacture of textiles. The single trademark license exclusion also includes collateral product licensing, where a trademark that is well known in one context (e.g., a soft drink logo) is licensed for use in another (e.g., on clothing or decorative items embossed with the soft drink logo).

2. *No More "First Personal Meeting" Disclosure Requirement:* In the past, many domestic and foreign franchisors have avoided the United States because they were required to commit considerable resources to the preparation of a disclosure document before even meeting with a prospective franchisee. Under the Amended FTC Rule's new process, however, a franchisor may now first test the waters for their concept before incurring the expense of disclosure compliance. Specifically, a franchisor now may exhibit at U.S. trade shows and engage in discussions with prospective franchisees without having to deliver an FDD. Prior to the Amended FTC Rule, a franchisor had to deliver disclosure documents to a prospective franchisee at the time of a first personal meeting to discuss a possible franchise relationship. This is no longer the case. The Amended FTC Rule now simply requires disclosures to be provided at least 14 calendar days before a prospective franchisee makes any payment to the franchisor or its affiliate or before signing any binding agreement in connection with the franchise sale.

   The benefit to would-be franchisors is they no longer have to incur the legal, accounting, and market research expenses necessary to prepare an FDD in order to attend trade shows and to

(continues)

Figure 5-1. (Continued)

evaluate franchise opportunities in the United States. Under the Amended FTC Rule, the time, effort, and expense of preparing the FDD (including audited financial statements and franchise agreements) may be deferred until one or more legitimate franchisee candidates are identified. These expenses can be significant, especially with respect to the preparation and audit of financial statements.

3. *Electronic Disclosure Is Specifically Permitted:* The Amended FTC Rule expressly permits franchisors to deliver the disclosure documents through electronic means, such as on a compact disc, through e-mail, through Internet downloads, or posted on Web pages. Although the disclosure documents must still be in writing, there is no longer a need to incur the expense of preparing and delivering paper copies of the often lengthy FDD.

4. *No More Waiting Period After Mutually Negotiating Changes to the Franchise Agreement:* Before the Amended FTC Rule, a prospective franchisee must have been furnished fully completed final form franchise and related agreements at least five business days before executing them. This meant that even nonmaterial fill-in-the-blank terms inserted into the standard form would trigger a new five-business-day waiting period. And if any negotiated terms of the standard agreements benefited the franchisor, the waiting period restarted. Under the Amended FTC Rule, however, there is no need to restart the waiting period after negotiating changes initiated by the prospective franchisee and revising the agreements accordingly. If a franchisor *unilaterally* and *materially* alters the terms of basic agreements attached to the FDD, however, a new waiting period will start.

5. *More Flexibility in Accounting and Audit Requirements for Financial Statements:* For foreign franchisors, the requirement to include audited financial statements in the FDD often requires significant time and expense. Before the Amended FTC Rule, a franchisor's financial statements were required to be prepared in accordance with U.S. Generally Accepted Accounting Principles (GAAP). However, foreign franchisors would typically prepare their financial statements according to their own country's GAAP. Further, the audit of the franchisor's financial statements was required to be done in accordance with U.S. Generally Accepted Auditing Standards (GAAS). This typically limited the choice of auditor to a U.S. accounting firm, which would not likely be familiar with the franchisor or its financial history.

❐ The company assists the buyer in any way with respect to securing accounts for the buyer, securing locations or sites for vending machines or rack displays, or providing the services of a person able to do either.

❐ The buyer is required to make a payment of $500 or more to the company or a person affiliated with the company at any time before to within six months after the business opens.

With the adoption of the Amended FTC Rule, however, the FTC created a separate regulation solely covering business opportunity ventures (16 CFR §437). The Amended FTC Rule no longer regulates business opportunity ventures.

The Registration States

Almost ten years before the FTC adopted the FTC Rule, California had already begun to regulate the offer and sale of franchises. In 1970, the California Franchise Investment Law was enacted by the California legislature. Many states followed the lead of California, and today 15 states regulate franchise offers and sales. The states that require full registration and merit review of a franchise offering prior to the "offering" or selling of a franchise are California, Maryland, Minnesota, New York, North Dakota, Rhode Island, Virginia, and Washington.

Other states that regulate franchise offers are:

❏ Hawaii, which requires the filing of a franchise disclosure document (FDD) and which will engage in a limited review of the franchisor's FDD documents.

❏ Indiana and Wisconsin, which require filing the FDD with the state authorities.

❏ Michigan, which requires filing of a Notice of Intent to Offer and Sell Franchises.

❏ Oregon, which requires only that presale disclosure be delivered to prospective investors, consistent with the Amended FTC Rule.

States that regulate the sale of business opportunities or seller-assisted marketing plans, such as Connecticut, Kentucky, Florida, Texas, Utah, and Nebraska, have exemptions available for franchisors that comply with the Amended FTC Rule or that offer a franchise including a license of a federally registered trademark. These states require the filing of a notice of exemption with the appropriate state agency.

Scope of the Amended FTC Rule

The Amended FTC Rule was adopted and is enforced by the FTC pursuant to its power and authority to regulate unfair and deceptive trade practices under the Federal Trade Commission Act (FTC Act). The relationship between the Amended FTC Rule and state franchise laws is noteworthy in that the Amended FTC Rule establishes a minimum level of protection that must be afforded to all prospective franchisees. If the state franchise law in a registration state provides prospective franchisees within its jurisdiction a greater level of protection, the Amended FTC Rule will not preempt state law. There is no private right of action under the Amended FTC Rule. However, the FTC itself may bring an enforcement action against a franchisor that does not meet its requirements, pursuant to its authority under Section 5 of the FTC Act, which prohibits unfair or deceptive acts or practices in interstate commerce. Penalties for noncompliance have included asset impoundments, cease and desist orders, injunctions, consent orders, mandated rescission or restitution for injured franchisees, and civil fines of up to $11,000 per violation. The individuals who formulate, direct, or control the franchisor's activities also can expect to be named individually for violations committed in the franchisor's name, together with the franchisor entity, and held personally liable for civil penalties and consumer redress.

Under Section 5 of the FTC Act, it is an unfair or deceptive act or practice for any franchisor or franchise broker:

❏ To fail to furnish prospective franchisees with an FDD all the information required by the Amended FTC Rule before taking a franchisee's payment or entering into a binding agreement in connection with the sale of a franchise.

❏ To make any representations about the actual or potential sales, income, or profits of existing or prospective franchisees except in the manner set forth in the Amended FTC Rule.

❏ To fail to return to prospective franchisees any funds or deposits (such as down payments) identified as refundable in the FDD.

The Amended FTC Rule has established a minimum federal standard of disclosure applicable to all franchisor offerings. As noted, however, individual states are permitted to provide additional protection to their citizens or to those operating businesses within their jurisdictions. Thus, the Amended FTC Rule will not preempt state law and regulations that either are consistent with the Rule or, even if inconsistent, would provide protection to prospective franchisees equal to or greater than that imposed by the Rule.

Examples of state laws or regulations that would not be preempted by the Rule include state provisions requiring the registration of franchisors and franchise salespersons, state requirements for escrow or bonding arrangements, and state-required disclosure obligations set forth in the Rule. Moreover, the Rule does not affect state laws or regulations that regulate the franchisor-franchisee relationship, such as termination practices, contract provisions, and financing arrangements.

Guidelines for Determining What *Is* and What *Is Not* a Franchise

Companies frequently seek advice on how to structure a relationship that avoids the definition of a franchise under federal or state laws. The first question I ask is why? And the answer usually is to avoid, for the appropriate legal or strategic reasons, having to comply with the registration and disclosure laws. Most such companies fall into one of the following categories:

❏ Overseas franchisors who are uncomfortable with the concepts of disclosure, which may not be required in their country of origin.

❏ Midsized or large companies that feel that (as pioneers) their industry is not ready for or will react adversely to the kinds of controls that a franchise relationship typically implies.

❏ Companies or individual officers with something in their pasts that they would prefer not to be disclosed (raising other legal problems).

❏ Small companies concerned about the perceived costs of preparing and maintaining the legal documents.

❏ Firms with the real or perceived belief that, by becoming a franchisor, they somehow increase their chances of being sued (a myth I usually try to debunk).

❏ Companies involved in some other specific circumstances or holding some other myth or fear about franchising.

When dealing with such companies, we usually try to solve their problem with creative thinking and structural alternatives before dealing with the parameters developed by the courts and regulatory authorities over the years that provide some (but not complete) insight into which relationships will be considered a franchise and which will not. For example, a foreign franchisor may want to set up a new subsidiary in lieu of disclosing the financial statements of the parent company (usually in the case of a privately held company). If the subsidiary is properly capitalized and certain other specific conditions are met, the confidentiality of the parent company's data may be preserved. For midsized or large companies, we have often created the nonfranchise franchisor, which is a company that has essentially agreed to prepare and provide a FDD even though the details of their relationships are in a regulatory gray area. Thus the franchisor appeases the regulators but also placates the industry participants who may be more comfortable with a strategic partner or licensee designation than with a franchisor-franchisee relationship.

If the company is insistent on avoiding the need to comply with federal and state franchise laws, we then determine from a cost-benefit analysis which leg of the three-legged stool (representing the three elements required to be a franchise) may be sacrificed. In today's brand-driven environment, the willingness to license the system without the brand to avoid the trademark license leg has not been very popular. Similarly, in an economy where cash flow is king, most of these clients have not been willing to waive the initial franchise fee or wait over six months for their financial rewards. And the age-old trick of hiding the franchise fee in a training program or initial inventory package was figured out by the regulators a long time ago.

So often the third leg of the stool—the one that is most difficult to interpret—is where the creative structuring must take place. The courts and the federal and state regulators have not provided much clear guidance as to the *degrees* of support or the *degrees* of assistance that will meet the definition and those that will not. The mandatory use of an operating system or marketing plan will meet the third element of the test, but what if use of the system is optional? What if the plan or system is not very detailed and provides the franchisee with a lot of room for discretion without penalty for adapting the plan or system to meet local market conditions? And if you choose this path, does allowing this degree of discretion and flexibility sacrifice your ability to maintain quality control? In addition, in a competitive environment where most growing companies are trying to provide more and more support and assistance to (as well as exerting more control over) their partners in the distribution channel, would providing less than the norm just to avoid the definition of a franchise really make sense? These legal and strategic decisions should not be made hastily without the long-term implications properly analyzed.

Analysis Under the Amended FTC Rule

Franchise is defined in Section 436.1(h) of the Amended FTC Rule as having three key components: (1) the franchisee's goods and/or services are to be offered and sold under the franchisor's trademarks; (2) the franchisee is required to make a minimum $500 payment to the franchisor; and (3) the franchisor exercises (or has authority to exercise) significant control over, or provide significant assistance to, the franchisee's method of operation. Each of these components is outlined below.

Trademark

This element is satisfied when the franchisee is given the right to distribute goods or services under the franchisor's trademark or service mark.

Required Payment

This element is met if a franchisee is required to pay the franchisor at least $500 as a condition of obtaining the franchise or of commencing operations. Payments made at any time prior to or within six months after commencing operations will be aggregated to determine whether the $500 threshold is met. The payments may be required by the franchise agreement, by an ancillary agreement between the parties, or by practical necessity (such as required supplies that are available only from the franchisor.

Significant Control and Assistance

The key to this element is that the control or assistance must be "significant." According to the "FTC's Franchise Rule Compliance Guide" (the "Compliance Guide"), the FTC explains significant control or assistance as follows:

> The more franchisees reasonably rely upon the franchisor's control or assistance, the more likely the control or assistance will be considered "significant." Franchisees' reliance is likely to be great when they are relatively inexperienced in the business being offered for sale or when they undertake a large financial risk. Similarly, franchisees are likely to reasonably rely on the franchisor's control or assistance if the control or assistance is unique to that specific franchisor, as opposed to a typical practice employed by all businesses in the same industry.

The "Compliance Guide" goes on to explain that "to be deemed 'significant,' the control or assistance must relate to the franchisee's overall method of operation—not a small part of the franchisee's business. Control or assistance involving the sale of a specific product that has, at most, a marginal effect on a franchisee's method of operating the overall business will not be considered in determining whether control or assistance is 'significant.'"

The presence of *any one* of the following types of control or assistance may suggest the existence of "significant control or assistance" sufficient to meet this part of the definition of a franchise:

Types of Control	*Types of Assistance*
Site approval	Formal sales, repair, or business training
Site design/appearance requirements	Establishing accounting systems
Dictating hours of operation	Furnishing management, marketing, or personnel advice
Production techniques	Site selection assistance
Accounting practices	Furnishing a detailed operations manual
Personnel policies and practices	
Required participation in, or financial contribution to, promotional campaigns	
Restrictions on customers	
Restrictions on sales area or location	

A wide variety of strategic questions and structural issues need to be considered in this analysis:

❐ Do we anticipate the relationship to be short term or long term?

❐ Are we ready to sacrifice the ability to build brand awareness and to increase the value of other intangible assets on our balance sheet in a brand-driven competitive environment?

❐ Are we prepared to deliver the level and the quality of training and support that is typically implied and expected in the franchisor-franchisee relationship?

❐ Will we be converting or keeping in place existing distributors, sales representatives, or other components of the current distribution channel? How will the franchising program *truly* differ?

❐ In considering the operational dynamics of the proposed relationship, how interdependent do we really need or want to be? Are you truly inextricably intertwined with synergistic and shared goals, or would a more casual commitment suffice? Would a joint venture or strategic partnering relationship adequately suffice?

❐ To what extent will training, support, marketing, and other key functions be uniform and centralized? Or will a more flexible system suffice?

❐ Could you unbundle the license of the intellectual properly being offered, making items an optional menu of support and services rather than making them mandatory and integrated?

❐ If you choose to operate in the gray area and without a FDD, how comfortable are you and your management team with living with the possibility of a regulatory investigation and/or a system-wide rescission offer if the relationship is subsequently deemed to be a franchise? How comfortable with this strategy are you if your company is publicly traded?

❏ To what extent will market conditions dictate that you maintain control over the product mix, warranty policies, discounting policies, and other business decisions or the need to conduct quality control audits or make pricing suggestions?

Again, weakening key strategic aspects of the program merely to avoid compliance with federal and state franchise laws does not make sense. The courts and the regulators are likely to examine the totality of the relationship, with an emphasis on reality and practice, rather than on the written word of the contract or offering materials. For example, if you take the position that the support services are optional but in practice 99 percent of your franchisees have elected to use and pay for them, then the reality of the situation will probably prevail. If the marketing plan or operating system is prescribed in substantial part by you in practice, and if there will be adverse consequences to the other party if these procedures and standards are not followed—whether or not your agreement says so—then you will have difficulty supporting your position that you are not a franchise. Although a "community of interest" is not generally a term that provides much insight, here are some factors directly considered by the court in arriving at this determination:

❏ The franchisor's advertising claims to prospective franchisees that a successful marketing plan is available.

❏ The contemplation of nationwide or area-wide distribution on an exclusive or semiexclusive basis, possibly with multiple levels of jurisdiction (such as regional and location distributorships and arrangements) designed to establish uniformity of prices and marketing terms.

❏ Reservation of control by the franchisor over matters such as customer terms and payments, credit practices, and warranties and representations made to customers.

❏ The franchisor's rendering of collateral services to the franchisee.

❏ Any prohibition or limitation on the franchisee's sale of competitive or noncompetitive products.

❏ A requirement that the franchisee observe the franchisor's direction or obtain the franchisor's approval for site selection, trade names, advertising, signs, appearance of the franchisee's business premises, fixtures and equipment used in the business, employee uniforms, hours of operation, housekeeping procedures, and other such issues.

❏ The franchisor's implementation of its requirements regarding the conduct of the business by inspection and reporting procedures.

❏ The franchisor's right to take corrective measures that may be at the franchisee's expense.

❏ Comprehensive advertising or other promotional programs, especially if the programs identify the location of the franchisee and if the franchisee's advertising or promotional activities require the franchisor's approval.

❐ Granting of an exclusive territory and the sale of products or services at bona fide wholesale prices.

❐ Percentage discounts (although insubstantial) and mutual advertising and soliciting by the franchisor and the franchisee.

❐ Volume discounts, attained by a system of distributors and subdistributors, and mutual advertising.

❐ Franchisee's use of the franchisor's confidential operating manuals or forms and mutual opportunity for profit.

❐ Granting of an exclusive patent and an exclusive territory, and a training program for which the franchisor receives payment from the franchisee.

❐ Required purchases from the franchisor, an exclusive territory, franchisor-supplied advertising, the provision of leads to the franchisee, and prohibitions on selling competitive products.

❐ Franchisee's selection of locations and required purchases through the franchisor.

❐ Performance of services devised by the franchisor, franchisor-approved forms, mutual service of customers, franchisor approval of the franchisee's presentations, and mutual financial benefit.

❐ Franchisee's production of products under the franchisor's patent, technical assistance, training, the franchisee's ability to subfranchise, and required record keeping.

❐ The franchisor's selection of locations, the franchisee's purchase of product from the franchisor for regularly serviced accounts, and required record keeping.

State Franchise Laws

Definitions of a Franchise under State Law

Each state franchise disclosure statute has its own definition of a franchise that is similar to, but different from, the definition set forth in the FTC Rule. If the relationship meets the definition of a franchise under applicable state law, then the franchisor must comply with the registration and disclosure laws in the state in question.

There are three major types of state definitions of a franchise:

1. *Majority State Definition.* In the states of California, Illinois, Indiana, Maryland, Michigan, North Dakota, Oregon, Rhode Island, Virginia, and Wisconsin, a franchise is defined as having three essential elements:

   • A franchisee is granted the right to engage in the business of offering, selling, or distributing goods or services under a marketing plan or system prescribed in substantial part by a franchisor.

- The operation of the franchisee's business is substantially associated with the franchisor's trademark or other commercial symbol designating the franchisor or its affiliate.

- The franchisee is required to pay a fee.

The definition in Virginia is limited to the offer, sale, or distribution of goods and services *at retail.*

2. *Minority State Definition.* The states of Hawaii, Minnesota, South Dakota, and Washington have adopted a somewhat broader definition of a franchise. In these states, a franchise is defined as having the following three essential elements:

- A franchisee is granted the right to engage in the business of offering or distributing goods or services using the franchisor's trade name or other commercial symbol or related characteristics.

- The franchisor and franchisee have a common interest in the marketing of goods or services.

- The franchisee pays a fee.

3. *New York Definition.* The state of New York has a unique definition. Under its law, a franchisee is defined by two guidelines:

- The franchisor is paid a fee by the franchisee.

- The franchisee either is essentially associated with the franchisor's trademark *or* operates under a marketing plan or system prescribed in substantial part by the franchisor.

Thus, New York requires a fee but specifies *either* association with franchisor's trademark *or* a marketing plan prescribed by the franchisor. Therefore, in New York no trademark license is required for a franchise relationship to exist. However, the regulations in New York exclude from the definition of a franchise any relationship in which a franchisor does not provide significant assistance to or exert significant controls over a franchisee.

Preparing the FDD

The FDD consists of 23 categories of information that must be provided by the franchisor to the prospective franchisee at least 14 business days prior to the execution of a binding agreement or before any payment is made to the franchisor. Because the Amended FTC Rule dictates the format and contents of the FDD, franchisors may not change the order in which information is presented, nor may any of the disclosure items be omitted in the document. In addition, many sections of the FDD must be a mirror image of the actual franchise agreement (and related documents) that the franchisee will be expected to sign. There should be no factual or legal inconsistencies between the FDD and the franchise agreement. Figure 5-2 sets out the required FDD contents and illustrates the specific topical sections that must be covered in every FDD. The exhibits are listed as an example of what would typically be included in the FDD in addition to the 23 disclosure items.

Figure 5-2. FDD table of contents.

Item	Contents
1	The Franchisor and Its Parents, Predecessors and Affiliates
2	Business Experience
3	Litigation
4	Bankruptcy
5	Initial Fees
6	Other Fees
7	Estimated Initial Investment
8	Restrictions on Sources of Products and Services
9	Franchisee's Obligations
10	Financing
11	Franchisor's Obligations, Assistance, Advertising, Computer Systems, and Training
12	Territory
13	Trademarks
14	Patents, Copyrights, and Proprietary Information
15	Obligation to Participate in the Actual Operation of the Franchise Business
16	Restrictions on What the Franchisee May Sell
17	Renewal, Termination, Transfer, and Dispute Resolution
18	Public Figures
19	Financial Performance Representations
20	Outlets and Franchisee Information
21	Financial Statements
22	Contracts
23	Receipt

Exhibits

Exhibit A	State-Specific Addendum
Exhibit B	Franchise Agreement and State Amendments
Exhibit C	Principal Owner's Guaranty
Exhibit D	Operations Manual Table of Contents
Exhibit E	Nonsolicitation, Noncompetition, and Confidentiality Agreement
Exhibit F	Franchisee Roster
Exhibit G	State Agencies and Agents for Service of Process
Exhibit H	Financial Statements
Exhibit I	Franchise Compliance Certificate
Exhibit J	Terms and Conditions of Use of Franchisor's Webmail
Exhibit K	Receipt

Data to Gather When Implementing a Franchising Program

The mandatory disclosures in the FDD will provide an appropriate starting point for a new franchisor in developing its franchising program. It may be useful to divide the 23 separate sections of the FDD into five general categories:

1. Background information about the franchise, its ownership, and key management employees, as well as recent involvement in litigation.

2. Financial performance information about the franchise, existing franchise outlets, and hypothetical new franchise outlets.

3. Franchisee required financial investment and available financing.

4. Basic contractual rights and responsibilities of franchisor and franchisee.

5. Operational rules and regulations with which franchisees must comply in running their particular franchise outlet.

The information in the FDD must be current as of the completion of the franchisor's most recent fiscal year. In addition, the FDD must be updated whenever there has been a material change in the information contained in the document.

The following is a more comprehensive list of data to be gathered and included in the FDD:

1. *Information Regarding the Company and Its Principals:*
   a. Present a history of the company's operations and business, and identify any predecessors and/or affiliated companies.
   b. Describe the market to be serviced by franchisees, including information about general or specific markets to be targeted, whether the market is developed or developing, and whether the business is seasonal. In addition, general information about industry-specific laws and regulations must be included, along with a description of the competition.
   c. Identify all of the company's directors, principal officers, and other executives who have management responsibility in connection with the operation of the company's business. For each, provide a summary of their job history for at least the past five years.
   d. Identify and describe all litigation in which the company, its officers, and its directors is involved or has previously been involved.
   e. Identify and describe any and all bankruptcy proceedings involving the company and its officers and directors.

2. *Initial Fees.* The disclosure document must disclose all payments a franchisee is required to make to the franchisor before opening the

franchised business. This will include the initial franchise fee and any other preopening purchases/leases from the franchisor. Before determining the initial franchise fee, you may want to compare the fees charged by competitors. The fee may be expressed as a single amount for all franchisees, or it may be a range of amounts, based on criteria you specify. In addition, the franchisor needs to state whether it has any plans for allowing the fee to be paid in installments and whether the fee will be refundable under certain conditions. The disclosure should also discuss the allocation of the initial franchise fees collected by the franchisor. For example, fees are often used to cover administrative and legal costs associated with the franchise offer, as well as to fund initial training programs and other preopening assistance provided by the franchisor.

3. *Royalty.* The royalty rate and method of payment must be determined. Again, a comparison of competitors' royalty structures may be helpful. The royalty formula (e.g., percentage of gross sales), payment frequency, and refundability must be disclosed.

4. *Advertising Fund.* Will franchisees be required to contribute to a regional or national advertising fund? Typically, advertising fund contributions are based on the same formula and are made with the same frequency as royalty payments. If such a fund is contemplated, what are the fund's objectives, administration, and participants (company-owned stores)? *Note:* All fees collected for the advertising fund *must* be used for that purpose.

5. *Other Fees Paid to Franchisor.* The disclosure document must identify all other fees that a franchisee is required to pay to the franchisor or to the franchisor's affiliate, including fees collected on behalf of third parties. Typically, these fees include ongoing training/consultant fees and expenses, real property and equipment leases, required supply purchases, transfer fees, renewal fees, and audit fees.

6. *Initial Investment.* The disclosure document must include a chart detailing all costs necessary to begin operation of the franchised business and to operate the business during the first three months (or some other initial phase more appropriate for the industry), including the costs of furniture, equipment, supplies, inventory, leasehold improvements, rent security, utilities, advertising, insurance, licenses, and permits. (Note that the initial phase is not the equivalent of a break-even point.) Many of the cost items will be stated in a low-high range, rather than as a specific amount.

7. *Sources for Products and Services.* What products and services must franchisees purchase: (a) only from the franchisor or its affiliates? (b) only from approved suppliers? (c) only in accordance with the franchisor's specifications? Will the franchisor derive any revenue from these purchases? For example, if proprietary items must be purchased from the franchisor or from a designated supplier, then this needs to be disclosed in the disclosure document.

8. *Franchisee's Obligations.* The franchisee's principal obligations under the franchise agreement are disclosed in a chart referencing 24 specific obligations. The chart also serves as a cross-reference for franchisees between the disclosure document and the franchise agreement. The list attached as Exhibit A (see Figure 5-3) details the specific franchisee obligations that must be addressed in this chart.

9. *Financing.* Will the franchisor or its affiliates offer any direct or indirect financing arrangements to franchisees? Indirect financing includes guaranteeing franchisee loans and facilitating arrangements with lenders. If so, then the terms of the loan must be disclosed.

10. *Franchisor's Obligations.* These obligations are broken down into two categories: obligations performed before the franchised business opens and ongoing obligations.

   a. *Preopening Obligations.* How will the franchisor assist franchisees (if at all) in locating a site for the business or in develop-

Figure 5-3. Exhibit A: Franchisee obligations.

a. Site selection and acquisition/lease

b. Preopening purchases/leases

c. Site development and other preopening requirements

d. Initial and ongoing training

e. Opening

f. Fees

g. Compliance with standards and policies/operating manual

h. Trademarks and proprietary information

i. Restrictions on products/services offered

j. Warranty and customer service requirements

k. Territorial development and sales quotas

l. Ongoing product/service purchases

m. Maintenance, appearance, and remodeling requirements

n. Insurance

o. Advertising

p. Indemnification

q. Owner's participation, management, staffing

r. Records and reports

s. Inspection and audits

t. Transfer

u. Renewal

v. Post-termination obligations

w. Noncompetition covenants

x. Dispute resolution

y. Other

ing the site so that it is suitable for the operation of the franchised business? Will the franchisor hire and/or train franchisees' employees?

b. *Ongoing Obligations.* What assistance (if any) will the franchisor provide with: (i) developing/improving the franchised business, (ii) operating problems encountered by franchisees, (iii) administrative, bookkeeping, and inventory control procedures? Specific details about the franchisor's advertising program and any computer systems or cash registers required to be used in the business must be provided.

In addition, a training program must be developed that will be offered to franchisees and/or the franchisees' manager. The training program should encompass instruction in the operation and management of a franchised business as well as instruction in the areas of advertising, marketing, personnel management, bookkeeping, inventory control, and any other issues unique to the operation of the franchised business. In connection with the training program, the following must also be determined:

a. Who will bear the costs for the training?

b. Who will pay the transportation, lodging, and other miscellaneous expenses associated with training?

c. How many people will be required to attend training, and who will be required to attend (i.e., the franchisee, franchisee's manager, franchisee's employees)?

d. If additional designees of the franchisee attend, will there be a charge?

e. Where will training be held, and what is the length of the training?

f. When will franchisee and its managers/employees be required to complete the training program (i.e., how many weeks prior to the opening of the store)?

The franchisor's training program must be described in detail, including information regarding its location, duration, and a general outline. What topics will be covered? What materials will be used? Who are the instructors? Is training mandatory?

11. *Territory.* Will franchisees be granted an exclusive territory? Will there be conditions on exclusivity? Will franchisees be subject to performance standards?

12. *Franchisee Participation.* Are franchisees required to participate personally in the direct operation of the franchised business?

13. *Restrictions on Goods and Services.* Are there any restrictions or conditions on the products that the franchisee may sell? For example, is the franchisee obligated to sell only those products approved by the franchisor?

14. *Renewal, Termination, Transfer, Dispute Resolution.*
    a. *Term and Renewal.* What will be the term of the franchise agreement? Will the franchisee be able to renew the agreement, and, if so, under what conditions? Will a fee be charged? Under what conditions may the franchisor terminate the agreement? Under what conditions (if any) may the franchisee terminate the agreement?
    b. *Termination.* What obligations are imposed on franchisees after the franchise agreement is terminated or expires? Will the franchisee be bound by a noncompete agreement? Will the noncompete restrict the franchisees' activities during and after the term of the agreement? What obligations (if any) are imposed on the franchisor after termination or expiration of the agreement?
    c. *Transfer.* May franchisees assign or transfer the franchise agreement? If so, under what conditions? Will a fee be charged? Will the franchisor have a right of first refusal to purchase the franchised business before it can be transferred or sold to a third party?
    d. *Dispute Resolution.* How and where will disputes be settled? (For example, must disputes be arbitrated? Will the arbitration or litigation take place in a specific location or jurisdiction?)

    Some state laws limit the franchisor's ability to enforce these provisions of the franchise agreement.

15. *Public Figures.* Will any public figure be involved in promoting or managing the franchise system?

16. *Financial Performance Representations.* The franchisor may include representations on financial performance or potential in the disclosure document.

17. *List of Outlets.* Although there are currently no franchisees, information about any company-owned stores must be disclosed, including the locations of the stores over the last three years and projections about the number of additional stores to be opened in the next fiscal year and their locations.

18. *Financial Statements.* The financial statements required will differ depending on which legal entity is selected to serve as the franchisor. If the franchisor is a newly established corporation or LLC, then it will need to include at least opening financial statements (i.e., an audited balance sheet).

The Mechanics of the Registration Process

Each of the registration states has slightly different procedures and requirements for the approval of a franchisor prior to offers and sales being authorized. In all cases, however, the package of disclosure documents is assembled, consisting of a disclosure document, franchise agreement, supplemental agreements, financial statements, franchise roster, mandated cover pages, acknowledgment of receipt, and the specific forms required by each state, such as corporation verification statements, franchise seller disclosure forms, and consent to service of process documents. The specific requirements of each state should be checked carefully by the franchisor and its counsel. Initial filing fees typically range from $250 to $750, with renewal filings usually ranging between $100 to $450.

The first step is for counsel to custom-tailor the FDD format to meet any special requirements or additional disclosures required under the particular state regulations. Once the documents are ready and all signatures have been obtained, the package is filed with the state franchise administrator, and a specific franchise examiner is assigned to the franchisor. Certain states require paper filings plus a soft copy on compact disc, and at least one state accepts only CD-ROM filings. The level of scrutiny applied by the examiner in reviewing the offering materials varies from state to state. The sales history, financial strength, litigation record, reputation of legal counsel, time pressures and workload of the examiner, geographic desirability of the state, and the general reputation of the franchisor will have an impact on the level of review and the timetable for approval. Franchisors should expect to see at least one so-called comment letter from examiners in certain states requesting certain changes or additional information as a condition of approval and registration. The procedure can go as quickly as six weeks or as slowly as six months or more, depending on the concerns of the examiner, the skills and experience of legal counsel, and the backlog of filings in the queue.

The initial and ongoing reporting and disclosure requirements vary from state to state. For example, the filing of an amendment to the disclosure document is required in the event of a material change (discussed in greater detail in Chapter 6); however, each state has different regulations as to the definition of a material change. Similarly, although all registration states require the annual filing of a renewal application or annual report, Maryland requires quarterly reports. When advertising materials are developed for use in attracting franchisees, they must be approved in advance by all registration states, except Virginia and Hawaii. (See discussion of advertising material requirements in Chapter 6.) All franchise registration states except Virginia require the filing of franchise seller disclosure forms. California requires certain additional forms. The franchisor's legal compliance officer must stay abreast of all of these special filing requirements.

The SBA Central Registry of Franchise Systems

Although the Amended FTC Rule has no federal registration requirements, the Small Business Administration (SBA) established a Central Registry of eligible franchise opportunities in 1998, with the intent of improving its loan guaranty program by eliminating:

1. Unnecessary review of franchise agreements and documents that creates lengthy processing delays.

2. Inconsistent decisions among different SBA field offices regarding the same franchise system.

In 2008, the SBA approved over 4,000 loans to franchisees with a total principal amount of over $1 billion. Historically, the typical transaction involves a franchisee that is unable to obtain financing on reasonable terms through normal lending channels but requires a loan guarantee from the SBA to obtain such financing. The process of obtaining such a loan guarantee has resulted in delays as well as conflicting policies and interpretations among SBA field offices regarding the same franchise system.

SBA Eligibility Guidelines

The eligibility guidelines set forth substantive criteria for determining whether a franchise system qualifies for SBA loan guarantees to the system's franchisees. The guidelines include restrictions on the franchisor's control of the franchisee's business; the franchisor's default, termination, and renewal rights; and the franchisor's right to approve transfers.

The guidelines also provide standards for screening each system based on five major criteria and loan conditions, which must be met during the term of the SBA-guaranteed loan.

1. *Control.* The franchisor may not control its franchisee to the point that the franchisee does not have the independent right to both profit from its efforts and bear the risk of loss commensurate with ownership. However, the franchisor may still impose quality controls with respect to the operations of the franchised business. The franchisor may not:

   - Set the franchisee's net profit from the franchised business.
   - Prescribe or strictly control the right of its franchisees to withdraw increases in the net worth of the franchised business.
   - Manage the daily operations of the franchised business for an extended period of time.
   - Hire, fire, or otherwise directly control its franchisee's employees.
   - Require its franchisee to deposit all revenues into an account that the franchisor controls, or from which the franchisor must consent to withdrawals.

2. *Leasing from Franchisor.* The franchisor may not terminate any real estate unless an uncured default has occurred under the terms of the real estate lease or the franchise agreement.

3. *Renewal.* The terms of the renewal agreement offered to the franchisee many not be less favorable to the franchisee than either (a) the terms of the franchisor's then current form of franchise agreement or (b) renewal terms offered by the franchisor to other comparable renewing franchisees.

4. *Transfer.* The franchisee must be free to transfer its interest in the franchised business at any time to a franchisee meeting the franchisor's qualifications. Consent must not be unreasonably withheld or delayed.

5. *Default and Termination.* The franchise agreement must identify:
   - All events of default.
   - Those events of default that constitute the basis for termination of the franchise agreement.
   - The written notice of termination of each default.
   - Defaults that are grounds for automatic termination and for which there is no opportunity to cure and all other defaults.
   - The time for cure that the franchisor will give for all other defaults.

During the term of the SBA-guaranteed loan, the franchisor may terminate the franchise agreement only for automatic terminations and uncured defaults. A series of cured defaults within a specified period of time, chronic deficiencies, or repeated violations can be considered an uncured default, if identified clearly as such in the franchise agreement.

Other Loan Conditions

The franchise agreement's term must be at least equal to the term of the SBA-guaranteed loan. If the franchisee leases or subleases the premises of the franchised business from the franchisor, the lease term must be equal to the loan term. The SBA will carefully evaluate and weigh the credit implications if a lease that is a sublease does not include an option for the franchisee to lease directly from the landlord if the franchisor defaults, rejects, disavows, or is unable to perform.

The franchisor is to give the lender or Community Development Corporation (CBC) and SBA, during the loan term, the same notice and opportunity to cure a default under a franchise agreement or lease that is given to the franchisee under the document. The franchisor must give the franchisee, lender, or CDC and SBA access to its pertinent books and records, if the franchisor:

- ❐ Provides billing and collection services.
- ❐ Controls accounts receivable.
- ❐ Accepts payments from franchisee's customers or third-party payors.
- ❐ Services the franchisee's accounts.

Related Federal and State Laws Affecting Franchisors and Franchising Systems

At any given time, Congress or state legislatures may be considering legislation that has a direct or indirect impact on franchisors and the operation of franchise systems. Over the past 20 years, multiple varieties of "franchise fairness" or "franchise rights bills" have originated with a member of Congress—usually at the urging of a constituent with a specific problem—and the legislation eventually dies due to a lack of interest by fellow legislators. Similar attempts at the state level have been introduced and defeated and are typically perceived as having a chilling effect on franchising.

At the federal level, legislation is often passed or considered that may have a direct impact on the franchisor's system or require modifications to its manuals on operating practices, especially in the areas of health care reform, wage and salary rules, pension regulations, workplace safety and ergonomics laws, tax laws, securities and accounting standards, environmental laws, and related matters. In addition, federal and state agencies may directly or indirectly regulate the underlying industry in which the franchisor operates, such as in medical services, personnel agencies, and financial services.

State Taxation of Franchise Fees and Royalties

The debate over whether the states have the power to collect income taxes from out-of-state franchisors on royalty and other income streams has been raging since the publication of the first edition of *Franchising & Licensing* in 1991. In the early days of the debate, the argument as to whether the out-of-state franchisor had sufficient presence, or "nexus," in a given state to be subject to their state income tax laws typically was ruled in favor of the franchisor. However, in recent years, state governments have become much more aggressive, driven by a general frustration that so much untaxed business activity goes on within their borders simply because the company has no traditional brick-and-mortar presence in the state. The advent and growth of the Internet and e-commerce have only compounded this frustration, and franchisors have been pulled into the range of target companies and industries in an attempt to turn the tide of shrinking state budgets and growing deficits.

As the states become more aggressive, the legal interpretation of "nexus" seems to have shrunk to the minimum level of physical presence; even services-based franchise systems who do not have offices in a state or whose contracts with the state are limited to field support visits have been subject to state income taxes. This area of law is evolving quickly, and current and prospective franchisors should consult with their legal and tax advisors regarding the need to file state income tax returns. Since the Supreme Court has yet to rule on this issue or set a uniform set of standards, compliance must be reviewed on a state-by-state basis. As of the publication of the fourth edition, the following states have been particularly aggressive and/or successful in enforcing their state income tax laws against franchisors and should be given special attention: California, Florida, Hawaii, Iowa, Louisiana, Massachusetts, New Jersey, New Mexico, North Carolina, Oregon, Pennsylvania, South Carolina, and Wisconsin.

CHAPTER 6

Compliance

he development of an in-house legal, quality control, and franchisor-franchisee relationship management compliance program and the designation of a compliance officer and support staff are *necessities,* not luxuries, for the growing and established franchisor operating in today's litigious society. In many cases, the compliance staff will be pitted against the sales and marketing staff, an outgrowth of the inherent tension between the need to market and grow aggressively and the need to market and grow legally. The growing franchisor must foster an attitude and a phi-

---

Box 6-1. Franchisor compliance best practices.

- Be sure to appoint a franchise compliance officer with enough accountability and authority to effectively enforce compliance policies. Toothless tigers or lip service will not keep the company out of legal hot water or effectively manage healthy relationships.

- Treat compliance as a leadership issue, putting it in the same category as the company's values and ethics, on *both* a top-down and bottom-up basis. To be effective, compliance must be part of the fabric of the company culture.

- Educate early and often. Establish budgets for ongoing compliance training and keep your content updated, easy to understand and navigate, and in touch with the latest developments. Maintain clear channels of communication and easy access to outside counsel. As a general rule, if in doubt, call compliance!

  Compliance is not just a headquarters issue; it must extend to regional offices, to overseas outposts, and to field support visits and audits.

losophy of teamwork early on in order to avoid tension within the company. The franchisor must make a commitment from day one to award franchises within the bounds of the law and to maintain complete and comprehensive compliance files. (See Figure 6-1 for contents of a typical compliance file.)

Personnel should be assigned to manage the establishment of compliance files for each candidate, whether or not a franchise is granted. The compliance files should contain everything from information about the initial meeting with the prospect to the execution of the franchise agreement to the termination of the relationship and beyond. The timing and content of the first few contacts with a prospective franchisee are the most critical for proper compliance. The franchisor should be subject to franchisor-imposed disclosure timing guidelines. (See Figure 6-2 for sample guidelines.) These record-keeping requirements and timing guidelines may seem burdensome, but they will go a long way in protecting the company if there is either a dispute with the franchisee or a federal or state regulatory investigation.

A compliance program means more than careful record keeping. A well-planned compliance system will require:

❐ Initial and ongoing training for the franchisor's sales and marketing personnel.

Figure 6-1. Developing a typical compliance file.

The typical compliance file that should be maintained by the compliance staff includes:

1. Acknowledgment of receipt of offering circular.
2. Completed applicant questionnaire.
3. Executed deposit agreement (if used).
4. Copy of the check for initial deposit.
5. The entire franchise agreement and any amendments/addenda, fully executed.
6. Area development agreement (if applicable).
7. Inventory purchase agreement (if applicable).
8. Option for assignment of lease.
9. Mandatory addendum to lease.
10. Receipt for manuals.
11. Written consent of board of directors of franchisee to enter into the agreements.
12. Proof of required insurance, including the franchisor as an additional insured.
13. Franchisor's written approval of site (if applicable).
14. Franchisee's certification of procurement of all licenses, permits, and bonds.
15. Franchisee's written notice of commencement of construction.
16. Franchisor's approval of the opening of the franchised business.
17. Copy of franchisee's lease.
18. Copy of the incorporation documents and shareholder agreements for the entity (or entities) operating the franchise business.
19. Copies of any key financing documents (SBA loan documents, key equipment leases, etc.) affecting the franchisee's business (anything that may create a lien on the franchisee's assets).
20. Certification of completion of basic training.
21. All ongoing material correspondence between franchisor and franchisee).
22. Inspection reports—periodic and special visits.
23. Notices of default and related correspondence.

Figure 6-2. Disclosure timing guidelines.

Following are the timing and content guidelines for the proper and efficient disclosure of prospective franchisees, formulated by an existing franchisor to ensure compliance as well as to ensure that only properly qualified candidates receive disclosure.

Step 1: Inquiry

Four or five basic questions, such as:
1. How did you hear of the opportunity?
2. Tell me about your current situation.
3. What other opportunities are you considering?
4. What is your timetable?
5. Do you understand that our opportunity requires $XXX,000 in readily available capital?

Step 2: Send Brochure/Application

1. Application to obtain more detailed information on location, etc.
2. If not registered, *stop here.*
3. If the prospective franchisee is registered *and* meets personal qualifications, then set up meeting.

Step 3: Meeting or Conference Call

1. Present overview of franchisor and its program.
2. Have a basic discussion of opportunity (OK to discuss basic terms, such as initial fee and capital requirements).
3. Determine whether the prospective franchisee has access to sufficient advisors.
4. If still a candidate, present FDD, starting the 14-day waiting period before any agreement may be signed by or any payment accepted from the franchisee.[1]
5. Present franchise and related agreements with all material terms filled in, starting the five-day period of required disclosure.

Step 4: Second Meeting

1. Further questions and/or closing.
2. Execution of documents, receipt of check.

[1]The 2007 Amendments changed the waiting period from 10 business days to 14 calendar days and also eliminated the requirement to deliver a disclosure document at the first personal meeting with the prospective franchisee. However, there is a lack of uniformity among state franchise laws (e.g., Maryland, New York, and Rhode Island have retained the 10-business-day waiting period and the first personal meeting delivery requirement; Michigan, Oregon, and Washington have retained the 10-business-day waiting period but eliminated the personal meeting trigger). The North American Securities Administrators Association (NASAA) adopted a Statement of Policy Regulatory Uniform Franchise Delivery Requirements in September 2009. The statement recommends, as the FTC Rule requires, the 14-day disclosure period before a franchisee may sign a binding agreement or pay any amount relating to the franchise relationship.

❏ The development of special forms and checklists.
❏ A management philosophy and compensation structure that rewards compliance and discourages noncompliance.
❏ A system for monitoring all registration and renewal dates.
❏ Custom-tailored verbal scripts and video presentations that must be used and strictly followed by the sales personnel.
❏ The development of a compliance manual and periodic policy statements.

❐ Special approval and renewal process for the award of new franchises.

❐ Periodic random and unannounced inspections of the franchise sales and compliance files in order to ensure that procedures are being followed.

The success of the compliance program should not be made dependent on outside legal counsel, but should rather be a priority for the franchisor's management team.

No compliance system is 100 percent perfect in preventing franchise law violations. Human nature may drive a franchise sales representative to "stretch the truth a little" if he or she has not had a sale in months and is facing the loss of a job or a home. Human error may result in a Maryland resident being disclosed with a New York offering document because the wrong package was hastily pulled off the shelf. The franchisor's ability to devote sufficient resources to the compliance program, select the right person as the compliance officer, and foster a positive attitude toward compliance among the sales staff all will affect the success or failure of the compliance program.

The franchise compliance officer must be selected carefully and charged with the responsibility of implementing the compliance program and enforcing its procedures. The officer serves as the in-house clearinghouse for franchise files and information, as well as the liaison with outside legal counsel. The compliance officer must gain (and maintain) the respect of the sales and marketing personnel or the system will fail. This will be achieved only if a senior executive within the company assumes responsibility for disciplining anyone who is apathetic about compliance.

Special Topics in Compliance: Financial Performance Representation

One common conflict in franchising is between prospective franchisees' desire to know what they are likely to earn as franchise owners and the strict rules governing the use of representations regarding financial performance (or earnings claims) in a sales presentation. The early days of franchising saw much abuse, with salespersons jotting down projections on the back of a hotel cocktail napkin to induce the prospect to buy a franchise. Eventually, federal and state regulators clamped down on these potentially deceptive practices and developed strict regulations for the use of an earnings claim.

A *financial performance representation* (or *earnings claim*) is defined under the law as any information given to a prospective franchisee by, on behalf of, or at the direction of a franchisor or its agent, from which a specific level or range of actual or potential sales, income, or profit from franchised or nonfranchised units may be easily ascertained. Information concerning costs is excluded from the definition, however, as long as the cost information does not lead the prospective franchisee to a calculation of profits. Earnings claims may include a chart, table, or mathematical calculation presented to demonstrate possible results based on a combination of variables (such as multiples of price and quantity to reflect gross sales). An earnings claim must include a *description of its factual basis* and the *material assumptions* underlying its preparation and presentation.

The original rules created a catch-22 because, even though prospective franchisees *wanted* to know what they were likely to earn and franchisors *wanted* to tell them, many franchisors could not do so and meet the strict standards contained in the federal and state regulations. Others feared that the earnings claim would be misused or misunderstood by the prospect and only come back to haunt them in subsequent litigation. As a result, the majority of franchisors did not provide prospective franchisees with earnings claims primarily because:

- ❏ The detailed substantiation required under federal and state law made compliance difficult and expensive, *especially for early-stage franchisors.*
- ❏ Many franchisors feared that the documents could be used against them in subsequent disputes with disgruntled or disappointed franchisees.
- ❏ Differences between the geographic location, actual performance, and number of units in the system made it difficult to have a sufficient foundation from which to compile the earnings information.

Pressure from members of the franchise community resulted in changes to the rules affecting earnings claims; the changes were designed to provide greater flexibility in franchise sales and marketing practices. The primary reasons cited for the changes, aside from political pressures, included the following: (1) Efforts by start-up and early-stage franchisors to sell franchises had been severely restricted. (2) Sophistication had grown (education, net worth, professional advisors, etc.) among prospective franchisees who *wanted* and *needed* to know what to expect financially when buying a franchise.

Special Topics in Compliance: Material Changes

As the franchise system grows, the franchisor is likely to experience a wide variety of challenges that may result in significant changes to the corporate structure, franchise program, financial statements, or relationships with its franchisees. When these significant structural or program changes occur, the FDD must be updated so that new prospects receive accurate disclosure. The laws that dictate how and when these updates must be made are commonly referred to as the "material change regulations."

The determination of what constitutes a material change can be difficult, and federal and state law provide for a significant degree of discretion. For example, the term *material change* is defined by the FTC as "any fact, circumstance, or set of conditions which has a substantial likelihood of influencing a reasonable franchisee or a reasonable prospective franchisee in the making of a significant decision relating to a named franchise business or which has any significant financial impact on a franchise or prospective franchisee."

With respect to the timing of FDD amendments, keep in mind the risk of continuing to grant franchises with knowledge of a material event or change that may require disclosure. The longer an amendment is deferred, the greater the risk is that sales made prior to the amendment may be successfully challenged as illegal or subject to rescission, which essentially grants the franchisee an "option" rather than a binding and enforceable franchise agreement. Amendments filed to the disclosure document in registration states will cause a short delay in the ability of the franchisor to offer and sell franchises in those states. However, the cost of this delay should be viewed as minor compared to the benefits of a "legal" sale.

Examples of Material Changes

The following list provides examples of facts and circumstances that have been considered by federal and state franchise regulators to constitute a material change:

1. A change in any franchise or other fee charged, or significantly increased costs of developing or operating a franchised outlet.

2. The termination, closing, failure to renew, or repurchase of a significant number of franchises. Whether the number is significant depends on the number of franchises in existence and whether the area in which the event occurred is the same area in which new franchises will be offered, except where specific state regulations define what constitutes a significant number (e.g., Hawaii and New York).

3. A significant *adverse* change in any of the following:
   - The obligations of the franchisee to purchase items from the franchisor or its designated sources.
   - Limitations or restrictions on goods or services that the franchisee may offer to its customers.
   - The obligations to be performed by the franchisor.
   - The key terms of the franchise agreement.
   - The franchisor's financial situation, resulting in a 5 percent or greater change in net profits or losses in any six-month period.
   - The services or products offered to consumers by the franchisees of the franchisor.
   - The identity of persons affiliated with the franchisor.
   - The current status of the franchisor's trade- or service marks.

4. Any change in control, corporate name, state of incorporation, or reorganization of the franchisor.

5. A significant change in status of litigation or administrative matters that have been disclosed in the FDD. In addition, a franchisor should be alert to provide for the addition of any new claims or counterclaims that have been filed against the franchisor that may need to be disclosed.

6. Any recent developments in the market(s) for the products or services sold by the franchisees that could increase competition or create operating problems for franchisees.

7. A change in the accuracy of earnings claims information disclosed (if applicable).

Compliance in the Nonregistration States

Prior to the 2007 Amendments, the FTC Rule 436.7(b) and (c) defined the terms *material, material fact,* and *material change* to include any fact, circumstance, or set of conditions that has a substantial likelihood of influencing a reasonable franchisee or a reasonable prospective franchisee in the making of a significant decision relating to a named franchise business or that has a significant financial impact on a franchisee or prospective franchisee. According to its Statement of Basis and Purpose for the 2007 Amendments, the FTC determined that these definitions were no longer necessary and that it was better to look to "long-established [FTC] jurisprudence." According to Section 436.7(b), the disclosure document must be updated within a reasonable time after the close of each quarter to reflect any material change in the information contained in the FDD. The material change disclosure may be attached to the FDD as an addendum.

Compliance in the Registration States

The following overview shows how each of the registration states handle the filing and registration of a material change.

California

California is a registration state that requires a franchisor to promptly notify the Commissioner of Corporations, in writing, by an application to amend the registration, of any material change in the information contained in the application as originally submitted, amended, or renewed.

Hawaii

Hawaii is a registration state that requires a franchisor to file with the director a copy of the offering circular as amended to reflect any *material event* or *material change* at least seven days before a sale of a franchise is made. Material event or material change may be, but is not limited to:

1. The termination, closing, or failure to renew during any three-month period of:
   - The greater of 1 percent or five of all franchises of a franchisor or subfranchisor regardless of location.

- The lesser of 15 percent or two of the franchises of a franchisor or subfranchisor located in Hawaii.

2. Any change in control, corporate name, state of incorporation, or reorganization of the franchisor whether or not the franchisor or its parent, if the franchisor or subfranchisor is a subsidiary, is required to file reports under section 12 of the Securities Exchange Act of 1934.

3. The purchase by the franchisor of more than 5 percent of its existing franchises during any three-month period on a continuous basis.

4. The commencement of any new product, service, or model line involving, directly or indirectly, additional investment by any franchisee or the discontinuation or modification of the marketing plan or system of any product or service of the franchisor where the total sales from such product or service exceeds 20 percent of the gross sales of the franchisor on an annual basis.

Illinois

Illinois is currently a registration state that requires a franchisor to promptly file with the administrator an amended disclosure statement reflecting any material change, defined as follows:

A change in information contained in the disclosure statement is material within the meaning of the act if there is a substantial likelihood that a reasonable prospective franchisee would consider it significant in making a decision to purchase or not purchase the franchise. Without limitation, examples of changes which could be material include:

1. Any increase or decrease in the initial or continuing fees charged by the franchisor

2. The termination, cancellation, failure to renew, or reacquisition of a significant number of franchises since the most recent effective date of the disclosure statement

3. A change in the franchisor's management

4. A change in the franchisor's or franchisee's obligations under the franchise or related agreements

5. A decrease in the franchisor's income or net worth

6. Limitations or significant prospective limitations regarding sources of supply that are known to or should reasonably be anticipated by the franchisor

7. Additional litigation or a significant change in the status of litigation including:

   ❏ The filing of an amended complaint alleging or involving violations of any franchise law, fraud, embezzlement, fraudulent conversion, restraint of trade, unfair or deceptive practices, misappropriation of property, or breach of contract;

- ❑ The entry of any injunctive or restrictive order relating to the franchise; or the entry of any injunction under any federal, state, or Canadian franchise securities, antitrust trade regulation, or trade practice law;
- ❑ The entry of a judgment that has or would have any significant financial impact on the franchisor. Such a judgment is considered to have significant financial impact if it equals 15 percent or more of the current assets of the franchisor and its subsidiaries on a consolidated basis.

8. The reincorporation of the franchisor or its merger into a corporation other than the registrant. In a merger where the surviving corporation changes its name to that of the original registrant, the material change has still occurred.

Maryland

Maryland is a registration state that requires a franchisor to promptly file an application for amendment of a registration statement with the Securities Commissioner in the Office of the Attorney General in the event of any material event or material change, which may be, but is not limited to:

- ❑ The termination, in any manner, of more than 10 percent of the franchises of the franchisor that are located in the state during any three-month period.
- ❑ The termination, in any manner, of more than 5 percent of all franchises of the franchisor regardless of location during any three-month period.
- ❑ A reorganization of the franchisor.
- ❑ A change in control, corporate name, or state of incorporation of the franchisor.
- ❑ The commencement of any new product, service, or model line requiring, directly or indirectly, additional investment by any franchisee.
- ❑ The discontinuation or modification of the marketing plan or system of any product or service of the franchisor that accounts for at least 20 percent of the annual gross sales of the franchisor.

Michigan

Michigan is a registration state that requires a franchisor to file with the Department of the Attorney General promptly in writing *any* change in the notice filing as originally submitted or amended. The notice includes only basic information about the franchisee, such as name, address, and type of franchise offered.

Minnesota

Minnesota is a registration state that requires a franchisor with a registration in effect to notify the Commissioner of Commerce in writing within 30 days of any material change in the information on file with the commissioner by an application to amend the registration. A material event or material change includes, but is not limited to:

1. The termination, closing, or failure to renew by the franchisor during any consecutive three-month period after registration of 10 percent of all franchises of the franchisor, regardless of location, or 10 percent of the franchises of the franchisor located in the state of Minnesota.
2. Any change in control, corporate name, or state of incorporation, or reorganization of the franchisor.
3. The purchase by the franchisor during any consecutive three-month period after registration of 10 percent of its existing franchises, regardless of location, or 10 percent of its existing franchises in the state of Minnesota.
4. The commencement of any new product, service, or model line involving, directly or indirectly, an additional investment in excess of 20 percent of the current average investment made by all franchises or the discontinuation or modification of the marketing plan or marketing system of any product or service of the franchisor where the average total sales from such product or service exceed 20 percent of the average gross sales of the existing franchisees on an annual basis.
5. Any change in the franchise fees charged by the franchisor.
6. Any significant change in:
   - The obligations of the franchisee to purchase items from the franchisor or its designated sources.
   - The limitations or restrictions on the goods or services the franchisee may offer to its customer.
   - The obligations to be performed by the franchisor.
   - The franchise contract or agreement, including all amendments thereto.

New York

New York is a registration state that requires a franchisor to promptly notify the New York State Department of Law, by application to amend its offering, of any material changes in the information contained in the prospectus as originally submitted or amended. As used in New York, the term "material change" includes, but is not limited to:

1. The termination, closing, or failure to renew, during a three-month period, of the lesser of ten or 10 percent of the franchises of a franchisor, regardless of location.

2. A purchase by the franchisor in excess of 5 percent of its existing franchises during six consecutive months.
3. A change in the franchise fees charged by the franchisor.
4. Any significant adverse change in the business condition of the franchisor or in any of the following:

   - The obligations of the franchisee to purchase items from the franchisor or its designated sources.
   - Limitations or restrictions on the goods or services the franchisee may offer to its customers.
   - The obligations to be performed by the franchisor.
   - The franchise contract or agreements, including amendments.
   - The franchisor's accounting system resulting in a 5 percent or greater change in its net profit or loss in any six-month period.
   - The service, product, or model line.

5. Audited financial statements of the preceding fiscal year.

North Dakota

North Dakota is a registration state that requires a franchisor to promptly notify the Securities Commissioner, in writing, by an application to amend the registration, of any material change in the information contained in the application as originally submitted, amended, or renewed. Although North Dakota is a registration state, the Commissioner of Securities has not defined what shall be considered a material change. Therefore, the definition used in nonregistration states should be consulted in preparing amendments to the offering circulars registered in North Dakota.

Oregon

Although Oregon is a registration state, the Director of the Department of Insurance and Finance has not defined what shall constitute a material change and therefore the definition used in the nonregistration states should be consulted.

Rhode Island

Rhode Island is a registration state that requires a franchisor to promptly notify the Director of Business Regulation in writing, by an application to amend the registration, of any material change in the information contained in the application as originally submitted, amended, or renewed. The director has not defined what constitutes a material change and therefore the definition used in the nonregistration states should be consulted.

Virginia

Virginia is a registration state that requires the franchisor to amend the effective registration filed at the commission upon the occurrence of any material change. Virginia defines material change to include any fact, circumstance, or condition that would have a substantial likelihood of influencing a reasonable prospective franchisee in making a decision related to the purchase of a franchise.

Washington

Washington is a registration state that requires a supplemental report to be filed as soon as reasonably possible (and in any case before the further sale of any franchise) if a material adverse change occurs in the condition of the franchisor or subfranchisor or if any material change occurs in the information contained in its offering circular. Because the terms "material adverse change" and "material change" are not defined, the definition of material change used in nonregistration states should be consulted.

Wisconsin

Wisconsin is a registration state that requires a franchisor to amend its registration in writing with the division of securities, by an application to amend the registration statement, within 30 days after any material event that affects a registered franchise. As defined in Wisconsin, the terms "material event" or "material change" include, but are not limited to:

1. The termination, closing, or failure to renew during any three-month period of (1) the greater of 1 percent or five of all franchises of a franchisor regardless of location or (2) the lesser of 15 percent or two of the franchises of a franchisor located in the state of Wisconsin

2. Any change in control, corporate name or state of incorporation, or reorganization of the franchisor whether or not the franchisor or its parent, if the franchisor is a subsidiary, is required to file reports under section 12 of the Securities Exchange Act of 1934.

3. The purchase by the franchisor in excess of 5 percent of its existing franchises during any three-month period on a running basis.

4. The commencement of any new product service or model line involving, directly or indirectly, additional investment by any franchisee or the discontinuation or modification of the marketing plan or system of any product or service of the franchisor where the total sales from such product or service exceeds 20 percent of the annual gross sales of the franchisor.

5. An adverse financial development involving the franchisor or the franchisor's parent company, controlling person, or guarantor of the franchisor's obligations. In this paragraph, "adverse financial development" includes, but is not limited to:

   • The filing of a petition under federal or state bankruptcy or receivership laws.

- A default in payment of principal, interest, or sinking fund installment on indebtedness that exceeds 5 percent of total assets that is
  not cured within 30 days of the default.

Special Topics in Compliance: Advertising Regulations

Certain states have enacted laws that regulate the use of franchisor advertising directed at prospective franchisees. Many of these states require the filing
and approval of these advertising and marketing materials *prior to their use*.
Most states exclude from regulation, however, advertising in a medium
where two-thirds of the recipients of the advertisement are outside the state.
(Internet marketing is discussed in the next section.) Following is a state-by-
state listing of special provisions that must be built into the overall compliance program.

California

No advertisement offering a franchise may be published in California unless
a true copy of the advertisement has been filed in the office of the California
Commissioner of Corporations at least three business days prior to the first
publication or unless such advertisement has been exempted by rule of the
commissioner. Additionally, all advertising must contain the following leg-
end (in not less than ten-point type):

> THESE FRANCHISES HAVE BEEN REGISTERED UNDER THE FRAN-
> CHISE INVESTMENT LAW OF THE STATE OF CALIFORNIA. SUCH REG-
> ISTRATION DOES NOT CONSTITUTE APPROVAL, RECOMMENDATION
> OR ENDORSEMENT BY THE COMMISSIONER OF CORPORATIONS NOR
> A FINDING BY THE COMMISSIONER THAT THE INFORMATION PRO-
> VIDED HEREIN IS TRUE, COMPLETE AND NOT MISLEADING.

Illinois

To publish, distribute, or use any offering to sell or to purchase a franchise in
the state of Illinois, the franchisor must file two true copies of the proposed
advertisement *at least* five days before its first publication, distribution, or
use, unless the advertisement has been exempted by rule of the administrator. If the advertisement is not in compliance with the Illinois Franchise
Disclosure Act, the Illinois attorney general will notify the franchisor of any
objections within five days of receipt of the advertisement. Failure of the
administrator to respond within five days does not constitute approval of
the advertisement but will preclude the administrator from objecting on the
grounds of the five-day filing requirement. (At the time of writing, legislation
is pending in the Illinois legislature under which the statutory provision for
the filing of advertisements with the Administrator may be deleted. Consult
any amendments to the Illinois Franchise Disclosure Act for current filing
requirements.)

Indiana

A copy of any advertising the franchisor intends to use in Indiana must be filed in the office of the Indiana Securities Commissioner at least five days prior to the first publication of such advertising.

Maryland

A franchisor may not publish any advertisement offering a franchise unless the advertisement (in duplicate) has been filed with the Securities Commissioner in the Office of the Attorney General at least seven *business* days before the first publication of the advertisement. An advertisement may not be used unless and until it has been cleared for use by the Division of Securities.

Michigan

The Michigan Department of the Attorney General *may* by rule or order require an advertisement to be filed that is addressed or intended to be distributed to prospective franchisees, as well as any other sales literature or advertising communication having the same purpose.

Minnesota

The franchisor must file one true copy of any advertisement, proposed for use in Minnesota, with the Office of the Commissioner of Commerce at least five *business* days before its first publication. If not disallowed by the commission within five business days from the date filed, the advertisement may be published.

New York

All sales literature must be submitted to the New York Department of Law at least seven days prior to its intended use. The franchisor must verify, in writing submitted with the sales literature, that it is not inconsistent with the filed prospectus. All sales literature must contain the following statement (in easily readable print) on the cover of all circulars, flyers, cards, letters, and other literature intended for use in New York:

> This advertisement is not an offering. An offering can only be made by a prospectus filed first with the Department of Law of the State of New York. Such filing does not constitute approval by the Department of Law.

In all classified advertisements that are not more than 5 inches long and no more than one column of print wide, and in all broadcast advertising that is 30 seconds or less in duration, the following statement may be used in lieu of the preceding statement:

> This offering is made by prospectus only.

North Dakota

The franchisor must file a true copy of any advertisement proposed for use in the state with the Office of the Commissioner of Securities at least five *business* days before the first publication.

Oklahoma

All sales literature and advertising must be filed with the administrator and approved prior to use. A filing shall include the sales literature and advertising package, a review fee of $25, and a representation by the seller that reads substantially as follows:

> I, _____, hereby attest and affirm that the enclosed sales literature or advertising package contains no false or misleading statements or misrepresentations of material facts and that all information contained therein is in conformity with the most recent disclosure document relating to the particular business opportunity offered thereby on file with the Administrator.

Rhode Island

No advertisements may be published in Rhode Island unless a true copy of the advertisement and required filing fee have been filed in the Office of the Director of Business Regulations at least five business days prior to its first publication.

South Dakota

At least three business days prior to the first publication, the franchisor must file two true copies of any advertisement offering a franchise subject to the registration requirements of South Dakota law with the Office of the Director of the Division of Securities.

Washington

The franchisor must file one true copy of any advertisement offering a franchise subject to the registration requirements of Washington law with the Office of the Director of Licensing at least seven days before publication.

Special Topics in Compliance: Franchise Sales and Marketing via the Internet

With the increased use of the Internet for conducting business, many issues have arisen regarding the application of the various federal and state fran-

chise laws to franchisors' use of the Internet. For example, do Internet advertisements for a franchise opportunity trigger state registration requirements
or state advertising filing requirements? Can a franchisor satisfy the federal
and state law disclosure requirements by providing its offering circular over
the Internet?

These questions have been addressed through statements of policy
adopted by the North American Securities Administrators Association
(NASAA), which various states follow, with some minor modifications.

With regard to state registration requirements, a majority of the registration states have adopted—or at least follow a policy of adoption of—an exemption from registration requirements for franchisors who simply post
information regarding their franchise opportunities on the Internet. The exemption applies to postings that are not specifically targeted to persons in a
registration state, and it requires that franchisors include a disclaimer on
their Web sites noting that they are not offering franchises to residents of any
jurisdiction in which the franchisor is not registered. The exemption terms
were adopted as a Statement of Policy by the NASAA on May 3, 1998.

As already noted, many state franchise laws require the filing of franchise solicitation advertising with franchise regulatory authorities. Because
Internet Web sites might be construed as franchise advertising and therefore
subject to these filing requirements, on September 9, 2001, NASAA adopted
a policy indicating that franchisor Web sites do not constitute advertising
subject to filing as long as the franchisor's Web site address is disclosed on
the cover of its FDD filing with the state or in a notice filed with the state,
and the advertisement is not directed to any person in the state by the franchisor or by someone acting with the franchisor's knowledge. Although the
policy exempts Web sites from filing requirements, a state can still bring an
enforcement action if it determines that the site is deceptive or misleading.

Historically, franchisors fulfilled their federal and state law disclosure
obligations by providing prospective franchisees with hard paper copies of
their FDDs. As technology improved and given the length of some of these
FDDs, franchisors sought to provide the FDD in electronic form. Recognizing
the need for guidance on this topic at the state level, in September 2003,
NASAA issued its Statement of Policy Regarding Electronic Delivery of Franchise Disclosure Documents, which has been incorporated into NASAA's
2008 Franchise Registration and Disclosure Conditions. The Statement of
Policy outlines certain conditions for electronic delivery, such as (1) that the
complete FDD be contained in one electronic file; (2) that the document contain no links to extrinsic information; (3) that the recipient be able to read,
store, and print the entire document; and (4) that the franchisor keep records
of the electronic delivery available for state administrators and be able to
prove the delivery in accordance with individual disclosure laws. The FTC
expressly allowed for electronic delivery of the FDD in the 2007 Amendments, however, it specifically prohibited features such as pop-up windows,
audio, video, and links to external documents, but allowing features that
facilitate reviewing the FDD, such as scroll bars, search capability, and internal links between a Table of Contents and the section referenced [§436.6(d)].

CHAPTER 7

Structuring Franchise Agreements, Area Development Agreements, and Related Documents

he principal document that sets forth the binding rights and obligations of each party to the franchise relationship and that contains the various terms and conditions to which the parties are bound for the term of their relationship is the franchise agreement. This agreement, therefore, must strike a delicate balance. On one hand, the franchisor must maintain enough control in the franchise agreement to enforce uniformity and consistency throughout the system. On the other hand, the franchise agreement must be flexible enough to anticipate changes in the marketplace and modifications to the franchise system and to address special considerations or demands resulting from the franchisee's local market conditions.

The franchise agreement can and should reflect the business philosophy of the franchisor and set the tenor of the relationship. A well-drafted franchise agreement is the result of hundreds of business decisions and hundreds of hours of strategic planning, market research, and customer testing. The length, term, and complexity of the franchise agreement will (and should) vary from franchisor to franchisor and from industry to industry. Many start-up franchisors make the critical mistake of borrowing terms from a competitor's franchise agreement. This practice can be detrimental to the franchisor and the franchisee because the agreement will not accurately reflect the actual dynamics and financial realities of the relationship.

Early-stage franchisors should resist the temptation to copy from the franchise agreement of a competitor or to accept the standard form and boilerplate from an inexperienced attorney or consultant. The relationship between the franchisor and franchisee is far too complex to tolerate such compromise in the preparation of such a critical document.

Franchise attorneys employ a wide variety of drafting styles and practices. Some prefer to roll everything into a single agreement (which can make for a huge document), while others prefer to separately document the equipment leases, product purchasing requirements, personal guarantee, site development obligations, security interests, options for assignment of leases, and other key aspects of the relationship in "supplemental agreements" apart from the actual franchise agreement. The advantage to the latter approach, which I have come to appreciate over the years, is that the franchisee and its counsel may not be as overwhelmed (or intimidated) as they would be by the complexity and depth of a single document. We will examine the key elements of a basic franchise agreement and then turn to some of the supplemental agreements that further define the long-term rights and obligations of the franchisor and franchisee.

Key Elements of the Basic Single-Unit Franchise Agreement

Regardless of size, stage of growth, industry dynamics, or specific trends in the marketplace, all basic single-unit franchise agreements should address the following key topics.

Box 7-1. Tips for the negotiation of franchise agreements.

Negotiation styles among franchise marketing representatives run the full spectrum. At one end is the no-negotiations camp that takes a hard line on negotiating and may fear reprimand from the franchisor's sales director and outside legal counsel. At the other end of the spectrum is the everything's-negotiable camp that fears the wrath of their spouses if there is no sales commission revenue to pay the monthly mortgage. Each of these camps represents an extreme approach in franchise sales and in franchise agreement negotiation. The franchise agreement is not to be presented as a contract of adhesion. It is within the human nature of the prospective franchisee (and its legal counsel) to request and expect some degree of negotiation of the agreement. This must be balanced against both the need for uniformity and consistency throughout the franchise system as well as the material change rules (which trigger an amendment to the offering circular), as discussed in the previous chapter. Certain states, such as New York and California, have developed strict regulations that address the negotiations of franchise agreements. Each request by the prospective franchisee to modify a key term of the franchise agreement should be carefully considered from an economic and quality control perspective, as well as reviewed by franchise counsel to identify potential legal problems and disclosure obligations.

Recitals

The introductory recital or preamble of the franchise agreement essentially sets the stage for the discussion of the contractual relationship. This section provides the background information regarding the development and ownership of the proprietary rights of the franchisor being licensed to the franchisee. The preamble should always contain at least one paragraph specifying that the franchisee will have to operate the business format in strict conformity with the operations manual and quality control standards provided by the franchisor.

Grant, Term, and Renewal

Typically, the initial section of the franchise agreement contains the grant of the franchise rights for a specified term. The length of the term will depend on a number of factors, including market conditions, the franchisor's need to periodically change certain material terms of the agreement, the cost of the franchise and the franchisee's expectations in relation to start-up costs, the length of related agreements necessary to the franchisee's operations such as leases and bank loans, and anticipated consumer demand for the franchised goods and services. The renewal rights granted to a franchisee, if any, will usually be conditional on the franchisee's being in good standing (e.g., no material defaults by franchisee) under the agreement. The other issues addressed in any provisions regarding renewal should include renewal fees, obligations to execute the then current form of the franchise agreement, and any obligations of the franchisee to upgrade its facilities to the latest standards and design. The franchisor's right to relocate the franchisee, to adjust the size of any exclusive territory granted, or to change the fee structure should also be addressed.

Legal Status of Franchisee

This section confirms the nature of the legal relationship between the franchisor and franchisee, confirming that the parties are *not* acting in the legal capacity or role of employer and employee, principal and agent, general partners, fiduciary, or any other status that might serve as a basis for a governmental agency or third party to assign liability to the franchisor for the actions of the franchisee. This characterization of the franchisee as an employee or as an agent should also be avoided because it otherwise may make termination more difficult (in terms of the enforcement of covenants against competition, minimum notice requirements, and even the possible mandatory payment of a severance compensation) in certain countries.

Rights Granted

The franchisor grants the franchisee the right to use the intellectual property developed by the franchisor. This intellectual property includes a set of trademarks, service marks, trade dress (signage, counter design, uniforms, special design features, etc.), the know-how (usually detailed in the operations manual, the initial training program, and the ongoing training and support programs), ongoing technical assistance and access to resources, and the right to manufacture or distribute the franchisor's proprietary products and/

or branded merchandise. These components help create the franchisee's ex-pectations regarding the value-added provided by the franchisor, the scope of the license (e.g., by clarifying what is intended and what is not), and they also serve as a type of due diligence for the franchisee and its advisors, evaluating the franchisor's level of preparedness for the challenges and demands of the local market.

Territory

The size of the geographic area granted to the franchisee by the franchisor is typically discussed in conjunction with any exclusive rights to be granted to the franchisee in the territory. The size of the territory may be defined as a specific radius, ZIP code, or a political boundary, such as city or county lim-its. The franchisor may provide for the right to either operate company-owned locations and/or grant additional franchises within the territory. Some franchisors designate a territory within which market research indi-cates a given number of locations could be successful without oversaturation and then sell that exact number of franchises, without regard to specific loca-tions within the geographic area. Any rights of first refusal for additional locations, advertising restrictions, performance quotas relating to territory, and policies of the franchisor with regard to territory are addressed in this part of the franchise agreement.

Site Selection

If the franchisee is free to choose the site, then the franchise agreement usu-ally will provide that any site selected is subject to the approval of the fran-chisor. Some franchisors provide significant assistance in site selection in terms of marketing and demographic studies, lease negotiations, and secur-ing local permits and licenses, especially if a turnkey franchise is offered. Because site selection may be the most critical aspect of business success, most franchisors are reluctant to assume full responsibility for this task, at least contractually. Some franchisors insist on leasing an approved site and then subletting to the franchisee through a mandatory sublease arrangement. This allows the franchisor to preserve the location if the franchisee does not succeed there. A more common and less burdensome way to secure similar protection is for the franchisor to insist on a right to assume the lease upon termination of the franchise.

Services to Be Provided by the Franchisor

The franchise agreement should clearly delineate which products and ser-vices will be provided to the franchisee by the franchisor or its affiliates, both in terms of the initial establishment of the franchised business (preopening obligations) and any ongoing assistance or support services provided throughout the term of the relationship (postopening obligations). The franchisor's preopening obligations generally include a trade secret and copyright license for the use of the confidential operations manual, the hiring and training of personnel, standard accounting and bookkeeping systems, inventory and equipment specifications and any purchase discounts, standard construction, building and interior design plans, and grand opening promotion and advertising assistance. The quality and extent of the training program is one of the most crucial preopening services provided by the franchisor and should include classroom as well as on-site instruction. Postopening services provided to the franchisee on a continuing basis generally include field support and troubleshooting, research and development for new products and services, development of national advertising and promotional campaigns (either in-house or working with an agency), and the arrangement of group purchasing programs and volume discounts.

Supplying the Products

Most product-driven franchise systems involve one or more proprietary or branded products, which the franchisor manufactures or controls. The franchisee must purchase these products, either for resale to the customers of the franchisee (e.g., ice cream) or for use by the franchisee in the delivery of the services (e.g., proprietary cleaning materials used in a home or commercial cleaning service franchise). In most jurisdictions and subject to applicable antitrust and commercial laws, the franchisor has a contractual or implied duty to deliver these products on a timely, high-quality basis at a reasonable price. Naturally, in a service-driven franchise system where the franchise relationship does not create a distribution channel for the franchisor's proprietary products, these provisions may not be necessary.

Franchise, Royalty, and Related Fees Payable to the Franchisor and Reporting

The franchise agreement must clearly set forth the nature and amount of fees payable to the franchisor by the franchisee, both initially and on a continuing basis. The initial franchise fee is usually a nonrefundable lump sum payment due upon execution of the franchise agreement. Essentially, this fee is compensation for the grant of the franchise, the trademark and trade secret license, preopening training and assistance, and the initial opening supply of materials, if any, to be provided by the franchisor to the franchisee.

Continuing fees usually take the form of a specific royalty on gross sales. This percentage can be fixed or based on a sliding scale for different ranges of sales achieved at a given location or on performance targets that have been met. Often minimum royalty payments will be required, regardless of the franchisee's actual performance. These fees may be payable weekly (either by check or via an electronic sweep of the franchisor's designated royalty account) and submitted to the franchisor together with some standardized reporting form for internal control and monitoring purposes. A weekly payment schedule generally allows the franchisee to budget for this payment from a cash flow perspective and provides the franchisor with an early warning system if there is a problem; it also allows the franchisee to react before the past-due royalties accrue to a virtually uncorrectable sum.

Another category of recurring fees involves advertising and usually takes the form of a national advertising and promotion fund. The franchise agreement must carefully describe how these funds will be used. For example, will funds be used solely for the production of advertising and marketing materials for use by the franchisees or for actual placement of the materials in the radio, television, or printed media? The fund may be managed by the franchisor, an independent advertising agency, or even a franchisee association. Either way, the franchisor must build some control of the fund into the franchise agreement to protect the company's trademarks and to ensure consistency in marketing efforts. Advertising fees should be carefully segregated from the franchisor's general accounts, and typically the franchisor provides some type of annual accounting or reporting regarding the use and application of these fees to the network of franchisees.

Other types of fees payable to the franchisor may include payments for the purchase of proprietary goods and services by the franchisee, consulting fees, audit and inspection fees, site design fees, lease management fees (where the franchisor is to serve as sublessor), renewal fees, and transfer fees.

The obligations of the franchisee to provide periodic weekly, monthly, quarterly, and annual financial and sales reports to the franchisor should also be addressed in the franchise agreement.

Quality Control

A well-drafted franchise agreement always includes a number of provisions designed to ensure quality control and consistency throughout the system. These provisions often impose restrictions on the franchisee's sources of products, ingredients, supplies, and materials, as well as setting strict guidelines and specifications for operating procedures. These operating procedures usually specify standards of service, trade dress and uniform requirements, condition and appearance of the facility, hours of business, minimum insurance requirements, guidelines for trademark usage, advertising and promotional materials, accounting systems, and credit practices. If the franchisor is the sole supplier or manufacturer of one or more products required by the franchisee in the day-to-day operation of the business, then such sole-sourcing should be justified by a truly proprietary or unique product.

Insurance, Record Keeping, and Related Obligations of the Franchisee

The franchise agreement should include requirements for the minimum amounts and types of insurance that the franchisee must carry in connection with the operation of the franchised businesses. Required coverages should include general liability policies, flood and hazard insurance, business interruption insurance, vehicle liability insurance, and, where possible, terrorism protection insurance. Typically the franchisor is named as an additional insured under the franchise's policies.

Related obligations of the franchisee in the franchise agreement may include:

- ❐ The keeping of proper financial records (which must be made available for inspection by the franchisor upon request).
- ❐ The obligation to maintain and enforce quality control standards with its employees and vendors.
- ❐ The obligation to comply with all applicable employment laws, health, and safety standards, and related local ordinances.
- ❐ The duty to upgrade and maintain the franchisee's facilities and equipment.
- ❐ The obligation to promote new and existing products and services of the franchisor.
- ❐ The obligation to reasonably process requests by patrons for franchising information.
- ❐ The obligation to produce only goods and services that meet the franchisor's quality control specifications and that are approved for offer at the franchisee's premises (such as the video games at a fast-food restaurant or no X-rated material at a bookstore).
- ❐ The obligation to solicit customers only within its designated territory.
- ❐ The obligation of the franchisee personally to participate in the day-to-day operation of the franchised business (required by many but not all franchisors).
- ❐ The general obligation of the franchisee to conduct itself in a manner that enhances the goodwill of the brand and to refrain from any activity that may reflect adversely on the reputation of the franchise system.

Protection of Intellectual Property and Covenants against Competition

The franchise agreement should always include a separate section on the obligations of the franchisee and its employees to protect against the misuse or disclosure of the trademarks and trade secrets being licensed as well as a clause clearly establishing that the trademarks and trade names being licensed are the exclusive property of the franchisor and that any goodwill is established to the sole benefit of the franchisor. The franchise agreement should state that the confidential operations manual is "on loan" to the franchisee under a limited use license and that the franchisee or its agents are prohibited from the unauthorized use of trade secrets both during and after the term of the agreement. To the extent that noncompete provisions are enforceable in local jurisdictions, the franchise agreement should contain covenants against competition by a franchisee, both during the term of the franchise agreement and following termination or cancellation. Additional guidance on these issues can be found in Chapter 9.

Termination of the Franchise Agreement

One of the most important sections of the franchise agreement is the termination section discussing how a franchisee may lose its rights to operate the franchised business. The so-called events of default should be defined and tailored to meet the needs of the specific type of business. Grounds for termination typically include the bankruptcy of a franchisee, failure to meet specified performance quotas or to abide strictly by quality control standards, and monetary defaults. Certain types of violations are grounds for termination, whereas other types of default provide the franchisee with an opportunity for cure. The termination section should address procedures for issuing a notice of breach and opportunity to cure, as well as the alternative actions that the franchisor may pursue to enforce its rights to terminate the franchise agreement. Certain state regulations limit franchise terminations to "good cause," and minimum procedural requirements must be considered in drafting this section. The post-termination obligations of the franchisee also must be clearly spelled out, such as the duty to return all copies of the operations manuals, pay all past-due royalty fees, and immediately cease using the franchisor's trademarks.

Miscellaneous Provisions

As with any well-prepared business agreement, the franchise agreement should include a notice provision, a governing law clause, severability provisions, an integration clause, and a provision confirming the relationship of the parties as independent contractors. Some franchisors may want to add:

❑ An arbitration clause.

❑ A hold-harmless and indemnification provision.

❑ A reservation of the right to injunctions and other forms of equitable relief, specific representations and warranties of the franchisee, and attorney's fees for the prevailing party in the event of dispute.

❑ A contractual provision acknowledging that the franchisee has reviewed the agreement with counsel and has conducted an independent investigation of the franchise and is not relying on any representations other than those expressly set forth in the agreement.

An Overview of Sample Supplemental Agreements Commonly Used in Franchising

In addition to the franchise agreement, a wide variety of other contracts may be necessary to govern the rights and the obligations of the franchisor and franchisee. These include:

General Release

The general release should be executed by all franchisees at the time of renewal of their franchise agreement and/or at the time of a transfer of the franchise agreement or their interest in the franchised business. The document serves as a release of the franchisor from all existing and potential claims that the franchisee may have against the franchisor. In recent years, however, some courts have restricted the scope of the release if it is executed under duress or where its effect will run contrary to public policy. Some state franchise laws also limit the use of a general release.

Personal Guarantee

For a variety of tax and liability purposes, many franchisees execute the franchise agreement in the name of a closely held corporation that has been formed to operate the franchised business. In that case, it is highly recommended that each shareholder of the franchise corporation personally guarantee the corporate franchisee's obligation under the franchise agreement. A sample personal guarantee, specially designed for multiple shareholders, is shown in Figure 7-1.

Sign Lease Agreement

A franchisor may want to separately lease the signage bearing its trademarks to the franchisee for a wide variety of reasons. The sign lease agreement sets forth the specific rental terms and conditions to which the franchisee is bound. Aside from the additional rental income, the sign lease should contain cross-default provisions that allow the franchisor to immediately remove the signs upon termination of the franchisee. A sample sign lease agreement is shown in Figure 7-2.

Site Selection Addendum to Franchise Agreement

A site selection addendum to the franchise agreement should be executed at the time that a *specific site* within the geographic area designated in the franchise agreement has been secured for a franchise location. The addendum will modify the initial designation of the territory initially agreed to at the time the agreement is signed.

Option for Assignment of Lease

The option for assignment of the lease agreement provides the franchisor with the option, exercisable upon the termination of the franchisee for any reason, to be substituted as the tenant under the franchisee's lease with its landlord for the premises on which the franchisee's center is located.

Figure 7-1. Sample personal guaranty for multiple shareholders.

In consideration of, and as an inducement to, the execution of the foregoing Franchise Agreement ("Agreement") dated _____ by Franchisor, each of the undersigned Guarantors, as shareholders of XYZ corporation, agree as follows:

1. The Guarantors do hereby jointly and severally unconditionally guarantee the full, prompt, and complete performance of the Franchisee under the Agreement of all the terms, covenants, and conditions of the Agreement, including without limitation the complete and prompt payment of all indebtedness to Franchisor under the Agreement and any revisions, modifications, and amendments thereto (hereinafter collectively referred to as the "Agreement"). The word indebtedness is used herein in its most comprehensive sense and includes without limitation any and all advances, debts, obligations, and liabilities of the Franchisee, now or hereafter incurred, either voluntarily or involuntarily, and whether due or not due, absolute or contingent, liquidated or unliquidated, determined or undetermined, or whether recovery thereof may be now or hereafter barred by any statute of limitation or is otherwise unenforceable.

2. The obligations of the Guarantors are independent of the obligations of Franchisee and a separate action or actions may be brought and prosecuted against the Guarantors, or any of them, whether or not actions are brought against the Franchisee or whether the Franchisee is joined in any such action.

3. If the Franchisee is a corporation or partnership, Franchisor shall not be obligated to inquire into the power or authority of the Franchisee or its partners or the officers, directors, or agents acting or purporting to act on the Franchisee's behalf and any obligation or indebtedness made or created in reliance upon the exercise of such power and authority shall be guaranteed hereunder. Where the Guarantors are corporations or partnerships, it shall be conclusively presumed the Guarantors and the partners, agents, officers, and directors acting on their behalf have the express corporations or partnerships and that such corporations or partnerships have the express power to act as the Guarantors pursuant to this Guaranty and that such action directly promotes the business and is in the interest of such corporations or partnerships.

4. Franchisor, its successors, and assigns may from time to time, without notice to the undersigned (a) resort to the undersigned for payment of any of the liabilities, whether or not it or its successors have resorted to any property securing any of the liabilities or proceeded against any other of the undersigned or any party primarily or secondarily liable on any of the liabilities; (b) release or compromise any liability of any of the undersigned hereunder or any liability of any party or parties primarily or secondarily liable on any of the liabilities; and (c) extend, renew, or credit any of the liabilities for any period (whether or not longer than the original period); alter, amend, or exchange any of the liabilities; or give any other form of indulgence, whether under the Agreement or not.

5. The undersigned further waives presentment, demand, notice of dishonor, protest, nonpayment, and all other notices whatsoever, including without limitation: notice of acceptance hereof; notice of all contracts and commitments; notice of the existence or creation of any liabilities under the foregoing Agreement and of the amount and terms thereof; and notice of all defaults, disputes, or controversies between Franchisee and Franchisor resulting from such agreement or otherwise, and the settlement, compromise, or adjustment thereof.

6. In the event any dispute between the Franchisor and the Guarantors cannot be settled amicably, the parties agree said dispute shall be settled in accordance with the Commercial Rules of the American Arbitration Association. The Arbitration shall be held at the Franchisor's headquarters in [Franchisor's headquarters]. The undersigned agrees to pay all expenses paid or incurred by Franchisor in attempting to enforce the foregoing Agreement and this Guaranty against Franchisee and against the undersigned and in attempting to collect any amounts due thereunder and hereunder, including reasonable attorneys' fees if such enforcement or collection is by or through an attorney-at-law. Any waiver, extension of time, or other indulgence granted from time to time by Franchisor or its agents, successors, or assigns, with respect to the foregoing Agreement, shall in no way modify or amend this Guaranty, which shall be continuing, absolute, unconditional, and irrevocable.

7. This Guaranty shall be enforceable by and against the respective administrators, executors, successors, and assigns of the Guarantors and the death of a Guarantor shall not terminate the liability of such Guarantor or limit the liability of the other Guarantors hereunder.

8. If more than one person has executed this Guaranty, the term *the undersigned*, as used herein shall refer to each such person, and the liability of each of the undersigned hereunder shall be joint and several and primary as sureties.

IN WITNESS WHEREOF, each of the undersigned has executed this Guaranty under seal effective as of the date of the foregoing Agreement.

Signature

Printed Name

Home Address

Home Telephone

Business Address

Business Telephone

Date

Employee Noncompetition and Nondisclosure Agreement

This agreement should be executed by all employees of the franchisees. It states that all information disclosed to said employees must be kept confidential and also imposes noncompetition restriction on employees of the franchisees.

Acknowledgment of Receipt of FDD

This document should be executed at the time the franchisor releases a franchise offering circular and franchise agreement to a prospective franchisee for review and consideration. It serves as an acknowledgment of receipt and notifies prospective franchisees that the documents remain the property of the franchisor and contain trade secrets that are confidential and that must be treated as such.

Special Disclaimer

The franchisee should sign and initial this document at the time of closing. It serves as a written acknowledgment that no earnings claims, representa-

(text continues on page 120)

Figure 7-2. Sample sign lease agreement.

SIGN LEASE AGREEMENT

THIS AGREEMENT made this ___ day of _____, by and between FRANCHISOR, a corporation organized under the laws of the State of, with its principal offices at (address of headquarters) (hereinafter referred to as "Franchisor"); and with its principal offices at _____ (hereinafter referred to as "Franchisee").

W I T N E S S E T H:

WHEREAS, on, _____ Franchisor and Franchisee entered into a written Franchise Agreement by the terms of which Franchisee has been licensed to operate a ("Center") to be operated in accordance with Franchisor's System and Proprietary Marks at the premises located at and has a valid lease for possession of, or has title to, said premises for that purpose; and

WHEREAS, the Franchisee is desirous of leasing certain building, window, and street signage (collectively "the Signage") for advertising and identifying the Center from the Franchisor for use at the Center.

NOW, THEREFORE, in consideration of the mutual covenants herein contained, it is mutually agreed as follows:

1. *Lease of Signs.* Franchisor hereby leases and rents Franchisee the Signage (which is more particularly described in Appendix "A" attached hereto and incorporated herein by this reference). The Signage shall be erected and used only at the premises of and in the operation of the Center as described herein.

2. *Title to Signs.* The parties acknowledge and agree that title to the Signage leased under this Agreement is in the Franchisor and the Signage shall always remain the property of Franchisor or its successors, assignees, or designees herein.

3. *Security Deposit and Rental.* Franchisee shall pay a security deposit of _____ Dollars ($_____) to Franchisor, as collateral to secure the care and maintenance of the Signage, upon the execution of this Agreement. Franchisee shall thereafter pay to the Franchisor as and for rent for the use of the Signage _____ Dollars ($_____) per year, payable monthly in advance, the first payment of _____ Dollars ($_____) to be made upon delivery of the Signage and each subsequent payment shall be made not later than the tenth day of each month thereafter together with any and all payments due to Franchisor pursuant to said Franchise Agreement. Any default in the payment of rent for the Signage shall be treated in the same manner as a default in the payment of franchise or royalty fees, except that the remedy provided in Paragraph Six (6) or Nine (9) below shall be in addition to and not in lieu of any other remedy available to the Franchisor under any other document for such default in payment of fees or royalties.

4. *Term.* The term of this Agreement shall commence at the time that the Signage is installed and shall continue for such period of time as Franchisee shall maintain and operate a Center at the premises described herein.

5. *Installation and Maintenance.* All Signage shall be installed by Franchisee at its expense pursuant to the plans and specifications of Franchisor. Franchisee shall not remove the Signage without first receiving written permission from Franchisor. Franchisee shall secure the necessary public permits and private permission to install all Signage. Franchisee shall pay the cost, if any, of such permits and

shall comply with all laws, orders, and regulations of federal, state, and local authorities. Franchisee shall be responsible for all repair and maintenance of the Signage as may be required from time to time and as may be specified by Franchisor. Franchisee shall pay all taxes and assessments of any nature that may be assessed against or levied upon the Signage before the same become delinquent.

6. *Right of Entry and/or Repossession.* If, for any reason, Franchisee should be in default of its obligations hereunder, its obligations under the Franchise Agreement, its obligations under the lease of the premises described herein, or any stipulation executed by Franchisee, Franchisor shall have the right to enter upon the premises of the Center at any hour to take possession of the Signage leased hereunder without liability thereof. Franchisee agrees that Franchisor shall not be required to obtain prior permission to enter upon the premises and remove the Signage. Franchisee hereby grants Franchisor the limited power of attorney to obtain an order and judgment in Franchisor's behalf in any court of competent jurisdiction that orders and authorizes the entry of Franchisor on the premises and the removal of the Signage. Franchisee further agrees that if Franchisor is forced to resort to this procedure by any interference with the Franchisor's rights hereunder or for any other reason, Franchisee shall pay all attorney's fees and other costs associated with Franchisor's obtaining such order and judgment on its behalf. Franchisee further agrees to reimburse Franchisor for any costs or expenses incurred in connection with any such removal or detachment. Franchisee shall be liable and hereby assumes responsibility for any damage done to the building, premises, or the Signage as a result of the removal thereof.

7. *Repairs.* The Franchisee shall keep the Signage in the same condition as when delivered and shall make all necessary repairs in order to maintain such condition. The Franchisee shall be responsible for any damage to the Signage and shall pay the Franchisor at Franchisor's option the current replacement cost of the Signage if destroyed or the cost of repairing the damage. If the Franchisee shall fail to make any necessary repairs, Franchisor shall have the right to repair the Signage on the premises, or off the premises if Franchisor resorts to its repossession under Paragraph Six (6) for the purpose of repairing the Signage. Franchisee shall pay to the Franchisor the cost of such repairs or the current replacement cost, to be paid in one lump sum along with the next royalty payment that becomes due under the Franchise Agreement. Franchisee agrees that his rental fee obligations under Paragraph two (2) for the term hereof shall continue even though the Signage is damaged or destroyed. Franchisee shall not make any alterations or additions to the Signage without the prior written consent of Franchisor.

8. *Transfers or Encumbrances.* Franchisee shall not pledge, loan, mortgage, or part with possession of the Signage or attempt in any other manner to dispose of or remove the Signage from the present location or suffer any liens or legal process to be incurred or levied thereupon.

9. *Default.* The occurrence of any of the following shall constitute an event of default hereunder:

(a) Failure of Franchisee to pay when due any installment of rent hereunder or any other sum herein required to be paid by Franchisee; and

(b) Franchisee's failure to perform any other covenant or condition of this Agreement or the Franchise Agreement or any stipulations thereunder.

Any default hereunder shall constitute and be considered a default of the Franchise Agreement, wherefore Franchisor shall be entitled to the enforcement of any and all rights under said Franchise Agreement or this Agreement.

10. *Warranties and Insurance.* Franchisor, upon written request of Franchisee, shall assign and transfer to Franchisee without recourse all assignable or transferable manufacturer's warranties, if any, which Franchisor may have with respect to the Signage. Franchisee agrees and acknowledges that

(continues)

Figure 7-2. (Continued)

Franchisor has made no representations or warranties, either express or implied, with respect to the Signage. Franchisee hereby assumes any and all risk and liability for the Signage including but not limited to the possession, use, operation, and maintenance thereof; injuries or death to person; and damage to property however arising or damage or destruction of the Signage however arising therefrom. Franchisee, at its own expense, shall carry adequate liability insurance coverage on the Signage, naming the Franchisor and Franchisee as named insureds, affording protection from and against damages, claims, and expenses however caused and shall provide Franchisor a copy of said insurance policy upon request.

11. *Return.* Upon termination of this Agreement, the Franchisee shall at its own expense return the Signage to the Franchisor at the Franchisor's place of business in the same condition as when received, less ordinary wear and tear. If Franchisee fails to return the Signage, the Franchisor may, by his agents, take possession of the Signage, with or without process of law, and for this purpose may enter upon any premises of the Franchisee without liability and remove all or any of the Signage in the manner provided in Paragraph Six (6) above. Franchisee shall pay to Franchisor and any third parties all costs and expenses incurred in connection with such removal.

12. *Joint Liability; Gender.* If there be more than one peon comprising the party designated as Franchisee, then all reference in this Agreement shall be deemed to refer to each such person jointly and severally, and all such persons shall be jointly and severally liable hereunder. Words of any gender used in this Agreement shall be construed to mean corresponding words of any other gender, and words in the singular number shall be construed to mean corresponding words in the plural, when the context so requires.

13. *Successors.* All terms and conditions of this Agreement shall be binding upon the successors, assignees, and legal representatives of the respective parties hereto.

IN WITNESS WHEREOF, the parties, intending to be legally bound hereby, have signed this Agreement and affixed their seals on the day and year above written.

WITNESS: FRANCHISOR:

_____   _____

                                                        FRANCHISEE:

_____   _____

---

tions, or warranties not contained in the offering circular have been made by the franchisor or relied on by the franchisee. It also serves as an acknowledgment that the proper offering circular and related documents were provided to the franchisee on a timely basis.

Inventory Purchase Agreement

The inventory purchase agreement defines the rights and obligations between the franchisor and the franchisee with respect to the purchase of certain items of inventory, supplies, and other items available for purchase through the franchisor or its affiliates. A sample inventory purchase agreement may be found in Figure 7-3 of this chapter.

Assignment of Franchise Agreement or Franchised Business

This agreement is executed at the time of an assignment by a franchisee of its rights, title, and interest in the franchise agreement or the franchised business. It serves as the formal assignment agreement as well as a consent to the assignment by the franchisor, and it imposes certain obligations on the franchisee (assignor) and the assignee.

Addendum to Lease Agreement

This addendum is executed at the time of closing. It contains various provisions that must be contained in the franchisee's lease agreement for the premises on which the franchised business is located.

Special Consulting Agreement

This agreement should be used in the event that the franchisor intends to provide special support services to a franchisee or assume interim control of a franchisee's facility in the event of death or disability of the franchisee.

Area Development Agreements and Subfranchising

Most franchises are sold to individual owner/operators who will be responsible for managing a single site in accordance with the franchisor's business format and quality control standards. So far in this chapter, the discussion has been in the context of the single-unit franchisee. Some franchise systems, however, offer multiple-unit franchises to more aggressive entrepreneurs who will be responsible for the development of an entire geographic region.

The two primary types of multiple-unit franchises are:

- ❑ *Subfranchisors*, who act as independent selling organizations that are responsible for franchisee recruitment, offer and sale of franchises, and ongoing support of franchisees within their given region.
- ❑ *Area developers*, who have no resale rights but rather are themselves directly responsible for meeting a mandatory development schedule for their region.

These two principal types of multiple-unit franchises vary widely in their characteristics. For example, some franchises that are initially single units wind up as multiple units through the use of option agreements or rights of first refusal. Other franchisors have experimented with codevelopment rights among adjacent franchisees of a nearby territory, franchises

(text continues on page 125)

Figure 7-3. Sample inventory purchase agreement.

INVENTORY PURCHASE AGREEMENT

THIS AGREEMENT is made and entered into this _____ day of _____ by and between FRANCHISOR, an _____ corporation, (the "Franchisor"), and _____ (the "Purchaser").

WITNESSETH:

WHEREAS, Franchisor has attained prominence in the industry and through its techniques and methods has developed numerous products;

WHEREAS, Purchaser entered into a Franchise Agreement with Franchisor, on , 20__ by the terms of which Purchaser as Franchisee has been granted the right and license to operate a (the "Center");

WHEREAS, Purchaser is obligated by the terms of the Franchise Agreement to purchase certain merchandise, products, and other supplies (the "Products") solely from Franchisor or its approved suppliers;

WHEREAS, Purchaser has agreed to maintain Franchisor's uniformly high standards of quality for its products and services, which Purchaser acknowledges to be critical to the Franchisor's positive image and the protection of Franchisor's good will, and which, if not maintained, would result in irreparable harm to the Franchisor and the Purchaser; and

WHEREAS, Purchaser desires to purchase from Franchisor and Franchisor desires to sell to Purchaser certain merchandise, products, and supplies to be used in connection with its operation of the Center.

NOW, THEREFORE, in consideration of the mutual promises, covenants, and conditions contained herein and for other good and valuable consideration, the receipt and sufficiency of which is hereby acknowledged, the parties agree as follows:

1. *Orders.* Orders for Products placed by Purchaser with Franchisor shall be subject to acceptance by Franchisor and Franchisor reserves the right to wholly or partially accept or reject any order placed by Purchaser. Franchisor also reserves the right to limit the amount of credit it will extend to Purchaser, to suspend shipments, to make shipments only after all prior orders shipped to Purchaser have been paid in full, to make shipments on a cash in advance or C.O.D. basis or on any other terms that Franchisor in its discretion deems to be appropriate.

2. *Price.* Franchisor agrees to sell the Products to Purchaser at the prices set forth in the Price Schedule attached hereto as Exhibit A and incorporated herein by this reference. The Price Schedule may be changed by Franchisor from time to time in the normal course of business. Any lists of suggested retail prices that Franchisor may provide to Purchaser for the sale of the Products to its customers shall be nothing more than suggested prices. Purchaser shall be free to set its prices for resale as it sees fit. Purchaser shall be free to set its prices for resale as it sees fit. Franchisor, in its sole discretion, shall make price adjustments in accordance with then current market conditions.

3. *Payments.* Purchaser shall submit full payment for its orders and all shipping and handling charges at the time that said order is submitted to the Franchisor in accordance with the Price Schedule attached as Exhibit A, which may be amended from time to time by the Franchisor. Purchaser agrees to pay Franchisor for all orders pursuant to Franchisor's then current payment terms and policies, which

terms and policies may be changed by Franchisor from time to time in its sole discretion without incurring any liability to Purchaser.

4. *Security Interest*. In order to secure prompt payment of all amounts due to Franchisor hereunder, the Purchaser grants Franchisor a security interest in Purchaser's accounts receivable, contract rights, inventory, equipment, fixtures, personal property, and all other assets whether now owned or hereafter acquired. Purchaser agrees to execute a Security Agreement and such financing statements as may be required under the Uniform Commercial Code in order to secure Franchisor's interest in the aforementioned assets of Purchaser.

5. *Delivery*. Franchisor understands that time is of the essence in the fulfillment of orders submitted by Purchaser and will make a good faith effort to fill all orders in a timely manner. Franchisor shall not be responsible for delays or failures in manufacture or delivery, due to any cause beyond its control.

6. *Warranties*. Franchisor hereby assigns to Purchaser, when such assignment may be made, each and every warranty for Products manufactured or supplied by others which is provided to Franchisor. Franchisor makes no other warranty of any nature concerning the Products supplied to Purchaser. FRANCHISOR MAKES NO OTHER WARRANTY, EXPRESSED, STATUTORY, OR IMPLIED, INCLUDING ANY WARRANTY OF FITNESS FOR A PARTICULAR PURPOSE OR WARRANTY OF MERCHANTABILITY. FRANCHISOR SHALL HAVE NO OTHER LIABILITY NOR DOES IT AFFIRM ANY REPRESENTATION BEYOND THE DESCRIPTION SET FORTH HEREIN OR ON THE LABEL OF ANY PRODUCT. Franchisor may, at its option, issue a credit to the Purchaser for damaged or defective merchandise provided that the Purchaser returns said merchandise to Franchisor in accordance with its standards and procedures for the return of merchandise. Franchisor will issue said credit upon receipt of the damaged or defective merchandise from Purchaser. Franchisor shall not be liable for incidental, consequential, or other damages suffered by the Purchaser due to defective products.

7. *Term*. The term of this Agreement shall be the same as the term of the Franchise Agreement dated _____, 20____ by and between Purchaser and Franchisor including all renewal terms. Upon termination or expiration of this Agreement, the Purchaser must return to Franchisor, within seven (7) days, any Products in the Purchaser's possession that have been provided on a consignment basis or that have been shipped to Purchaser by Franchisor for which payment has not been received.

8. *Waiver*. The failure of either party to enforce at any time of the provisions hereof shall not be construed to be a waiver of such provisions or of the right of any party thereafter to enforce any such provisions.

9. *Assignment*. This Agreement and the rights hereunder are not assignable by Purchaser and the obligations imposed on Purchaser are not delegatable without the prior written consent of Franchisor.

10. *Modification*. No renewal hereof, or modification or waiver of any of the provisions herein contained, or any future representation, promise, or condition in connection with the subject matter hereof, shall be effective unless agreed upon by the parties hereto a signed writing.

11. *Independent Contractor*. This Agreement shall not be construed so as to characterize Purchaser as an agent, legal representative, joint venturer, partner, employee, or servant of Franchisor for any purpose whatsoever; and it is understood between the parties hereto that the Purchaser shall be an independent contractor and in no way shall Purchaser, its officers, directors, agents, or employees, be authorized to make any contract, agreement, warranty, or representation on behalf of Franchisor or to create any obligation, express or implied, on behalf of Franchisor.

(continues)

Figure 7-3. (Continued)

12. *Guaranty of Franchisee's Shareholder.* All shareholders of the Purchaser hereby undertake to guarantee the performance by the Purchaser of any and all obligations imposed upon the Purchasers under this Agreement.

13. *Notices.* Any and all Notices required or permitted under this Agreement shall be in writing and shall be personally delivered or mailed by certified or registered mail, return receipt requested, to the respective parties at the addresses set forth below, unless and until a different address has been designated by a written Notice to the other party. Notice by mail shall be deemed received five (5) days after deposit with the United States Postal Service.

14. *Entire Agreement.* This instrument contains the entire agreement between the parties. This Agreement supersedes and is in lieu of all existing agreements or arrangements between the parties relating to the Products heretofore sold or delivered to Purchaser, and with respect to any fair trade agreement that may be in existence as of the effective date hereof.

15. *Execution of Documents.* Purchaser agrees to execute any and all documents or agreements and to take all action as may be necessary or desirable to effectuate the terms, covenants, and conditions of this Agreement.

16. *Binding Effect.* This Agreement shall be binding upon the parties hereto, their heirs, executors, successors, assigns, and legal representatives.

17. *Severability.* If any provision of this Agreement or any part thereof is declared invalid by any court of competent jurisdiction, such act shall not affect the validity of this Agreement and the remainder of this Agreement shall remain in full force and effect according to the terms of the remaining provisions or part provisions hereof.

18. *Remedies.* The rights and remedies created herein shall be deemed cumulative and no one of such rights or remedies shall be exclusive at law or in equity of the rights and remedies that Franchisor may have under this Agreement or otherwise.

19. *Attorney's Fees.* If any action is instituted by any party to enforce any provision of this Agreement, the prevailing party shall be entitled to recover all reasonable attorney's fees and costs incurred in connection therewith.

20. *Construction.* This agreement shall be governed by and construed in accordance with the laws of the State of _____.

IN WITNESS WHEREOF, the parties hereto have caused this Purchase Agreement to be executed on the day and year first above written.

ATTEST   FRANCHISOR:

_____   By: _____
            Secretary

ATTEST   PURCHASER:

_____   By: _____
            Secretary

coupled with management agreements (under circumstances where the franchisee deserves to be more passive), equity participation by franchisors in franchisees (and vice versa), employee ownership of franchisor-operated units, and codevelopment rights between the franchisor and franchisee.

As a general rule, the inclusion of multiple-unit franchises in a franchisor's development strategy allows for even more rapid market penetration and less administrative burdens. Often the franchisee demands the right to develop and operate multiple units. However, a wide range of legal and strategic issues must be addressed when multiple-unit franchises are included in the overall franchising program.

Structuring Area Development Agreements

The key issues in structuring an area development agreement usually include the size of the territory, fees, the mandatory timetable for development, and ownership of the units. The franchisor usually reserves certain rights and remedies in the event that the franchisee defaults on its development obligations. The area developer may pay an umbrella development fee for the region, over and above the individual unit fee that is to be due and payable as each unit becomes operational in the territory. The amount of the fee varies, depending on factors such as the strength of the franchisor's trademarks and market share, the size of the territory, and the term (and renewal) of the agreement. This development fee is essentially a payment to the franchisor that prevents the franchisor from offering any other franchises in that region (unless there is a default). Sample key provisions of the area development agreement may be found in Figure 7-4.

Structuring Subfranchising Agreements

Subfranchise agreements present a myriad of issues that are not raised in the sale of a single-unit franchise or in an area development agreement, primarily because the rights and responsibilities of the subfranchisor differ from those of the area developer or single-unit operator. In most subfranchising relationships, the franchisor will share a portion of the initial franchise fee and ongoing royalty with the subfranchisor in exchange for the subfranchisor's assuming franchisor-like responsibilities in the region. The proportions in which fees are shared usually have a direct relationship to the exact responsibilities of the subfranchisor. In addition, the subfranchisor receives a comprehensive regional operations manual that covers franchise sales and promotions, training, and field support over and above the information contained in the operations manuals provided to the individual franchisees. The key challenge for the franchisor is to develop and deliver an adequate training program, not just to replicate a store but rather to replicate *themselves,* because the subfranchisee must be able to deliver on its obligations and provide services as if it was the franchisor. Some of the key issues that must be addressed in the subfranchise relationship are:

(text continues on page 129)

Figure 7-4. Selected key provisions from a typical area development agreement.

A. *Recitals*

WHEREAS, Franchisor, as the result of the expenditure of time, skill, effort, and money, has developed and owns a unique system (hereinafter, the "System, development, and operation of _____ (the "Franchised Business" or "Center");

WHEREAS, the distinguishing characteristics of the System include, without limitation, unique _____ techniques; technical assistance and training in the operation, management, and promotion of the Franchised Business; specialized bookkeeping and accounting methods; and advertising and promotional programs, all of which may be changed, improved, and further developed by Franchisor;

WHEREAS, Franchisor is the owner of certain rights, title, and interest in the trade name, trademark, and service mark and such other trade names, trademarks, and service marks as are now designated (and may hereafter be designated by Franchisor in writing) as part of the System (hereinafter referred to as the "Proprietary Marks");

WHEREAS, Franchisor continues to develop, expand, use, control, and add to its Proprietary Marks for the benefit and exclusive use of itself and its franchisees in order to identify for the public the source of products and services marketed thereunder and to represent the System's high standards of quality and service;

WHEREAS, Area Developer desires to obtain the exclusive right to develop, construct, manage, and operate a series of Centers within the marketing territory specified hereunder as the "Designated Marketing Territory" (a geographic map of which is attached hereto as Exhibit "A") under the System and Proprietary Marks, as well as to receive the training and other assistance provided by Franchisor in connection therewith; and

WHEREAS, Area Developer understands and acknowledges the importance of Franchisor's uniformly high standards of quality and service and the necessity of operating the Centers in strict conformity with Franchisor's quality control standards and specifications.

B. *Grant*

1. Franchisor hereby grants to Area Developer the right and license to develop, construct, operate, and manage _____ (_____) Centers in strict accordance with the System and under the Proprietary Marks within the marketing territory ("Designated Marketing Territory") as described in Exhibit "A" attached hereto. Each Center shall be operated according to the terms of the individual Franchise Agreement with respect thereto.

2. If the Area Developer complies with the terms of this Agreement, the Development Schedule, and the individual Franchise Agreement for each Center, then Franchisor will not franchise or license others, nor will it itself directly or indirectly develop, own, lease, construct, or operate in any manner, any Centers in the Designated Marketing Territory during the term hereof.

3. This Agreement is not a franchise agreement and Developer shall have no right to use in any manner the Proprietary Marks of Franchisor by virtue hereof.

C. *Development Fee*

Area Developer shall pay to Franchisor a nonrefundable development fee of Five Thousand Dollars ($5,000) per Center to be developed by Area Developer, which shall be paid upon execution of this Agreement, which fee shall be fully earned by Franchisor in consideration of its execution of the Agreement and its services and forbearance in offering franchises in the Designated Marketing Territory that is the subject of this Agreement. With respect to all Centers to be developed under this Agreement, Franchisor and Area Developer shall enter into an individual Franchise Agreement for each such Center within thirty (30) days prior to the grand opening thereof, which Agreement shall be in the form of the then current Franchise Agreement offered to new franchisees; provided, however, that the royalty fees shall remain the same as those royalty fees set forth in the individual Franchise Agreement being executed currently herewith.

D. *Development Schedule*

Area Developer shall open and continuously operate the Centers in accordance with the System and the development schedule set forth in Exhibit B (the "Development Schedule"). In the event that Area Developer opens and operates a greater number of Centers than is required to comply with the current period of the Development Schedule, the requirements of the succeeding period(s) shall be deemed to have been satisfied to the extent of such excess number of Centers. Except as otherwise provided herein, nothing herein shall require Area Developer to open Centers in excess of the number of Centers set forth in the Development Schedule, nor shall Area Developer be precluded from opening additional Franchised Businesses subject to the prior approval of Franchisor.

E. *Location of Centers*

The location of each Center shall be selected by Area Developer, within the Designated Marketing Territory, subject to Franchisor's prior approval, which approval shall take into account the marketing information and report provided by Area Developer. The acquisition of any proposed site by Area Developer prior to approval of Franchisor shall be the sole risk and responsibility of Area Developer and shall not obligate Franchisor in any way to approve the same. The approval of a proposed site by Franchisor does not in any way constitute a warranty or representation by Franchisor as to the suitability of such site for location of a Center.

F. *Assignment and Ownership of the Centers*

1. *By Franchisor.* Franchisor shall have the absolute right to transfer or assign all or any part of its rights or obligations hereunder to any person or legal entity.

2. *By Area Developer*

A. Area Developer understands and acknowledges that the rights and duties set forth in this Development Agreement are personal to Area Developer and are granted in reliance upon the personal qualifications of Area Developer. Area Developer has represented to Franchisor that Area Developer is entering into this Development Agreement with the intention of complying with its terms and conditions and not for the purpose of resale of the development and option rights hereunder.

B. Neither Area Developer nor any partner or shareholder thereof shall, without Franchisor's prior written consent, directly or indirectly sell, assign, transfer, convey, give away, pledge, mortgage, or otherwise encumber any interest in this Agreement or in Area Developer. Any such proposed assignment occurring by operation of law or otherwise, including any assignment by a trustee in bankruptcy, without Franchisor's prior written consent shall be a material default of this Agreement.

(continues)

Figure 7-4. (Continued).

C. If Area Developer is in full compliance with this Agreement, Franchisor shall not unreasonably withhold its approval of an assignment or transfer to proposed assignees or transferees who are of good moral character, have sufficient business experience, aptitude, and financial resources and otherwise meet the Franchisor's then applicable standards for area developers and are willing to assume all obligations of Area Developer hereunder and to execute and be bound by all provisions of the Franchisor's then current form of Area Development Agreement for a term equal to the remaining term hereof. As a condition to the granting of its approval of any such assignee or transferee, Franchisor may require Area Developer or the assignee or transferee to pay to the Franchisor its then current transfer fee as specified in Subsection F to defray expenses incurred by the Franchisor in connection with the assignment or transfer, legal and accounting fees, credit and other investigation charges and evaluation of the assignee or transferee, and the terms of the assignment or transfer. Franchisor shall have the right to require Area Developer and its owners to execute a general release of Franchisor in a form satisfactory to Franchisor as a condition to its approval of the assignment of this Agreement or ownership of Area Developer.

G. *Change in Territory*

The parties acknowledge that the development of the Designated Marketing Territory as anticipated hereunder has been determined according to the needs of the existing individuals who constitute Area Developer's targeted market in the Designated Marketing Territory, as determined by Franchisor, as of the date of execution of this Agreement. The parties agree that if there is an increased public demand for the products and services offered by Franchisor due to an increase in the number of individuals in the Designated Marketing Territory, as may be determined by a future demographic study, Franchisor shall have the right to demand that additional Centers be established within the Designated Marketing Territory. Area Developer shall have the right of first refusal to establish any such additional Centers deemed necessary and Franchisor agrees that such additional Centers shall be established only under the following terms and conditions:

(i) Any additional Centers shall be governed by the then current individual Franchise Agreement; and

(ii) Additional Centers will only be deemed necessary if the number of individuals in the Designated Marketing Territory increases by persons.

H. *Acknowledgments*

1. Area Developer acknowledges and recognizes that different terms and conditions, including different fee structures, may pertain to different Development Agreements and Franchise Agreements offered in the past, contemporaneously herewith, or in the future, and that Franchisor does not represent that all Development Agreements or Franchise Agreement are or will be identical.

2. Area Developer acknowledges that it is not, nor is it intended to be, a third-party beneficiary of this Agreement or any other agreement to which Franchisor is a party.

AREA DEVELOPER REPRESENTS THAT IT HAS READ THIS AGREEMENT, THE OFFERING CIRCULAR, FRANCHISE AGREEMENT, AND ALL EXHIBITS THERETO IN THEIR ENTIRETY AND THAT IT HAS BEEN GIVEN THE OPPORTUNITY TO CLARIFY ANY PROVISIONS AND INFORMATION THAT IT DID NOT UNDERSTAND AND TO CONSULT WITH AN ATTORNEY OR OTHER PROFESSIONAL ADVISOR. AREA DEVELOPER UNDERSTANDS THE TERMS, CONDITIONS, AND OBLIGATIONS OF THIS AGREEMENT AND AGREES TO BE BOUND THEREBY.

- ❐ How will the initial and ongoing franchise fees be divided between franchisor and subfranchisor? Who will be responsible for the collection and processing of franchise fees?

- ❐ Will the subfranchisor be a party of the individual franchise agreements? Or will the legal contract be between the franchisor and the individual subfranchisee?

- ❐ What is the exact nature of the subfranchisor's recruitment, site selection, franchising, training, and ongoing support to the individual subfranchisees in its region?

- ❐ Who will be responsible for the preparation and filing of franchise offering documents in the states where the subfranchisor must file separately?

- ❐ What happens if the subfranchisor defaults or files for bankruptcy? How will the subfranchisees in the region be handled?

- ❐ What mandatory development schedules and related performance quotas will be imposed on the subfranchisor?

- ❐ Will the subfranchisor be granted the rights to operate individual units in the territory? If yes, how will these units be priced?

- ❐ What will the subfranchisor be obligated to pay the franchisor initially for the exclusive rights to develop the territory?

- ❐ What rights of approval will the franchisor retain with respect to the sale of individual franchises (e.g., background of the candidate, any negotiated changes in the agreement, decision to terminate, etc.)?

- ❐ What rights does the franchisor reserve to modify the size of the territory or repurchase it from the subfranchisor?

A subfranchisor enters into what typically is referred to as a *regional development agreement* or *master franchise agreement* with the franchisor, pursuant to which the subfranchisor is granted certain rights to develop a region. The regional development agreement is *not* a single-unit franchise agreement to operate any individual franchise units; rather, it grants the subfranchisor the right to award and grant franchises to individuals using the franchisor's system and proprietary marks solely for the purpose of the recruitment, management, supervision, and support of individual franchisees. If the subfranchisor itself develops units, then a separate single-unit franchise agreement for each such unit must be executed. Some of the key terms, conditions, and obligations that make up the subfranchising relationship are discussed in this section.

Grant

The franchisor grants the subfranchisor the right and exclusive license to develop or grant franchises for the establishment and operation of franchises in a stated geographic region for a stated term (generally ten years or more).

Fees

The subfranchisor generally pays to the franchisor a development fee in exchange for the grant of the right and exclusive license to operate and sell franchises in the designated region. Typically, this development fee is paid upon execution of the regional development agreement, although it may be paid in installments.

Development of Region

The subfranchisor is obligated to develop and operate a franchise sales, marketing, and development program for its designated region that will include advertising and promotion of the franchisor's system, the offer and sale of franchises in the designated region, and the provision of support and assistance to franchisees in the establishment and ongoing operation of their franchises.

Traditionally, a performance schedule is set in the regional development agreement for the development of the designated region. This schedule will set forth the number of franchises the subfranchisor will be required to develop and/or sell in the designated region over the term of the agreement. Generally, if the subfranchisor fails to meet the development schedule, the franchisor may do one or more of the following:

1. Accelerate or modify the development schedule.
2. Withdraw the territorial exclusivity granted to the subfranchisor.
3. Redefine the designated region to encompass a smaller territory.
4. Terminate the regional development agreement.

Franchisor's Obligations

Most of the franchisor's obligations under a franchise agreement with an individual franchisee, in turn, become obligations of the subfranchisor to the subfranchisee in a subfranchising relationship. The franchisor, however, typically has several distinct obligations to the subfranchisor, including:

❑ Provision of training.
❑ Provision of materials, layouts, promotional items, operations, and other manuals (sometimes including a regional development manual).
❑ Oversight of subfranchisor's operations and techniques and suggesting improvements thereto.
❑ Promotion of the business and goodwill of the franchisor's system and proprietary marks.

Subfranchisor's Obligations

The most extensive portion of the regional development agreement is the recitation of the subfranchisor's obligations. These obligations flow to the franchisor and may benefit the individual subfranchisees in the designated region as well. They include the obligations to:

- ❐ Locate and maintain an office within the designated region.
- ❐ Submit for the franchisor's prior approval all proposed advertising, promotional, and sales materials that relate to the recruitment of franchisees.
- ❐ Offer and sell franchises only to persons/entities who meet franchisor's qualifications for experience, competence, reputation, and financial responsibility.
- ❐ Submit to the franchisor written applications for all qualified prospective franchisees for approval.
- ❐ Ensure the proper execution of franchise and related agreements by the franchisee.
- ❐ Ensure that each franchise in its designated region is developed and operated in accordance with the franchisor's standards and specifications.
- ❐ Comply with all federal and state laws and all regulations enacted by appropriate regulatory bodies with respect to the offer and sale of franchises.
- ❐ Provide ongoing support and assistance to franchisees in the designated region, including on-site supervision, inspection, training, and the provision of marketing/advertising techniques and materials.
- ❐ Submit all periodic reports required by the franchisor.

Remuneration of the Franchisor and Subfranchisor

- ❐ *Initial Franchise Fees Paid by Franchisees.* Generally, the franchisor and subfranchisor split the initial franchise fee charged to and collected from individual franchisees in the designated region. Typically, at the outset (e.g., the first 25 franchises), the franchisor is entitled to a higher percentage of the initial franchise fee. The percentages are gradually adjusted (as an incentive to stimulate sales in the region) as the subfranchisor sells more franchises.
- ❐ *Royalty Fees.* Additionally, the franchisor and subfranchisor share the royalty fees collected from each franchisee in the designated region. Similarly, the franchisor collects a greater percentage of royalties at the outset (e.g., the first 25 or so franchises sold by the subfranchisor), but as more franchises are sold, the subfranchisor's percentage of royalties increases.
- ❐ *Product Sales.* The franchisor's business format may revolve around the sale of proprietary goods and services through the franchised distribution channel. The role of the subfranchisor, if any, in this channel must be clearly defined with respect to pricing issues, warehousing and distribution issues, warranty policies, customer training, and product support. Some franchisors will view their subfranchise relationships as

regional warehouses or centralized commissaries, whereas other franchisors would prefer to see their subfranchisor stay focused on franchise sales and support and require only minimal responsibility from the subfranchisor with respect to product distribution and support.

The relationship between franchisor and subfranchisor is unique and somewhat complicated. If the appropriate individual is chosen for this role, the relationship can be mutually beneficial. The advantages of such a relationship to the franchisor include rapid market penetration, the delegation of obligations it would otherwise be required to fulfill to each franchisee in its network, and the ability to collect a percentage of the initial franchise fee and royalty fees from each franchisee, generally without the same level of effort that would be required in a single-unit relationship.

Managing Multiparty Franchise Relationships

The management of subfranchisor relationships by the franchisor presents a host of challenges. It is in some ways akin to a set of grandparents who disagree over how their children are raising their grandchildren. Everyone is in the same family, and a balance must be struck between the needs of the system overall to ensure that the parents are not doing anything to harm or mistreat the children against the parents' need not to feel micromanaged by the grandparents. The franchisor must create a culture where the franchisor and its team, the various subfranchisees and their teams, and each individual franchisee and their staffs have unified thinking and shared objectives toward the overall goals, mission, and values of the company. These common strategic objectives and operational focus ensure that the efforts and focus of all key parties are aligned and that all energies are directed at serving the needs of the customer. The franchisor must be committed to keeping technology-driven lines of communication open at all levels, to empowering the subfranchisors and subfranchisees to participate in business planning and in the development of shared goals, and to building systems that ensure accountability at all levels and in all directions, as set forth in Figure 7-5.

Figure 7-5. Managing subfranchise relationships.

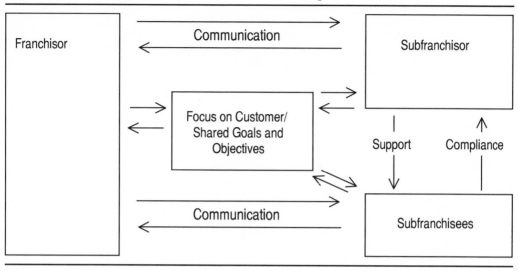

CHAPTER 8

Protecting the Intellectual Property of the Franchise System

t the foundation of every successful franchise system is the franchisor's intellectual property that has been developed, improved, and expanded over the years to create a unique concept, product, or service readily identifiable by consumers. The intellectual property of a franchise system consists primarily of (1) trademarks and service marks, (2) trade secrets, (3) copyrights, and, in some cases, (4) traditional and business method patents.

This chapter first examines the basics of understanding and protecting these key intangible assets. The second part focuses on building systems to better manage these assets.

Trademarks and Service Marks

A *trademark* or *service mark* is a word, name, symbol, or device used to identify and distinguish the products or services of one person from those of another and to indicate the source of the products or services. A trademark identifies a product and is used on the product, on containers or labels for the product, or on displays associated with the product. A service mark is used in the sale and advertising of services and generally appears in advertising and promotional materials.

A trademark or service mark also provides a guarantee of quality and consistency of the product or service it identifies. It assures the consumer that the products and services purchased today at one location are of the same quality as those purchased at another location tomorrow. Consumer recognition of and confidence in the product or service identified by the trademark or service mark is the lifeline of a successful franchise system.

In a franchise system, the franchisor grants the franchisee a *nonexclusive* license to use the franchisor's trademarks and/or service marks in connection with the franchisee's sale of the products and services in connection with the business that constitutes the franchise system.

Types of Marks

Not all words or phrases are entitled to trademark or service mark protection. The mark must, preliminarily, identify the products or services as coming from a particular source. The goodwill and name recognition established by the franchisor are the most valuable components of the franchise for the franchisee. Generally, marks that are protectable are those that are coined, fanciful, arbitrary, or suggestive. Generic marks are not protectable, and marks that are merely descriptive of the products or services they identify may not be protected without a showing of acquired distinctiveness or secondary meaning (as defined in the following list).

❑ *Coined, Fanciful, or Arbitrary.* This is the strongest category of mark that can be protected. The mark is either a coined word, such as XEROX, or a word in common usage that has no meaning when applied to the goods and services in question, such as DOVE for dish detergent or body soap. These marks are inherently distinctive and readily distinguish the products or services of one person from those of another.

❑ *Suggestive.* A suggestive mark requires the consumer to use some degree of imagination in determining the product or service represented. As such, it is the next strongest category of mark that may be protected. Owners of suggestive marks are not required to establish secondary meaning. Examples of suggestive marks include ORANGE CRUSH for orange drinks and ROACH MOTEL for insect traps.

❑ *Descriptive.* Marks that are descriptive of the goods or services they identify *cannot* be protected unless the manufacturer can establish that its mark has acquired distinctiveness. Proving this requires demonstration that the public associates the particular mark with the goods or services of the specific producer (known as secondary meaning). This category would include marks like HOLIDAY INN for motels, which is descriptive but nevertheless registered because it has acquired distinctiveness.

The host of marks that will be refused registration are those that:

❑ Are immoral, deceptive, or scandalous.

❑ May disparage or falsely suggest a connection with persons, institutions, beliefs, or national symbols or bring them into contempt or disrepute.

❑ Consist of or simulate the flag or coat of arms or other insignia of the United States, or of a state or municipality or any foreign nation.

❑ Are the name, portrait, or signature of a particular living individual unless he or she has given written consent, or are the name, signature, or portrait of a deceased president of the United States during the life of his widow, unless she has given her consent.

❑ So resemble a mark already registered in the U.S. Patent and Trademark Office (USPTO) as to be likely, when applied to the goods and/or services of the applicant, to cause confusion, to cause a mistake, or to deceive.

❒ Are merely descriptive or deceptively misdescriptive of the goods or services of the applicant.

❒ Are primarily geographically descriptive or deceptively misdescriptive of the goods or services of the applicant.

❒ Are primarily a surname.

Sometimes a mark may not be refused registration on the grounds that it is (1) merely descriptive or deceptively misdescriptive of the goods or services of the applicant, (2) primarily geographically descriptive or deceptively misdescriptive of the goods or services of the applicant, or (3) primarily a surname. In these cases, the applicant must show that, through use in commerce, the mark has acquired distinctiveness so that it now identifies to the public the applicant's products or services. Marks that are refused registration on these grounds may also be registered on the Supplemental Register if such marks are in use on or in connection with the goods and/or services identified in the subject application. The Supplemental Register contains terms or designs that are considered capable of distinguishing the registrant's goods or services but that have not yet acquired secondary meaning.

Protections Afforded by Registration

Trademark or service mark rights arise from either (1) use of the mark or (2) a bona fide intention to use the mark along with the filing of an application to federally register the mark on the Principal Register. Federal registration of a mark under the U.S. Trademark (Lanham) Act is not required to protect a mark, and a mark may be used without securing registration. However, registration provides a number of advantages, as listed in Figure 8-1.

A mark that is in actual use in commerce but that does not qualify for registration on the Principal Register for one or more reasons (i.e., it is merely descriptive or a surname) may be registered with the USPTO on the Supplemental Register. Registration on the Supplemental Register does not give a mark the same level of protection afforded by registration on the Principal Register, but it does give the registrant:

❒ The right to use the registration symbol (®) in association with the mark.

❒ The right to sue in federal court and obtain statutory remedies for infringement.

❒ In foreign countries whose laws require prior registration in the home country, a possible right to foreign registration.

❒ Protection against federal registration by another identical or confusingly similar mark.

Registration on the Supplemental Register allows the owner of the mark to put the world on notice of the use and rights to the mark. Further, registra-

Figure 8-1. Advantages of registration.

---

1. The filing date of the application becomes a constructive date of first use of the mark in commerce, giving the registrant nationwide priority as of that date, except as to prior users.

2. The right to bring legal action in federal court for trademark infringement.

3. Recovery of profits, damages, and costs in a federal court infringement action and the possibility of triple damages and attorneys' fees.

4. Constructive notice of a claim of ownership (which eliminates a good faith defense for a party adopting the mark subsequent to the registrant's date of registration).

5. The right to record the registration with U.S. Customs in order to stop the importation of goods bearing an infringing mark.

6. Prima facie evidence of the validity of the registration, registrant's ownership of the mark, and registrant's exclusive right to use the mark in commerce in connection with the goods or services specified in the registration certificate.

7. The possibility of incontestability, in which case the registration constitutes conclusive evidence of the registrant's exclusive right, with certain limited exceptions, to use the registered mark in commerce.

8. Limited grounds for attacking a registration once it is five years old.

9. Availability of criminal penalties and triple damages in an action for counterfeiting a registered trademark.

10. A basis for filing trademark applications in foreign countries.

---

tion of a descriptive mark on the Supplemental Register may be advantageous for a period of time while the mark's use is increased to the point where it becomes so substantial as to acquire secondary meaning. At that time, the mark may qualify for registration on the Principal Register. It may be advantageous for a start-up franchisor to take advantage of registration on the Supplemental Register, if registration is denied on the Principal Register, until a few franchises are sold and the mark, through increased use, gains secondary meaning. This would bolster the marketability of the franchise more than would an unregistered mark licensed by the franchisor.

Overview of the Registration Process

Prior to the passage of the Trademark Law Revision Act of 1988 (TLRA), a trademark owner was eligible for federal registration only if the mark had *actually been used* in interstate commerce. This requirement was different from that of most other countries, which generally allow a company to register a mark even if no actual use has been established. As a result, a substantial amount of time and expense might be invested in a proposed trade identity for a new product or service, with virtually no assurance that the mark could ever be properly registered and protected.

Under the TLRA, a franchisor may file an application to register a mark based on actual use *or* upon a bona fide intention to use the mark in interstate commerce. This allows the franchisor to conduct some market research and further investigation without the need to actually put the mark into the stream of commerce as a prerequisite to filing for federal protection.

The United States Patent and Trademark Office (USPTO) has developed the following procedures for registration under TLRA's so-called intent to use provisions:

1. Company files application for registration, which is subject to all of the current tests for registrability (e.g., likelihood of confusion, descriptiveness, etc.). If the mark is used in interstate commerce prior to approval of the application by the examiner, an amendment to the application may be made to allege that use of the mark in interstate commerce has occurred.

2. When the application is approved by the examiner, a Notice of Allowance is issued, advising the applicant that it has approximately three years from the date of the Notice of Allowance to use the mark, or the application will be abandoned.

3. If actual use does not occur until after the application is approved, the applicant will then have six months from the date of the Notice of Allowance to use the mark in interstate commerce and to file a Statement of Use, which must be accompanied by examples of the mark as used (i.e., specimens). Specimens may include labels evidencing use of a trademark on a product or brochures marketing services under a particular service mark. After review and approval of the Statement of Use and specimens, the mark will be registered. An applicant may request extensions of time for filing of the Statement of Use for up to five successive six-month periods. Failure to file by this deadline will result in abandonment of the application.

Regardless of whether a franchisor files under the actual use or intent to use provisions, an application must be prepared and filed at the USPTO for the mark in the classification that is appropriate for the goods and services offered. An examiner will then review the application to determine whether it meets the statutory requirements and whether similar marks have already been registered for the same or similar goods and/or services. The examiner's concerns are usually enumerated in a formal office action. An applicant is then required to respond to all of the issues raised by the examiner within six months. This process continues until the application is either finally refused or recommended by the examiner for publication in the *Official Gazette*, which serves as notice to the general public.

Anyone who believes that he or she would be injured by registration may file a Notice of Opposition or an extension of time to file a Notice of Opposition within 30 days of publication in the *Official Gazette*. A potential opposer may request extensions of time to file a Notice of Opposition of up to 180 days from the date of publication. The filing of a Notice of Opposition initiates an adversarial proceeding (akin to a litigation) before the Trademark

Trial and Appeal Board (TTAB). In an opposition, the TTAB decides whether the applicant is entitled to *register* its mark but does not decide whether the applicant is entitled to *use* it. The TTAB is also the appropriate body to appeal the examiner's final refusal to register.

Registration is a complex and often lengthy process (taking from 12 to 18 months even if there are only minimal problems), but the commercial rewards may be substantial if the registered mark is properly used to provide the franchisor with a competitive edge. Registration under the Lanham Act is effective for 10 years and may be renewed for additional 10-year terms thereafter as long as the mark is still in actual use in interstate commerce. The registration will, however, be canceled unless an affidavit demonstrating the continued use of the mark is filed with the USPTO between the fifth and sixth years of registration.

International Trademark Protection

According to the International Franchise Association, more than 500 U.S. franchisors offer international franchising opportunities. However, as any U.S. franchisor that has entered the international marketplace can attest, obtaining and maintaining trademark portfolios in each country where the franchisor expands can be an expensive and complex process with respect to trademark filing fees as well as legal fees associated with retaining trademark counsel throughout the world. However, U.S. franchisors and other trademark owners may take advantage of an international filing system called the "Madrid Protocol" that permits the simultaneous filing of marks in as many as 79 countries using a single, standardized application.

The Madrid Protocol is administered by the World Intellectual Property Organization (WIPO) located in Geneva, Switzerland. For U.S. franchisors and other companies that maintain international trademark portfolios, access to the Madrid Protocol is an opportunity to streamline and significantly reduce the cost of global trademark acquisition and management. The Madrid Protocol became available to U.S. trademark owners on November 2, 2003.

For U.S. trademark owners in need of international trademark protection, the Madrid Protocol, in many cases, may eliminate the need to file separate applications in each country where trademark protection is required. For example, under this protocol, a U.S. company in need of trademark protection in China, Japan, the United Kingdom, and Morocco (all members of the Madrid Protocol) may simply file one standardized application in the USPTO, pay one fee, and obtain a single registration covering those countries, provided the marks pass examination and publication in the jurisdictions filed. The resulting registration will have one registration number and one renewal date.

However, the Madrid Protocol is *not* a substantive trademark law, and an application filed under it does not result in a Madrid Registration. In other words, although the registration issued under the Madrid Protocol is often referred to as an "international registration," it differs from registrations issued under the auspices of such collective organizations as the European

Union because it is not a freestanding, supranational registration. Instead, the Madrid Protocol provides a *centralized filing mechanism* for simultaneously obtaining, in effect, separate national registrations based either on a pending application or existing registration on file in the national trademark office of the applicant's home country.

To file an application under the Madrid Protocol, the applicant must be a qualified owner of either a pending application or a registration on file in the national trademark office of the applicant's home country.

Maintaining Rights in the Trademarks

Because a trademark provides consumers with a guarantee of quality, the owner of a trademark is responsible for protecting and ensuring the quality of the products or services associated with it. For a franchisor that has licensed its marks to franchisees who are located all over the country, maintaining a certain level of quality of the products and services identified by the marks is certainly a challenge.

Along with the rights conferred as the owner of a registered mark, there are responsibilities. The licensor/franchisor must actively police its marks to ensure that an established level of quality is maintained by the licensees/ franchisees. A carefully drafted franchise/license agreement should set forth in detail the specific obligations of the franchisee with respect to the marks. The franchise/license agreement must provide the franchisor with supervisory control over the quality of the products or services that the mark represents. If such control is not retained by the franchisor, the license could be considered "naked" and found to be invalid. A franchisor therefore must provide its franchisees with both guidelines for use of the marks and guidance on the level of quality and uniformity that must be maintained for the products and services that bear the marks.

Protecting the Trademarks Under the Franchise Agreement

Every franchise agreement should have a section devoted to the proper use and care of the franchisor's marks, which should stipulate at least the following:

- ❒ The identity of the marks that are being licensed to the franchisees for use in the franchised business
- ❒ That the franchisee use only the marks designated by the franchisor and only in the manner authorized and permitted by the franchisor
- ❒ That the franchisee use the marks only in connection with the right and license granted to the franchisee
- ❒ That the franchisee identify itself as a licensee/franchisee on all documentation, such as invoices, order forms, receipts, business stationery, and contracts; that the franchisee must also display a notice at its locations stating its status as a licensee/franchisee

- ❒ That the franchisee's right to use the marks is limited to uses authorized under the franchise agreement, and that any unauthorized use is an infringement of the marks and grounds for termination of the franchise agreement
- ❒ That the franchisee not use the license or the marks as collateral to incur or secure any obligation or indebtedness
- ❒ That the franchisee not use the marks as part of its corporate or other legal name without the prior written authorization of the franchisor
- ❒ That the franchisee comply with the franchisor's instructions and any local jurisdictions' requirements for filing and maintaining trade name or fictitious name registrations
- ❒ That the franchisee promptly notify the franchisor if it learns of any third-party improper uses of the marks in the territory
- ❒ That the franchisee (1) promptly notify the franchisor if litigation involving the marks is instituted or threatened against the franchisee and (2) cooperate fully in defending or settling such litigation

Additionally, the franchisee should be required to expressly acknowledge that:

- ❒ The franchisor is the owner of all right, title, and interest in the marks and the goodwill associated with and symbolized by the marks.
- ❒ The marks are valid and serve to identify the franchisor's system and those who are licensed to operate a franchise in accordance with the system.
- ❒ The franchisee will neither directly or indirectly contest the marks' validity nor the franchisor's ownership of the marks.
- ❒ The franchisee's use of the marks according to the franchise agreement does not give the franchisee any ownership interest or other interest in or to the marks, except a nonexclusive license.
- ❒ Any and all goodwill arising from the franchisee's use of the marks in accordance with the franchisor's system is solely and exclusively to the franchisor's benefit, and upon expiration or termination of the franchise agreement, no monetary amount will be assigned as attributable to any goodwill associated with the franchisee's use of the system or the marks.
- ❒ The license and rights to use the marks granted to the franchisee are nonexclusive, and the franchisor may therefore (1) itself use the marks and grant franchises and licenses to others to use them; (2) establish, develop, and franchise other systems different from the one licensed to the franchisee, without offering or providing the franchisee any rights in, to, or under such other systems; and (3) modify or change, in whole or in part, any aspect of the marks so long as the franchisee's rights are not materially harmed.
- ❒ The franchisor reserves the right to substitute different names and marks for use in identifying the system, the franchise, and other franchised businesses operating under the franchisor's system.

❐ The franchisor has no liability to the franchisee for any senior users that may claim rights to the franchisor's marks.

❐ The franchisee will neither register nor attempt to register the marks or marks confusingly similar thereto in the franchisee's name or that of any other person, firm, entity, or corporation.

Trademark Protection and Quality Control Program

Every franchisor should develop an active trademark protection program designed to educate the franchisor's field staff, key vendors, advisors, officers, employees, and all of its franchisees about the proper usage and protection of the marks. The development of a franchise agreement that imposes all of the relevant obligations is a vital component of this program, but alone it is insufficient to prevent misuse of the marks and enforce quality control standards. A Trademark Use Compliance Manual, which contains more detailed guidelines for proper trademark usage and quality control, also plays an important role in a successful trademark protection program. The compliance manual may comprise a section of the franchisor's operations manual and specify the following:

❐ Proper use and display of the marks (including use of ®,™, and/or ᔆᴹ symbols)

❐ Information and instructions regarding state filings (fictitious name registrations) required to reflect the franchisee's status as a licensee of the marks

❐ All documents, correspondence, and other materials on which the franchisee must display the marks and identify itself as a licensee/franchisee

❐ All authorized uses and all prohibited uses of the marks (i.e., they may not be used as part of franchisee's corporate name)

In addition to a compliance manual, strategies should be developed to monitor franchisees, competitors, and other third parties to detect and prevent improper usage or potential infringement of the marks. A staff member of the franchisor should be designated to read trade publications, business press, marketing materials of competitors, and in-house production, labeling, and correspondence to ensure that the mark is properly used by the franchisees and not infringed by competitors. If an infringing use is discovered by a clipping service, company field representative, franchisee, trade association, or supplier, the franchisor must be vigilant in its protection of the marks by working with trademark counsel to ensure that all potential infringers are dealt with appropriately and in a timely manner. This may include warning letters demanding the immediate cessation of use of the franchisor's mark and destruction of the infringing materials. As much evidence as possible should be gathered on each infringer and accurate files kept in the event that trademark infringement litigation is necessary to settle the dispute. Each possible infringement should be carefully studied and weighed. The risks of continued use in the marketplace and the effect that continued use will have on subsequent infringements by other third parties must be considered in light of the likelihood of success in stopping any such alleged infringement. Although the goal is to keep the marketplace and the Trademark Office Register free from confusingly similar marks, the realities of the marketplace and associated costs of enforcement versus the potential loss of goodwill and market share must be considered. In those cases where the risk of damage to goodwill and the effect on subsequent third-party infringers is low, allocating the funds to advertising, to further build the goodwill in the mark, might be wiser than spending them paying legal fees.

Trademark Infringement and Dilution

The principal reason a trademark monitoring program must be maintained by every franchisor is to guard against trademark infringement and/or dilution. Under the Lanham Act, infringement of a registered mark is demonstrated by establishing that an unauthorized third party is using a reproduction, counterfeit, copy, or colorable imitation of the registered mark in connection with the sale, offering for sale, distribution, or advertising of any goods or services when such use is likely to cause confusion, mistake, or deception on the part of the ordinary purchaser.

The standard for determining "likelihood of confusion" varies slightly from circuit to circuit. However, the focus is on whether the ordinary purchaser of the product in question is likely to be confused as to the source of origin or sponsorship. The courts weigh a wide variety of factors in determining whether likelihood of confusion exists, including:

❒ The degree of similarity and resemblance of the infringer's mark to the registered mark (in terms of appearance, pronunciation, meaning and commercial impression, etc.).

❒ The strength of the registered mark in the relevant industry or territory.

❒ The good faith/bad faith of the infringer.

❒ The similarity and/or relatedness of the goods or services offered by the infringer and the owner of the registered mark.

❒ The overlap (if any) in the distribution and marketing channels of the infringer and the owner of the registered mark.

❒ The extent to which the owner of the registered mark can demonstrate that consumers were actually confused (usually demonstrated with consumer surveys and affidavits).

❒ The quality of the infringer's product.

❒ The sophistication of the buyers.

In addition to a federal cause of action for trademark infringement, the Federal Trademark Dilution Act expands the scope of rights granted to "famous" marks. Dilution differs from trademark infringement in that there is no need to prove a likelihood of confusion to protect a mark. Instead, all that is required is that unauthorized use of a famous mark by a third party causes the dilution of the "distinctive quality" of the mark. The determination of whether a mark is famous for purposes of availing of this act requires consideration of the following factors:

❏ Duration and extent of use of the mark and advertising of the mark
❏ The geographic area in which the mark has been used
❏ The degree of distinctiveness of the mark
❏ The degree of recognition of the mark
❏ The channels of trade in which the goods/services are distributed and marketed
❏ Whether the mark was federally registered

Although a claim for dilution is very attractive, it is only available to trademark owners who can establish that their marks are famous, meaning that the mark enjoys very strong consumer loyalty, recognition, and goodwill.

Strengthening the Franchisor's Trademark Portfolio

There are at least two methods of strengthening the franchisor's portfolio of core trademarks through intellectual capital leveraging management strategies. The first way is to *expand the registered uses* of the mark through brand extension licensing. For example, The Coca-Cola Company started using Coca-Cola® as the brand name for a carbonated beverage. But the uses for this mark has expanded over time, and it can now be seen on everything from playing cards to clothing to retail store services. In fact, The Coca-Cola Company retail store in Las Vegas features hundreds of licensed merchandise items bearing The Coca-Cola Company's recognized brands. Because The Coca-Cola Company has used its various marks on almost all types of retail goods and registered them for nearly every use imaginable, they are protected from third-party use of similar marks on nearly anything and have created new streams of protectable revenues through brand extension licensing.

McDonald's Corporation, as a franchisor, is an example of a second common strategy for strengthening a trademark portfolio. McDonald's Corporation has *created a "family" of marks* that makes it difficult for a third party to develop branding strategies within the range of its marks. A family of marks is created by using multiple marks with a common feature. For example, McDonald's Corporation has used and registered many marks comprising the "Mc" prefix for goods and services associated with its restaurants, such as Chicken McNuggets®, McRib®, McSkillet®, McCafe®, McDeals®, McFamily®, and others. McDonald's Corporation uses and promotes these marks together in such a manner as to create among purchasers an association of common ownership based upon the Mc family characteristic. A family of marks argument can be an effective tool against third-party use of a mark that contains the particular family characteristic and that is used for similar or related goods or services. Such an argument would likely be successful against an unauthorized third-party use of McPizzas. It may even support a claim of infringement against a bicycle retailer who uses the mark McBikes because the consumer should not be led to believe that bicycles are affiliated with McDonald's Corporation.[1]

Trade Dress

Trade dress generally refers to the characteristics of the visual appearance of a product or its packaging. It can also be a combination or arrangement of elements that comprise the total image of a retail or restaurant business. Trade dress may include external building features, interior designs, signage, uniforms, product packaging, and similar features designed to build brand awareness and to distinguish one company's products or services from those of another. Trade dress may be subject to protection if:

1. The *combination* of features used in the presentation, packaging, or "dress" of the goods and services are determined to be distinctive of the goods or services being offered.
2. The elements, either individually or in combination, are deemed to be *nonfunctional*; that is, they are an arbitrary aspect of the business used for identification, not to facilitate business operations.

For example, in the case of *Taco Cabana International, Inc. v. Two Pesos, Inc.*, which was affirmed by the Supreme Court, a jury found the following combination of restaurant decor features to be protectable trade dress:

❐ Interior and patio dining areas decorated with artifacts, bright colors, paintings, and murals

❐ Overhead garage doors sealing off the interior from the patio areas

❐ Festive exterior paintings having a color scheme using top border paint and neon stripes

❐ Brightly colored awnings and umbrellas

❐ A food-ordering counter set at an oblique angle to the exterior wall and communicating electronically with the food preparation and pickup areas

❐ An exposed food preparation area accented by cooking and preparation equipment visible to the consumer

❐ A condiment stand in the interior dining area proximate to the food pickup stand

---

1. *See McDonald's Corp. v. McBagel's Inc.* (holding that selling food under the name "McBagel's" infringed McDonald's trademark); *McDonald's Corp. v. Druck and Gerner* (holding that dentists providing dental services to customers under the name "McDental" infringed McDonald's trademark).

This case and others like it suggest the increased availability of protection for nonfunctional components of a franchisor's system. The franchisor looking to enhance the strength of its image and to gain protection for its trade dress would be wise to follow these suggestions:

❑ Adopt a combination of several features.

❑ Try to use as many unique features as possible in the combination.

❑ Avoid features that may be viewed as functional or necessary to better operate the business.

❑ Use the features consistently and continuously.

❑ Include the trade dress in advertising and promotional literature for the goods and/or services with which it is associated to build source recognition in the marketplace.

❑ Advertise the trade dress as extensively as possible,

❑ Carry the theme of the trade dress throughout the entire business.

❑ Obtain federal registration of as many components of the trade dress as possible.

❑ Keep competitors from adopting similar combinations of features and from using features unique to your trade dress.

In today's competitive marketplace, trademark and service mark rights are often the most valuable assets of the franchise system. The goodwill and consumer recognition that trademarks and service marks represent have tremendous economic value and are therefore worth the effort and expense to properly register and protect. Management must also implement and support a strict trademark compliance program that includes usage guidelines for all franchisees, as well as suppliers, service providers, and distributors.

Trade Secrets

A franchisor's advantage over its competitors is gained and maintained in large part through its trade secrets and proprietary information. A franchisor's trade secrets will typically consist of its confidential formula, recipes, business format and plan, prospect lists, pricing methods, and marketing and distribution techniques.

Not all ideas and concepts are considered to be trade secrets. Courts have generally set forth three requirements for information to qualify for trade secret protection:

1. The information must have some commercial value.

2. The information must not be generally known or readily ascertainable by others.

3. The owner of the information must take all reasonable steps to maintain its secrecy. To preserve legal protections for its trade secrets, a franchisor must follow a reasonable and consistent program for

ensuring that the secrecy of the information is maintained. This presents a difficult problem in the franchising context where the franchisor, as the owner of the trade secrets, licenses sometimes hundreds (and even thousands) of people and/or companies to use its trade secrets. It is therefore important to continuously strive to maintain the secrecy of the trade secrets in the hands of franchisees and their employees.

In deciding the extent to which protection should be afforded for trade secrets, however, courts have considered many other factors. Among the factors most often cited are:

❐ The extent to which the information is known by others outside the company.
❐ The measures employed within the company to protect its secrets.
❐ The value of the information to its owner, including the resources expended to develop the information.
❐ The amount of effort that would be required by others to duplicate the effort or reverse-engineer the technology.
❐ The nature of the relationship between the alleged infringer and the owner of the trade secret.

Implementing a Trade Secret Protection Program

Franchisors can readily adopt some fundamental, affordable, and practical measures to protect the trade secrets that constitute the heart of their competitive advantage.

Steps to Be Taken by the Franchisor and Its Franchisees

Even in an effort to protect trade secrets, there is such a thing as overkill. In fact, like the boy who cried wolf, if a franchisor tries to protect every aspect of its operation by classifying everything in sight as a trade secret, virtually nothing at all will likely be afforded protection when put to the test. Genuine trade secrets may be diluted if you try to protect too much.

The process of establishing a trade secret protection and compliance program should start with a trade secret audit to identify which information is *genuinely* confidential and proprietary. Although each franchisor has its own priorities, all types of franchised businesses should consider financial, technical, structural, marketing, engineering, distribution documents, recipes, business plans, operations manuals, and pricing techniques to be candidates for protection. A portion of the franchisor's operations manual should identify all information the franchisor considers to be trade secrets and address their proper use and protection as part of the licensing process to franchisees.

Trade secret protection must be a part of the franchisee's training program, during which a full briefing should be given on their continuing duty and legal obligation to protect the secrets of the franchisor. In fact, the franchisor should maintain a written statement of its trade secret security policy to prevent unwritten rules from being followed or the lax enforcement and eventual ignoring of rules. It's easier to persuade a court that the company viewed its security procedures as a primary concern if they are committed to writing.

Franchisees should be instructed that trade secrets should be disclosed only to employees who have a genuine need to know the information in order to perform their jobs. Employees who have access to the franchisor's trade secrets should also be informed of their continuing duty and legal obligation to protect the secrets. For certain key employees, it may be advisable to require them to execute a Confidentiality and Noncompetition Agreement.

The critical rules of the franchisor's compliance program to which franchisees must adhere are as follows:

☐ Ensure that adequate security measures are taken, which may include restricting access to certain proprietary documents and information (recipes, manuals); implementing log-in procedures prior to gaining access to locked desks, files, and vaults for proprietary documents; and posting signs and notices in all appropriate places.

☐ Label trade secret documents clearly with a proprietary notice, and instruct all employees about the meaning of the designation; restrict the photocopying of these documents to limited circumstances.

☐ Designate a Trade Secret Compliance Officer to be in charge of all aspects relating to the proper care and monitoring of trade secrets.

☐ Carefully review advertising and promotional materials, press releases, public speeches, and other corporate communications, as well as patent applications, to ensure that they do not contain any trade secrets. Each of these provides a competitor with ample opportunity to discover a trade secret.

☐ Ensure that *all* key employees, marketing representatives, service providers, franchisees, prospective investors or joint venturers, customers, suppliers, or anyone else who has access to the company's trade secrets has signed a carefully prepared Confidentiality and Nondisclosure Agreement. See Figure 8-2.

☐ Police the activities of former employees, suppliers, and franchisees; include post-term obligations in agreements that impose a duty on the employee to maintain the secrecy of confidential information/trade secrets after employment has terminated.

☐ If trade secrets are contained on computers, use passwords and data encryption to restrict access to terminals and telephone access through modems.

☐ Establish controlled routing procedures for the distribution and circulation of documents containing trade secrets.

(text continues on page 152)

Figure 8-2. Noncompetition and nondisclosure agreement (for execution by employees of franchisee).

This AGREEMENT is made and entered into this _____ day of _____, 20__, by and between _____, a corporation, (the "Franchisee"); Prof-Finders, a corporation, (the "Franchisor"); and _____ ("Employee").

WITNESSETH

WHEREAS, the Franchisor and Franchisee have entered into a franchise agreement dated _____, (the "Franchise Agreement"), pursuant to which Franchisee shall receive access to Confidential Information [as that term is defined in Paragraph __ of the Franchise Agreement] and trade secrets of the Franchisor, which Franchisee may, in certain instances, need to convey to Employee, in order to operate its Prof-Finders academic referral centers (the "Center"); and

WHEREAS, Franchisor and Franchisee desire to protect said Confidential Information and trade secrets from disclosure and unauthorized use by the Employee.

NOW, THEREFORE, in consideration of the employment of Employee by Franchisee and the mutual promises and covenants herein contained, and other valuable consideration the receipt and sufficiency of which is hereby acknowledged, the parties hereto, intending to be legally bound, hereby agree as follows:

A. *Covenant Not to Compete*

Employee specifically acknowledges that due to its employment by Franchisee, Employee will receive valuable, specialized training and Confidential Information [as that term is defined in Paragraph of the Franchise Agreement] and information regarding academic referrals, operational, sales, and marketing methods and techniques of Franchisor and its System. Employee covenants that during the term of his employment and subject to the post-termination provisions contained herein, except as otherwise approved in writing by Franchisor, Employee shall not, either directly or indirectly, for himself or through, on behalf of, or in conjunction with any person, persons, partners, or corporation:

1. Divert or attempt to divert any business, customer, or employees of the Franchisor or Franchisee to any competitor, by direct or indirect inducement or otherwise, or do or perform, directly or indirectly, any other act injurious or prejudicial to the goodwill associated with Franchisor's Proprietary Marks and the System.

2. Employ or seek to employ any person who is at that time employed by Franchisor or Franchisee, by any other franchisee or developer of Franchisor, or otherwise directly or indirectly induce such person to leave his or her employment.

3. Own, maintain, engage in, be employed by, advise, assist, invest in, franchise, or have any interest in any business which is the same as or substantially similar to that of the Franchisor or Franchisee.

4. Employee covenants that, except as otherwise approved in writing by Franchisor, Employee shall not, for a continuous uninterrupted period commencing upon the expiration of termination of his employment with Franchisee, regardless of the cause for termination, and continuing for ( ) years thereafter, either directly or indirectly, for himself or through, on behalf of, or in conjunction with any person, persons, partnership, or corporation, own, maintain, engage in, be employed by, advise, assist, invest in, franchise, make loans to, or have any interest in any business that is the same as or substantially similar to that of

the Franchisor or Franchisee and that is located within a radius of (___) miles of the Franchisee's Designated Territory, or the location of any Center operated under the System [as that term is defined in the Franchise Agreement] that is in existence on the date of termination of Employee's employment relationship with Franchisee. Employee acknowledges and agrees that these covenants will survive the termination of his employment. This Section shall not apply to ownership by Employee of less than a five percent (5%) beneficial interest in the outstanding equity securities of any publicly held corporation.

B. *Nondisclosure and Confidentiality*

1. Franchisor and Franchisee may make available to Employee certain designate materials, operational techniques, and information pertinent to the franchise being operated by the Franchisee pursuant to the Franchisor's System and Proprietary Marks.

2. Employee acknowledges and agrees that all materials and information shall be used solely for the purposes of conducting his duties as an employee of the Franchisee's Center.

3. Employee agrees to hold in strict trust and confidence all such materials and information that the Franchisor or Franchisee furnishes or otherwise makes available to Employee.

4. Neither the Employee nor his/her relatives, agents, or representatives will use such material or information for any purpose other than stated herein and shall not copy, reproduce, sell, reveal, or otherwise disclose any such materials and information to any persons or parties.

5. Employee shall not be subject to the restrictions imposed herein with respect to any information or data obtained by it from the Franchisor or Franchisee during his employment with Franchisee if the information or data:

(a) was known to the Employee or has been independently developed by the Employee at the time of the receipt of the proprietary materials and information thereof from the Franchisor or Franchisee; or

(b) was or hereafter is obtained by Employee from another source; however, the burden of proof shall rest on the Employee to demonstrate that such information or materials were not provided by the Franchisor or Franchisee.

C. *Not an Employment Agreement*

Employee is being employed by Franchisee under separate arrangements that form no part of this Agreement. Franchisee is not obligated by this Agreement to continue to employ Employee for any particular time period, or under any specific terms or conditions. This Agreement does not create an employment relationship between Franchisor and Employee.

D. *Severability*

The parties agree that each of the foregoing covenants shall be construed as independent of any other covenant or provision of this Agreement. If any or all portions of the covenants in this Section are held unreasonable or unenforceable by a court or agency having valid jurisdiction in an unappealed final decision to which Franchisor and Franchisee are parties, Employee expressly agrees to be bound by any lesser covenant subsumed within the terms of such covenant that imposes the maximum duty permitted by law, as if the resulting covenant were separately stated in and made a part of this Agreement.

(continues)

Figure 8-2. (Continued)

E. *Governing Law*

This Agreement shall be construed in accordance with the laws of the State of _____, which law shall govern in the event of a conflict of laws.

IN WITNESS WHEREOF, the parties have signed this Agreement and affixed their seals on the day and year above written.

Employee
_____

Prof-Finders
_____

By: _____
Franchisee

☐ Purchase a paper shredder and use it when appropriate.

☐ Restrict the photocopying of documents and *prohibit* photocopying of confidential operations manuals; use legends and maintain logbooks on the status and location of the originals.

☐ Monitor the trade press and business journals for any news indicating a possible compromise and/or exploitation of your trade secrets by others.

☐ Conduct exit interviews with all employees who have had access to the franchisor's trade secrets; remind employees of their obligations not to use or disclose confidential and proprietary data owned by the franchisor, and of the costs and penalties for doing so; include provisions in confidentiality agreements requiring an employee to notify future employers in writing of its duty of confidentiality, especially in situations where the new employment is directly or indirectly competitive; conversely, to avoid litigation as a defendant, remind new employees of the franchisor's trade secret policies and that they are being hired for their skills and expertise, *not* for their knowledge of a former employer's trade secrets

Confidentiality Provisions in the Franchise Agreement

An important component of the trade secret protection program is the franchise agreement. A properly drafted agreement should contain confidentiality provisions, covenants against competition (both in-term and post-termination), and obligations with respect to the use and care of the franchisor's proprietary operations manuals.

Provisions regarding the franchisor's proprietary operations manuals should contain the following:

☐ Franchisee will conduct its business in strict compliance with the operational systems, procedures, policies, methods, and requirements prescribed in the franchisor's manual(s) and in any supplemental bulletins, notices, revisions, modifications, or amendments thereto.

☐ Franchisee acknowledges receipt of a copy of the franchisor's manual that has been provided *on loan* for the term of the franchise agreement; franchisor should have an identifying number on each manual it distributes to franchisees.

☐ Franchisee acknowledges that the franchisor is the owner of all proprietary rights in and to the system and manual(s) and any changes or supplements to the manual(s); franchisee acknowledges that all of the information contained in the manual(s) is proprietary and confidential, and franchisee shall use all reasonable efforts to maintain such information as confidential.

☐ Franchisee acknowledges, knows, and agrees that designated portions of the manuals are trade secrets known and treated as such by the franchisor.

☐ The trade secrets must be accorded maximum security consistent with franchisee's need to make frequent reference to them; franchisees shall strictly limit access to the manuals to employees who have a demonstrable and valid need to know the information contained therein to perform their jobs and strictly follow any provisions in the manuals regarding the care, storage, and use of the manuals and all related proprietary information; the franchisor should reserve the right to designate which employees of the franchisee shall execute confidentiality agreements, in a form provided by the franchisor.

☐ Franchisee shall not at any time, without franchisor's prior written consent, copy, duplicate, record, or otherwise reproduce in any manner any part of the manuals, updates, supplements, or related materials, in whole or in part, or otherwise make the same available to any unauthorized person.

☐ The manuals at all times remain the sole property of franchisor; upon the expiration or termination, for any reason, of the franchise agreement, franchisee shall return to franchisor the manuals and all supplements thereto.

☐ Franchisor retains the right to prescribe additions to, deletions from, or revisions to the manuals, which shall become binding upon franchisee once mailed or otherwise delivered to franchisee; the manuals and any additions, deletions, or revisions thereto shall not alter franchisee's rights and obligations under the franchise agreement.

☐ Franchisee shall at all times ensure that its copies of the manuals are kept current and up-to-date; in the event of any dispute as to the contents of the manuals, the terms contained in the master set (#0001) of the manuals maintained by franchisor at franchisor's headquarters shall be controlling.

☐ If one or more of the volumes comprising the manuals is lost, stolen, or destroyed, franchisee shall immediately notify franchisor so that procedures can be taken to minimize any loss of confidential/trade secret information. Franchisee shall also pay franchisor a nonrefundable fee for replacement manuals.

Misappropriation of Trade Secrets

The first step in protecting against the unauthorized use or misappropriation of trade secrets is to establish that those who come in contact with the information have a duty not to disclose or use it in any way not authorized and in the best interest of the franchisor. Generally, this duty must be established and then breached before a cause of action will arise. The only exception to this rule is wrongful misappropriation by improper means, such as theft or bribery, ascertained according to applicable state criminal statutes.

The simplest way to create such a duty is by agreement. In addition to the franchise agreement, the franchisor should have a written employment agreement with each of its employees who may have access to the franchisor's trade secrets. The employment agreement should contain provisions regarding the nondisclosure of proprietary information as well as covenants of nonexploitation and noncompetition, applicable both during and after the term of employment. In most states, these covenants will be upheld and enforced by a court if they are reasonable, consistent with industry norms, and not overly restrictive.

Agreements like these, as well as similar provisions in the franchise agreement, will go a long way toward proving to a court that the franchisor intended to and in fact took reasonable steps to protect its trade secrets in the event of any subsequent litigation. These agreements should only be the beginning, however, of an ongoing program to make franchisees and franchisee employees mindful of their continuing duty to protect the trade secrets of the franchisor.

Proving an Act of Misappropriation

Generally, the key elements of a civil cause of action for the misappropriation of trade secrets are:

1. Existence of a trade secret.
2. *Communication* of it pursuant to a confidential relationship.
3. Use of the trade secret in violation of the confidence (some duty not to disclose).
4. Information constituting the trade secrets *used* by the defendant to the *injury of the plaintiff.*

In analyzing whether these essential elements are present, the courts may consider the following factors:

1. Was any *relationship of trust and confidence,* either by express agreement or implied, breached?

2. How much in time, value, money, and labor has been expended in developing the trade secret?

3. Has the trade secret reached the public domain? If so, through what channels?

4. Has the franchisor maintained a conscious and continuing effort to maintain secrecy (agreements of nondisclosure, security measures, etc.)?

5. What were the mitigating circumstances surrounding the alleged breach or misappropriation?

6. What is the value of the secret to the franchisor?

Remedies for Misappropriation

The most important and immediate civil remedies available in any trade secret misappropriation case is the temporary restraining order and preliminary injunction. These remedies immediately restrain the unauthorized user from continuing to use or practice the trade secret, pending a hearing regarding the charge of misappropriation. Prompt action is necessary to protect the trade secret from further unauthorized disclosure. If the case continues to trial, the court's decision will address the terms of the injunction (i.e., permanent injunction) and may award damages and profits resulting from the wrongful appropriation of the trade secret.

Franchisors, however, should evaluate certain risks before instituting a trade secret suit. The franchisor may face the risk that the trade secret at issue, or collateral trade secrets, may be disclosed during the course of the litigation. Certain federal and state rules of civil procedure and laws of evidence will protect against this risk to a limited extent. Trade secret litigation is very fact intensive. Establishing the paper trail needed to prove all of the elements of misappropriation may be virtually impossible in some cases. Such lengthy litigation is likely to be prohibitively expensive for the average early-stage franchisor. This is all the more reason why preventative and protective measures are far more attractive alternatives than litigation.

Criminal Penalties for Trade Secret Misappropriation

Under the Economic Espionage Act of 1996 (EEA), trade secret theft or misappropriation is a federal crime. The EEA contains a broad definition of *trade secret*, including tangible as well as intangible property, whether "stored, compiled or memorialized physically, electronically, graphically, photographically or in writing." Penalties for conviction under the EEA are fines of up to $500,000 per offense and imprisonment of up to 15 years for individuals, and fines of up to $10 million for organizations.

A violation of the EEA occurs if a person or entity: (1) steals, or takes without authorization, or by fraud or deception obtains a trade secret; (2) copies, photographs, downloads, uploads, alters, transmits, sends, mails, or otherwise communicates or conveys a trade secret without authorization; or

(3) receives, buys, or possesses information knowing that it has been stolen or misappropriated. Before a violation may be found, however, it must be proven that the person or entity committed the act knowingly, intended to convert the trade secret to someone else's economic benefit, and knew that the offense would injure the owner of the trade secret. (These requirements differ slightly when a foreign entity is involved.)

The EEA also prohibits attempted theft as well as conspiracy to commit a theft. Consequently, if an employee of one company goes to work for a competitor who expects that employee to bring with him information belonging to his former employer, both the new employer and the employee may be violating the EEA. This situation would apply equally to a franchisee who leaves one system and joins another. Aside from possibly violating noncompete provisions in the former franchise agreement, the franchisee may be accused of violating the EEA if he or she attempts to use any of the former franchisor's trade secrets in the new business. The new franchisor may similarly be liable if it knows the franchisee will bring trade secrets for use in the new business. Whether in the employment or franchising scenario, corporations must educate employees about the dangers in hiring employees or in recruiting franchisees who have worked for the competition.

Copyrights

The legal basis for copyright protection is found in the United States Constitution, which empowers Congress to enact legislation to promote the progress of science and the useful arts by assuring authors, for a limited period of time, the exclusive right to their respective creations.

Pursuant to the power granted by the Constitution, Congress enacted the Copyright Act, which provides protection to all "original works of authorship fixed in any tangible medium of expression." This definition includes not only literary materials but also pictorial, graphic, and sculptural works. Operations manuals, promotional and advertising materials, training films and videos, forms, architectural plans, and computer programs typically developed and used by franchisors may be copyrightable works within the definition of the act.

Protections Afforded to Owner of Copyright

The act provides that the owner of a copyright has the exclusive right to:

1. Reproduce the work.
2. Prepare derivative works.
3. Distribute copies of the work.
4. Perform the work publicly.
5. Display the work publicly.

The owner's copyright is infringed if any of these exclusive rights is violated.

A copyright protects only the *expression of an idea,* not the idea itself.

In other words, a copyright protects *only* the original labor of the author that gave substance to the idea, *not* the underlying abstract idea or concept of the author. Once the copyrightable work is created in a tangible form, it automatically enjoys federal copyright protection and may be transferred or licensed to others.

How to Obtain Copyright Protection

Unlike trademark rights, which arise under common law based on use, copyright protection is a creature of statute. According to the act, copyright protection arises *as soon as the work is created and fixed in a tangible medium of expression*. The work need not be registered prior to its publication; however, registration is necessary before the copyright owner may commence legal proceedings against an infringer. The right to sue for infringement includes the ability to obtain injunctive relief and damages. However, in the absence of a notice of copyright (as described later in the chapter), an innocent infringer will not be liable for actual or statutory damages before receiving actual notice of the copyright. Prior to registration, it is advisable to consider whether registration would compromise the confidentiality of any trade secrets contained in the work. For example, the contents of a new marketing brochure are a natural candidate for copyright registration; however, the contents of a confidential operations manual should not be registered due to its proprietary nature.

The author of a work protectable by copyright should use the copyright notice, which puts the world on notice that the author claims copyright ownership in the work. The prescribed notice consists of (1) the copyright symbol (©) or the word "Copyright" or the abbreviation "Copr.," (2) the year of first publication of the work, and (3) the name of the copyright owner: for example, ©2011 Andrew J. Sherman.

Work Made for Hire

Typically, the author of the work is the owner of the copyright. Works developed by someone on behalf of another, however, may be considered works made for hire. The act defines a *work made for hire* as:

1. A work prepared by an employee within the scope of his or her employment.
2. A work specially ordered or commissioned for use as a contribution to a collective work, as a part of a motion picture or other audiovisual work, as a translation, as a supplementary work, as a compilation, as an instructional text, as a test, as answer material for a test, ". . . if the parties expressly agree in a written instrument signed by them that the work shall be considered a work made for hire . . . ."

A work made for hire, therefore, must either be prepared by an employee or fit within one of the narrow categories enumerated in entry 2 of the preceding list. With respect to agreements with independent contributors, if the work to be commissioned falls within one of those narrow categories, the agreement must clearly set forth that the work is intended by both parties to be a work made for hire under the act and owned by the commissioning party. Absent such express written agreement, the work would be presumed to be owned by its creator, not the person who paid for its creation.

Many companies overlook the need to get assignments of copyright from advertising agencies, label designers, and computer programmers in order to secure the copyright rights in their creative work and to prevent its being copied by the competition. In situations where the work to be commissioned does *not* fall within the work for hire definition, it is extremely important that the agreement specifically state that the independent contributor assigns all rights, title, and interest in the work to the party paying for the work. Otherwise, the work will be owned by its creator.

All materials used by the franchisor that constitute original works of authorship may be protected by the act. Registration is advisable for all major nonproprietary works that are an integral part of a franchise system, and the appropriate notice should appear on all such products.

Patents in a Franchising System

For many years, the intellectual property portfolio of the typical franchisor did not include patents. Only a handful of systems had core intellectual property assets that were based on patented technology, usually limited to home or business services where a particular process, machine, or technique supported the legal basis for patent protection. However, in today's market, where technology may be your competitive edge, patents can be an attractive option for protecting certain types of assets in the business and for providing an additional revenue stream. Therefore, patent protection may be a viable option for franchise systems that have patentable assets and that are looking to build a strong intellectual asset foundation.

A patent grants the inventor the right to exclude others from making, using, selling, or offering to sell the invention throughout the United States, or from importing the invention into the United States for a limited period of time. To obtain a patent, an application must be submitted with the United States Patent and Trademark Office (USPTO). A patent for an invention will not be granted if the subject matter of the claimed invention was publicly used or on sale in the United States by anyone, including the inventor, more than one year before the effective filing date of the application, or if the subject matter of the claimed invention was patented by anyone, anywhere in the world, more than one year before the effective filing date of the U.S. application.

The following categories of patents are available:

1. *Utility patents*, which are the most common, protect a new and useful process, machine, manufacture, or composition of matter, or any new and useful improvement thereto, for a period of 20 years from the filing date of the application.

2. *Design patents* protect the visual ornamental characteristics embodied in, or applied to, an article of manufacture, *not* its utilitarian features, for a period of 14 years from the date the patent is granted.

3. *Plant patents*, the least used, are issued to protect certain new varieties of plants that have been asexually reproduced for a term of 20 years from the filing date of the application.

Business Method Patents

Another type of patent to consider is a business method patent. Business method patents are a class of patents that disclose and claim new methods of doing business. A business method may be defined as a method of operating any aspect of an economic enterprise.

The appropriateness of patenting business methods has been the subject of numerous court actions over the years. For many years, the USPTO took the position that methods of doing business were not patentable. However, with the increased popularity of the Internet, many ways of doing business in cyberspace started to be viewed as novel and patentable, and it was no longer practical to determine whether a particular computer-implemented invention was a technological invention or a business invention. Novel methods of business were deemed patentable in the late 1990s by the United States Circuit Court for the Ninth Circuit in the landmark case of *State Street Bank v. Signature Financial Group, Inc.*, wherein the court found that Signature's patent for its "hub and spoke" mutual fund management process was valid. Perhaps the best-known Internet-related *business model patents* issued are for Priceline.com's reverse auction method and Amazon.com's one-click purchase feature.

However, in recent years, the case law has changed the landscape with respect to the patentability of business methods. In 2008, the court in *In re Bilski* determined that the test set forth in *State Street Bank* should no longer be relied on in determining the patentability of business method patents and concluded that a method of claim is patentable subject matter if it transforms an article into a different state or thing *or* if the process is tied to a particular machine or apparatus. In 2009, *In re Bilski* went up to the Supreme Court for argument, and to date a decision has not yet been issued, but it is anticipated that the decision will have an impact on the world of business method patents.

If a company's franchise system is dependent on a proprietary business method or system, as is the case with so many franchises, then it should consider whether the process may be patentable under the current laws. A patent attorney well versed in the area of business method patents can walk you through the issues, as well as the costs and benefits of patent protection, to determine whether this area is worth exploring.

In general, the patent application and registration process can last from two to five years and can be very costly. Therefore, before attempting to obtain a patent, you should conduct a cost-benefit analysis to determine whether the benefits of being able to exclude others from making, using, or

selling the invention outweigh the significant costs of prosecuting and protecting the patent. As part of this analysis, you should consider:

1. The projected commercial value of the invention.
2. Out-of-pocket expenses to obtain the patent, including legal fees, advertising, marketing, and retooling costs.
3. The invention's proximity to existing patented and nonpatented
   technology (from an infringement and a commercial development
   perspective).
4. The ability to exploit the invention during the time frame of exclusivity granted by a patent.
5. The market value of the invention two to five years down the road,
   after completion of the patent application process.
6. The availability of adequate alternatives for protecting the invention,
   such as trade secret law.

If the franchisor decides to pursue a patent, it is important to *compile
and maintain careful records* relating to the research, development, and testing of the invention before retaining a patent attorney. The records should
contain key dates, including the date the invention was conceived and the
date it was put into practice (that is, the date the invention was well beyond
the conceptual stage and either was actually developed and tested or was so
clearly described in the application that a third party skilled in the particular
art could understand and actually develop the technology). The records
should also demonstrate your diligence in developing and testing the invention. Make sure the records contain the corroboration of independent witnesses who are capable of understanding the nature and scope of the
invention and who will verify the recorded dates.

The next step is to *conduct a search* at the USPTO Public Search Room,
located in northern Virginia, just outside Washington, DC. An attorney experienced in this area usually conducts the search. The search will reveal patents in your field that have already been issued and how these patents may
affect your application. The ramifications of any previously issued patents
should be thoroughly discussed with your advisor and may factor into your
decision to apply for a patent.

The Application Process

The prosecution of a patent application is a complex process. First, the actual
application must be compiled. The application consists of the following distinct parts:

❏ The oath or declaration attesting to certain particulars regarding the filing of the application.
❏ Drawings of the invention (where applicable and necessary).
❏ One or more claims of exclusivity (These claims define the actual
  boundaries of the exclusive rights you hope to be granted; if drafted

too narrowly, imitators and competitors may be able to develop similar technologies and processes without fear of infringement; if drafted too broadly, you run the risk of rejection by the USPTO examiner or subsequent challenge to the patent's validity by a competitor.)

❏ The appropriate filing fees

Once the application is filed, a patent examiner at the USPTO, having knowledge of the subject matter to which the application pertains, will review it. The examiner will make a thorough review of the prior art relating to the subject matter of the application to determine whether the claimed invention meets the requirements of patentability. The examiner will also review the application for compliance with the statute. If the examiner determines that the claims do not meet the formal requirements of the Patent Act or if prior art presents a bar, the examiner will issue an official action setting forth specific reasons for denying the application.

Also as part of this review, the examiner will determine whether you have met the following statutory requirements:

❏ The invention consists of *patentable subject matter* (i.e., a process, machine, composition of matter or article of manufacture, or a new and useful improvement to one of these).

❏ You are the *original inventor* or discoverer of the subject matter described in the patent application.

❏ The subject matter is *new or novel* (i.e., it is not already known to or used by others, has not been previously described in a printed publication, and is not merely a new use of an existing product).

❏ The subject matter is *useful* and not merely of scientific or philosophical interest.

❏ The subject matter is *nonobvious* to others in that particular trade or industry, as determined in the broad discretion of the USPTO examiner (i.e., the differences between the subject matter of the application and the current body of knowledge of those skilled in that area are more than marginal).

Protecting Your Patent

To preserve your rights and to continue to protect your interests, you need to institute an aggressive patent protection program once you secure your patent. Although the costs of such a program may be high, especially if you undertake any patent litigation, the rewards will be worthwhile. Should you successfully pursue an infringer, you may be entitled to an award of damages (which may be tripled by the court in extraordinary cases), as well as equitable relief, such as an injunction or accounting for profits.

Your patent protection program should include:

1. The use of proper notices of the existence of the patent on all labeling and marketing of the invention.

2. Ongoing monitoring of new industry developments.

3. Policing (and limiting) the activities of employees, licensees, and others who come into contact with the subject matter of the patent.

4. Exploiting and saturating the market created by the patented product.

5. Pursuing known or suspected infringers of the patent.

Intellectual Property and the Internet

Many franchisors and franchisees have established a presence on the Internet either to directly offer franchises, goods, or services, or to advertise and promote these items. The increasing importance of communicating and obtaining information over the Internet presents several unique intellectual property protection issues. Therefore, taking certain steps to protect the company's intellectual property on the Internet and to avoid misappropriating someone else's intellectual property on the Internet is important.

Trademarks

The trademark infringement prevention activities established by a company should be extended to the Internet, which is just another medium for third-party infringement. Franchisors should monitor the use of their marks on the Internet by franchisees, as well as by third parties, to police against unauthorized uses. Similarly, a company should monitor the sites linking to its Web pages. These links may not present the sort of image the company wants associated with its marks, and, if this occurs, the owners should be asked to disengage the link.

Companies who have a presence on the Internet tend to use their trademark or service mark as their domain name as well. They do so because those who are looking for information regarding a particular product or service tend to seek that information by putting the product or service name into the search engine or by typing it in as a domain name address. Therefore, using your mark as a domain name is always a good choice. A domain name is typically used as the address for a Web site. However, if the domain name is also going to be used in a trademark/service mark sense, that is, as a brand name for goods and/or services, such as AMAZON.COM®, MONSTER.COM®, and EXPEDIA.COM®, the domain name may also be entitled to registration in the USPTO.

A number of domain name registrars are accredited by the Internet Corporation for Assigned Names and Numbers (ICANN) to manage the reservation of Internet domain names in accordance with the guidelines of the designated domain name registries and to offer such services to the public. Until 1999, Network Solutions, Inc. (NSI), located in Virginia, operated the .com, .net, and .org registries. Today, in addition to NSI, GoDaddy is also a very popular registrar. In general, domain names are awarded on a first-come/first-serve basis and, provided other requirements are met, are typically issued as long as no one else has an identical domain name. Consequently, someone could register someone else's trademark as their own domain name.

Several actions are available to gain ownership of a domain name from a third party. The most common is the Uniform Domain Name Dispute Resolution Policy (UDRP) complaint, heard by any of a number of arbitration bodies such as the World Intellectual Property Organization and the National Arbitration Forum. Additionally, the United States Anticybersquatting Consumer Protection Act (ACPA) provides a federal court action that is similar to a UDRP proceeding. Further, there is a Registrar Transfer Dispute arbitration policy. Each action has its own set of requirements for bringing a claim, but the outcome is substantially the same: the transfer of the domain name to its rightful owner. Therefore, guarding and protecting your domain names in the same manner that you guard and protect your trademarks are important.

Copyrights

Prior to posting any information on the Internet that is subject to copyright protection, a company should ensure that the material does not contain any confidential information. Copyright notices should be prominently displayed on various pages of the site, and ownership information and disclaimers should be conspicuously displayed on the Web site. Franchisors should provide strict guidelines with respect to the posting of their copyrightable information on their own Web sites.

Trade Secrets

Trade secrets should *not* be posted on the Internet under any circumstances. Once posted, a trade secret could become part of the public domain and lose its trade secret status. Franchisors should constantly monitor their own Web sites and those of their franchisees to ensure that trade secrets are not placed on the sites.

Developing Intellectual Asset Management Systems and Intellectual Property Audits

As discussed in Chapter 1, the management and protection of intangible assets and intellectual property rights are at the heart of every franchise system. Franchisors must constantly protect these rights by ensuring the proper use of their intellectual property, proper notice of ownership of these rights, and protection of these rights against misuse by others. These core requirements are essential whether dealing with trademarks, copyrights, patents, or trade secrets and regardless of the medium in which they are used.

One key strategic step in developing an effective IAM system is to conduct an intellectual property (IP) audit, explained in Chapter 1. The IP audit has seven primary phases, ranging from data gathering to the development of policies and procedures, as shown in Figure 8-3. A wide range of issues and action items need to be addressed during each phase, depending on the results of the audit and overall IP objectives.

Figure 8-3. Seven primary phases in the IP audit for franchise systems.

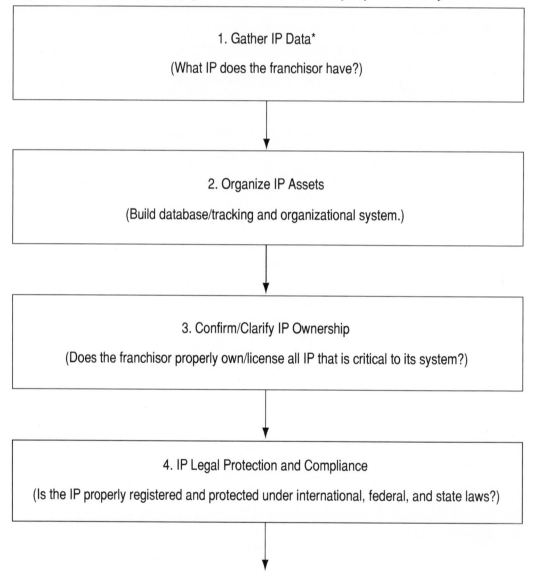

*In addition to the traditional categories of the IP discussed earlier in this chapter, IP assets of a growing franchisor might include software, license agreements, training programs, field support systems and techniques, proprietary advertising and marketing materials, recipes, customer databases, and the like.

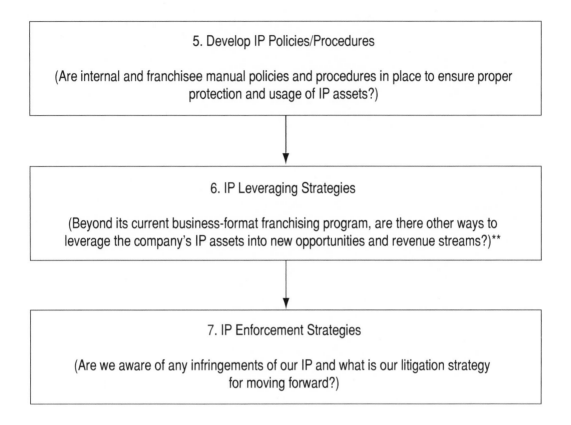

5. Develop IP Policies/Procedures

(Are internal and franchisee manual policies and procedures in place to ensure proper protection and usage of IP assets?)

6. IP Leveraging Strategies

(Beyond its current business-format franchising program, are there other ways to leverage the company's IP assets into new opportunities and revenue streams?)**

7. IP Enforcement Strategies

(Are we aware of any infringements of our IP and what is our litigation strategy for moving forward?)

**This may include the development of new or spin-off franchising programs, joint ventures, co-branding, brand-extension licensing, overseas development, other channels of distribution, and so on.

CHAPTER 9

Managing Disputes

I n a franchise system, conflict between the franchisor and franchisee is inevitable. Resolving conflicts with franchisees through formal litigation, however, is an expensive and time-consuming process that can significantly impede the growth of a franchisor as well as distract the franchisor from the attainment of its business objectives. In my experience, protracted litigation yields no winners, only successful or unsuccessful litigants.

As a result, most franchisors prefer to engage in battle in the marketplace or in the boardroom rather than in the courtroom. Nevertheless, in some instances an amicable resolution or settlement of a conflict seems unattainable. If a dispute with a franchisee or prospective franchisee matures into a courtroom battle, franchisors must understand the fundamental rules of litigation as well as alternate means of resolving disputes.

Problems Leading to Litigation

Inherent in the franchisor-franchisee relationship is a certain level of tension. The franchisor has invested a great deal of time, effort, and money in establishing a business-format franchise system. Hence quality control guidelines must be followed. The franchisee, on the other hand, often may resist any restrictions that are perceived as unfair or oppressive and from time to time may not see the ongoing value in paying royalties to remain a part of the system. The tension can often create a dynamic and volatile atmosphere that fuels disputes and ill will. In many instances, however, the tension that is part and parcel of every franchise relationship leads to conflict and strife that distract the parties from their common objectives.

Another key factor leading to many of the disputes between franchisors and franchisees is the potential *gap between expectation and reality*. In an effort to recruit franchisees, some franchisors raise the expectation level of the prospective franchisee regarding the training and support and other key aspects of the relationship, leading to disappointment and frustration by the

franchisee when the realities of the franchisor's actual capabilities are revealed.

Ten Common Areas of Conflict

Franchisors must recognize and understand the problems that typically give
rise to litigation and attempt, if at all possible, to resolve them in an effort to
avoid legal action. The following are ten common areas of conflict.

1. Franchisee Recruiting

A franchised operation is only as strong as the franchisees operating it. The
franchisor must carefully evaluate and screen prospective franchisees to ensure that only qualified individuals are accepted. Because the initial franchisees in a system set the tone for and may establish the criteria for later
applicants, they must be carefully scrutinized to ensure they have the financial background and experience to successfully operate a franchise.

An applicant should possess the requisite financial strength to meet the
demands that can reasonably be expected to arise in a franchised business,
including sufficient working capital for payroll, rent, unexpected complica-
tions, product purchases, taxes, and so on. Ideally, the candidate should have
a background in some business similar to or compatible with the franchised
business or other sufficient experience as a business owner or manager. The
intangible factors that contribute to a franchisee's success, such as motivation, loyalty, and commitment, are, of course, almost impossible to evaluate
from a written application, and the franchisor should at least speak with the
applicant's references and his or her current employer, if there are any. A
franchisee's level of motivation can also be evaluated by analyzing the franchisee's ownership interest or risk in the enterprise. A franchisee who is
gambling with someone else's money will be far less committed to the business than one who has invested his or her own hard-earned dollars and personal savings. A franchisor can also learn a great deal about an individual
simply through the initial screening process. An applicant who is hostile,
contentious, and untruthful in the interview and negotiation process will in
all likelihood be hostile, contentious, and untruthful as a franchisee. Almost
inevitably, such a franchisee will cause discord and dissension that may lead
to litigation.

Many franchisors have discovered that claims of fraud, misrepresentation, and mistakes can grow out of misunderstandings in the recruiting and
sales process. Franchisors or their sales staff may unintentionally make comments about other franchisees who have earned certain sums of money, and
the prospective franchisee may view this as a guarantee of a certain dollar
amount. The sales staff may promise assistance and support that the franchisor does not commonly offer. These misunderstandings commonly lead
to litigation.

For example, an Indiana district court held that General Foods, then the
parent of Burger Chef, had made actionable misrepresentations to its fran-

chisees that it planned to actively develop and promote its restaurant system when in fact General Foods planned to sell Burger Chef to Hardee's. On appeal, the decision was reversed on the ground that General Foods' statements amounted to mere puffery and opinions, not statements of existing fact (*Vaughn v. General Foods Corp.*). Similarly, a Missouri district court recently held that statements that the franchisee was "going to be driving a truckload of money away . . . every year" and that she was "not going to have to worry about paying . . . bills" were mere predictions about future profitability and puffery. As such, they could not support fraud and misrepresentation claims (*Bath Junkie Branson, L.L.C. v. Bath Junkie, Inc.*). As these cases demonstrate, courts attempt to draw a line between statements of existing fact on the one hand and opinions or predictions on the other. When sales statements exceed mere puffery or opinionated sales talk, there is a heightened risk of litigation.

Although it is understandable that emerging franchisors are anxious to make sales, this eagerness should not be allowed to displace the franchisor's need for careful scrutiny of applicants and prudent communications with them. In this regard, franchisors should take heed of the adage, "If you want it badly, that's exactly how you'll get it."

2. Site Selection and Territorial Rights

Even the best franchise in the world cannot take root and flourish in a very poor location. The franchise agreement typically imposes a duty on the franchisee to select a site for the location of the business. Often the franchisor lends some assistance in site selection and has the right to reject a site located by the franchisee. A franchisor should develop criteria to assist in determining whether a site selected by the franchisee is acceptable. Some of the factors considered by franchisors in such a determination include size of the site, suitability of the location and surrounding area for the type of business being franchised, adequate parking, costs of development, zoning and traffic patterns, proximity and access to major thoroughfares, compatibility with other businesses in the area, population centers, and proximity to competing businesses.

Franchisees often expect a great deal of assistance in site selection and are quick to demand compliance with the terms of agreements that bind the franchisors to offer that support. For example, Avis Service, Inc., a subsidiary of the rental car company, was besieged by lawsuits alleging that Avis failed to help franchisees find sites for quick-lube businesses and rejected sites found by them as being too expensive or unsuitable. In many instances the franchisees demanded refunds and alleged fraud and misrepresentation. Franchisors must ensure that site selection staff fulfill their obligations to find and develop suitable locations and guard against oversaturation of the market.

Franchisees have also attempted to hold franchisors responsible when they approve sites that later prove unsuitable, although some courts have rejected such claims. For example, in *RHC, LLC v. Quizno's Franchising, LLC*, the franchise agreement gave the franchisor site approval rights. The agreement also provided that the franchisor could not unreasonably with-hold approval and that approval provided no guarantee with respect to the suitability of the site. After the franchisee's business failed, it filed suit against the franchisor, arguing that it breached the implied duty of good faith and fair dealing by approving the site. The court rejected the franchisee's claims, finding there was no implied duty to ensure that the site would be suitable and that such a duty would be inconsistent with the parties' reasonable expectations.

A franchisee will sometimes be granted an exclusive area or territory within which to operate the business. As long as the franchisee performs its obligations under the franchise agreement, the franchisor will not establish any other franchises in this territory. The territory is often defined by population or some geographical criteria such as ZIP code or a certain radius area around the franchised business. Although franchisors may be tempted to offer an existing franchisee a right of first refusal to expand into adjacent or surrounding territories, such a right places burdensome restrictions on the franchisor, which is then precluded from selling in certain areas unless time-consuming and complicated notice procedures are followed. A franchisor's failure to follow a right of first refusal and provide the appropriate notice to an existing franchisee who has been granted such a right may lead to litigation, and courts often consider these rights.

An area of conflict that has gained much attention is encroachment. Essentially, encroachment involves the franchisor's allegedly competing with the franchisee by opening other businesses (franchised or company-owned, under the same or a different trade name) near the franchisee's location. This situation often arises when a franchisor acquires another franchise system. In such cases, franchisees sometimes claim that the franchisor has breached its agreement with the franchisee or, where the contract language is ambiguous or absent, that the franchisor has failed to fulfill a duty of good faith and fair dealing that it owes to the franchisee.

In some cases, if the franchise agreement prohibits the franchisor from operating a competing business under the same name as that licensed under the contract, operation of a competing business under a *different* name will not be considered a breach of the contract. (See, e.g., *John Keenan Company, Inc. dba Norrell Temporary Services v. Norrell Corporation, fka Norrell Services, Inc. and Interim Services, Inc.*) At least one case, however, has held that a franchisor may violate a franchise agreement by operating a competing business under a competing name despite the language of the franchise agreement (*Re/Max of Georgia v. Real Estate Group of Peachtree*). In that case, however, the court found that, although the infringing office did not operate under the Re/Max name, it used the same operating system and was a *de facto* Re/Max office. To avoid this type of conflict, franchisors should ensure that their franchise agreements affirmatively grant them the right to operate or franchise a competing business under a different name and, to avoid the *de facto* franchise argument, the two competing systems should operate separately, with different systems and support staff, and should not share their competitive business information.

An alternative theory used by a franchisee who feels harmed by the franchisor's conduct may be invoked even when the contract does not afford any territorial protection. Essentially, the theory suggests that the operation of a competing business (under any name) that negatively impacts an existing franchisee violates the covenant of good faith and fair dealing implied in every contract. The case law in this area of encroachment has varied from state to state. In general terms, however, most courts will not allow the covenant to be used to rewrite or modify the express terms in a contract. Nor will they allow the covenant to be used to render a provision in a contract meaningless.

When the contract contains language regarding exclusivity, the covenant cannot be used to defeat that language. [See, e.g., *Clark v. America's Favorite Chicken* (affirming trial court's finding that AFC's acquisition and operation of a competing franchise system did not violate the implied covenant of good faith and fair dealing because the contract contained express language that the franchisor was permitted to operate and establish competing businesses under different marks, even within the franchisee's market area).] Some cases hold that, if no language of exclusivity exists (or if it is ambiguous), a franchisor may not establish, by exercising its discretion in bad faith, competing operations under a different mark that serve to capitalize on a franchisee's business. (See *Scheck v. Burger King Corp.*) For example, in *Photovest Corp. v. Fotomat*, no exclusivity clause existed in the agreement. The court found a breach of the covenant of good faith and fair dealing because the company had determined corporate stores were more profitable than franchise units and then took action to drive down franchisee sales in an effort to get them to sell out to the franchisor. The *Scheck* case extends a bit further to suggest that a franchisor may not, in the absence of an express reservation of rights, establish competing businesses in a franchisee's market area, even if there is no effect on the existing franchise. Importantly, however, some courts, such as the Court of Appeals for the 11th Circuit in *Burger King v. C. R. Weaver*, have criticized and declined to follow *Scheck*.

Again, the best chance for a franchisor to avoid a claim of encroachment is for the franchise agreement to expressly permit the franchisor to establish competing businesses, regardless of their proximity to the franchisee's location. This type of provision, obviously, may not be agreeable to franchisees. In an attempt to strike a balance between the competing concerns, some franchise systems have adopted so-called impact policies that provide the franchisee an opportunity to raise concerns about the development of a new business by the franchisor (or its franchisee) within the existing franchisee's market. The policy typically provides for an independent analysis of the anticipated effect of the new business on the existing franchisee's sales. Once the impact is determined, the policy may offer various means to compensate the existing franchisee or to quash the proposed new location altogether.

An additional theory of liability that a franchisee might raise is a claim that the franchisor has breached a fiduciary duty owed to the franchisee. The vast majority of cases, however, state that the ordinary franchisor/franchisee relationship does not rise to a level whereby the franchisor owes the franchisee any fiduciary duty. (See, e.g., *Vaughn v. General Foods Corp.*) An exception may be when a franchisor, through its actions, has given a franchisee a reasonable expectation that it will provide for that franchisee's welfare, such as by assuming the role of advisor to the franchisee. Clearly, to avoid the existence of a fiduciary relationship, franchisors should not assume this role.

3. Accounting Practices and Procedures

The franchise agreement will impose various requirements on the franchisee to provide records, reports, and accounting information to the franchisor. Such records are needed to enable the franchisor to determine whether royalties are being calculated correctly, whether contributions to funds for advertising are being paid on time, whether gross sales are accurately reported, and so forth.

A clearly written franchise agreement sets forth the manner and timing of such reporting, and the franchisor must act swiftly and efficiently to enforce the deadlines, if necessary. As soon as a royalty or advertising payment is overdue or an accounting report is tardy, the franchisor should notify the franchisee and demand compliance with the appropriate provision of the franchise agreement. Repeated failures by the franchisee to pay or to report and account may justify termination of the franchise agreement.

Franchisors should be vigilant in observing and documenting these defaults because they may be warning signs of a failing franchisee in need of extra supervision and monitoring. Failure to notify a franchisee properly and in a timely manner may result in an assertion by the franchisee that the franchisor has given up or waived its right to insist on timely compliance with payment and record-keeping deadlines.

4. Misuse of Advertising Funds

Many franchisors require all franchisees to pay an advertising fee to be used for regional and/or national promotions and advertising programs. Franchisees who are unhappy with the use of their advertising fees may file suit. For example, in a recent case filed in the Delaware Chancery Court, a franchisee-dominated advertising council alleged that Kentucky Fried Chicken's recent advertising campaigns improperly featured grilled chicken at the expense of fried chicken. As a result, the franchisees claimed, sales decreased. KFC's parent company, Yum Brands!, maintains that the suit is baseless. Undoubtedly, however, this type of litigation is time-consuming and costly.

Fees paid into the advertising fund should be kept separate from the funds used by franchisors for their operating expenses and from the funds allocated to advertising by the franchisor to attract new franchisees. Franchisors that experience temporary financial difficulties are often inclined to borrow from the advertising fund until their financial condition improves. Such borrowing may give rise to litigation based on the failure of the franchisor to use the funds for the specified purposes. A California case focuses on this very issue. Thirty-six franchisees sued Pioneer Take Out, a fast-food restaurant franchise, alleging, among other claims, that various rebates and allowances received by the franchisor when it purchased supplies and food products were not deposited into the advertising fund as required. The franchisees further alleged that Pioneer, without informing the franchisees, used their advertising contributions to pay advertising bills incurred by Pioneer prior to the date the franchisees purchased their franchises. These kinds of lawsuits can be avoided by establishing separate accounts and an advertising committee composed of franchisees as well as key members of the franchisor's management team.

5. Supervision and Support

Although franchisees are usually independent individuals who desire to operate a business on their own, they are also attracted to franchising because of the guidance and support offered by a franchisor with an established and proven business concept. A successful franchisor not only meets the contractual commitments established by the franchise agreement but may go beyond the agreement to offer additional support and supervision to the franchisees. This increased support results in two bonuses to the franchisor: The supervision (1) alerts the franchisor to difficulties that a franchisee may be having and (2) demonstrates the franchisor's commitment to the system (which never hurts when prospective franchisees are talking to existing franchisees). Although overzealous supervision by a franchisor is usually not needed and in fact may interfere with a franchisee's ability to run the business, routine phone contact and occasional visits to the franchisee's place of business show a willingness to assist with problems and an assurance that the franchisor is committed to the franchisee's goals, depending on the type of franchise involved.

A lack of such support often leads to conflict in the system and ultimately to litigation, as seen in the Pioneer case, in which the franchisees also alleged that the franchisor had diverted the chains' operating capital to other ventures and had failed to develop new products or to support the franchisees. This contention is increasingly being leveled against franchisors. Franchisees are likewise alert to spin-offs, mergers, and other restructuring attempts by franchisors and view them as an abdication of the franchisor's duty to offer assistance and support. Burger King franchisees successfully blocked an attempt by Pillsbury to spin off the Burger King franchise system as a defense against a takeover bid. Franchisees of the Diet Center system sued the weight loss company following its leveraged buyout, which allegedly resulted in a 41 percent increase in royalty fees. When Marriott tried to sell its Straw Hat Pizza chain to Pizza Hut, many of the franchisees broke away and became their own franchisor by forming a cooperative. These disputes all arose out of a perceived lack of support and guidance by the franchisor and a fear that the franchisees would be burdened with a debt-ridden and undercapitalized new franchisor.

Support by the franchisor can be made available through regular meetings and seminars, newsletters, conventions, retraining programs, and the dissemination of published materials related to the franchised business, again depending on the type of franchise involved.

Franchisors should respond promptly and in writing to specific franchisee questions and concerns. Failure to respond to and manage the franchisees will not make the problem go away but rather will only compound it by creating an adversarial relationship. In this regard, franchisors should not attempt to interfere with or impede franchisees' efforts to form a franchisee association, and, in fact, many states specifically declare any such interference to be unlawful.

Franchisors can also support franchisees by offering to provide management consulting services for special projects or general assistance at specified fees.

Communication between the parties and the support and assistance offered by the franchisor serve not only to promote harmonious relations between the franchisor and franchisee but negate any argument that the franchisor was interested only in the initial franchisee fee and not in a long-term and mutually satisfactory relationship.

6. Quality Control

A key characteristic of a successful franchisor is the protection of its business format, image, trademarks, the quality and nature of the goods and services sold, and the uniformity of its business operations. The franchisor must strictly protect and defend these interests; failure to do so will result in a weakened system with no identifiable image. Franchisors with a need for increased revenues may be tempted to force a franchisee to purchase goods, services, supplies, fixtures, equipment, and inventory from the franchisor on the basis that such items are integral to the franchisor's system and cannot be obtained elsewhere. Because courts strictly scrutinize such franchisor requirements, many franchisors no longer sell supplies but rather regulate the items franchisees purchase by requiring that they go to suppliers approved by the franchisor or purchase in accordance with the franchisor's specifications. Many franchisors pass through to the franchisees any discounts or rebates received by the franchisor from its suppliers. This practice greatly allays any misgivings about the franchisor's profiting on items that can be easily obtained from other suppliers at a lower cost. One of the issues in the Pioneer Take Out litigation was an allegation by the franchisees that the franchisor was charging an excessively high price for one of its special product mixes. Similarly, a change in the product mix of Steve's Home-Made Ice Cream resulted in litigation by a franchisee who alleged fraud and breach of contract (*Stewart v. Integrated Resources, Inc., et al.*).

Franchisors need to be watchful to ensure that franchisees do not substitute unapproved goods or items in place of those that meet the franchisor's quality control standards. Such action by franchisees erodes the goodwill and regional or national recognition that distinguish the franchised business from other businesses. If the practice is not stopped, the franchisor signals to other franchisees that it is not interested in protecting its investment in the system.

7. Unequal Treatment

Although some circumstances may justify a decision by a franchisor to offer a benefit to one franchisee only, such as a grace period for the payment of royalties in the event of financial trouble, such advantages should be offered sparingly and only after a thorough analysis of the circumstances. Franchisees expect the system to operate uniformly, and any perceived arbitrariness or inequality in treatment will lead to resentment and hostility, especially when the favorable treatment is afforded to company-owned stores. In addition to creating an atmosphere of tension, any deviation by the franchisor from established operating procedures will also raise the perception that the franchisor has waived or foregone the right to demand compliance with the franchise agreement.

Just as some franchisees should not be singled out for more favorable treatment than others, franchisees who are difficult and demanding should not be subjected to any form of treatment that could be viewed as retaliatory or discriminatory. Any defaults or breaches of the franchise agreement by troublesome franchisees should be carefully documented and handled strictly in accordance with the franchise agreement. Franchisees who have made valid complaints against the franchisor or the system may not be subjected to any practice that a court would interpret as a reprisal for exercising their contractual rights. Such retaliatory treatment by franchisors leads only to litigation and further disruption of the system.

8. Transfers by Franchisees

A franchisee who wants to sell the franchised business should be assisted by the franchisor because an unhappy or unmotivated franchisee is unproductive and weakens the system. The franchisor may be able to steer potential buyers to the franchisee or even purchase the location and operate it as a company-owned store until a suitable purchaser can be found, unless otherwise prohibited by applicable statutory provisions. However, the franchisor should carefully evaluate the decision to purchase a franchisee's business because word of the repurchase will invariably spread to other franchisees, who may believe that such a practice is the established policy of the franchisor and an absolute right of a disgruntled or noncomplying franchisor.

If a franchisee presents a prospective purchaser to the franchisor for approval, the franchisor must ensure that the purchaser satisfies the selection criteria established for all applicants. In one case involving the transfer of an ice cream franchise, the court held that a "reasonableness" requirement should be read into the franchise agreement and that the franchisor should not be allowed to arbitrarily reject a transfer without reference to some reasonable and objective standards (*Larese v. Creamland Dairies, Inc.*). If the purchaser fails to meet such objective standards and thus to qualify, a written notification should be provided to the franchisee explaining the rejection and its basis.

9. Training for Franchisor's Management and Sales Team

Many of the problems that lead to litigation are caused by improperly trained members of the franchisor's staff. Salespeople are so eager to make a sale that they sometimes ignore the FTC regulation requiring provision of the franchise disclosure document to a prospective franchisee at least 14 days before the signing of the franchise agreement. Information that must be included in the disclosure document may also be neglected. [See, e.g., *FTC v. Transnet Wireless Corp.* (granting summary judgment in favor of the FTC where the franchisor's sales staff omitted required information from a disclosure document).] On other occasions, the salespeople make claims to prospective franchisees regarding anticipated earnings or bind the franchisor to a new contract term such as a lower initial franchise fee or payment of the fee in installments. Although such acts might not be directed or authorized by the franchisor, the principles of agency law may result in the franchisor's being bound by such acts performed by its agents. Therefore, the franchisor must have in place a training and compliance program to instruct the management and sales team with regard to the FTC requirements and the franchisor's philosophy and goals. Often legal counsel for the franchisor will participate in training and instructing the franchisor's staff. Form letters and checklists should be developed for routine transactions. Managers or salespeople who are "loose cannons" should be dealt with firmly to ensure that they do not "give away the store" in an effort to make a sale or retain a franchisee.

10. Documentation

Although the goal of every successful franchisor is to manage the business rather than to manage disputes, when disputes arise, the franchisor should be well prepared to discuss and resolve the conflict. Resolution cannot be accomplished unless the franchisor has kept adequate records, including notes of all conversations, telephone message slips, memos reflecting understandings reached at meetings, correspondence between the franchisor and franchisee, copies of all documents provided to or received from the franchisee, and notices to the franchisee. The franchisor should develop procedures for such record keeping and file management, and it should designate a reliable individual to assume responsibility for it. Meetings with a troubled franchisee should be attended by at least two of the franchisor's employees to verify the nature of the meeting and what was said.

Dealing with the Danger Signs

The problems arising from these areas of potential conflict often lead to litigation. It should be apparent that the common thread running through all such problems is lack of or poor communication with the franchisee and inadequate documentation to support the franchisor's position. However, franchisors can be on the lookout for several warning signs, such as those listed in Figure 9-1, which are often seen in troubled franchisees and which should be noted and managed before they erupt into a need for legal intervention.

Figure 9-1. Warning signs of troubled franchisees.

Danger Signal	Franchisor's Action
1. Late payment or nonpayment of royalties	Notice of default to be followed by termination, if default is not remedied
2. Cancellation of franchisee's insurance by insurance company	Notice of default and if not remedied, procurement of policy by franchisor who assesses franchisee for said payment
3. Steadily declining royalties	Meet with franchisee to discuss problem, analyze financial statements, consider an increase in the advertising budget, study competitive marketplace, perform an audit to ensure reporting of sales is accurate; check the potential franchisee "burnout"
4. Complaints by franchisee's customers	Meet with franchisee, retrain franchisee and/or franchisee's staff, send "test" customers to franchisee's place of business to monitor and ensure compliance
5. Inability to contact or communicate with franchisee	Increase supervision of franchisee and make frequent unannounced visits to franchisee's business
6. Use of unauthorized products or unapproved advertising	Notice of default, retraining, and termination of franchise, if default is not remedied
7. Standards of cleanliness and hygiene not followed	Notice of default and increased supervision of franchisee, including sending "test" customers to franchisee
8. Misuse of franchisor's proprietary marks	Notice of default and termination of franchise, if default is not remedied after notice; immediately stop the distribution of unauthorized materials
9. Understaffing of franchisee's business	Increase supervision and inspections and retrain franchisee and franchisee's staff
10. Unhappy or troubled franchisee	Increase communication with franchisee and offer to meet to resolve conflict; consider facilitation of a transfer of the unit to a third party

Litigation Planning and Strategy

If and when a franchisor determines that litigation is the most sensible and efficient way to resolve a business dispute or when a franchisee brings suit, the franchisor must develop plans and strategies. In addition, the franchisor:

❐ Must develop goals and objectives and communicate them to legal counsel. A broad strategy such as "kick the franchisee out" is not sufficient. Rather, counsel must be made aware of any specific business objectives, budgetary limitations, or time constraints that affect the franchisor well before the litigation is initiated.

❒ Must gather all documents relevant to the dispute and organize them in advance of when the opponent serves the first discovery request.

❒ Should explore alternative methods of dispute resolution, clearly define parameters for settlement, and communicate them to legal counsel.

❒ Should discuss with legal counsel the risks, costs, and benefits of entering into litigation.

❒ Should review with counsel the terms of payment of legal fees (as well as those of any experts needed).

❒ Should review the terms of its insurance policies with its risk management team to determine whether there is insurance coverage for its defense costs or any judgment rendered against the franchisor.

❒ Should develop a litigation management system for monitoring and controlling costs.

❒ Should maintain clear lines of communication with legal counsel throughout all phases of the litigation and appoint a responsible individual to serve as a liaison with counsel.

Although litigation of franchise disputes does not significantly differ in some respects from litigation of other matters, the decision to resolve a dispute through litigation must be based on a clear understanding of the legal rights, remedies, and defenses available. For example, suppose that a franchisee has stopped paying royalties with the argument that payment is excused by the franchisor's failure to provide adequate field support and supervision. Before filing a complaint to terminate the agreement, the franchisor should carefully review:

❒ Alternative methods for resolving the dispute.

❒ The elements of proving a breach of the franchise agreement in the jurisdiction that governs the agreement.

❒ The defenses that will be raised by the franchisee, such as lack of field support and supervision.

❒ The perceptions and opinions of the other franchisees regarding this litigation.

❒ The direct and indirect costs of litigation.

❒ The damages that may accrue if a breach is successfully established.

❒ The probability that the location can be easily sold to a new franchisee if the franchise agreement is terminated.

The franchisor should pursue formal action only after being satisfied that all these considerations indicate that litigation is a viable alternative. Similarly, if the franchisor is sued by a franchisee, it should consider attempting to resolve the dispute before responding with a formal answer.

Where Do We Do Battle? Forum Selection Clauses

Most franchisors will designate their home turf as the battlefield in the event of a dispute. The franchise agreement will designate a specific city or county

Box 9-1. Dealing with the financially distressed franchisee.

Franchisors rely on the financial health of their franchisees for both royalty cash flow (the lifeblood of the franchisor's income statement) and for the continued growth of the system. Continuing to recruit new franchisees is impossible if a high percentage of current franchisees are failing financially and operationally. If more than 10 to 15 percent of franchisees are in financial distress at any given point in the evolution of the franchise system, then some analysis may be needed to determine the viability of the business model. A high percentage of financially distressed franchisees is also likely to lead to litigation in connection with the franchisor's attempt to collect past-due royalty payments and/or enforce its ability to collect past-due payments and related rights if the franchisee files for bankruptcy.

If a high failure rate pattern is beginning to emerge, there are two levels of analysis: at the system level and at the franchisee level.

A. System Analysis

- Is a fundamental flaw in our economic model causing these distressed franchisees?

- Is there a pattern among the financially distressed franchisees? By size or type of unit? By region? By number of years in the system?

- Should additional special training or support programs be developed to address this disturbing trend?

- Are financial reports from our franchisees being gathered and analyzed on a timely basis?

- Were adequate minimum capitalization requirements set in the franchise disclosure document?

- Should changes or stricter enforcement of our collection policies in dealing with our franchisees be considered?

- Are the single-unit franchisees being allowed to add additional units too quickly?

B. Situational Analysis

In dealing with an individual distressed franchisee, the following questions need to be asked:

- Does the franchisor want to work with this franchisee (or specific location) to attempt to keep it in the system—or not? If not, what additional steps need to be taken? Are the franchisor's claims to past-due payments secured or unsecured?

continues

Box 9-1. (Continued)

- How well has the franchisor documented the property of its obligations under the franchise agreement, as well as the franchisee's financial and nonfinancial defaults?

- Is the franchisee facing any short-term or long-term personal problems that may have lead to the poor financial performance (e.g., health problems, alcohol or drug abuse, death in the family, gambling, divorce, etc.)? If so, will these problems have a permanent impact on the performance of the business? In the case of a divorce or death of a spouse, what involvement did the spouse play in the management of the business? Are other key employees or family members capable and/or available to run the business on a short- or long-term basis? If not, would the franchisee consider the sale of their business before all potential value is lost?

- Where does the franchisee stand with respect to its other vendors, equipment, lessors, lenders, etc.? Has it fallen behind on its obligations or only with respect to its obligations to the franchisor? Has a Uniform Commercial Code (UCC) search been conducted?

- Has an analysis been performed to determine the extent to which the problem rests with the franchisee as an individual (e.g., incapability, laziness, lack of motivation, burnout, inability to focus, etc.) versus a flaw in the system overall or some external cause, such as weak or changing demographics at the location, increased competition, etc.?

- If action to terminate is initiated, is the franchisee likely to file counterclaims? If yes, has an analysis been performed on the strength of the counterclaims?

- If the franchisee files for bankruptcy, what protections are provided by the franchise agreement? Have you been in touch with other major creditors (e.g., SBA lenders, the landlord, etc.) to discuss what actions they may be taking on recommending or to formulate an overall strategy?

courthouse and usually force the defendant to incur the time and expense of doing battle in a foreign jurisdiction. However, these forum selection clauses in franchise agreements have come under attack lately by many courts, state legislatures, and state franchise administrators. For example, in *Kubis & Perszyk Associates v. Sun Microsystems, Inc.*, the New Jersey Supreme Court held that forum selection clauses in franchise agreements are presumptively invalid. According to that decision, to overcome this presumption, franchisors must establish that the forum selection clause was not imposed on the franchisee unfairly by means of the franchisor's superior bargaining position. To sustain any such burden of proof, if applicable, a franchisor could provide evidence of negotiations over the inclusion of the forum selection clause in exchange for specific concessions to the franchisee.

The enforcement of forum selection clauses in franchise agreements has recently become more complex. The ability to enforce them depends not only on the wording of the clause itself, but also on such factors as:

❐ The state in which a proceeding is commenced.

❐ The forum in which the determination is made (judicial or arbitral).

❐ The choice of law determinations.

❐ In the case of judicial proceedings, whether the matter is commenced in federal or state court and the procedural context in which the issue of the enforceability of the forum selection clause is determined.

State Franchise Statutes Regulating Forum Selection

California, Connecticut, Illinois, Indiana, Iowa, Louisiana, Maryland, Michigan, Minnesota, North Carolina, North Dakota, Rhode Island, and South Dakota all have statutes, rules, or policies that regulate where franchise-related litigation and/or arbitration may occur. In Iowa, Rhode Island, and South Dakota, which have similar restrictive though not uniform statutes, a provision in a franchise agreement restricting venue or jurisdiction to a forum outside the state is void with respect to any claim otherwise enforceable under the state's franchise protection law.

California's Franchise Relations Act invalidates all contractual provisions restricting venue to a forum outside the state, declaring that "a provision in a franchise agreement restricting venue to a forum outside the state is void with respect to any claim arising under or relating to a franchise agreement involving a franchise business operating with this state." California's antiwaiver statute is broader than those of Iowa, Rhode Island, and South Dakota in that it applies to all claims brought by a California franchisee, as opposed to only claims brought under state franchise laws. No distinction is drawn between litigation and arbitration.

The Mechanics of Litigation

The first step when beginning civil litigation is preparing and filing a Complaint, in which the plaintiff must set forth the claim(s) against the other party. Each allegation should be set forth in a separate paragraph and written in a clear and concise manner, with any necessary exhibits attached to the end of the Complaint or filed as an exhibit, depending on local practice. Each allegation should relate to a claim by which you are entitled to relief and to make a demand for judgment. If the Complaint meets all statutory and procedural requirements, the clerk of the court will then prepare a Summons, which is served with the Complaint on the other party, the defendant. The Summons directs the defendant to serve an Answer upon the plaintiff's lawyer, often within 20 days after service of process is made, depending on the applicable court rules or statutes.

In lieu of answering your specific allegations, the defendant may file certain preliminary motions, which, in some cases, must be filed prior to the filing of an Answer or they are waived. These motions, which are essentially specific requests for the court to act, can include a motion to dismiss (due to a lack of jurisdiction, improper service or process, etc.), a motion to dismiss due to failure to state a claim on which relief can be granted, a motion to strike, or a motion for a more definite statement.

Once the Answer is filed, it must contain three principal components:

❑ Admit the allegations contained in the Complaint that are true.

❑ Deny the allegations that, in the opinion of the defendant, are not true or cannot be admitted for lack of information.

❑ Allege any affirmative defenses to the causes of action raised by the plaintiff.

The defendant must also file any counterclaims that it may have against the plaintiff that may have arisen out of the same transaction or occurrence. Failure to raise such claims will often prevent the defendant from raising them later. The Complaint, Answer, and any Counterclaims and Answers to Counterclaims are usually collectively referred to as the "Pleadings."

Once all of the Pleadings and preliminary motions are filed, the parties are then permitted to begin the process of discovery. *Discovery* is a pretrial procedure for obtaining information that will be necessary for the disposition of the dispute. Discovery serves a number of important purposes, including:

❑ Narrowing down the issues that are actually in dispute.

❑ Preventing surprise by allowing each party to find out what testimony and other evidence is available for each issue in dispute.

❑ Preserving information that may not be available at the actual trial, such as the statement of a very ill witness.

❑ Encouraging resolution of the dispute prior to trial.

Despite these many benefits, discovery also tends to significantly increase the legal fees and related expenses of the company in connection with the litigation, as well as the amount of time needed to resolve the dispute.

The five principal discovery devices available to litigants are depositions, written interrogatories, requests for production of documents, physical and mental examinations, and requests for admissions (see Figure 9-2).

One of the key issues to consider is the permissible *scope* of the discovery. The general rule is that information that is reasonably calculated to lead to the discovery of admissible evidence and not subject to any category of evidentiary privilege is subject to discovery. These privileges are usually limited to information exchanged between a doctor and patient, attorney and client, priest and penitent, or husband and wife.

Once the parties have completed the discovery process, the litigation

Figure 9-2. Five commonly used discovery devices.

1. *Deposition.* A deposition generally involves the pretrial examination and cross-examination of a live witness by legal counsel of any person who has information relevant to the case, whether or not they are a party to the action. The written record of the deposition may sometimes be admitted at trial as substance evidence and may be used to impeach a witness whose testimony at trial is inconsistent with the testimony given during the deposition. Depositions are often the most productive discovery devices and are the most frequently used, despite their cost.

2. *Written Interrogatories.* An interrogatory is a written question that one party may pose to another party, which must be answered in writing, under oath, within 30 days (or other similar time frames). Unlike depositions, interrogatories may be served only on parties to the litigation. Some courts or rules will limit the number of interrogatories that may be filed and the scope of the questions so that they are not overly burdensome and to prevent parties from engaging in so-called fishing expeditions. To object to a specific interrogatory, a party must specify its grounds for refusing to answer, at which time the burden shifts to the proponent of the question to convince the court why an answer is necessary. An answer to an interrogatory may also include a reference to a particular business document or set of records, provided that the other party is given an opportunity to inspect the documents.

3. *Requests for Production of Documents or Inspection of Land.* A party may request another party to produce and permit inspection, copying, testing, or photographing business documents, tangible assets, financial books and records, or anything else that may be relevant to the litigation. Similarly, a party may request entry to the business premises of another party for inspection, photographing, surveying, or any other purpose that is relevant and not subject to an evidentiary privilege. These requests are limited to parties to the litigation, with the exception of a subpoena duces tecum, which is a demand to produce certain documents and records in connection with the deposition of a non-party.

4. *Physical and Mental Examinations.* A party may request that another party submit to a mental or physical examination by a physician or psychiatrist. The mental or physical condition of the party, however, must be relevant to the issues in dispute. The court will grant such a request only if good cause is shown and will usually limit the scope of the examination to the actual issues in controversy. This is the only discovery device that involves court intervention and is generally used in personal injury and paternity cases.

5. *Requests for Admissions.* A party may serve a request for admission on another party in order to ascertain the genuineness of specific documents, to obtain the admission or denial of a specific matter, or to confirm the application of a certain law to a given set of facts. For example, this procedure may be employed to confirm a set of facts to save the time and expense of having to prove them later. Failure to respond to a request will be deemed to be an admittance. Therefore, the party on which a request has been served must either deny the request, explain why it is unable to admit or deny, or file an objection to the request as improper, typically within 30 days or any other applicable required time frames.

    i. If a party refuses to comply with discovery requests, the court may impose monetary sanctions, and in cases of willful or repeated refusals, the court may dismiss a plaintiff's complaint or enter judgment against a defendant.

will proceed to the pretrial conference, the actual trial, the appeal, and any post-trial proceedings. Although a comprehensive discussion of the mechanics of a trial is beyond the scope of this chapter, suffice it to say that this process consumes two of the most important resources to an emerging growth business: *time* and *money*. As a result, the various alternatives to litigation, which are likely to be less expensive and less time-consuming, should be considered when disputes must be resolved.

Alternatives to Litigation

Franchise dispute litigation is not only invariably time-consuming and expensive, but also the adverse counsel can portray a franchisor in a number of unflattering ways, all designed to engender the jury's support and emotion: as a huge impersonal corporate entity with no feeling for the small and defenseless franchisee; as a greedy corporate conglomerate interested in increasing its coffers at the expense of its loyal and diligent franchisees; as a vindictive and retaliatory entity motivated to get even with a franchisee who has merely exercised its contractual rights; or as a poorly managed business that has mishandled its affairs to the ruin of its franchisees. Because litigation involves these drawbacks and uncertainties, many franchisors seek to resolve their disputes with franchisees through alternative methods.

A broad range of methods and procedures are available to expedite the resolution of disputes without the need for litigation and are broadly referred to as *alternative dispute resolution* (*ADR*) *methods*. These methods are more attractive than litigation to franchisors because proprietary information, trade secrets, and the like can be protected whereas in a judicial proceeding, the commercial information can result in intense efforts by competitors to misappropriate and use the information due to the right of access by the general public and news media.

The most commonly known ADR method is arbitration, in which a neutral third party is selected by the disputants to hear the case and render an opinion, which may or may not be binding on the parties depending on the terms of the arbitration clause or agreement. In addition to arbitration, various forms of mediation, private judging, minitrials, and moderated settlement conferences are available to companies who are unable to independently resolve their disputes but who wish to avoid the expense and delay of a trial.

Each method offers particular advantages and disadvantages that may make one process far more appropriate for resolving a particular dispute than another. Therefore, the procedures, costs, and benefits of each ADR method should be carefully reviewed with experienced legal counsel.

Benefits of ADR

❏ *Faster Resolution of Disputes.* Reducing delays in dispute resolution was one of the driving forces behind the ADR movement. As the number of civil filings increased, it became clear that courts cannot expeditiously accommodate the influx without parties seeking alternatives to such filings.

❐ *Cost Savings.* In a study by the Deloitte & Touche accounting firm, 60 percent of all ADR users and 78 percent of those characterized as extensive users reported that they had saved money by using ADR. The amount of savings ranged from 11 to 50 percent of the cost of litigation.

❐ *Preserving Relationships.* ADR offers the opportunity for parties to resolve a dispute without destroying a relationship, whether it is business or personal.

❐ *Preserving Privacy and Confidentiality.* Traditional litigation often results in the public disclosure of proprietary information, particularly in business disputes. ADR procedures allow the parties to structure a dispute resolution process while protecting confidential information.

❐ *Flexibility.* ADR allows the parties to tailor a dispute resolution process that is uniquely suited to the matter at hand. Parties can select the mechanism, determine the amount of information that needs to be exchanged, choose their own neutral ground, and agree on a format for the procedure, all in a way that makes sense for the issue at hand.

❐ *Durability of the Result.* Resolutions achieved by consensus of the disputants are less likely to be challenged than resolutions imposed by third parties.

❐ *Better, More Creative Solutions.* By giving litigants early and direct participation, ADR provides a better opportunity for achieving a resolution based on the parties' real interests. Such agreements often involve terms other than the distribution of dollars from one party to another, and they may well produce a solution that makes more sense for the parties than one imposed by a court.

Situations in Which ADR Is Successful

❐ *An ADR Contract Clause in Place.* The most important indicator of possible ADR success is the existence of an effective contract clause that provides for the use of ADR in the event of a future dispute.

❐ *Continuing Relationships.* If a continuing relationship between the parties is possible (as with franchisors and franchisees or suppliers and customers), the chances of ADR success are greatly enhanced. It makes more sense for the parties to continue making money from each other over the duration of an agreement than severing the relationship and suffering the cost and disruption of litigation.

❐ *Complex Disputes.* If a case is based on, for example, highly complex technology, a jury and even a judge may very well become confused. Under these circumstances, ADR may be the best option, particularly if the proceedings are conducted before a neutral person who is an expert in the subject matter of dispute. In addition, the American Arbitration Association has enacted rules specifically designed for use in complex cases.

❏ *Relatively Little Money at Stake.* If the amount of money in dispute is relatively small, the cost of litigation may approach or even exceed that amount.

❏ *The Need for Confidentiality.* The parties can maintain confidentiality more effectively in an ADR proceeding than in litigation. The need for confidentiality can prove to be more important than any other consideration in the dispute resolution process.

Situations in Which ADR Is Not Successful

❏ *Skeptical and Mistrusting Adversary.* The adversary may see the overture to use ADR as a ploy designed to get an edge in litigation.

❏ *Parties or Counsel with Harsh Attitudes.* When the parties or their counsel are particularly emotional, belligerent, and abusive, the chances for a successful nonbinding ADR are significantly diminished.

❏ *One of Many Cases.* If the case at issue is just one of many that are expected to be filed, then the defendant is not likely to be motivated to agree to the use of ADR. In such a setting, there is little, if any, hope for a successful nonbinding ADR, at least at an early stage. This may be one of those rare situations where full-blown litigation is actually more cost-effective due to the efficiencies of consolidation.

❏ *Delays.* If a delay will benefit one of the parties, then the chances for the successful use of ADR are diminished.

❏ *Monetary Imbalances.* If there is a monetary imbalance between the parties, and the wealthier party thinks it can wear down the other through traditional litigation, then getting the wealthier party to agree to ADR is likely to be difficult.

Arbitration

Of the many forms of formal arbitration, each involves a process for the parties in dispute to submit arguments and evidence to a neutral person or persons for the purpose of adjudicating the differences. The evidentiary and procedural rules are not nearly as formal as in litigation, and the timing of the proceeding and the selection of the actual decision makers tend to be relatively flexible.

Arbitration may be a voluntary proceeding that the parties have selected before a dispute arises, such as in a contract, or it may be a compulsory, court-annexed procedure that is a prerequisite to full-blown litigation. Owners and managers of growing franchisors who wish to avoid the cost and delay of litigation should consider adding arbitration clauses prior to entering into a contract. The clause should specify:

❏ That the parties agree to submit any controversy or claim arising from the agreement or contract to a binding (or nonbinding) arbitration.

- ❏ The choice(s) of location for the arbitration.
- ❏ The method for selecting the parties who will hear the dispute.
- ❏ Any limitations on the award that the arbitrator may tender.
- ❏ Which party shall be responsible for the costs of the proceeding.
- ❏ Any special procedural rules that will govern the arbitration.

Importantly, however, a battle has been brewing regarding mandatory arbitration clauses in contracts. The *University of Michigan Journal of Law Reform* recently stated, "[t]here is a new bad boy in the contract law block: the mandatory arbitration clause. Increasingly pervasive in the boilerplate portion of mass contracts, the mandatory arbitration clause controls the manner by which aggrieved parties can vindicate their rights, and—according to a widely held view—effectively diminishes access to justice."[1] To help support enforceability in your key contracts, any arbitration provisions should be clearly and prominently displayed, often in bold or in a larger font. The following clause is recommended by the American Arbitration Association (AAA):

Any controversy or claim arising out of or relating to this contract, or the breach thereof, shall be settled by arbitration in accordance with the Commercial Arbitration Rules of the American Arbitration Association, and judgement rendered upon the award rendered by the arbitrator(s) may be entered in any court having jurisdiction thereof.

Because the arbitrator selected is usually an attorney whose expertise may be negotiating rather than adjudicating, arbitration often results in "splitting the baby down the middle," not providing a clear award for one party or the other. Additionally, because no jury is involved, the likelihood of recovering punitive or exemplary damages from an attorney or experienced arbitrator is reduced because appeals to emotion are not as effective. See Figure 9.3.

A key factor is whether the decision of the arbitrator will be binding or nonbinding. If the parties agree that the award will be binding, then they must live with the results. Binding arbitration awards are usually enforceable by the local court, unless there has been a defect in the arbitration procedures. On the other hand, the opinion rendered in a nonbinding arbitration is advisory only. The parties may either accept the result or reject the award and proceed to litigation. In a court-annexed arbitration, the court will order the arbitration as a nonbinding proceeding that is intended to work out the differences between the parties without the need for litigation. Another drawback of nonbinding arbitration is that, after the award is made, the losing party often threatens litigation (a trial de novo, or new trial) unless the monetary award is adjusted. Thus, the party that wins the arbitration is often

---

1. Omri Ben-Shahar, "How Bad Are Mandatory Arbitration Terms?" 41 *UMIJLR* 777 (2008).

(text continues on page 190)

Figure 9-3. Sample Arbitration Procedures Letter Agreement.

[NAME AND ADDRESS OF FRANCHISEE COUNSEL]

Dear Sir/Madam:

The purpose of this letter is to propose for your consideration a set of basic ground rules for informal discovery regarding the relationship between Franchisee, Inc. ("FRANCHISEE"), and our client Franchisor, Inc. ("FRANCHISOR"). Please call to discuss at your earliest convenience, as it is anticipated that this letter and your response will form the basis of a Stipulation and Agreement concerning these rules and their effect.

In an effort to set the ground rules, we propose the following:

1. *Scope.* Unless otherwise modified by this agreement, the Federal Rules of Civil Procedure shall govern the manner and method of discovery. The materials produced pursuant to this agreement may be used only for purposes of settlement or in any subsequent arbitration between the parties, subject in any event to the Covenant of Confidentiality at paragraph 5 below.

2. *Definitions.* As used herein, a reference to "party" or "parties" means FRANCHISOR, FRANCHISEE, and the following individuals: _____. This agreement does not provide for discovery against third parties other than persons to be designated pursuant to paragraph 3(c) herein.

3. *Written Interrogatories and Production of Documents.* Each party may once seek the other party's response to written interrogatories and requests for production of documents pursuant to Rules 33 and 34 of the Federal Rules of Civil Procedure. All interrogatories and requests for production of documents shall be exchanged by close of business on [DATE]. Failure to meet this deadline shall make any response by the receiving party optional.

a. A party receiving a set of interrogatories will be allocated one day to answer each separate interrogatory (a subpart of an interrogatory is here included as a separate interrogatory), the response to all interrogatories coming due at the close of business on the last day allocated to the last interrogatory. For example, if the interrogating party asks ten interrogatories, the tenth consisting of five subparts, the responding party shall have 15 days to respond, the response coming due close of business on the 15th day. A party may not respond to an interrogatory by a general reference to documents.

b. A party receiving a request for production of documents shall respond to it within thirty days or at the time the responses to any interrogatories are due pursuant to paragraph 3(a) above, whichever is later.

c. Within fifteen days of the Effective Date or within five days of receipt of documents produced to it pursuant to subparagraph 3(b) herein, whichever is later, a party shall designate for deposition by name or title no more than three individuals who are or who act as an officer, director, high level employee, or other managing agent employed by or affiliated with the other party and who have knowledge regarding that party's answer to the interrogatories. There shall be no other depositions.

4. *Depositions.* Each party may take the deposition of any other party pursuant to the following:

a. Deponents shall be limited to persons identified pursuant to paragraph 3(c) hereof;

b. Depositions of the parties shall occur in [CITY/STATE], at the offices of [LOCATION] commencing 15 business days after the production of documents by all parties as described in paragraph 3(b). The parties shall agree on a schedule for all depositions consistent with this paragraph 4, and FRANCHISEE shall take the first deposition.

c. Each deposition shall be limited to four hours of examination, excluding any breaks called for by counsel defending the party-deponent, to be followed by no more than one hour of any examination by counsel defending the party-deponent, to be followed by one half-hour of any examination by counsel for the party seeking the deposition. No time may be reserved.

d. There shall be two depositions per day until all witnesses identified pursuant to subparagraph 3(c) are completed. The depositions shall be staggered so that the deposition of one party will follow the deposition of the other party until all persons designated by a party have been deposed.

5. *Covenant of Confidentiality.* This letter, all documents that may be exchanged or produced pursuant to this letter and any subsequent agreement on procedure, and all testimony that may be given in the depositions to occur pursuant to them, shall be held strictly confidential by the parties and the persons designated pursuant to paragraph 3(c) hereof. This covenant of confidentiality shall survive the termination of this agreement by further agreement or otherwise. It is expressly understood and agreed that this covenant of confidentiality is a material condition of the process described by this agreement. Each party agrees that it shall be liable to the other party for all, and not an allocable portion of, damages suffered by that other party resulting in any way, in whole or in part, from a breach of this covenant of confidentiality by the breaching party or one or more of its representatives, agents, or affiliates.

6. *Objections.* Either party may reserve the right to limit or withhold disclosure of information or material in the course of discovery contemplated by this agreement only on the basis of attorney-client privilege or to the extent that the information or material sought exceeds the scope of the dispute between the parties. There shall be no "speaking objections" at any deposition.

7. *No Action.* Except as expressed in the Covenant of Confidentiality herein, the parties to this agreement, its performance by any party, including party-deponents designated pursuant to this agreement, and the conduct of the parties in connection with or in any way arising out of this agreement or its performance shall not create or support any right, obligation, liability, cause of action, demand, or claim in law or equity.

8. *Notice and Costs.* Each party agrees to produce documents, answer interrogatories, and produce witnesses for deposition pursuant to this agreement without the necessity of any subpoena or other notice. Each party agrees to bear its own costs.

9. *Miscellaneous*

a. All deadlines may be met by providing documentation to counsel for each party via overnight delivery, ordinary mail, or facsimile as follows:
  (1) If to FRANCHISOR, to:

  [NAME/ADDRESS/TELEPHONE NUMBER]

  (2) If to FRANCHISEE, to:

  [NAME/ADDRESS/TELEPHONE NUMBER]

(continues)

Figure 9-3. (Continued)

---

b. The materials, including transcripts of testimony, produced pursuant to this agreement shall bear the following title only: "In Re Arbitration of Franchising Dispute in [LOCATION]."

c. The headings herein are for ease of reference only and do not necessarily reflect the terms of the agreement.

d. Any dispute arising in any way out of this agreement, including but not limited to any allegations of fraud, shall be subject to arbitration in the manner and place prescribed by the parties in the Agreement between FRANCHISOR and FRANCHISEE dated on or about [DATE].

e. This agreement may be signed by counsel.

Very truly yours,

[COUNSEL FOR FRANCHISOR]

---

coerced into paying or accepting less than the award simply to avoid a trial after arbitration.

There are many sources of arbitration rules. Unless the parties have specific rules and procedures in mind that will govern the arbitration, the two best known in the United States are the American Arbitration Association (www.adr.org) and the International Chamber of Commerce (www.iccwbo.org). Both offer their rules at no cost; the fees for handling arbitration proceedings vary for these and other such organizations. Other sources include the U.N. Commission on International Trade Law Arbitration Rules and the Inter-American Commercial Arbitration Commission.

Whether arbitration is faster and cheaper than litigation really hinges on the parties and their interests. In some cases, the parties can escalate arbitration costs and length to rival those of litigation. For example, in *Advanced Micro Devices Inc. v. Intel Corp.*, the proceeding lasted seven years, cost about $100 million, and included several rounds of collateral litigation. Intel's vice president and general counsel described the dispute as a basic contract dispute, but a predispute arbitration clause routed the issue into arbitration. Ultimately the arbitrator's ruling led the parties to settle in a mediation proceeding.

Over the last several years, the court decisions concerning the enforceability of arbitration clauses, particularly those that mandate venue contrary to state law, have been conflicting. The issue is whether the Federal Arbitration Act preempts state laws governing the unconscionability of contract provisions. The case law continues to differ state by state and circuit by circuit, and it also often depends on the court's determination of whether the agreement is a contract of adhesion or one that was freely negotiated by both parties. Before deciding to include an arbitration provision in its franchise agreements, a franchisor should look closely at the most recent relevant case law in the affected area.

Mediation

Mediation differs substantially from arbitration because an arbitrator renders a decision that is often binding. In the mediation process, the parties decide how to resolve their dispute by discussing their differences with a mediator only making suggestions or recommendations. The mediation process typically consists of five stages:

1. Presentation of positions.
2. Identification of interests.
3. Generation and evaluation of options.
4. Narrowing of options to resolve the dispute.
5. Executing a written settlement agreement.

A sample mediation clause in an agreement is as follows:

Any dispute arising out of or relating to this Agreement shall be resolved in accordance with the procedures specified in this Agreement, which shall be the sole and exclusive procedures for the resolution of such disputes. Each party shall continue to perform its obligations under this Agreement pending final resolution of any dispute arising out of or relating to this Agreement, unless to do so would be impossible or impracticable under the circumstances.

Upon becoming aware of the existence of a dispute, a party to this Agreement shall inform the other party in writing of the nature of such dispute. The parties shall attempt in good faith to resolve any dispute arising out of or relating to this Agreement promptly by negotiation between executives who have authority to settle the controversy. All negotiations pursuant to this Agreement shall be confidential and shall be treated as compromise and settlement negotiations for purposes of the applicable rules of evidence. If the dispute cannot be settled through direct discussions within days of the receipt of such notice, the dispute shall be submitted to {Name of Mediator} (or such substitute mediation service specified by the parties in writing prior to receiving notice of the existence of such dispute) for mediation by notifying {Mediator} (or the specified substitute service) and the other party in writing. The notification shall specify: (1) the nature of the dispute, and (2) the name and title of the executive who will represent the party in mediation and of any other person who will accompany the executive. Following receipt of the notice, {Mediator} (or the specified substitute service) will convene the parties, in person or by telephone, to establish the mediation procedures and a schedule. If the parties are unable to agree on mediation procedures, {Mediator} (or the specified substitute service) will set the procedures. The mediation shall be completed within seven (7) days of submitting the dispute to mediation, or such longer time as the parties may agree. Each party will participate in the mediation process in good faith, will use their best efforts to resolve the dispute within the seven (7) day time period and will make available executives or representatives with authority to resolve the controversy to participate personally and actively in the mediation. The parties shall share equally pay the fees, charges and expenses of {Mediator} (or the specified substitute service).

Mediation costs are minimal and generally include only payment on an hourly basis to the mediator for his or her services. However, because the mediator has no authority to render a binding decision, the mediation process is effective only if both parties are committed to achieving a voluntary resolution. The participants always have the ultimate authority in the mediation process, and they are free to reject any suggestion by the mediator and can ultimately pursue litigation.

The controversies surrounding mediation typically include how the mediator should resolve disputes and how to determine the ethical standards of conduct for mediators. Some experts believe mediation should facilitate the parties' own resolution of the problem by digging deep into the interests and feelings underlying the surface dispute. Others say the proper purpose of mediation is to bring the parties into an amicable accord. Still others contend that mediators should provide subject matter expertise, acting essentially as sounding boards to help the parties evaluate the merits of the dispute or the proposed settlement. The American Bar Association's Section on Dispute Resolution, the Society of Professionals in Dispute Resolution, and the AAA, in an attempt to draft ethical standards of conduct, concluded that mediators should try only to facilitate the parties' own resolution and admonished professionals who serve as mediators (including lawyers) to "refrain from providing professional advice." Florida, New Jersey, and Hawaii are the only states to have adopted qualification requirements for mediators. Many states merely require completion of 40 hours of training, while in others a law license is enough. Florida is the only state to take the next step of implementing a disciplinary process for mediators.

The International Franchise Association, working in conjunction with the CPR Institute for Dispute Resolution in New York City (www.cpradr.org), recently established the National Franchise Mediation Program, which outlines the process for resolving disputes for participating franchisors and their franchisees. The program includes sample forms, agreements, and model procedures, and 100 major franchisors have agreed to try to resolve their disputes with franchises through mediation, including Midas, Pizza Hut, Dunkin' Donuts, 7-Eleven, Jiffy Lube, and McDonald's.

Private Judging

In many communities, retired judges are available at an hourly fee (sometimes at $500 per hour or higher) to hear and resolve disputes. Parties may agree in advance whether the decision will be legally binding. The disadvantages of nonbinding arbitration also apply to nonbinding private judging.

Although private judging costs are substantially higher than court-annexed arbitration costs, private judging is considerably more flexible. A private judge may be retained without court intervention and without litigation first being instituted. The parties are free to select a judge and a mutually convenient date for the hearing. The hearing itself tends to be informal, and the rules of evidence are not strictly applied. The private judge often uses a settlement conference approach as opposed to a trial approach to achieve a resolution.

Moderated Settlement Conferences

After litigation begins, a court may insist that the parties participate in settlement discussions before a judge. If the court does not schedule a settlement conference, the parties can usually request one, often with a particular judge.

The attorneys are often required to prepare settlement briefs to inform the judge of each party's contentions, theories, and claimed damages. Parties, as well as attorneys, attend so that the judge may explain his or her view of the case and to obtain their consent to any proposed settlement. If a resolution is reached in the judge's chambers, the litigants often proceed to the courtroom so that the settlement (and the parties' consent to it) can be entered in the record to eliminate any further disputes. Because moderated settlement conferences produce no out-of-pocket costs (other than attorney's fees), and because the information obtained or revealed is for settlement purposes only, these settlements serve as excellent last-ditch efforts for resolving a dispute prior to trial.

Small Claims Matters

Matters that involve a small monetary amount (usually no greater than $2,500) are often best resolved in small claims court. Generally, litigants represent themselves and describe the dispute in an informal manner to a judge, who renders a decision at the time of the hearing. Court filing fees are moderate, and a trial date usually is set for within two or three months. Often representing the franchisor is a bookkeeper or credit manager who is knowledgeable about the dispute and has supporting documentation. Unfortunately, however, even when an award is made, actually collecting the judgment is difficult. As a result, many courts have small claims advisers who can assist litigants in collecting the money awarded.

Owners and managers of growing franchisors must be committed to developing programs and procedures within the organization that are specifically designed to avoid the time and expense of litigation. Business conflicts are inevitable, but lengthy trials are not if prompt steps are taken to resolve business conflicts and legal disputes. If disputes cannot be resolved amicably, then the costs and benefits of litigation and its alternatives must be understood well before the pleadings are filed. If litigation is, in fact, the only alternative available, then growing companies must work closely with counsel to establish specific strategies, objectives, and budgets for each conflict that matures into a formal legal dispute.

CHAPTER 10

Developing Sales and Marketing Strategies at the Target Franchisee and Target Consumer Levels

A t the heart of a successful franchise program are the viability and effectiveness of the franchisor's sales and marketing strategies. In fact, most early-stage franchisors are quick to recruit an aggressive franchise sales force well before they hire other key management positions, such as in the areas of operations, administration, and finance. Despite this overall commitment to marketing, if you were to ask most franchisors in this country to show you a recent copy of their formal franchise sales and marketing plan, you would see a dumbfounded expression on their faces. When asked how they go about marketing franchises, most would respond, "Trade shows and advertisements in the Thursday edition of the *Wall Street Journal.*"

These traditional approaches are simply not good enough in today's competitive and complex marketplace. Today's franchise sales and marketing plans require a genuine understanding of the needs and wants of the modern and more sophisticated franchisee (who may be a wealthy individual, a former senior executive, a recent college graduate Gen Y'er, a stay-at-home mom reentering the workforce, an overseas government, or a large corporation). Other requirements are a keen sense of target marketing, an understanding of how technology (such as the Internet and Web 2.0) can enhance and support the marketing effort, access to sophisticated databases, a detailed and well-designed strategic marketing plan, a well-educated sales team, and an ability to truly understand your competition. Each franchisor must understand the fears, uncertainties, and doubts of the targeted candidate and then deal with those issues in the initial and follow-up presentations. *The days of the fast-talking, leisure-suited, gold-chained, blue-suede-shoe franchise salesperson are long gone.* In fact, as discussed in Chapter 6 in the context of special legal compliance issues and challenges, today's prospective franchisees are much more likely to gather data on a program from the franchisor's own Web site or from a social networking site than they would from any other more traditional method of marketing.

Franchisors operating in different industries must also custom-tailor their marketing plans according to the demographics of the target franchisee, competitive trends, and the stage of the underlying product or service's life cycle. The total capital required on a per-unit basis is also likely to influence the overall sales and marketing plan. For example, a hotel franchisor will market to candidates very differently than a housecleaning services franchisor, which has a much lower project capital cost. A franchisor who is virtually alone in its industry group may market differently than a franchisor that is operating a highly competitive sector like chicken, pizza, or bagels, where the targeted franchisee may have 30 to 50 franchisors to choose from and therefore may need to more strongly differentiate its offering. A franchisor whose core product is late in the life cycle (e.g., cinnamon buns) may need to market differently than a franchisor whose product or services are still in their infancy, who may be facing the added burden of educating the marketplace. Finally, large franchisors may have very different marketing strategies and systems than their early-stage counterparts, and candidates who are attracted to a more developed franchise system may be very different from and more risk adverse than those willing to take a chance on an early-stage system. The prospective franchisees more attracted to an early-stage system are typically more entrepreneurial in nature and may welcome the opportunity to influence the development and evolution of the franchising system.

For the early-stage franchisor, attracting qualified leads and closing the sales are becoming increasingly difficult. The crowded field of inquirers range from wannabees and tire kickers to genuine "suspects and prospects." Some have access to the necessary capital but no expertise and some have all the expertise but no money, especially in light of stock market fluctuations and tightening lending standards for home equity lines of credit. Some small franchisors have had such a tough time attracting qualified candidates that they have abandoned franchising altogether. Among the hurdles that early-stage franchisors must overcome in the sales and marketing process are:

- ❐ A shrinking pool of qualified candidates who have the business acumen or financial resources to invest in some of today's high-ticket retail and food franchises.

- ❐ A growing number of franchisors who are all competing to attract qualified franchisee candidates as an increasing number of companies of all sizes and in virtually every industry launch new franchise programs each year.

- ❐ A difficult time competing against larger and well-financed franchisors who can afford sophisticated media campaigns and marketing resources.

- ❐ A fierce competition for quality retail sites, which is often won by the larger franchisors.

- ❐ A reluctance by commercial lenders to extend financing to the franchisees of start-up franchisors.

- ❐ A growing sense of prudence, skepticism, and cautiousness in the pool of qualified franchisees, as more and more reports of failing and failed franchisors (especially early-stage franchisors) find their way into the press.

❏ A growing pressure to recoup the often significant sums spent for franchise development costs through franchise sales.

The pressure to quickly achieve rapid franchise sales can result in a lowering of the standards initially set to qualify a lead. Such a compromise will significantly lower the franchisee's likelihood of success, resulting in damage to the franchisor's goodwill and probably in litigation. Proper franchise sales and marketing requires *patience* and *planning*, two characteristics not often found among the entrepreneurial pioneers of franchise systems.

Before examining the details of each component of a target franchisee and/or target consumer sales and marketing plan, let's take a look at the critical factors in understanding the discipline of marketing.

What Is Marketing?

Marketing is the ongoing process of:

❏ Determining the level of consumer demand for the company's products and services.

❏ Matching the company's strengths and weaknesses with the established demand.

❏ Delivering the products and services more effectively and more efficiently than do competitors.

❏ Monitoring changes in consumer demand; in industry trends; in political, social, environmental, and legal issues; in technology; and in competition, in order to ensure that the company's products and services remain competitive and consistent with consumer demand.

In the context of franchising, this must always be done on two levels:

❏ Marketing to the prospective franchisee.

❏ Marketing to the prospective consumers of the franchisor's proprietary products and services.

Academics and consultants often identify the well-known marketing mix as the foundation of a marketing program: product, price, place, and promotion. All marketing plans and decisions stem from one or more of these components of the marketing mix. Here are some of the typical issues raised by each element of the marketing mix, as applied to franchising.

Product

❏ What products and services will the franchisor offer to the consumer through its franchisees and company-owned centers?

❏ What are the various features, options, and styles that each product or service will include as being unique, of better quality, or proprietary?

❏ How will these products and services be packaged and offered to the consuming public?

❏ How will franchises be packaged to attract prospective franchisees?

Place

❏ In what manner will the franchisor's products and services be distributed to the marketplace? Dual distribution or exclusively through franchisees? Why has this strategy been selected?

❏ What are the various advantages and disadvantages of the distribution channels that are alternatives to franchising?

❏ In what geographic markets should the franchisor's products and services be offered (determined through, say, demographics and population analysis, primary versus secondary market studies, local competitor analysis, analysis of local and regional consumer habits)? Will the franchisor be able to attract franchisees in these targeted markets?

Price

❏ What will consumers be willing to pay for the franchisor's products and services? How are prices determined? To what extent can price ranges be suggested to franchisees?

❏ What pricing policies will be developed with respect to discounts, credit terms, allowances, and introductory or special pricing schedules when products are sold directly by the franchisor to the franchisee? By the franchisees to the consumers? If the franchisor (or its franchisees) does engage in introductory or promotional pricing, have such policies been reviewed by legal counsel in connection with (1) Robinson-Patman Act considerations, (2) deceptive pricing regulations established by the Federal Trade Commission, or (3) prohibited predatory pricing practices?

Promotion

❏ What strategies will be implemented to ensure that targeted franchisees are aware of the franchisor's business format?

❏ What strategies will be implemented to ensure that the consuming public is *aware* of the company's products and services?

❏ What sales, advertising, and public relations plans, programs, and strategies will be adopted?

❏ How will human and financial resources best be allocated to these various advertising and promotional programs?

Key Components of the Marketing Program

The key components of a well-developed marketing program fall into three distinct stages: (1) marketing planning and strategy formulation, (2) implementation, and (3) monitoring and feedback. The balance of this chapter discusses these stages.

Stage 1: Marketing Planning and Strategy Formulation

Effective marketing planning and strategy formulation typically fall into three distinct stages: marketing research, market analysis, and the development of a marketing plan. Each has its own set of management team activities.

Marketing Research

Effective marketing planning begins with the development of a database of information regarding the history of the franchisor; of its products, services, and personnel; of trends in its industry; of the size of its total marketplace; of the characteristics of its typical customers and targeted franchisees; of the strengths and weaknesses of its current competitors; and of the various barriers to entry for prospective competitors. This information is typically the end result of *market research* that must be conducted prior to the development of a formal marketing plan. Market research need not be expensive and time-consuming for companies with minimal resources to devote to collecting data about the marketplace.

Essentially two types of data are needed for conducting market research: external and internal. External data has many sources that are available virtually free of charge, from state and local economic development agencies, chambers of commerce, trade associations such as the International Franchise Association, public libraries, local colleges and universities, and even federal agencies such as the Small Business Administration or the U.S. Department of Commerce. Internal sources of information include surveys; meetings with suppliers, customers, and the company staff to collect additional information regarding industry trends; consumer preferences; and the strengths and weaknesses of current marketing efforts.

Market Analysis and Segmentation

The information collected during the franchisor's market research must then be properly organized in order to be effective in the planning process. Unorganized data collected in a haphazard manner will have minimal benefit to the development of marketing plans and strategies. The end result of the marketing research should be a *market analysis*, which should include information on the segmentation of the franchisor's targeted markets, trends in its industry, and an assessment of the franchisor's direct and indirect competitors.

Box 10-1. Marketing resources.

Advertising Age
www.adage.com
American Marketing Association
www.marketingpower.com
Business Marketing Association
www.marketing.org
Direct Marketing Association
www.the-dma.org
Emarketing Association
www.emarketingassociation.com
PRWeek
www.prweek.com
Public Relations Society of America
www.prsa.org
Word of Mouth Marketing Association
www.womma.org

One of the key objectives of market research is the segmentation and targeting of the franchisor's market—the starting point for market planning. *Market segmentation* is the division of the total market into distinct groups of buyers based on either demographic variables (e.g., age, income levels, gender, or race), geographic location of consumers, or even social-political trends and preferences. *Market targeting* is the evaluation and selection of one or more of these market segments toward which marketing efforts and resources will be directed. Once specific markets have been targeted, the franchisor must develop plans and strategies to *position* its franchise offering, as well as its products and services, in such a way as to attract these desired market segments. Market positioning involves the manipulation of the elements of the marketing mix in order to effectively and efficiently reach the targeted consumer/franchisee.

Development of the Marketing Plan

A well-written marketing plan becomes the blueprint for the franchisor to follow in positioning its franchise offering, as well as its products and services, in the marketplace in order to meet its long-term growth objectives. The marketing plan becomes an integral part of the franchisor's overall strategic plan. Like strategic planning, marketing planning must be an ongoing process that will allow the franchisor to respond to changes in the marketplace, law, or technology so that its marketing strategies do not remain static or risk becoming quickly obsolete. Even more importantly, marketing planning must be *consistent* with the franchisor's overall strategies and objectives. Therefore, managers of *all* departments and at *varying levels* of the company must be involved in the marketing planning process and kept in-formed of marketing strategies as they are developed on an ongoing basis. For example, an aggressive marketing plan that is likely to triple the company's franchise sales should not be adopted without consulting the training and field support departments of the organization. Otherwise, neglected and im-properly trained franchisees can cripple the company.

Key Elements of the Marketing Plan

Naturally, the content of the marketing plan varies for each franchisor in terms of topics to be addressed, relevant trends, extent of the market re-search, and resources that can be committed to the implementation of the plan. The elements of the plan vary from franchisor to franchisor depending on the specific industry in which the franchisor operates, the total cost of the franchise, and the desired profile of the targeted franchisee. Nevertheless, the following key components can and should be included in the marketing plan of franchisors of all types and sizes:

❏ *Executive Summary.* This section should provide an overview of the principal goals and strategies that the marketing department of the fran-chisor plans to adopt. This summary should be distributed to all mem-bers of the franchisor's management team for review and comment *before* devoting time and resources to the completion of the plan.

❏ *Assessment of the Current State of Affairs.* This section must answer the classic planning question, "Where are we, and how did we get here?"—but this time from a marketing perspective. Although this section is pri-marily *historical* in nature, it is also *analytical* because it must do more than simply tell a story; it must also *explain* why the franchisor's mar-keting strategies have evolved and ensure that these strategies are con-sistent with current market trends and available technology. This will often require a *marketing audit*, which seeks to identify and assess cur-rent marketing programs and strategies. This section should describe the franchisor's current products and services, the size and growth of its marketplace, a profile of its current and targeted franchisees, and an assessment of its competitors.

The importance of competitive analysis should not be overlooked. Many entrepreneurs often make the statement, "Our product/service is so unique that we have no competition." Such a statement is very dan-gerous and naive because it often reveals both a misunderstanding of the market and the likelihood of poorly conducted market research. For example, suppose that a franchisor has developed a new form of recre-ational activity. To the best of the franchisor's knowledge, no other com-pany is offering this activity to consumers or this type of business format to prospective franchisees. However, this belief could mean that the franchisor has not conducted sufficient market research and/or that the company has not recognized that *all* forms of recreation indirectly com-pete for the prospective franchisee's investment income and/or the con-sumer's disposable income that will be allocated for leisure activities or investment in these types of businesses. Therefore, direct and indirect competitors must be discovered through detailed market research and then described in the marketing plan in terms of size, financial strength, market share, sales and profits, product/service quality, and differentiation from the company's products and services, marketing strategies, and any other characteristics that may be relevant to the development of a comprehensive marketing plan.

❑ *Discussion of Current Issues and Opportunities.* This section should summarize the principal opportunities and threats, strengths and weaknesses, and issues and concerns that affect the franchisor's products and services as well as the market conditions affecting its ability to sell franchises. The principal question to be answered is, "What market trends and factors should be exploited, and what are the external/internal barriers that must be overcome before marketing strategies can be successfully implemented?" The "opportunities and threats" subsection should address the key *external* factors in the macroenvironment affecting the company's marketing strategies, such as legal, political, economic, or social trends. The exact impact of these trends will vary depending on the company's products and services. For example, a forthcoming recession could be a threat to automobile dealers because consumers will hold onto their cars longer (creating an opportunity for the automobile aftermarket services franchisors). Yet a recession could be an opportunity for a franchisor of miniature golf courses because market research has proved that consumers tend to spend even more money on low-cost entertainment during troubled economic periods. The same recession could be damaging to a franchise system featuring upscale furniture or expensive clothing.

❑ *The Strengths and Weaknesses Subsection.* This section should address the key *internal* factors in the microenvironment affecting the franchisor's marketing strategies, such as resource limitations, research and development, organizational structure and politics, protection of intellectual property, distribution channels, service and warranty policies, pricing strategies, and promotional programs. Once all of the strengths, weaknesses, opportunities, and threats have been identified, the last subsection should discuss strategies and tactics for exploiting the franchisor's marketing strengths and compensating for its marketing weaknesses.

❑ *Marketing Objectives and Strategies.* This section should define the goals and objectives identified by the managers of the marketing department with respect to market share, advertising/promotion expenditures, franchise sales, and promotional methods. Strategies should then be discussed, outlining the specific steps and timetables required to achieve marketing goals and objectives. Marketing strategy is essentially the game plan that must be adopted to achieve with respect to targeted markets, positioning of products and services, budgets for advertising, sales and public relations, and the delegation of responsibility within the organization for specific projects. Because this section also involves

dealing with sales and profitability projections, the franchisor's marketing staff must work closely with the finance department to ensure accuracy and consistency. As is true for all forms of planning, the statement
of marketing objectives and strategies should be clear and succinct and
not leave the reader (or user) hanging as to methodology. For example,
a marketing objective of increasing franchise sales revenue by 10 percent could be achieved by increasing the franchise fee, increasing the
total number of franchise units with the franchise fee structure remaining at current levels, or increasing fees *and* unit sales volume. Marketing
managers must identify which course of action will be taken, based on
information ascertained from the market research as well as data and
input received from other departments within the organization.

❐ *Execution of Marketing Program.* This section of the plan should set
forth timetables for achieving specific goals and objectives, identify the
persons who will be responsible for implementation, and project the
anticipated resources required to meet the goals.

❐ *Monitoring of Marketing Plans and Strategies.* This section should discuss the establishment and operation of management systems and controls designed to monitor the franchise marketing plans and strategies
implemented by the company. The relative success or failure of these
programs should be measurable, so that performance can be properly
assessed. Periodic reports should be prepared by the marketing department for distribution to other key members of the franchisor's management team.

❐ *Alternative Marketing Strategies and Contingency Plans.* This final section should address the alternative strategies available to the franchisor
in the event of changes in the marketplace as identified in the plan. The
ability to predict these positive or negative changes that may occur in
the marketing plan and adopt alternative strategies in the event that they
do occur is at the heart of effective strategic marketing planning.

Remember that the marketing plan will continue to evolve and may be
changed as often as monthly, or it may be revised for specific targeted markets. Either way, the ability to quickly respond to consumer demands and
prospective franchisee investment preferences is critical.

Stage 2: Implementation of the Marketing Program

Once market research has been conducted and a marketing plan prepared,
the next step in the development of a marketing program is the actual *implementation.* At most growing franchisors, a separate marketing department
is responsible for the implementation of the marketing plan. The franchise
marketing director and staff must constantly interact with other departments,
such as operations, finance, and administration, as well as outside with legal
counsel in order to coordinate marketing efforts and to keep the marketing
program consistent with the overall strategic plans and objectives of the franchisor. This will require the marketing department to establish certain proce-

dures and controls to monitor marketing performance and to take corrective action as necessary to keep the franchisor on its course of growth and development. These periodic performance audits should also aim to make the franchisor more efficient by reducing unnecessary promotional expenditures and managing advertising costs.

Early-stage and growing franchisors typically experience four distinct stages in the evolution of the department responsible for the development and implementation of sales and marketing functions within the organization.

- ❏ At the inception of the company, all founders are responsible for sales and marketing efforts. During this initial stage, marketing plans are virtually nonexistent, marketing strategies are developed with a whatever-works approach, and sales are to anybody who will buy the franchise offered.

- ❏ Eventually, the founders of the company are too busy with other demands to continue the sales function, and as a result a professional franchise sales staff is developed.

- ❏ As the franchisor reaches the third stage of its growth, all sales and marketing efforts must be centralized into a formal department. Typically at this phase, formal marketing plans start being prepared by top marketing executives with guidance and input from managers of other departments.

- ❏ As the franchisor experiences changes in its external and internal operating environment, the marketing department experiences the fourth and final phase of reorganization, during which modifications in organizational structure are made in order to adapt and respond to these environmental changes.

Developing the Franchise Sales Plan

The responsibility for managing the franchise sales program is typically vested with the vice president of sales or the director of franchise development. This individual is responsible for development of the *franchise sales plan*, which is a critical step in the implementation of the overall marketing plan. The sales plan identifies the specific steps and resources required to attract prospective franchisees. Different sales plans have to be developed for each type of franchise offered by the company. For example, designing a program to attract a qualified prospect to serve as a subfranchisor for the state of New York is quite different from attracting a candidate for a single-unit franchise for the suburbs of Des Moines. (See Figure 10-1.)

The key to developing a successful franchise sales plan is to ascertain a genuine understanding of the targeted franchisee. Doing so requires the development of a detailed profile of the prospect, which includes an analysis of targeted age, gender, education, business sophistication, income levels, net worth, family size, health, communication skills, personality traits, hob-

Figure 10-1. Crafting a franchising sales strategy.

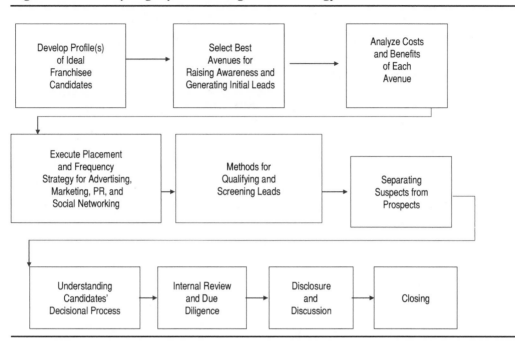

bies, habits, and career objectives. Much of this information will be obtained through the use of a confidential franchise application and personal interviews. See Figure 10-2 for a sample franchise application. Many sophisticated franchisors have turned to detailed psychological testing methods as part of the qualification process for prospective franchisees. If the tests reflect a personality that resists following rules and procedures or lacks a certain attention to detail, then many franchisors will reject the candidate regardless of business acumen or financial net worth. Franchisors look for a wide range of qualities and characteristics in developing criteria for the appropriate type of franchisee. Naturally, the criteria vary from franchisor to franchisor and from industry to industry. Neither the know-it-alls nor the naive are likely to make very good franchisees. Those who understand the importance of rules and procedures and who display a willingness to follow them are likely to make the best franchisees. The franchisor is looking to attract those individuals whose personalities and experience are more suited to serve as sergeants, not as generals.

Once an accurate and objective set of criteria is developed for identifying the "model" franchisee, a sales plan must be developed to attract this prospect. Shots should always be fired with a rifle, not a cannon. For example, if experience has demonstrated that a model franchisee for your franchise system is an executive, college-educated female, between the ages of 34 and 45, then an advertisement in *Working Woman* may be a better allocation of resources than an advertisement in *Inc.* magazine. The key elements of a franchise sales plan are shown in Figure 10-3, and Figure 10-4 diagrams the steps in the process.

(text continues on page 212)

Figure 10-2. Sample franchise application.

CONFIDENTIAL APPLICANT QUESTIONNAIRE

FOR PROSPECTIVE FRANCHISEES

Thank you for your initial inquiry about _____. The information you provide will help us consider your application to become a member of our franchise network. This application will be carefully reviewed by our Franchise Selection Committee and your responses will be kept confidential. The completion of this questionnaire in no way obligates either party in any manner.

PERSONAL DATA

Applicant Name _____
                        First   Middle   Last

Social Security # _____ Date of Birth _____

Marital Status: _____ Married   _____ Single   _____ Divorced

Home Address _____

City, State _____ Zip _____

Home Phone (____)_____   Business Phone (____)_____

Is Co-Applicant your spouse?   [ ] Yes   [ ] No

Co-Applicant's Name _____
                        First   Middle   Last

Social Security # _____ Date of Birth _____

Marital Status: _____ Married   _____ Single   _____ Divorced

Home Address _____

City, State _____ Zip _____

Home Phone (____)_____   Business Phone (____)_____

May we contact your business number?   [ ] Yes   [ ] No

Best time to contact:

THIS APPLICATION WHEN COMPLETED
DOES NOT OBLIGATE EITHER PARTY IN ANY MANNER

Why do you feel you are suited for the retail food and beverage business?

What is your philosophy regarding retail food and beverage sales?

What experience do you have with the retail food and beverage industry?

Do you feel that you possess the qualities necessary to:

1. Train and supervise staff members?   [ ] Yes   [ ] No

2. Handle the everyday ongoing problems that arise when dealing with customers and staff?
   [ ] Yes   [ ] No

3. Handle staff scheduling in both regular and flex-time modes?   [ ] Yes   [ ] No

Briefly explain why:

_____

_____

_____

Who will operate the franchise?   [ ] Self   [ ] Spouse   [ ] Other

Will one of you continue to work at your current place of employment after the franchise is awarded?   [ ] Yes   [ ] No

If yes, who?   [ ] Self   [ ] Spouse   [ ] Co-Applicant   [ ] Other

In what city, county, and state would you like to own a franchise?

City _____

County _____

State _____

Do you have a specific mall or shopping center in mind?

How soon would you be available to operate the Center?

[ ] Immediately   [ ] Within ___ months

Do you now own any other franchises or businesses?   [ ] Yes   [ ] No

If yes, please describe:

(continues)

Figure 10-2. (Continued).

APPLICANT'S EDUCATIONAL HISTORY

Dates of Attendance	School/College	Major	Degree

CO-APPLICANT'S EDUCATIONAL HISTORY

Dates of Attendance	School/College	Major	Degree

APPLICANT'S EMPLOYMENT HISTORY

Dates From—To	Company	Position	Annual Income

CO-APPLICANT'S EMPLOYMENT HISTORY

Dates From—To	Company	Position	Annual Income

Other business affiliations (officer, director, owner, partner, etc.):

_____

_____

_____

Have you ever failed in business or filed voluntary or involuntary bankruptcy?   [ ] Yes   [ ] No
(If yes, please list when, where, circumstances, including any remaining liabilities.)

_____

_____

_____

Are there any lawsuits pending against you?   [ ] Yes   [ ] No

If yes, please describe: _____

_____

Have you ever been charged with or convicted of a crime or act of moral turpitude?   [ ] Yes   [ ] No

If yes, please describe: _____

_____

Are you a U.S. Citizen?   [ ] Yes   [ ] No

If no, in which country do you hold a citizenship? _____

Where will the funds come from to meet the requirements of the estimated start-up costs? Enter source
and dollar amounts: _____

Do you plan to have a partner (other than your spouse or co-applicant)?   [ ] Yes   [ ] No

If you own your own home, do you plan to borrow against it?   [ ] Yes   [ ] No

Amount of equity $_____

Amount of loan $_____

Do you anticipate obtaining a loan to assist you in funding this franchise opportunity?   [ ] Yes   [ ] No

If co-applicant is other than your spouse, please copy the remainder of the form and have each co-
applicant fill out the appropriate information.

(continues)

Figure 10-2. (Continued).

DEPOSIT ACCOUNT INFORMATION

Personal bank accounts and savings and loan deposits carried at:

Bank Contact Name _____

Account No. _____ Phone No. (___)_____

Bank Contact Name_____

Account No. _____ Phone No. (___)_____

Bank Contact Name_____

Account No. _____ Phone No. (___)_____

ASSETS

Cash in banks _____

Savings and loan deposits _____

Investments: Bonds and stocks _____

Accounts and notes receivable _____

Real estate owned (see schedule) _____

Automobiles: Year _____ Make _____

Personal property and furniture _____

Life insurance cash surrender value _____

Other assets—itemize _____

_____

Profit sharing _____

Retirement funds _____

True business *net* worth_____

Attach current financial statement _____.

TOTAL ASSETS _____

SCHEDULE OF STOCKS AND BONDS

Amount or Number of Shares	Description	Marketable (actual market value)	Nonmarket (unlisted securities—estimated worth)

SCHEDULE OF REAL ESTATE

Description and Location	Date of Purchase	Cost	Value	Market Value	Percentage of Ownership	Mortgage Due To Owner	Monthly Payment

LIABILITIES

Notes Payable: Name Payee

To banks _____

To relatives _____

To others _____

Installment accounts payable:

Automobile _____

Other (attach separately) _____

Other accounts payable _____

Mortgage payable on real estate _____

Unpaid real estate taxes _____

Unpaid income taxes _____

Secured loans _____

(continues)

Figure 10-2. (Continued).

Loans on life insurance policies _____

Other debts—itemize _____

TOTAL LIABILITIES _____

NET WORTH (Assets—Liabilities) _____

TOTAL LIABILITIES
& NET WORTH _____

SCHEDULE OF NOTES AND ACCOUNTS PAYABLE

Includes installment debts, revolving charge accounts, bank notes, etc. Specify any assets pledged as collateral indicating the liabilities that they secure:

To Whom Payable	Date	Amount Due	Interest	Monthly Payment	Assets Pledged as Security

I certify that the information I have provided on this application is complete and correct. I hereby authorize _____ or its authorized agent to obtain verification of any of the above information and I authorize the release of such information to _____ or its authorized agent.

Signature of applicant_____ Date_____

Signature of applicant_____ Date_____

Stage 3: Marketing Program Monitoring and Feedback

Once marketing and sales plans are developed and implemented, systems must be put into place that monitor the performance of the sales and marketing department, in addition to gathering market and competitor intelligence. The market research division is usually responsible for acquiring data and intelligence, which are sometimes used as the first step in the development of the marketing plan and at other times used in tracking the performance of marketing efforts in order to modify and refine the plans. Either way, systems must be developed to *gather and analyze the effectiveness of franchise sales*

Figure 10-3. *Key elements of a franchise sales plan.*

A. Introduction
  1. Description of the targeted franchisee
  2. Overview of the techniques and procedures to be implemented to generate the maximum number of leads and prospects whose characteristics match those of the model franchisee
  3. Procedures for meeting, disclosing, and closing the sale
  4. Postclosing procedures
B. State of the Nation
  1. *Why People Buy Franchises.* Corporate restructuring and downsizing in corporate America and abroad have lead to an all-time low in job security. A wide variety of well-educated and financially secure executives and professionals lack the dreams and excitement they so sorely need to continue the daily grind or the loyalty or sense of security from the current employer. Franchising offers these individuals an opportunity to be in business for themselves, but not by themselves. It is an opportunity to be an entrepreneur, but without the risk and difficulty inherent in starting a nonfranchised business. It is an opportunity to avoid the job loss risks of downsizing and restructuring by large corporate employers. For many of these individuals, franchising offers a happy compromise between being a middle-level executive paper pusher and a total maverick. In short, it is an opportunity to control their own destiny.
  Once you understand *why* people buy franchises, you need to figure out why they will buy *your* franchise. A common misconception is that people currently operating within their industry are the best candidates for their franchise offering. Remember that considerably more frustrated accountants have purchased quick-lube and tune-up centers than have trained mechanics. With the notable exception of conversion franchising (e.g., Century 21), those with years of training and experience in a given industry are not likely to perceive the benefits of franchising in the same light as does a novice.
  2. *Why People Buy* Your *Franchise.* As a general rule, people will want to buy *your* franchise because of one or more of the following reasons:
    a. They have an interest in your industry but lack the training skills to pursue this interest without assistance.
    b. They have a friend, relative, or business associate who is already a franchisee within your system. (Happy franchisees tend to lead to more happy franchisees.)
    c. They have been consumers or employees of a franchise (or company-owned store) within your system and were impressed by the quality and consistency of your products and services.
    d. They recognize your underlying product or service as being at the leading edge and want to take advantage of a ground floor opportunity.
    e. They were impressed by the quality and professionalism of your advertising materials, the integrity of your sales staff, and the enthusiasm and passion of your management team.
C. Lead Generation and Qualification
  1. Selection of effective media and methods.
    a. *National/Regional/Local Newspapers and Magazines.* Direct advertising in specific publications with focuses such as business, income opportunity, general interest, topic-specific. Which are the most likely to attract the model franchisee? Which publications have rates within our budgets? How do we get the biggest bang for the buck? What should our advertisements say about the company? What image do we want to project?
    b. *Direct Mail.* Which mailing lists are readily available and most likely to contain a large number of our model franchisees? At what cost? In the design of the marketing piece, what should the text say? What should the prospect's next step be? How often do we mail? What are the procedures for follow-up?

(continues)

Figure 10-3. (Continued).

---

c. *Trade Shows.* What is the quality of the trade show organizer and promoter? [I strongly recommend the trade shows sponsored by the International Franchise Association.] Of the facility? Of the average attendee? How elaborate should we make our booth? What type of promotional displays should be developed? How many people should we send? What literature should be available? How often should we participate? In what regions?

d. *Public Relations.* What story do we tell to the media? What makes our franchise system and company different from the competition? How often do we send press releases? To whom? Saying what? When should we hold press conferences? For what events?

e. *Internet Web Site and Social Media.* In today's technology-driven information age, a steadily increasing number of prospective franchisees are using the Internet to gather data about franchising as well as to narrow the field of potential franchisors to consider. The development of an informative and interactive Web site where you can exchange data with prospective candidates is a critical marketing tool that must be carefully considered. One strategic issue is whether the Web address will be a stand-alone site or part of an umbrella site that features a wealth of information about franchising opportunities overall and has a section on your specific offering alongside other franchisors. One advantage of umbrella sites is that the host company invests the advertising dollars to promote the site overall, thereby increasing your visibility and the chances of attracting qualified leads on the Internet. Also critical is articulating a Web 2.0 social networking media strategy to ensure that candidates can learn about your program on Facebook, MySpace, YouTube, Yelp, Digg, and other networking sites.

f. *Internal Marketing.* This effort includes developing lead generation and incentive programs from the existing network of franchisees, signs and brochures within the franchisee's facilities, and rewards to franchisees and employees for generating qualified leads and actual franchise sales.

g. *Miscellaneous Sources of Lead Generation.* Leads for prospective franchisees can come from a variety of nontraditional sources such as military bases, college placement offices, local business organizations, outplacement offices of large corporations that have been downsized, charitable organizations, personnel agencies, and investment clubs.

2. Procedures for qualifying a lead and making a presentation

a. *Where and How Should Franchises Be Awarded?* Avoid the hotel bar. Get the prospect to the franchisor's headquarters, if at all possible. Make prospects feel special once they arrive. Give them the red-carpet treatment and full-blown tour. Doors should be open, not closed. People should be smiling, not frowning.

b. *Qualities of an Effective Franchise Salesperson and Presentation.* The sales staff should be there to *assist, not pressure,* the prospect. Many prospects base their decision more on the personality traits of the salesperson than on the cold hard facts contained in the offering circular. The sales staff should *listen* to the *needs* and *questions* of the prospect; let the prospect make the decision to buy the franchise. The sales staff should be *confident, not pushy.* Franchises are *awarded, not sold.*

c. *Data Gathering on the Prospect.* All relevant historical and financial data must be collected and verified. No detail should be overlooked. Employment and credit references should be checked carefully. Aptitude and psychological tests are commonplace and recommended. Carefully study the prospect, looking for any early warning signs of subsequent failure. A premium should be placed on the sales representative's "gut feel" assessment of the candidate's likelihood of success.

    d. *Materials and Tools for the Sales Team.* Beyond the personal presentation, brochures, flip charts, and inspection of the franchisor's facilities, audiovisual materials are strongly recommended. Many franchisors have produced 15-minute videotapes designed to educate the prospect and help close the sale. *Legal compliance* (timing of disclosures, avoidance of unauthorized or improper earnings claims and misrepresentations concerning support and assistance, etc.) is *critical.* (See Chapters 5 and 6.)

D. Closing the Sale
    1. Stay in touch during the 14-day waiting period in order to offset the inevitable negative input, sweaty palms, and cold feet that the average prospect will be experiencing.
    2. Resolve all the mystery and confusion regarding the rights and obligations of each party *before signing the franchise agreement.*
    3. Consider the franchise closing *an event, not a mere procedure.* This is likely to be the biggest financial transaction of the prospect's life. Make it special.
    4. Stay in touch with the franchisee after execution of the franchise documents until formal training begins.

E. Managing the Sales Team
    1. Establishment of group and individual sales goals and objectives
    2. Timing and timetable for franchise sales
    3. Travel and promotional budgets to support sales efforts
    4. Personal, ethical, and professional expectations from your sales team (no leisure suits, no gold chains, no lies, and no unauthorized earnings claims)
    5. Reporting and record-keeping requirements (careful documentation of communications with prospects; see Chapter 6)
    6. Respect for prospect review and qualification procedures (data gathering and verification, committee approval, profile testing, etc.)
    7. Ongoing sales and compliance training for the team (sales and closing methods and techniques, legal documents, etc.)
    8. Coordination of efforts with other departments (operations, training, finance, legal, etc.)
    9. Costs and benefits of the use of an outside sales organization

and marketing efforts. Such systems also enable franchisors to study relevant market characteristics and trends affecting their industry-competitive analysis and to monitor general business and economic, legal, political, and technological conditions. These intelligence-gathering systems are indispensable tools of a well-managed franchise marketing department and overall franchise organization. For example, very few franchisors actively follow up with qualified leads that arrived at the decision *not* to become a franchisee of their particular system in order to find out the reason for the decision and to learn from what they hear. Conversely, not enough time is spent in focus groups with franchisees who *did* select their system to make their favorable decision a learning experience.

A comprehensive monitoring and review system helps the franchise sales department identify strengths and weaknesses of the plans and strategies initially adopted and implemented to attract prospective franchisees, measure the performance of those efforts, refine plans to adapt to changes in the marketing macroenvironment, and totally eliminate failed marketing strategies and sales techniques.

The key components of an effective monitoring and intelligence-gathering system include:

(text continues on page 218)

Figure 10-4. Sales and marketing decision chart.

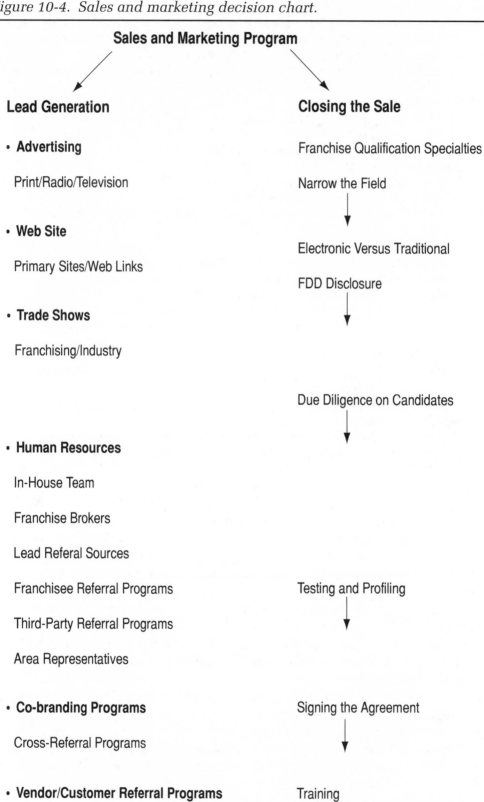

Box 10-2. Common marketing mistakes made by franchisors of all shapes and sizes.

Overlooking the Warts. The importance of the candidate's character and attitude are often overlooked by the overeager franchisor who focuses too much on the candidate's personal net worth or is feeling the pressure to meet payroll costs. The acceptance of this franchisee into the system just to solve a short-term cash flow problem creates a long-term systematic or legal problem. A franchisee with a bad attitude is destined to fail and likely to bring litigation.

Looking for Love in All the Wrong Places. The failure to really understand how and where your targeted candidate will be evaluating opportunities will result in slow growth and probable failure of the franchisor. The franchisor must be *focused* in its marketing efforts and allocate resources to those marketing activities that yield the best results.

Passion and a Sense of Teamwork. To be successful, a franchisee must have a passion and excitement level for the underlying business and enter the relationship with a proper understanding of the roles of each party. The franchisor must *screen* candidates carefully to ensure this level of passion and commitment as well as *educate* the candidate on the respective roles of each party in order to avoid any confusion (or potential litigation) down the road.

Consensus among the Decision Makers. Some franchisors spend too much time with the proposed operator and not enough time with the other decision makers (spouses, parents, investors, lenders, etc.) who may play a critical role in the final decision-making process. The failure to address the needs and questions of all critical players will often lead to a lost sale.

Matching Experience and Skills with Your Opportunity. An age-old question in franchising is how much experience, if any, do you want your ideal candidate to have in your underlying industry? Some franchisors prefer to train from scratch and look for strong general attitudes and business backgrounds. Others prefer their candidates to have some direct prior experience in their core industry. Other franchisors can award franchises *only* to candidates with special technical skills, professional licenses, or personality types. Franchisors must decide on these qualifications in advance and then stay focused on their pursuit of candidates who meet their criteria.

Armchair Marketing. Franchisors who draft marketing plans from their armchairs, who do not get out into the field to see what competitors are really doing, who do not react to what candidates are really saying, or who do not understand what market trends will really affect their growth plans, are destined to fail. Franchise marketing is a very down-in-the-trenches business; it is *proactive,* not *reactive.*

(continues)

Box 10-2. (Continued)

The Wrong Person for the Wrong Job. Particularly in the early stages, the marketing is sometimes handled by the CEO/founder and/or a lost-soul family member in an act of nepotism. Bad idea. These competitive times require a genuine marketing professional who has trade show experience and strong interpersonal skills and who has been trained in techniques that prevent the big fish from getting away. Today's franchise marketing professionals are experienced in dealing with sophisticated prospective multiunit operators. They are trained to develop and execute an automated multistep marketing process and follow-up system, and they do not expect success with a haphazard advertising strategy and an index-card-driven follow-up system.

Reality and Patience. Another classic marketing mistake made by franchisors is the failure to carefully check candidates' willingness to work very hard and to be patient before enjoying a return on their investment and efforts. Candidates who come into the meeting thinking that their location will be an overnight success with minimal effort and maximum financial returns are sorely misguided. Many franchising marketing professionals don't want to burst the excitement bubble and never throw a little cold water on such candidates as a dose of reality until it's too late. Again, this gap between the *expectations* of the franchisee and the *reality* of the challenge and performance of the underlying franchised business is a major source of litigation between franchisors and franchisees.

- ❐ Acquiring and maintaining sufficient computer equipment capability to manage and organize market data.
- ❐ Tracking the development and problems of competitors.
- ❐ Remaining active in industry groups and trade associations.
- ❐ Regularly reading trade journals and industry publications.
- ❐ Meeting with key suppliers and customers to understand industry trends and preferences.
- ❐ Buying the products of competitors to observe pricing, packaging, labeling, and features.
- ❐ Keeping track of the information that may be readily available from federal, state, and local governments.
- ❐ Staying abreast of political, economic, social, and legal trends and developments affecting marketing plans and strategies.

Franchisors should continue to monitor their sales and marketing efforts by interviewing prospects who chose not to acquire the franchise (to find out their reasons), as well as to collect data from recent franchisees (to find out why they did). If the lost prospect bought a franchise from another franchisor, then finding out why is critical. Ask the lost prospect as well as the recent franchisee what they liked and didn't like about the sales presentation and offering process. The franchise director should hold weekly meetings with staff to analyze and deal with the common concerns and objections raised by the typical prospect. Tools and data should then be developed to overcome these concerns.

Franchisors of all sizes and stages of development should understand that effective sales and marketing are at the end of the day all about *leadership*. Franchisors must have a strong leader who is trusted and respected by both employees and current franchisees. The business of awarding franchises is at its heart the process of commencing new relationships. Prospective franchisees will want to have a confidence level in the franchisor's leadership team and believe that this team is absolutely dedicated to their success and to the overall health of the franchise system. Without this feeling of trust and perception of commitment, awarding a franchise is all but impossible.

Embracing Today's Marketing Tools and Technologies

In the relatively short seven years between the publishing of the third and fourth editions of this book, we have moved from Web 1.0 (marketing from an outward-facing unidimensional Web site) to Web 2.0 (marketing from a multidimensional, user-driven content and community). The impact of this one advance on franchisee recruitment is immensely significant. Building a robust and interactive Web site for prospective franchisees is now basic blocking and tackling when just a short time ago it was advanced Internet playmaking. The rules of the game and the paradigm for success have completely changed and will probably do so again before the fifth edition is published. Franchisors of all sizes and in all industries must keep up or will be left behind.

For example, just in the area of lead generation, the world has changed dramatically:

❑ *Go It Alone or Join a Portal.* It is increasingly difficult to solely maintain a stand-alone presence on the Web without being part of the heavily promoted Web portals that are designed to generate enough interest from your listing to drive the candidate to *your* site and complete an application. These portals are, among many, many others, Franchise-Works.com, FranchiseGator.com, Bison.com, FranchiseExpo.com, Franchise.com, and FranchiseSolutions.com. Effectiveness and listing rates will vary. Do your homework!

❑ *Pay per What?* Some Web tolls drive traffic and candidates to your site as paid "wranglers" or as pay-per-click or cost-per-click models. These include Google AdWords, Yahoo Search Marketing, MSN Live Search, and the like. You may want also to use an automated CMS (Contact

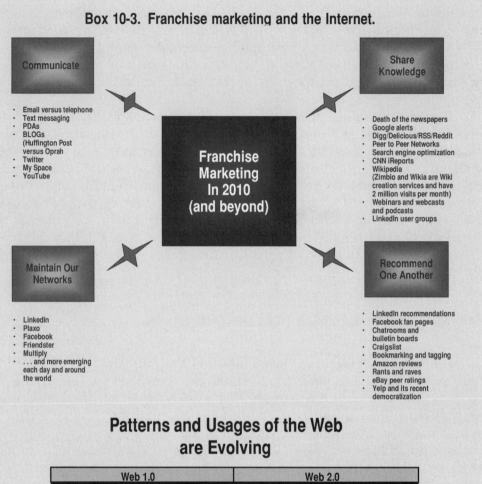

Box 10-3. Franchise marketing and the Internet.

Communicate

- Email versus telephone
- Text messaging
- PDAs
- BLOGs
  (Huffington Post
  versus Oprah
- Twitter
- My Space
- YouTube

Franchise Marketing In 2010 (and beyond)

Share Knowledge

- Death of the newspapers
- Google alerts
- Digg/Delicious/RSS/Reddit
- Peer to Peer Networks
- Search engine optimization
- CNN iReports
- Wikipedia
  (Zimbio and Wikia are Wiki
  creation services and have
  2 million visits per month)
- Webinars and webcasts
  and podcasts
- LinkedIn user groups

Maintain Our Networks

- LinkedIn
- Plaxo
- Facebook
- Friendster
- Multiply
- . . . and more emerging
  each day and around
  the world

Recommend One Another

- LinkedIn recommendations
- Facebook fan pages
- Chatrooms and
  bulletin boards
- Craigslist
- Bookmarking and tagging
- Amazon reviews
- Rants and raves
- eBay peer ratings
- Yelp and its recent
  democratization

Patterns and Usages of the Web are Evolving

Web 1.0	Web 2.0
250,000 Web sites (build it and they will come)	80,000,000 Web sites (How will they find us?)
45 million global users	1.5 billion global users
One to one, one to many	Many to many
Directive	Interactive
Customer feedback	Crowdsourcing
Document-centric	People-centric
Structured	Freeform
Getting online	Search engine optimization
Folders	Tagging
Knowledge management	Knowledge sharing
Need-to-know	Need-to-share
Centralized	Distributed
Heavyweight	Lightweight
Firewalls	Wonderwalls
Long time-to-market cycles	Short time-to-market cycles

Consider the following:

- *Social networking sites have overtaken personal e-mail as the third most common use of the Internet. Business e-mail is second. You know what number one still is.*

- *The fastest growing demographic is the 35- to 49-year-old age group, and the fastest growing applications are for business purposes.*

- *People are just as inclined to e-mail someone in a LinkedIn or Facebook account as they are to use such systems to find firms, as opposed to using the firms' Web sites.*

- *In January 2009, Facebook had 200 million worldwide users in 40 languages, up from 50 million in January 2008—a fourfold growth in 12 months.*

- *Fourteen million users visited Twitter.com, 99 million times in September 2008, a 1300 percent growth rate since January 2008.*

- *LinkedIn had 11.9 million unique visitors in September 2008, a 198 percent increase from January 2008.*

- *If you want to bookmark (i.e., share) an article you read (or wrote) on the Internet, you have over 50 sites and services to choose from (Digg, Reddit, Propeller, Technocrati, Faves, Kaboodle, etc.).*

Management System) such as those offered by a eMaximization, IFX, MyBravo, or Franconnect.

❏ *V-4 Versus V-8.* Search engine optimization (SEO) is one way to make sure that candidates looking for the best new bagel franchise opportunity do not find your company on page 37 of a Google search where they will never see it. Consultants are available to help you and your site with SEO strategies and tools to keep you on pages 1 or 2 of all major search engines. URL addresses, key words, content, strategic links, meta-tags, and other strategies will help keep you above the fold.

❏ *Knock, Knock, Who's There?* Franchisors need to know *who* is visiting the site, *what* they are reading, *how* long they are staying, and other information. Web analytic tools help you understand and analyze their habits. Tools range from basics offered by Google Analytics (for free) to more sophisticated and more expensive ways to measure Web traffic, unique visitors, conversion rates, exit pages, repeat visitors, referral traffic (from portals and search engines), bounce rates, and the like, so that you can better manage and update your Web site, capture more qualified leads, understand your cost per lead, and know where to invest in additional research and development.

❏ *Always on the Run.* Franchisors cannot assume any longer that Internet searches on franchise opportunities will be done from a desktop computer. Web sites, messaging, outbound marketing initiatives, and other communications must be tailored for the Webbook-, laptop-, and PDA-driven world where key data may be read and consumed on a screen that is smaller than a credit card. Being mobile friendly and mobile driven is critical in an Internet-based marketing environment. Displaying it is not enough to get your target audience to see it, use it, or be influenced by it unless you adjust to the likely methods of viewing. And be aware of the significant shift to mobile Internet marketing and advertising dollars and budgets, which are likely to reach $3.3 billion by 2013 and which were already a robust $648 million in 2008. As of the winter of 2010, the AppStore for the Apple® iPhone offered over 100,000 programs, which have been downloaded well over one billion times. The CTIA estimates that over 120 billion text messages are sent per month, well over one trillion per annum. How can you be sure that sources of these texts are focused on how great your franchise system performs?

The impact of these new Web 2.0 tools and strategies is not limited to lead generation. These tools are also used for overall branding, positioning, and awareness aimed both at the existing or prospective franchisee and at the existing and prospective customer basis, from overall corporate strategy to basic couponing. In addition to the messaging and branding on your Web site, franchisors in 2010 and beyond need to have a presence on all major social networking sites, such as MySpace®, Facebook®, Yelp®, Ning®, Flickr®, and others, including social networks abroad. Consider that Facebook® and MySpace® boast over 250 million regular users on their two networks and your goal is not only to accumulate "friends" but also to establish FanPages for a community that follows developments in your system.

Social media strategies also include:

❏ A presence on Wikipedia® and other community-built information sites.

❏ Being active on business-driven networking sites such as LinkedIn® and Plaxo.®

❏ Joining key user groups dealing with franchising or industry issues.

❏ Embracing bookmaking tools, such as Dig® and Delicious®, to allow candidates, franchisees, and customers to save your URL as a favorite and share it with others.

❏ Posting content from your team as well as from satisfied franchisees and customers on YouTube® and other content-sharing Web sites.

❏ Preparing and disseminating blogs (or even podcasts or webcasts) on a weekly or biweekly basis to stay in front of your target audience(s) as a thought leader and to keep them informed of new developments. Blogs help drive traffic to your Web site and can be optimized with keyword phrases for RSS (really simple syndication) feeds, tagged for the technorati audience, and uploaded instantly to your Facebook® and MySpace® sites. Interested readers can even blog about your blog or include hyperlinks to your blog, Web site, or social networking pages.

❒ Posting online contests, promotions, coupons, and other specials to drive more traffic to your Web site, to increase lead generation, and/or to step up the pace of e-commerce.

Last, but certainly not the least, is the tweet. Twitter® has arisen quickly as a very robust messaging platform that is limited to 140 characters for succinct messaging. Twitter® can be used to share updates with those who choose to "follow" you or your company, including vendors, customers, sources of finances, and franchisees. Your tweets may include:

❒ New products or capabilities at your business.
❒ New cases or regulations.
❒ Best practices, trends, and strategic nuggets.
❒ Critical client updates and news with.
❒ New transactions of interest to your community.
❒ Recent awards, recognition, or honors.
❒ Upcoming speeches, articles, or events.
❒ Links to recent media coverage of Jones Day partners or other clips of interest.

The Changing Landscape

Changing at a pace and with a complexity never before experienced are the paradigm and rules of engagement as to how we:

❒ Communicate and express ourselves.
❒ Share news.
❒ Exchange information.
❒ Find one another and maintain our networks.
❒ Make referrals or seek advice.
❒ Brand ourselves as a firm and as individuals.

CHAPTER 11

Taking Your Franchise Program Overseas

Just as the overwhelming popularity of franchising has captured the attention of U.S. business leaders over the past 30 years, it has also attracted genuine attention in the overseas markets over the past 20 years and is likely to be a major trend in the future, especially as our own economy recovers from a deep recession, subject to global geographical trends and concerns. For example, U.S.-based franchisors are currently operating in more than 160 countries worldwide, and many successful overseas franchisors have successfully penetrated the U.S. market as well as many other markets beyond their domestic roots. The reasons for this foreign expansion are strikingly similar to the reasons for domestic growth, including a heightened demand for personal services, raised levels of disposable income, a developing infrastructure, an increase in the size of the middle-class consumer, and a stepped-up desire for individual business ownership. Foreign franchisees are responding eagerly with greater levels of profitability and lower levels of risk that are inherent in the marketing of an established franchised system.

U.S.-based franchisors bringing their branded products to another country in many ways face an already receptive consumer market. The established fascination in most countries with American products and lifestyles can often pave the way for successful business operations overseas. Beyond the fundamental interest in our branded products, many countries, particularly the less developed ones, view franchising as a readily acceptable source of retail technological development and system support that cost-effectively brings know-how to a fledgling business community.

Avoiding the Square-Pegs-in-Round-Holes Syndrome

Many U.S. and overseas franchisors decide to enter a new market without *really* understanding the dynamics of the local marketplace. For example, one global coffee shop chain based in the United States had to significantly alter their trade dress and store design specifications based on average times that overseas consumers sit down and enjoy their beverage, either alone or with friends. Excluding for the moment the small number of customers who sit with laptops enjoying wi-fi for hours at a time, the average sitting time in the United States is seven minutes, but in the United Kingdom it is 21 minutes, and in India it is 45 minutes. Abroad, people *actually* take the time to talk to each other and enjoy their beverages! But this difference in sitting times means that store design and the number of seats and tables need to be rearranged for the store to succeed, and rearrangement affects construction costs and rental rates.

The lesson is that variables such as speed, convenience, consumption, priorities, purchasing power, disposable income, age trends and demographics, work habits, communications norms, and cultural values all need to be carefully considered from market to market.

Each franchisor considering global expansion should build its own decisional and strategy map in order to assess the viability of the overseas franchising business model. it must include variables that will be relevant to the success of the particular franchising system and the underlying products and services. Franchisors must be sensitive to potential variations in size, price, consuming patterns, frequency of consumption, competitive analysis, and other factors as they build their models. Figure 11-1 depicts a typical strategy map. The franchisor's willingness to invest meaningful time and resources into an international expansion program will ultimately define success.

When embarking on an international expansion program, franchisors must always consider:

❏ *Language Barriers.* Although at the outset translating the operations manual into the local language may seem simple enough, marketing the

Figure 11-1. International franchising strategy and assessment model.

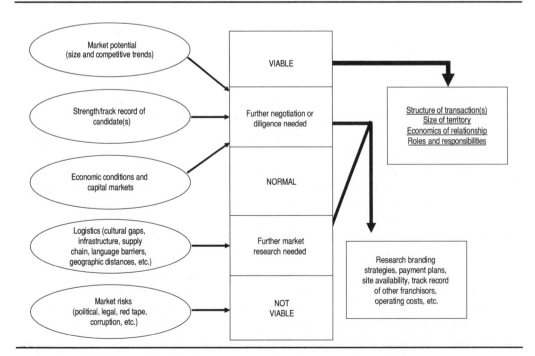

system and the product may present unforeseen difficulties if the concept itself does not "translate" well. The local country's standards for humor, accepted puns or jargon, or even subtle gestures may not be the same as your domestic country's norms or idioms, and so the manual may need to be adjusted accordingly.

☐ *Taste Barriers.* Franchisors marketing food products have frequently found that foreign tastes differ greatly from those of American. These factors should be carefully reviewed with the assistance of local marketing personnel and product development specialists before undertaking any negotiations with suppliers and distributors. The challenge is how to modify the particulars without losing the essence of the core product or service.

☐ *Marketing Barriers.* These types of barriers most frequently go to the deepest cultural levels. For example, whereas many overseas markets have developed a taste for fast-food burgers and hot dogs, differences in culture may dictate that the speed aspect is less important. Many cultures demand the leisure to be able to relax on the premises after eating a meal rather than taking a meal to go. These cultural norms can, in turn, be affected by factors such as the cost and availability of retail space. Direct and subtle messages in advertising campaigns may need to be modified, the appeal of using a particular celebrity in a campaign may vary, and the channels for promotion may also need to be modified to meet the educational patterns and needs of the local consumer. Even marketing methodologies may need to be modified. In certain cultures, coupons are widely accepted and used by people who are both rich and poor (such as in the United States), but in other cultures coupons are not widely used or accepted. In some cultures, even the use of comparative advertising, which is now commonplace in the United States since the late 1980s, could be viewed as offensive or destructive.

☐ *Legal Barriers.* Domestic legislation may not be conducive to the establishment of franchise and distributorship arrangements. Tax laws, customs laws, import restrictions, corporate organization, and agency/liability laws may all prove to be significant stumbling blocks. (See Figure 11-2.)

☐ *Access to Raw Materials and Human Resources.* Not all countries offer the same levels of access to critical raw materials and skilled labor that may be needed to operate the underlying franchised business. The franchisor may want to consider what changes in the system may be feasible to accommodate this challenge without sacrificing the core business format.

☐ *Government Barriers.* The foreign government may or may not be receptive to foreign investment in general or to franchising in particular. A given country's past history of expropriation, government restrictions, and limitations on currency repatriation may all prove to be decisive factors in determining whether the cost of market penetration is worth the potential benefits.

Figure 11-2. Strategic challenges in international franchising.

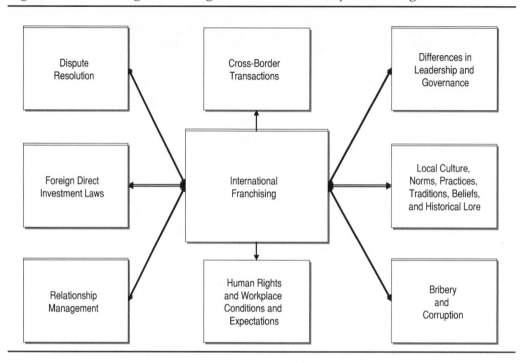

☐ *Business Formation.* The structure that the international franchising transaction will take must be determined (i.e., foreign corporation, area developer, single-unit operators, joint venture).

☐ *Choice of Territory.* A territory overseas may consist of a major city, an entire country, or even a geographic region encompassing several countries. The chosen territory may well affect sales, distribution, and the ability to expand.

☐ *Intellectual Property and Quality Control Concerns.* The protection of trademarks, trade names, and service marks is vital for a domestic franchisor's licensing of intellectual property overseas. The physical distance between the franchisor's domestic headquarters and the overseas franchisee will make the protection of intellectual property and the monitoring of quality control more difficult than maintaining protection domestically.

☐ *Local Laws.* Domestic legislation needs to be examined as well as issues arising under labor law, immigration law, customs law, tax law, agency law, and other producer/distributor liability provisions. The need for import licenses and work permits will also need to be considered.

☐ *Sources of Financing.* The territory chosen may affect the ability to maintain and sustain financing for the undertaking, as well as the ability to receive risk insurance both publicly and privately. The franchisees in the targeted markets must have access to the financing necessary to establish single-unit franchises.

❒ *Expatriation of Profits.* This can frequently be the most decisive factor in deciding whether to enter a market. If a franchisor is restricted in the ability to convert and remove earned fees and royalties from a foreign jurisdiction, then the incentive for entering the market may be completely eliminated.

❒ *Taxes.* The presence or absence of a tax treaty between the franchisor's home country and the targeted foreign market can raise numerous issues and may well affect the business format chosen.

❒ *Dispute Resolution.* The forum and governing law for the resolution of disputes must be chosen. On an international level, these issues become hotly negotiated due to the inconvenience and expense to the party who must come to the other's forum.

❒ *Use of a Local Liaison.* The domestic franchisor must have a local liaison or representative in each foreign market. This local agent can assist the franchisor in understanding cultural differences, interpreting translational problems, understanding local laws/regulations, and explaining the differences in protocol, etiquette, and customs. Offering employment and equity to these foreign nationals might be advisable so that they have a vested interest in the success of your operations abroad.

Naturally, these opportunities also bring certain challenges for which appropriate strategies must be developed. For example, the world's leading franchisor, McDonald's Corporation, recently opened its first outlet in Iceland but had to build an underground heated parking lot to attract customers. In Israel, McDonald's spent months fighting with the Israeli agriculture ministry over the importation of the proper strain of potatoes for its french fries. Such seemingly insurmountable problems are not enough of a barrier to reconsider overseas expansions, but they are enough to warrant a thorough investigation of the company's readiness to expand internationally and a thorough knowledge of the targeted markets. (See Figure 11-3.)

Developing an International Franchising Strategy

The Eight Commandments of developing an effective international franchising strategy are set forth below are some basic guidelines for the development of an effective international franchise program.

1. Know Thy Strengths and Weaknesses

Before expanding to another country, be sure to have a secure domestic foundation from which the international program can be launched. Make sure that adequate capital, resources, personnel, support systems, and training programs are in place to assist your franchisees abroad.

Figure 11-3. Franchising around the world (as of December 2008).

Country	Number of Franchise Systems	Number of Franchise Outlets
Brazil	1,013	62,500
France	600	30,000
United Kingdom	432	26,400
Germany	500	18,000
Italy	387	19,000
Netherlands	309	11,005
Spain	550	25,950
Sweden	200	6,800
Austria	170	2,700
Norway	125	3,500
Belgium	90	3,200
Portugal	55	800
Denmark	42	500

2. Know Thy Targeted Market

Going into a new market blindly can be costly and lead to disputes. Market studies and research should be conducted to measure market demand and competition for your company's products and services. Take the pulse of the targeted country to gather data on economic trends; political stability; currency exchange rates; religious considerations; dietary restrictions; lifestyle issues; foreign investment and approval procedures; restrictions on termination and nonrenewal (where applicable); regulatory requirements; access to resources and raw materials; availability of transportation and communication channels; labor and employment laws; technology transfer regulations; language and cultural differences; access to affordable capital and suitable sites for the development of units; governmental assistance programs; customs laws and import restrictions; tax laws and applicable treaties; repatriation and immigration laws; trademark registration requirements; availability and protection policies; the costs and methods for dispute resolution; agency laws; and availability of appropriate media for marketing efforts. Also, specific industry regulations may affect the product or service you offer to consumers (e.g., health care, financial services, environmental laws, food and drug labeling laws, etc.).

Many overseas franchisors have made the mistake of awarding a single master license to a company for the development of the United States or even all of North America, only to discover that they lack the resources and the expertise to adequately develop this vast marketplace, which encompasses well over 300 million people. To avoid the fallacy of the single master licensee in large and diverse markets, franchisors are well advised to pursue a regional approach, more closely tied to the actual capability of the regional licensee as well as the anticipated market demand for the products and services offered by the business format within the targeted region.

3. Know Thy Partner

Experienced international franchising executives around the world will tell you that the ultimate success or failure of the program will depend on three critical things: finding the right partner, finding the right partner, and finding the right partner. Regardless of the specific legal structure selected for international expansion into a particular market (discussed shortly), the master developer or subfranchisor in the local market should always be philosophically and strategically viewed as your partner. And, just as a dating period precedes a marriage or a due diligence period comes before an acquisition, such is the case in selecting an international partner. There is no substitute for face-to-face negotiations between parties, regardless of whether the individual is interested in a master development agreement or a single-unit franchise.

The most promising candidates will often be those with proven financial resources who have already established a successful business in the host country. They should have experience and relationships with the local and regional real estate and financial communities, have capital and management resources, and language and communications capabilities. They should also have knowledge of the underlying industry, contacts with key suppliers, and a working familiarity with computer and communications technology.

Critical strategies and procedures should be in place to ensure that you make the right selection before embarking overseas.

❐ What systems do you have in place for recruiting and selecting the right candidates?

❐ What procedures will you employ for reviewing their qualifications?

❐ What fallback plan do you have in place if you wind up selecting the wrong person or company?

Beyond a certain point, however, only careful negotiating and contract preparation will provide any degree of protection for a franchisor risking entry into a new market.

4. Know Thy Value

Many franchisors entering overseas markets for the first time have grandiose ideas about the structure of the master license fee and the sharing of single-unit fees and royalties. However, *reality* and *patience* are the two key words. If you overprice, you'll scare away qualified candidates and/or leave your partner with insufficient capital to develop the market. If you underprice, you'll be lacking the resources and incentive to provide quality training and ongoing support. The fee structure should fairly and realistically reflect the division of responsibility between you and your partner. Impatience is another factor that has defeated many international franchising programs. It often takes time for another culture to absorb and welcome your products and services and begin respecting and recognizing your brand. Other factors influencing the structure will be currency exchange and tax issues, pricing strategies, market trends, the franchisor's availability of resources and personnel to provide on-site support, and which party will bear responsibility for the translation of the manuals and marketing materials as well as the adaptation of the system, products, and services to meet local demand trends and cultural differences.

Franchisors must be patient in the expectations of return on investment and profits from overseas expansion. In addition to normal economic cycles and break-even analysis, certain countries dictate legal structures that are essentially forced joint ventures, placing restrictions on a franchisor's ability to quickly pull capital out of the targeted country. In structuring the actual master franchise agreement, the franchisor should carefully consider the structure of the relationship, the term of the agreement, and the scope and length of nondisclosure and noncompete clauses. These provisions and their enforceability will take on increased importance when complicated by distance and differences in legal systems. Franchisors should also give careful thought to the structuring of the financial provisions of the franchise agreement. It is tempting to try to mitigate potential downstream losses by raising the initial fee. This alternative, however, often results in uneasiness on the part of the prospective franchisees with respect to the franchisor's long-term commitment to the host country as a whole. In light of these considerations, a more balanced approach to fees and ongoing royalties should be considered.

5. Know Thy Trademark

As a general matter, trademark laws and rights are based on actual *use* (or on the bona fide intent of use) in a given country. Unlike international copyright laws, your properly registered domestic trademark does not automatically confer any trademark rights in other countries. Be sure to take steps to ensure the availability and registration of your trademarks in all targeted markets. Also be sure that your trademark translates effectively in the targeted country and native language. Many franchisors have had to modify their names, designs, or slogans because of translation or pirating problems in new targeted markets.

6. Know Thy Product and Service

The format of proprietary products or services that are successful in the United States may or may not be successful in another country. Franchisors must be sensitive to different tastes, cultures, norms, traditions, trends, and habits in a country before making final decisions on prices, sizes, or other product or service characteristics. Conversely, they must be careful not to make drastic changes in their product or service at the cost of sacrificing quality, integrity, uniformity, or consistency. Many comical (yet expensive) lessons and stories can be told about domestic franchisors who have learned the hard way that what works well at home may have a very different effect abroad.

Box 11-1. Expect the unexpected.

What works in your home market will not always work or translate effectively abroad. Too often franchisors misjudge, misread, or misunderstand the demand patterns or business model adjustments that will be necessary to be successful abroad.

Some of the more unexpected and unpleasant surprises include anecdotal observations such as:

- We really thought that the joint venture partner would be more trustworthy.
- We cannot understand why the master subfranchisor won't listen to us.
- We thought that the work ethic in ＿＿＿ would be stronger.
- We thought our brand awareness would be higher.
- We expected health, safety, and hygiene standards to be higher and taken more seriously.
- We really thought that the local supply chain would be more efficient and reliable.
- We didn't realize how loyal consumers would be to local competitors.
- We thought it would be easier to obtain reliable accounting data and timely reports.
- Why are the single-unit franchisees not following or using our operations manuals?
- We never realized there would be so much red tape, politics, nepotism, and bureaucracy that got in the way of our growth plans.
- Man, the local employment, labor, and related laws in ＿＿＿ were way worse than in the United States!
- We really thought there would be more reliable sites available at affordable rental rates.
- We could not seem to establish critical mass or concentration of units in a given market to establish efficient management regimes or sufficient brand recognition and dominance.
- Our local franchisees had a heck of a time attracting and retaining a properly trained workforce.
- We never realized how tough it would be to go after trademark infringers and intellectual capital pirates and copycats.
- Man, did we mistime our entry into that particular market due to ＿＿＿＿＿'s [political unrest, natural disasters, war, capital market adjustments, regulatory constraints, currency fluctuations, or you fill in the blank]!

7. Know Thy Resources

Access to resources and experienced advice is a major factor in the success of an international franchising program but does not always require the help of expensive advisors or market research studies. In addition to the extensive resources available at the International Franchise Association in Washington, D.C. (202-628-8000), over 30 countries have established national and regional franchise associations that may be excellent starting points for gathering data about a targeted market. In addition, the International Trade Administration within the U.S. Department of Commerce, the U.S. Chamber of Commerce, and the economic bureaus of most embassies maintain extensive economic and political data on countries around the world.

8. Know Thy Rationale

Franchisors often have widely varying reasons for selecting a targeted country or market. Sometimes they are pulled into a market by an interested prospect who is familiar with their concept (often as a result of being a temporary resident, tourist, or student in the franchisor's home country). This avenue is especially dangerous if the franchisor relies only on the assurances of the interested candidate that there is a demand for products and services. Other franchisors push their way into a targeted foreign market (sometimes due to market saturation or a lack of opportunity in their domestic market) by ranking the likelihood of their success in terms of certain factors of overseas markets. These factors include language and cultural similarities, geographical proximity, market and economic growth trends, risk level, cooperative attitude, and potential return on investment.

Structuring International Master Franchising Relationships

An international franchising program can take a wide variety of forms, each with its respective advantages and disadvantages. Although an extensive discussion of these issues is beyond the scope of this chapter, franchisors should consult with experienced counsel as to whether joint ventures, subfranchising, regional development, area franchising, direct franchising or direct product or service distribution strategies, or even more creative strategies or structures should be pursued.

Most international franchising transactions are structured as:

❑ *Either* an award of multiple-unit franchise development rights to aggressive entrepreneurs who will be responsible for the development of an entire geographic region, either through their own resources or by subfranchising to third parties.

❑ *Or* some joint venture structure, as discussed in Chapters 7 and 20.

The Regulation of Franchising Abroad

Although most countries do not encourage or discourage franchising specifically, the attitude toward foreign investors seeking to penetrate local markets through master or direct franchising is subject to a balancing of competing policy objections. On the one hand, local government is interested in attracting capital investment, creating employment, bringing in new technology, and increasing tax revenue, all of which a new franchise system may provide. On the other hand, the local government may want to control the remittance of local currency to foreign investors, whether paid as licensing fees, royalties, or profits. The local government may also be committed to protecting local franchisees from paying the franchisor an excessive amount for the rights to operate the franchise and wants to protect the local franchisee from onerous clauses in the franchise agreement that unduly restrict the franchisee's operations. Therefore, restrictive clauses that require the franchisee to use only raw materials furnished by the franchisor, limit the franchisee's production, or prevent the franchisee from selling outside a particular geographical area may be invalid under local franchising or antitrust law.

The success of franchising both in the United States and around the world has resulted in a surge of franchise-specific legislation. Thirty years ago, only one country (the United States) had any national franchise disclosure requirements. Twenty years later, in 1992, only three countries (France, Mexico, and the United States) had any such laws. Since 2005, however, many jurisdictions around the globe have passed some version of laws affecting either initial disclosure laws and ongoing relationship—or both. (See Figure 11-4.) Some of these laws have been outgrowths of older technology transfer laws, and some are brand new, reflecting the significant role that franchising has begun to play in the economy of these countries, ranging from Belgium to Macau and from Venezuela to Kazakhstan. And in many countries, sophisticated prospective franchisees are asking for copies of the U.S. FDD and related documentation as a matter of disclosure and negotiation best practices, even if their host country laws do not require them.

Not all of these countries require a disclosure document as detailed as the FDD requirements discussed in Chapter 5. Some countries have disclosure documents that are relatively limited in nature and require only basic background on the franchisor, its management personnel, franchising fees, and territory. Prospective and current franchisors and their lawyers need to monitor this area on an ongoing basis with the assistance of local counsel. (See Figure 11-5.)

Region-by-Region Analysis

Our global economy is developing quickly with changes in economic conditions, government regimes, and general receptiveness to the importation of American franchise systems becoming commonplace in many countries. The relative conditions and risk of each region and each country should be studied carefully. The strategic and regulatory conditions discussed in this section were effective as of fall of 2009 and are intended to be summaries only and not a substitute for comprehensive market research.

Figure 11-4. Survey of international franchising laws.

Countries with Disclosure and Relationship Laws

United States: Federal disclosure laws and registration and relationship laws vary by state,

Canada: Alberta has both laws, Ontario is disclosure only, and PEI is relationship only.

Mexico	Romania	China
Italy	Albania	Japan
Australia	Georgia	Taiwan
Indonesia	Moldova	Vietnam
Malaysia		

Disclosure Laws Only

Brazil	Spain	Macau
Belgium	Sweden	
France		

Relationship Laws Only

Venezuela	Russia
European Union (as a region via	
primarily antitrust laws)	Ukraine
Estonia	Belarus
Lithuania	

Other Notes

Certain countries, such as South Africa, set forth a mandatory code of conduct for franchising through its industry association, but there are limited or no rights for governmental or private cause of action enforcement.

Many countries have antitrust, intellectual property, tax, foreign direct investment, employment, and other laws that directly or indirectly affect the franchising relationship, unless an exception is available.

Asia

The size and strength of the developing and established economies in the Asian market alone make it an attractive target for franchising expansion. More than half of the world's population lives in this region, and nearly a quarter live in China alone. Furthermore, the consumer market is strong, with a growing middle class and strong economic growth rates. Multinational corporations are finding receptive local businesspeople and governments throughout the region. Several governments, including those of Malaysia, Singapore, and Indonesia, have taken steps to encourage franchising by introducing laws, developing programs, and establishing organizations to support the effort.

Although the Asian market has many benefits, it also has its challenges. Some markets, such as the Philippines, are oversaturated relative to disposable income. Others, such as Malaysia, Taiwan, and Singapore, are facing

Figure 11-5. Sales compliance decisional matrix.

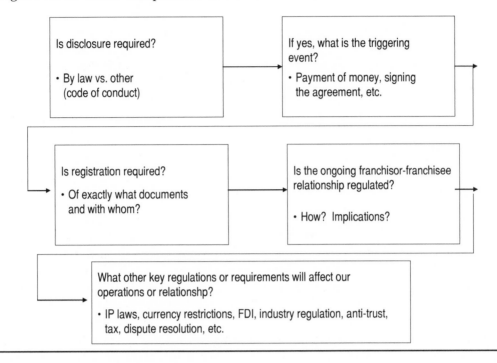

trouble with labor and site availability shortages. The biggest obstacle, however, is the existence of strict foreign investment regulations in most Asian countries; these regulations normally do not forbid foreign investment but are extremely complex and present challenges to inexperienced companies.

China

For many reasons, China is among the most coveted countries by international franchisors. The most important of the reasons is the enormous size of the population, a slow but steady embracing of capitalism, and its rapidly growing economy. Regulations that are both vague and restrictive present a major obstacle in China, and it is difficult for a company to establish its system in China without first franchising in Taiwan, Singapore, Japan, or Korea. The forecast is that this impediment will be alleviated in the future, however, as the Chinese government has been genuinely trying to create regulations favorable to foreign investors.

Indonesia

This country is gaining in interest among franchisors as a very attractive market because of its economic growth. However, there is still a big gap between the nation's rich and poor, and Indonesian law requires that foreign retail establishments are operated by Indonesians, leaving foreign partners to be involved only as consultants.

Singapore and Malaysia

Franchising activity is actively growing in both of these countries. This activity is bolstered by government encouragement and the belief by locals that investing in franchises has a greater chance of success than investing in local business. For example, the Malaysian Franchise Association boasts 250 franchisors with over 8,000 franchisees throughout the country. The Malaysian franchising laws do, however, tend to favor local companies over foreign franchisors, and the government plays a very strong role in regulating commercial activities.

The Middle East

The Middle East has been steadily gaining popularity among franchisors in recent years, particularly in the grant of regional master franchising rights. The population of the region is large (particularly in Dubai), has a growing amount of disposable income, and is increasingly more sophisticated. Many members of the population are well educated and well traveled, and they are aware of the world's latest fashions and trends. Finally, several countries are realizing the economic development benefits of franchising and are introducing laws and offering incentives to encourage continued growth. The level of anti-Americanism at any given time will vary and should be considered carefully prior to expansion.

A major obstacle in the region is domestic political unrest, and some countries have complex legal procedures and bureaucratic procedures that can slow down the launch of new business enterprises. An important aspect is the importance of cultural differences. Certain actions, products, or business methods may be unacceptable in the region, and how this possibility impacts your business model must be considered carefully (e.g., the inability to sell alcohol could significantly impact some bar/restaurant chains).

In general, the countries that are most attractive to foreign investors are Israel, Jordan, the United Arab Emirate, Saudi Arabia, Kuwait, and Egypt, because of suitable conditions and local interest. Unattractive markets may be Syria, Iran, and Lebanon because of their political instability and a generally anti-Western bias. The opportunities for franchise system expansion in a postwar Iraq are interesting but should be approached very carefully.

Central and South America

U.S., Canadian, and European franchise systems have generally enjoyed success in Central and South America, particularly when the transactions are well researched and the franchisor is patient on its expected development schedule. The most common franchising in this region has been with fast-food chains, but there is clearly room for entry with franchises in cleaning services, automotive services, rental services, hotels and motels, and supermarkets. Political and economic unrest in Columbia, Argentina, and Venezuela taints what would otherwise be very attractive franchising markets. Franchisors considering international development should also strongly consider the growing economies of Guatemala, El Salvador, Honduras, Nicaragua, Costa Rica, and Panama, as well as Puerto Rico and the U.S. Virgin Islands. The Caribbean nations of the Dominican Republic, Jamaica, and the Bahamas offer stable economies, high rates of tourism, and a relatively high standard of living relative to the region, and they are also worth serious consideration, especially for test pilot international franchising given their close geographic proximity to the United States.

Brazil

After facing some difficult times in the 1990s, Brazil has rebounded and is experiencing steady economic growth as one of the BRIC nations (Brazil, Russia, India, and China). The country has over 180 million in population, is accustomed to franchising, and is the region's leader with over 1,000 homegrown and overseas franchisors offering opportunities in Brazil with over 62,500 franchised outlets, representing over $20 billion in system-wide sales. Furthermore, the market has been more open to foreign investment since 1995 when it implemented drastic regulatory changes affecting its financial markets to encourage trade and stabilize its currency. As inflation in the country decreases along with regulation on investment, the country promises to be an excellent franchise target in the future.

Chile and Uruguay

These countries have been commonly used by franchisors as test markets for their entry into South America. Both have high growth rates, highly educated populations, and few restrictions on foreign investment. The problem with these countries is that they have very small populations—a total of approximately 20 million combined. In addition, these countries have been slow to adopt principles of entrepreneurship, and patience is key to developing these markets.

Colombia

At the present, Colombia has the third largest number of franchises in South America and is open to this kind of investment. It has several dangerous disadvantages, however, which include a high poverty rate (40%), the threat of guerilla and drug violence, and a small local market.

Mexico

The first franchised business in Mexico opened its doors more than 20 years ago, and franchising now represents over 15 percent of the retail economy. Franchise systems are developing very quickly in Mexico, including companies based in the region.

In Mexico, the nation's Industrial Property Law regulates the offer and sale of franchises, and the Mexican Congress recently modified legislation to provide enhanced enforcement and disclosure provisions.

There is a vast market to penetrate in Mexico, especially outside the capital of Mexico City. Mexico tends to be a centralized nation, so the rest of the country is still pretty much untouched. Franchising grew 17 percent during 2006 through 2009. There are more than 800 franchisors in 72 industries.

Western Europe

Franchising in Western Europe continues to grow at a steady rate. The United Kingdom is a common entry point into Europe for many U.S. and Canadian franchisors and has no precontract disclosure laws—or really any specific franchisee legislation whatsoever. Franchisee systems in France, Germany, and Italy continue to flourish, both homegrown and foreign. Spain is emerging as a powerful force in European franchising, and the number of franchisors operating in Spain has grown 150 percent over the past five years. Statistics recently released by the Spanish Franchise Association demonstrate that franchising sales now make up over 6 percent of total retail sales and employ over 8 percent of the nation's workforce. Franchising in Northern Europe has also grown at a slow but steady rate, particularly in Denmark, Belgium, and Switzerland, whose early-stage homegrown franchise systems are starting to expand into other parts of Europe and have their long-term eye on the North American market.

Eastern Europe

Eastern Europe continues to navigate through challenging economic times and has not been an attractive market for franchising in the past, but this may be changing. The region's economy is stabilizing, governments are gradually lifting regulatory restrictions, disposable income is increasing, and the public is attracted to Western goods. It is apparent that the region will at some point be an excellent place for international franchisors, but the challenge is deciding when to enter this market, particularly now when competition is limited. At the present, a barrier is that local entrepreneurs generally do not have access to the needed capital or the experience to develop franchises. They understand their limitations, and this leads them to be afraid of taking advantage of such an opportunity. Industries that are expected to succeed in this region are cleaning services, fast food, book and music retailing, professional training, and hotels and motels. The two countries in Europe that are most attractive are Russia and Poland. Hungary, the Czech Republic, Yugoslavia, and Bulgaria also promise to be attractive franchising markets in the future.

Russia

Russia boasts a very large consumer market with a population of 150 million. It has many negatives, however, that must be overcome. The economy is tainted by high crime rates, political problems, bribery, and poverty. Further-more, many Russian entrepreneurs and consumers are unfamiliar with and unconvinced of the advantages of franchising. The difficulties are further complicated by access to capital issues, which is very limited, and by entre-preneurs' fear of putting their own money on the line for such a venture. Finally, government regulation has been unkind to franchisors and places many restrictions on them.

Poland

Poland is far more attractive than Russia. It is the second largest country in Eastern Europe (with a population of 40 million), and it welcomes franchis-ing as a step toward its economic development. Locals are educated and receptive to Western business and customs. There are some obstacles con-cerning land rights, tight investment loans, and high rental rates, but these can be overcome. Some of the emerging post-USSR nations are developing stable economies and a growing middle class that may lend themselves to successful franchising in the not too distant future. Some U.S. franchise sys-tems have already been established in the Ukraine, Azerbaijan, and Kazakh-stan, including Yum! Brands systems, such as KFC and Pizza Hut, as well as Subway and Baskin-Robbins. Other types of franchise systems, such as automotive care, home services, and business services, may flourish as these economies stabilize.

Regional Trade Agreements

NAFTA

On January 1, 1994, the North American Free Trade Agreement (NAFTA) among Canada, Mexico, and the United States began to take effect. NAFTA mandates the eventual elimination of all tariff and nontariff barriers to trade between Mexico and the United States over 15 years. Between 1993 and 1997, combined real U.S. manufactured exports to its NAFTA partners rose by 40 percent, with 34 percent and 54 percent increases to Canada and Mex-ico, respectively.

Mercosur

Mercosur was created by Argentina, Brazil, Paraguay, and Uruguay in March 1991 with the signing of the Treaty of Asuncion. Mercosur is, since January 1, 1995, a customs union, whereby the member states (Argentina, Paraguay, Uruguay, and Brazil) have eliminated all tariff and nontariff barriers to recip-rocal trade and adopted a common external tariff for third-party countries. In 1996, association agreements were signed with Chile and Bolivia estab-lishing free trade areas with these countries. This regime is not, at present, fully in effect. The Member States of Mercosur negotiated what has come to be called an "adaptation regime," by which some products traded among the four countries will, for a time, continue to pay duties. Lists of exceptions to the common external tariff for a group of specific products also exist. The customs union will be in full effect on January 1, 2006. Mercosur as an international commitment is today something between NAFTA and the European Union.

EU

The European Union (EU) was set up after World War II. The process of European integration was launched on May 9, 1950, when France officially proposed to create "the first concrete foundation of a European federation." Six countries (Belgium, Germany, France, Italy, Luxembourg, and the Netherlands) joined from the very beginning. Today, after four waves of accessions (1973: Denmark, Ireland, and the United Kingdom; 1981: Greece; 1986: Spain and Portugal; 1995: Austria, Finland, and Sweden), the EU has 15 member states and is preparing for the accession of 13 Eastern and Southern European countries. The European Union, which has its origins in the 1957 Treaty of Rome, has traveled a long road of conciliation and negotiation in order to form today one single market, and it is striving to adopt common policies inside and outside Europe. This single market includes the free movement of goods, free movement of workers, right of establishment and freedom to provide services, and free movement of capital. As of January 1, 2002, the EU launched the euro and achieved its single currency goal, which has helped fuel the growth of franchising systems across Europe.

Protecting Intellectual Property Rights Abroad

International Trademark Protection

As a general rule, trademark rights are based on actual use in each country. Entrepreneurs and leaders of growing companies doing business abroad can take advantage of an international system (the Madrid System) that permits the simultaneous registration of trademarks in as many as 56 countries using a single, standardized application.

The Madrid System is comprised of two treaties: the Madrid Agreement Concerning the International Registration of Marks (Madrid Agreement) and the Madrid Protocol for the International Registration of Trademarks (Madrid Protocol). Both are administered by the World Intellectual Property Organization (WIPO), located in Geneva, Switzerland. On November 2, 2002, President George W. Bush signed the implementing legislation for the Madrid Protocol. For U.S. franchisors and other companies that maintain international trademark portfolios, access to the Madrid System presents an opportunity to streamline and to significantly reduce the cost of global trademark acquisition and management.

For U.S. trademark owners in need of international trademark protection, the Madrid System, in many cases, may eliminate the need to file separate applications in each country where trademark protection is required. For example, the availability of the Madrid System will mean that a U.S. company in need of trademark protection in China, Japan, the United Kingdom, and Morocco (all members of the Madrid Protocol) will simply file one standardized application in the United States Patent and Trademark Office (USPTO), pay one fee, and obtain a single registration covering the series of underlying national applications in each of the named countries. The resulting registration will have one registration number and one renewal date.

However, the Madrid System is *not* a substantive trademark law, and an application filed under it does not result in a Madrid Registration. In other words, although the registration issued under the Madrid System oftentimes is referred to as an "international registration," it differs from registrations issued under the auspices of such collective organizations as the European Union because it is not a freestanding, supranational registration. Instead, the Madrid System provides a *centralized mechanism* for simultaneously obtaining, in effect, separate national registrations based either on a pending application or existing registration on file in the national trademark office of the applicant's home country.

To file an application under the Madrid System, the applicant must be a qualified owner of either a pending application or a registration on file in the national trademark office of the applicant's home country.

International Patent Rights

As a general rule, protection provided by a patent is limited to the country in which it was granted. For example, a patent granted in the United States would not be infringed by a company manufacturing an identical product abroad, unless or until the foreign company starts manufacturing or selling the patented product in the United States. Limited international intellectual property rights (IPR) may offer alternative protection to national rights. A number of international conventions govern IPRs, including:

❏ Paris Convention for the Protection of Industrial Property (1883).
❏ Berne Convention for the Protection of Literary and Artistic Works (1886).
❏ Patent Co-operation Treaty (PCT, 1970).
❏ WTO—Agreement on the Trade Related aspects of Intellectual Property Rights (TRIPS, 1994).

None of these conventions establishes an international form of IPR valid in several countries. Rather, each convention tries to harmonize IPR protection or simplify the application process.

❏ The Paris Convention has two main principles: national treatment (i.e., foreigners from other signatory states are to be treated the same as domestic citizens so far as patent protection for inventions is concerned);

and right of priority (i.e., provided the correspondent application in country B is filed within 12 months of a filing in Country A, then it is backdated to the date of first filing).

❏ The PCT's aim is to reduce unnecessary effort, work, and cost on the part of patent applicants. Once a single international patent application is filed at the patent office of a member state, it has the effect of being filed in both the first country and all other designated states in which the applicant is interested. The home patent office transmits the international patent application to an international searching authority for a prior art search, which is forwarded to all designated states. The local patent office of each designated state then continues with the application in accordance with its own normal procedures.

❏ TRIPS' aim is to narrow the gaps in how IPR is protected around the world and covers five broad issues:

1. How basic principles of the trading system and other intellectual property agreements should be applied
2. How to give adequate protection to IPRs
3. How countries should enforce those rights adequately
4. How to settle IPR disputes between members of the WTO
5. Special transitional arrangements in less developed countries

Within Europe, a similar system has existed under the European Patent Convention (EPC) since 1973. A single application, once filed, is examined by the EPO; once a patent is granted, it gives the same level of legal protection as a national patent in any of the contracting states that are designated in the application. There are currently 27 contracting countries with another four expected to become members in due course.

PART THREE

FINANCIAL STRATEGIES

CHAPTER 12

Business and Strategic Planning for the Growing Franchisor

 n today's highly competitive and rapidly changing marketplace, the management teams of early-stage, growing, and established franchisors must be clear on their (1) overall strategic plan, (2) current business plan, and (3) the efficacy of their business model. (See Figure 12-1.) All three documents must be updated from time to time to reflect the company's medium- to long-range growth and development plans, but each plays a difficult role in articulating the course that the company will follow and the resources that it will require along the way.

Figure 12-1. The three key planning documents.

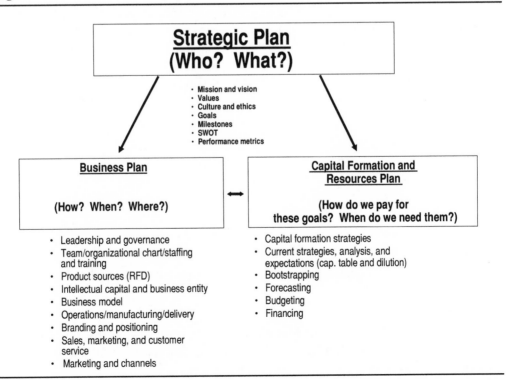

Understanding the Business Plan

Founders and leaders of growing franchisors have come to understand that meaningful and effective business planning is critical to the long-term success and viability of its underlying business and to its ability to raise capital. Before you read about the various methods of financing available to fuel the growing franchisor in Chapter 13, you must understand the key documents that virtually any source of capital will want to review as a condition to closing. One of the critical documents is a business plan that charts a path for the growth of the franchise company.

Regardless of the financing method or the type of capital to be raised, virtually any lender, underwriter, venture capitalist, or private investor will expect to be presented with a well-drafted and viable business plan. A well-prepared business plan demonstrates the franchisor's management team's ability to focus on long-term achievable goals, provides a guide to effectively implement the articulated goals once the capital has been committed, and constitutes a yardstick by which actual performance can be evaluated.

Business plans should be used by newly formed franchisors as well as by established ones. The following is a broad outline of the fundamental topics to be included in a typical franchisor's business plan.

Executive Summary

This introductory section of the plan should explain the nature of the business and highlight the important features and opportunities offered by an investment in the company. The executive summary should be no longer than one to three pages and include (1) the company's history and performance to date, (2) distinguishing and unique features of the products and services offered to *both* consumers and franchisees, (3) an overview of the market, (4) a summary of the biographies of the leadership team, and (5) the amount of money sought and for what specific purposes. This information must be included in some way or the other in the Executive Summary.

History and Operations of the Franchisor

In this first section, the history of the franchisor should be discussed in greater detail:

- ❐ Its management team (with resumes included as an exhibit)
- ❐ The specific program, opportunity, or project being funded by the proceeds
- ❐ The prototype
- ❐ An overview of the franchisor's industry, with a specific emphasis on recent trends affecting the market demand for the franchises
- ❐ The products and services offered by the franchisee

Figure 12-2 provides a list of questions to be addressed in this section.

Many of these issues will be described in greater detail in later sections of the plan. Therefore, each topic should be covered summarily in two or three paragraphs.

Marketing Research and Analysis

This section must present to the reader all relevant and current information regarding the size and strength of the market for both franchisees and consumers, trends in the industry, marketing and sales strategies and techniques, assessments of the competition (direct and indirect), estimated market share and projected sales, pricing policies, advertising and public relations, strategies, and a description of sales personnel. The following questions should also be addressed:

- ❐ *The Typical Consumer.* How and why is the consumer attracted to patronize the franchisee's facility? What relevant market trends affect the consumer's decision to purchase products and services from the franchisee's facility?

- ❐ *The Typical Franchisee.* How and why is the prospective franchisee attracted to the franchisor's business format? What factors have influenced the prospect's decision to purchase the franchise? What steps are being taken to attract additional candidates who meet these criteria?

- ❐ *The Market.* What is the approximate size of the total market for the services offered by the franchisee? The approximate market for franchisees?

- ❐ *The Strategy.* What marketing strategies and techniques have been adopted to attract franchisees and consumers? Where do referrals for prospective franchisees come from? Do existing franchisees make referrals? Why or why not? (Include sample promotional materials as an exhibit.)

- ❐ *The Performance of the Typical Franchisee.* Are current stores profitable? Why or why not? What factors influence their performance?

Figure 12-2. Questions to address in Section 1.

1. When and how was the prototype facility first developed? How has it performed? Will this be typical when the franchise system is built?

2. Why has the company decided to expand its market share through franchising? What other alternatives have been considered and why did the company select franchising?

3. What are the company's greatest strengths and proprietary advantages with respect to its franchisees? Consumers? Employees? Shareholders? Competitors?

4. What are the nature, current status, and future prospects in the franchisor's industry?

5. Has an economic model and pro forma been built to demonstrate the viability of the franchise system to both franchisor and franchisee?

Rationale for Franchising

This section should explain the underlying rationale for selecting franchising in lieu of other growth and distribution strategies that may be available. Discuss whether a dual distribution strategy will be pursued. Under what circumstances will company-owned units be established? Explain to the reader which method(s) of franchising will be selected. Single units only? Sales representatives? Area developers? Subfranchisees? Special risks and legal issues that are triggered by the decision to franchise should also be discussed.

The Franchising Program

This section should provide an overview of the franchising program with respect to key aspects of the franchise agreement, a description of the typical site, an overview of the proprietary business format and trade identity, the training program, operations manual, support services to franchisees, targeted markets and registration strategies, the offering of regional and area development agreements, and arrangements with vendors. A detailed analysis of sales and earnings estimates and personnel needed for a typical facility should also be included. Discuss marketing strategies relevant to franchising such as trade shows, industry publications, and sales techniques. Explain the typical length of time between the first meeting with a prospect through the grand opening and beyond. What are the various steps and costs during this time period (from the perspective of both the franchisor and the franchisee)? Discuss strategies for the growth and development of the franchising program over the next five to ten years.

Corporate and Financial Matters

This section should briefly describe the current officers, directors, and shareholders of the corporation. An overview of the capital contributed to the company thus far should be provided, along with an explanation of how these funds have been allocated. Discuss the anticipated monthly operating costs to be incurred by the corporation, both current and projected, not only for operating and managing the prototype facility but also for the administrative expenses incurred in setting up a franchise sales and services office. Explain the pricing of the franchise fee, royalties, and promotional fund contributions. Discuss the payment histories of the franchisees thus far. Are they complying with their obligations under the franchise agreement? Why or why not?

What portion of the fees collected from the franchisee will be net profit? Discuss the amount of capital that will be required for the corporation to meet its short-term goals and objectives. How much, if any, additional capital will be required to meet long-term objectives? What alternative structures and methods are available for raising these funds? How will these funds be allocated? Provide a breakdown of expenses for personnel, advertising and marketing, acquisition of equipment or real estate, administration, professional fees, and travel. To what extent are these expenses fixed, and to what extent will they vary depending on the actual growth of the company?

Operations and Management

Provide the current and projected organizational and management structure. Identify each position by title, with a description of duties and responsibilities and compensation. Describe the current management team and anticipated hiring requirements over the next three to five years. What strategies will be adopted to attract and retain qualified franchise professionals? Provide a description of the company's external management team (attorney, accountant, etc.).

Exhibits

Include in the presentation copies of the franchisor's trademarks, marketing brochures, press coverage, and sample franchise agreements and area development agreements.

The Ongoing Strategic Planning Process

In a franchisor's early stages, the emphasis is on the business plan: How does it properly launch the franchising program to attract qualified candidates, and what resources will it need to sustain the program?

Then, what happens later? Once a franchisor reaches 50 to 100 units or more, the focus shifts away from mere business planning and to strategic planning. In the context of franchising, strategic planning is an ongoing process that seeks to *build* and *improve* the following key areas (see Figure 12-3):

❐ The quality and performance of the franchisees
❐ The quality and sophistication of the technology used by the franchisor to support franchisees

Figure 12-3. Key strategic planning questions.

- What are the common characteristics of our top 20 percent franchisees?
- What can we do to attract more people like this in the recruitment and selection process?
- What are the common characteristics of our bottom 20 percent franchisees?
- How do we screen these out? What can we do to improve their performance?
- What are the five greatest strengths of our system?
- What is being done to build on these strengths?
- What are the five biggest problems in our system?
- What are we doing to resolve these problems?

❐ The quality and sophistication of the training and support systems

❐ The value and recognition of the franchisor's brand from a customer awareness perspective

❐ The development and communication of the franchise system's best practices throughout the system as well as general best practices in franchise overall

❐ The exploration of new domestic and international markets

❐ The organization of franchisee advisory councils, supplier councils, co-branding alliances, and other key strategic relationships

❐ The development of strategies for multiunit franchising, alternative sites, and related new market penetration strategies

❐ The development of advanced branding and intellectual property protection strategies

The strategic planning process should manifest itself in periodic meetings among the franchisor's leadership, periodic strategic planning retreats, and a written strategic plan that is updated annually. The strategic planning meetings and retreats could be focused on a specific theme, such as brand building and leveraging, rebuilding trust and value with the franchisees, litigation prevention and compliance, international opportunities in the global village, leadership and productivity issues, financial management and per-unit performance issues, the improved recruitment of women and minorities, technology improvement and communications systems, alternative site and nontraditional location analysis, co-branding and brand extension licensing, or building systems for improving internal communication. Any or all of these topics are appropriate for one meeting or for discussion on a continuing basis. The strategic planning meeting could be led by an outside facilitator, such as an industry expert, or by the franchisor's senior management team. A model agenda for a general strategic planning retreat is shown in Figure 12-4.

The end result of an effective strategic planning meeting is to develop a list of specific action items. Some action items may be implemented right away and some may take time. Here is a list of possible specific action items:

1. Consider the entry into new domestic and international markets. You can start with our neighbors to the north and south. Many franchisors are currently exploring opportunities in markets such as Canada, Mexico, and South America due to their close geographic proximity to the United States.

2. Consider implementing various types of multiunit development strategies.

3. Consider alternative territorial penetration strategies such as kiosks, satellites, carts, miniunits, seasonal units, limited service units, in-store units, resorts units, military base units, and related alternative site selection strategies.

Figure 12-4. Model strategic planning meeting agenda.

Evaluating Our Strategic Assets and Relationships

1. *Overview*
   - Goals and objectives of the meeting
   - Reiteration of our mission, values, goals, and culture
   - Key trends in domestic and international franchising

2. *Assessing the Strengths of Our Franchise Relations*
   - Franchising state of the union
   - Common critical success factors by and among our franchisees

3. *Evaluating Our Team*
   - Code of values—reality and practice
   - Motivating and rewarding employees
   - Protecting the knowledge worker
   - Providing genuine leadership

4. *Our Strategic Partners*
   - What do we expect from our vendors and professional advisors?
   - What can we do to enhance the efficiency and productivity of these relationships?
   - Building the national accounts program
   - Do all of our strategic relationships truly provide mutual reward?

5. *Our Targeted Customers*
   - Identifying and dealing with the competition
   - Customer perceptions of quality and value
   - Franchisor–customer communications
   - Customer satisfaction surveys
   - Exploring two-tier marketing strategies

Asset-Building Strategies

1. *Building and Leveraging Brand Awareness*
   - Building overall brand awareness
   - Brand leveraging strategies
   - Building an arsenal of intangible assets

2. *Co-branding and Strategic Alliances*
   - Identifying goals and objectives
   - Targeting and selecting partners
   - Structuring the deal

3. *Shared Goals and Values*
   - Enhancing intracompany communications
   - Building trust and respect

4. *Role and Value of Technology*
   - How technology is changing the way we work and consume products/services
   - The impact of technology on recruiting, training, and supporting franchises
   - The impact of technology on how our franchisees will market their products/services to targeted customers

5. *Development of Branded Products and Services to Strengthen Revenue Base*
   - Business training and assistance resources for clients
   - Home cleaning and refinishing products
   - Co-branded products and services (e.g., securities sales, financial planning, home improvement and remodeling, etc.)
   - Affinity/group purchasing programs

4. Consider joint ventures and co-branding opportunities with other franchisors or nonfranchisors and complementary but noncompeting markets. These could include joint site developments such as in the coffee and muffin industries or automobile minimalls and other related operational joint ventures. Many food-related franchisors are actively developing co-branding programs as a vehicle for growth and new market penetration.

5. Be aggressive and proactive in commercial leasing strategies, especially in a weakened marketplace. Consider subleasing and turnkey development strategies, as well as stricter site selection criteria to lower the failure rate and to improve the financial performance of each franchisee, and so on.

6. Reevaluate your internal and external management team. Get rid of internal deadwood, and don't be afraid to demand more and better from your outside advisors. Continue to evaluate your management team for any individuals who may be engaged in a course of action that is unproductive, hostile, or harassing to your current or prospective franchisees. Ask your outside advisors, "What are you doing to help us grow, and do you truly care about the future direction of our company?"

7. Carefully evaluate the future of the baseless rabble rousers and nonperformers with your franchise system. These negative influencers spread like wildfire. Put these fires out while they are just sparks, not flames. Separate the good constructive criticism and proactive franchisee from the whiners, whom you will never satisfy.

8. Build up your arsenal of protectable and registered intellectual property (e.g., trademarks, copyrights, trade dress, etc.).

9. Be proactive in creating franchisee advisory councils and other methods in improving franchisor/franchisee communications to maximize franchise relationships. Bear in mind that happy franchisees keep litigation costs down and new franchise sales up.

10. Venture into the world of being a product and service provider to your network of franchisees. These activities should be subject to applicable antitrust laws—but quite lucrative—provided that you are within legal boundaries, you are not too greedy, and the economic relationships are properly structured. These products and service provider relationships can be done directly or through joint ventures with third-party suppliers.

11. Reread your FDD tomorrow as if you were a prospective franchisee. Do the documents convey your company's philosophies? Do the documents adequately tell your company's story? Do they convey a sense of trust, fairness, and reasonableness? Are the documents user friendly to the reader and to the advisors of the franchisee? Would you buy this franchise? You will be able to discover a lot about your FDD and your ability to use the document as a marketing tool if you reread the document as if you were buying the franchise.

12. Strengthen effectiveness and the strategic use of your data gathering systems for the financial performance and other key metrics involving the operations of your franchisees. Use this data to compile sample profit and loss statements and balance sheets of some of the strong, medium, and weak franchisees in the system. Circulate these documents, subject, of course, to confidentiality and earning claims regulations, among your existing franchisees to increase their performance and to point out flaws in their financial management.

Box 12-1. The four habits of highly successful franchisors.

1. *An Ability to Adapt to Challenges and Changes in the Marketplace*
   - How do we react to inevitable and constant changes in the environment?
   - How well do we plan in advance, anticipate change, and face the reality of what's really happening in the trenches?
   - Do we really listen to our franchisees?

2. *A Genuine Commitment to the Success of Each and Every Franchisee*
   - A chain is only as strong as its weakest link.
   - How is this commitment demonstrated?
   - Is this how our franchisees truly perceive our commitment?

3. *A Culture Committed to Overcoming Complacency*
   - Are we committed to research and development?
   - What steps are in place to constantly improve and expand our systems and capabilities?
   - How quickly do we abandon a failing franchisee?

4. *A Team Ready to Break Old Paradigms*
   - Are we committed to thinking outside the box?
   - What recent examples do we have where creative thinking solved a problem or created a new opportunity?

In sum, the strategic planning process is a commitment to strive for the *continuous improvement* of the franchise system. The process is designed to ensure that maximum value is being delivered, day in and day out, to the franchisor's executive team, employees, shareholders, vendors and suppliers, and, of course, franchisees. Do not be afraid to ask: Where are we? Where do we want to be? What do we need to do to get there? What is currently standing in our way of achieving these objectives? Make sure that the company takes the time to develop a mission statement, to define a collective vision, and then to develop a series of plans to achieve these goals.

Executives must stay *focused* on these objectives and provide leadership to both the balance of the franchisor's team as well as to the franchisees as to *how* these objectives will be achieved. The focus must be on brand equity, franchisee value, customer loyalty, and shareholder profitability. The guidelines and protocols for internal communications must encourage honesty and openness, without fear of retaliation or politics.

CHAPTER 13

Capital Formation Strategies

ne of the most difficult tasks faced by the leadership team of a growing franchisor is the development and maintenance of an optimal
capital structure and access to the resources needed to stay strong
and to execute its growth plans. Access to affordable debt and equity
capital continues to be a problem for franchisors, even though franchising
has matured as a viable method of business growth.

Only recently have the investment banking, private equity, venture capital, and commercial lending communities given franchising the recognition
it deserves. There are finally enough franchisors with respectable balance
sheets who have participated in successful public offerings, who have played
(and won) in the merger and acquisition game, and who have demonstrated
consistent financial appreciation and profitability. These developments have
played a role in providing young franchisors access to affordable capital in
recent years.

Nevertheless, a growing franchisor must be prepared to *educate the
source of capital* as to the unique aspects of financing a franchise company.
And franchise companies do have their differences. Franchisors have different balance sheets (heavily laden with intangible assets), different allocations of capital (primarily as expenditures for "soft costs"), different types of
management teams, different sources of revenues, and different strategies for
growth. The amount of capital potentially available, as well as the sources
willing to consider financing a given transaction, depends largely on the
franchisor's current and projected financial strength, as well as on the experience of its management team and a host of other factors, such as trademarks
and its franchise sales history.

The Initial and Ongoing Costs of Franchising

Before examining capital formation strategies, we need to explain the
specific nature of the capital requirements of the early-stage and emerging
franchisor. Although franchising is less capital intensive than is internal

expansion, *franchisors still require a solid capital structure.* Grossly under-capitalized franchisors are on a path to disaster because they will be unable to develop effective marketing programs, attract qualified staff, or provide the high-quality ongoing support and assistance that franchisees need to grow and prosper.

Bootstrap franchising has been tried by many companies, but very few have been successful with it. In a bootstrap franchising program, the franchisor uses the initial franchise fees paid by the franchisee as its capital for growth and expansion. This approach has a catch-22, however, if the franchisor has not properly developed its operations, training program, and materials prior to the offer and sale of a franchise. Such a strategy could subject the franchisor to claims of fraud and misrepresentation because the franchisee has good reason to expect that the business-format franchise is complete, not still under construction. A second legal problem with under-capitalization is that many examiners in the registration states will either completely bar a franchisor from offering and selling in their jurisdictions until the financial condition improves, or they will impose restrictive bonding and escrow provisions in order to protect the fees paid by the franchisee. A third possible legal problem is that if the franchisor is using the franchise offering circular to raise growth capital, then the entire scheme could be viewed as a securities offering, which triggers compliance with federal and state securities laws (as discussed in this chapter).

The start-up franchisor must initially put together a budget for the developmental costs of building the franchise system. This budget should be incorporated into the business plan (see Chapter 12). The start-up costs include the development of operations manuals, training programs, sales and marketing materials, personnel recruitment, accounting and legal fees, research and development, testing and operation of the prototype unit, outside consulting fees, and travel costs for trade shows and sales presentations. Naturally, a number of variables influence the amount that must be budgeted for development costs, including:

- ❐ The extent to which outside consultants are required to develop operations and training materials.
- ❐ The franchisor's location and geographic proximity to targeted franchisees.
- ❐ The complexity of the franchise program and trends in the franchisor's industry.
- ❐ The quality, experience, and fee structure of the legal and accounting firms selected to prepare the offering documents and agreements.
- ❐ The extent to which products or equipment will be sold directly to franchisees, which may require warehousing and shipping capabilities.
- ❐ The extent to which personnel placement firms will be used to recruit the franchisor's management team.
- ❐ The use of a celebrity or industry expert to endorse the franchisor's products, services, and franchise program.

- ❐ The difficulty encountered at the United States Patent and Trademark Office in registering the franchisor's trademarks.

- ❐ The extent to which direct financing will be offered to the franchisees for initial opening and/or expansion.

- ❐ The compensation structure for the franchisor's sales staff.

- ❐ The difficulty encountered by franchise counsel in the registration states.

- ❐ The extent to which the franchisor gets embroiled in legal disputes with the franchisees at an early stage.

- ❐ The quality of the franchisor's marketing materials.

- ❐ The type of media and marketing strategy selected to reach targeted franchisees.

- ❐ The number of company-owned units the franchisor plans to develop.

- ❐ The length and complexity of the franchisor's training program.

- ❐ The rate at which the franchisor will be in a position to repay the capital (or provide a return on investment), which will influence the cost of the capital.

The Capital Formation Process

First and foremost, the franchise management team has to understand that a capital formation strategic plan is *not* the same as a business plan, but rather is one component of the business plan. However, it is a key component, and the management team has to keep certain important facts in mind:

- ❐ They must have a realistic assessment of current growth opportunities; leave the emperor's new clothes at home in the closet.

- ❐ Capital is the fuel that makes the company bigger, better, faster, and more profitable. Without adequate capital, investors will take a pass on the company's shares. Management's job is to demonstrate and prove that investment in their business plan and presentations is prudent and will be profitable.

- ❐ Capital has both a *quantitative* and a *qualitative* cost in terms of the financial dilution of ownership as well as the intangible loss of control.

With this mindset, the team is ready to undertake the capital formation task (see Figure 13-1).

Strategic Planning for the Capital Formation Process

Capital formation is a process (unfolding in stages); *it is not* an event. The franchisor must be prepared to invest the *time* and *resources* into the process. This means, among other things, that the management team must:

Figure 13-1. The capital formation process: Pathways to a closing.

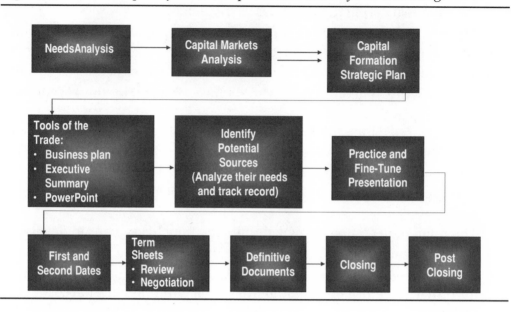

- [ ] Have the *right advisors* in place.
- [ ] Be realistic in their valuation expectations (reflective of industry trends, market conditions, growth plans, operating margins, etc.) to avoid making the enterprise look like a pie-in-the-sky entrepreneurial lark.

In developing the overall capital formation strategy, the franchisor has to make reviews of and decisions about:

- [ ] Using debt as opposed to equity or some hybrid of these sources.
- [ ] Market conditions.
- [ ] The proposed allocation of proceeds and sensitivity analysis.
- [ ] Analysis of current balance sheet.
- [ ] Development and analysis of forecast and growth projects.
- [ ] Needs analysis and timetable (openness to staging).

In addition, regardless of what kind of capital you're raising—or how—any lender, underwriter, venture capitalist, or private investor will expect the franchisor and the management team to be able to prepare a meaningful business plan. That plan will have to address specific financial questions, such as these:

- [ ] What market problems and financial opportunities have you identified?
- [ ] What services, products, and projects are planned to exploit these opportunities or to solve these problems?
- [ ] How much capital will you need to obtain the resources necessary to bring these projects to fruition?

❑ How soon do you really, really need the money?

❑ Exactly how will you *allocate* the capital? How will this infusion of capital increase sales, profits, and the overall value of the company?

❑ How will you meet your debt service obligations and provide a meaningful return on investment to your investors and lenders?

❑ How much equity in the company are you offering to investors? How is it being valued?

❑ What exit strategies will be available to the equity investors?

Other considerations to be addressed in the business plan are listed in Figure 13-2.

Private Placements

Small and medium-sized franchisors often initially turn to the private capital markets to fuel their growth and expansion. The most common method selected is the sale of a company's (or its subsidiary's) securities through a private placement. In general terms, a private placement may be used as a vehicle for capital formation any time a particular security or transaction is exempt from federal registration requirements under the Securities Act of 1933, as amended (as explained shortly).

The private placement generally offers a number of benefits. It entails reduced transactional and ongoing costs because of its exemption from many of the extensive registration and reporting requirements imposed by federal and state securities laws. The private placement usually also offers the ability to structure a more complex and confidential transaction, since the offeree will typically be a small number of sophisticated investors. In addition, a private placement permits a more rapid penetration into the capital markets than would a public offering of securities requiring registration with the Securities and Exchange Commission (SEC). To determine whether a private

Figure 13-2. Strategic assessment of current capitalization table and shareholder list.

Politics

Perceptions and expectations of capital sources

Controls and restrictions

Rights of first refusal

Antidilution rights

Disenchanted or distressed shareholders

State law protections for minority shareholders

Down rounds

Willingness to provide additional capital or "piggybacking"

placement is a sensible strategy for raising capital, franchisors must (1) have a fundamental understanding of the federal and state securities laws affecting private placements, (2) be familiar with the basic procedural steps that must be taken before such an alternative is pursued, and (3) have a team of qualified legal and accounting professionals who are familiar with the securities laws to assist in the offering.

An Overview of Regulation D

The most common exemptions from registration that franchisors rely on in connection with a private placement are contained in the Securities and Exchange Commission's Regulation D of the Securities Act of 1933, as amended. The SEC promulgated Regulation D in 1982 to facilitate capital formation by small companies. Since its inception, Regulation D has been an extremely successful vehicle for raising capital, with billions of dollars being raised each year by small and growing businesses. Regulation D offers a menu of three transaction exemptions:

- ❏ *Rule 504* under Regulation D permits offers and sales of not more than $1 million during any 12-month period by any issuer that is not subject to the reporting requirements of the Securities Exchange Act of 1934, as amended (the Exchange Act), *and* that is not an investment company. Rule 504 places virtually no limit on the number or the nature of the investors that participate in the offering. *But even if accreditation is not required, it is strongly recommended that certain baseline criteria be developed and disclosed in order to avoid unqualified or unsophisticated investors.* Even though no formal disclosure document (also known as a "prospectus") needs to be registered and delivered to offerees under Rule 504, many procedures still must be understood and followed, and a *disclosure document is nevertheless strongly recommended.* An offering under Rule 504 is still subject to the general antifraud provisions of Section 10(b) of the Exchange Act and Rule 10b-5; thus, every document or other information that is actually provided to the prospective investor must be accurate and not misleading by virtue of its content or its omissions in any material respect. The SEC also requires that its Form D be filed for all offerings under Regulation D within 15 days of the first sale and thereafter under certain circumstances. Finally, a growing franchisor seeking to raise capital under Rule 504 should examine applicable state laws very carefully because, although many states have adopted overall securities laws similar to Regulation D, many of them do not include an exemption similar to 504; as a result, a formal memorandum (discussed later in this chapter) may need to be prepared.
- ❏ *Rule 505* under Regulation D is selected over Rule 504 by many companies as a result of its requirements being consistent with many state securities laws. Rule 505 allows for the sale of up to $5 million of the issuer's securities in a 12-month period to an unlimited number of so-

called accredited investors and up to 35 nonaccredited investors (regardless of their net worth, income, or sophistication), but note that the company must satisfy certain information requirements a reasonable time prior to the sale of securities if it sells securities to a nonaccredited investor. An *accredited investor* is any person who qualifies for (and *must* fall within one of) one or more of the eight categories set out in Rule 501(a) of Regulation D. Included in these categories are officers and directors of the franchisor who have policy-making functions, as well as outside investors who meet certain income or net worth criteria. Rule 505 has many of the same filing requirements and restrictions imposed by Rule 504 (such as the need to file a Form D), in addition to an absolute prohibition on advertising and general solicitation for offerings and restrictions on which companies may be an issuer. Any company that is subject to the so-called bad boy provisions of Regulation A is disqualified from being a 505 offeror; this stipulation applies to persons who have been subject to certain disciplinary, administrative, civil, or criminal proceedings, or sanctions that involve the franchisor or its predecessors.

❏ *Rule 506* under Regulation D is similar to Rule 505; however, the issuer may sell its securities to an unlimited number of accredited investors and up to 35 nonaccredited investors. For those requiring large amounts of capital, this exemption is the most attractive because it has no maximum dollar limitation. The key difference under Rule 506 is that any nonaccredited investor must be sophisticated. A *sophisticated investor* (in this context) is one who does not fall within any of the eight categories specified by Rule 501(a) but who is believed by the issuer to "have knowledge and experience in financial and business matters that render him capable of evaluating the merits and understanding the risks posed by the transaction (either acting alone or in conjunction with his 'purchaser representative')." The best way to remove any uncertainty over the sophistication or accreditation of a prospective investor is to request that a comprehensive confidential offeree questionnaire be completed before the securities are sold. If exclusively accredited investors participate in the transaction, Rule 506 eliminates the need to prepare and deliver disclosure documents in any specified format. Like Rule 505, Rule 506 absolutely prohibits advertising and general solicitation.

The Relationship Between Regulation D and State Securities Laws

Full compliance with the federal securities laws is only one level of regulation that must be taken into account when a franchisor is developing plans and strategies to raise capital through an offering of securities. Whether or not the offering is exempt under federal laws, registration may still be required in the states where the securities are to be sold under applicable blue sky laws. This requirement often creates expensive and timely compliance burdens for growing franchisors and their counsel, who must contend with this bifurcated scheme of regulation. Generally speaking, there is a wide variety of standards of review among the states, ranging from very tough merit reviews (designed to ensure that all offerings of securities are fair and equitable) to very lenient notice-only filings (designed primarily to promote full disclosure). The securities laws of each state where an offer or sale will be made should be checked very carefully prior to the distribution of the offering documents.

Subscription Agreement

A private offering under Regulation D requires the preparation of certain subscription documents. The two principal documents are the subscription agreement and the offeree questionnaire.

The subscription agreement represents the contractual obligation of the investor to buy and of the issuer to sell the securities that are the subject of the offering. The subscription agreement should also contain certain representations and warranties by the investor that serve as evidence of the franchisor's compliance with the applicable federal and state securities laws exemptions. The subscription agreement may also contain relevant disclosure issues addressing investment risks and may also contain operative clauses that will enable the franchisor to execute documents and effect certain transactions after the closing of the offering.

Offeree and Purchaser Questionnaires

Offeree questionnaires are developed in order to obtain certain information from prospective offerees, which then serves as evidence of the required sophistication level and the ability to fend for themselves in a private offering. Generally, questionnaires will contain personal information relating to the prospective investor's name, home and business addresses, telephone numbers, age, Social Security number, education, and employment history, as well as investment and business experience. The requested financial information will include the prospective investor's tax bracket, income, and net worth. The offeror must exercise reasonable care and diligence in confirming the truthfulness of the information provided in the questionnaire; however, the offeree should be required to attest to the accuracy of the data provided.

Venture Capital

A rapidly growing franchisor should also strongly consider venture capital. This source of equity financing is suitable when the franchisor needs additional capital to bring its business plans to fruition but lacks the collateral or current ability to meet the debt service payments that are typically required to qualify for traditional debt financing from a commercial bank. This source is especially appropriate for franchisors, whose capital needs are often soft costs such as personnel and marketing, for which debt financing may be very difficult to obtain. Because franchising as a method of expanding a business matures, a growing number of private investors and venture capitalists have been willing to consider a commitment of capital to an emerging franchisor.

The term "venture capital" has been defined in many ways but refers generally to the early-stage financing of young, emerging growth companies at a relatively high risk, which is usually attributable to the newness of the company itself or even the entire industry. The professional venture capitalist is usually a highly trained finance professional who manages a pool of venture funds for investment in growing companies on behalf of a group of passive investors. Another major source of venture capital for growing franchisors is the Small Business Investment Company (SBIC). An SBIC is a privately organized investment firm that is specially licensed under the Small Business Investment Act of 1958 to borrow funds through the Small Business Administration, for subsequent investment in the small business community. Finally, some private corporations and state governments also manage venture funds for investment in growth companies.

Some recent trends in the venture capital industry may increase the chances for early-stage franchisors to obtain venture capital. For example, many venture capital firms have recently expressed an interest in smaller transactions in more traditional industries, with less risk and more moderate (but stable) returns. Many franchisors that do operate in basic industries (e.g., food, hospitality, entertainment, personal services) can meet these investment criteria. There has been a definite shift away from high-tech deals, which largely depend on a single patent or on the completion of successful research and development, and toward investments in more traditional industries, even if the investment results in less dynamic returns.

Negotiating and Structuring the Venture Capital Investment

Assuming that the franchisor's business plan is favorably received by the venture capitalist, the franchisor must then assemble a management team that is capable of negotiating the transaction. The negotiation and structuring of most venture capital transactions revolves around the need to strike a balance between the concerns of the founders of the franchisor, such as dilution of ownership and loss of control, and the concerns of the venture capitalist, such as return on investment and mitigating the risk of business failure.

The typical result of these discussions is a *term sheet,* which sets forth the key financial and legal terms of the transaction, which will then serve as a basis for the negotiation and preparation of the definitive legal documentation. Franchisors should ensure that legal counsel is familiar with the many traps and restrictions that are typically found in venture capital financing documents. The term sheet may also contain certain rights and obligations of the parties. These may include an obligation to maintain an agreed valuation of the franchisor, an obligation to be responsible for certain costs and expenses in the event the proposed transaction does not take place, or an obligation to secure commitments for financing from additional sources prior to closing. Often these obligations will also be included as part of the "conditions precedent" section of the formal investment agreement.

Negotiation regarding the *structure* of the transaction between the franchisor and the venture capitalist will usually revolve around the types of securities to be used and the principal terms, conditions, and benefits offered by the securities. The type of securities ultimately selected and the structure of the transaction will usually fall within one of the following categories:

❐ *Preferred Stock.* This is the most typical form of security issued in connection with a venture capital financing to an emerging franchisor because of its many advantages. Preferred stock can be structured so as to offer an investor convertibility into common stock, dividend and liquidation preferences over the common stock, antidilution protection, mandatory or optional redemption schedules, and special voting rights and preferences.

❐ *Convertible Debentures.* This type of security is basically a debt instrument (secured or unsecured) that may be converted into equity securities under specified terms and conditions. Until converted, it offers the venture capitalist a fixed rate of return and offers tax advantages (e.g., deductibility of interest payments) to the franchisor. A venture capitalist will often prefer a convertible debenture in connection with higher-risk transactions because the venture capitalist is able to enjoy the elevated position of a creditor until the risk of the company's failure has been mitigated. Sometimes these instruments are used in connection with bridge financing, pursuant to which the venture capitalist expects to convert the debt to equity when the subsequent rounds of capital are raised. Finally, if the debentures are subordinated, commercial lenders will often treat them as the equivalent of an equity security for balance sheet purposes, enabling the franchisor to obtain institutional debt financing.

❐ *Debt Securities with Warrants.* Venture capitalists will prefer debentures or notes in connection with warrants often for the same reasons that convertible debt is used, namely the ability to protect their downside by enjoying the elevated position of a creditor and the ability to protect their upside by including warrants to purchase common stock at favorable prices and terms. The use of a warrant enables the investor to buy common stock without sacrificing the position as a creditor, as would be the case if only convertible debt were used in the financing.

❐ *Common Stock.* Venture capitalists will rarely prefer to purchase common stock from the franchisor, especially in the early stages of development. So-called straight common stock offers the investor no special rights or preferences, no fixed return on investment, no special ability to exercise control over management, and no liquidity to protect against downside risks. One of the few times that common stock might be selected is when the franchisor wishes to preserve its Subchapter S status under the Internal Revenue Code, which would be jeopardized if a class of preferred stock were to be authorized. If the company wishes to preserve its Subchapter S status, the company must make sure that the ownership of common stock by the venture capitalist does not jeopardize its status under applicable IRS guidelines.

Once the type of security is selected by the franchisor and the venture capitalist, steps must be taken to ensure that the authorization and issuance of the security are properly effected under applicable state corporate laws. For example, if the franchisor's charter does not provide for a class of preferred stock, then articles of amendment must be prepared, approved by the board of directors and shareholders, and filed with the appropriate state corporation authorities. These articles of amendment will be the focus of negotiation between the franchisor and the venture capitalist in terms of voting rights, dividend rates and preferences, mandatory redemption provisions, antidilution protection (ratchet clauses), and related special rights and features. If debentures are selected, then negotiations will typically focus on term, interest rate and payment schedule, conversion rights and rates, the extent of subordination, remedies for default, acceleration and prepayment rights, and underlying security for the instrument, as well as the terms and conditions of any warrants granted along with the debentures. The legal documents involved in a venture capital financing must reflect the end result of the negotiation between the franchisor and the venture capitalist. These documents will contain all of the legal rights and obligations of the parties, striking a balance between the needs and concerns of the franchisor and the investment objectives and necessary controls of the venture capitalist.

Private Equity Funds

In the closing years of the first decade, a wide variety of institutional and specialized private equity funds emerged to fuel the growth and acquisition of franchising companies. These include specialized funds such as Roark Capital, The Riverside Company, Envest, American Capital Partners, Castle Harlan, and Sentinel Capital. However, many general-purpose private equity funds, such as Bain, Carlyle Group, Thomas H. Lee Partners (who joined together to buy Dunkin' Donuts in March 2006), Nautic, Summit, JHW Greentree Capital, Argosy, Palladium Equity Partners, Sun Capital Partners, and ACON have also taken investment positions in emerging and mature franchisors. The traditional controls and covenants often mirror those of their venture capital brethren, but typically private equity funds will want to own the lion's share of the equity in the company. Be sure to check the firm's typical investment criteria on its Web site to ensure that its deal terms are aligned with your goals and objectives.

To prepare for your first meeting with a private equity fund (and generally to increase the drivers of raising growth capital), the franchisor's leadership team must take the following steps:

❐ Update their strategic plans, business plans, and business model (as discussed in Chapter 12).

❐ Have a strong management team, organizational structure, and succession plan/emergency contingent plan in place.

❏ Be ready to demonstrate a high degree of franchisee satisfaction, loyalty, renewal rates, and overall healthy franchisor-franchisee dynamics, all of which are going to be a key area of the private equity firm's due diligence.

❏ Develop charts and tables to support strong company-owned and franchise unit economics, including overall sales and profitability rates, growth rates, seasonal trends, and the like.

❏ Ensure that the franchisor's financial statements are transparent, well footnoted, and trending in the right direction. Demonstrate that internal controls and accounting clarity are in place to support the accuracy and predictability of the current financials and forecasts.

Debt Financing Alternatives for the Growing Franchisor

Early-stage franchisors have not had much luck with commercial banks over the past two decades because most lenders prefer to see hard collateral on the balance sheet of a borrower, which is often lacking with start-up franchisors who have only their intellectual property, a projected royalty stream, and a business plan to pledge. A second problem is that most lenders prefer to see proceeds allocated primarily to the purchase of hard assets (to further serve as collateral), and this is the opposite of what many franchisors want to do with their capital. Most early-stage franchisors need capital for soft costs, such as the development of manuals, advertising materials, and recruitment fees. Often these banks are more interested in providing financing to the franchisees rather than directly to the franchisor. Certainly these intangible assets can be pledged; however, they are likely to be given far less weight than are equipment, inventory, and real estate. By the time the franchise system has matured to the point that a lender is willing to extend capital based on the franchisor's balance sheet, royalty stream, and track record, the franchisor is likely not to need the capital.

Despite these problems, the optimal capital structure of a growing franchisor will likely include a certain amount of debt on the balance sheet. The use of debt in the capital structure, commonly known as "leverage," will affect both the valuation of the franchisor and its overall cost of capital. The maximum debt capacity that a growing franchisor will ultimately be able to handle usually involves a balancing of the costs and risks of a default of a debt obligation *against* the desire of the owners and managers to maintain control of the enterprise by protecting against the dilution that an equity offering causes. Many franchisors prefer preservation of control over the affairs of their company in exchange for the higher level of risk inherent in taking on additional debt obligations. The ability to meet debt service payments must be carefully considered in the franchisor's financial projections.

If a pro forma analysis reveals that the ability to meet debt service obligations will put a strain on the franchisor's cash flow or that insufficient collateral is available (as is often the case for early-stage franchisors who lack significant tangible assets), then equity alternatives should be explored. Driving the franchisor into voluntary or involuntary bankruptcy solely to maintain a maximum level of control is simply not worthwhile. Overleveraged franchisors typically spend so much of their cash servicing the debt that capital is unavailable to develop new programs and to provide support to the franchisees, triggering the decline and deterioration of the franchise system. In addition, the level of debt financing selected by the franchisor should be compared against key business ratios in its industry, such as those published by Robert Morris Associates or Dun & Bradstreet. Once the optimum debt-to-equity ratio is determined, owners and managers should be aware of the various sources of debt financing as well as the business and legal issues involved in borrowing funds from a commercial lender.

Sources of Debt Financing

Although most franchisors turn to traditional forms of financing such as term loans and operating lines of credit from commercial banks, debt financing comes from a wide variety of sources:

☐ *Trade Credit.* The use of credit with key suppliers is often a practical means of survival for rapidly growing corporate franchisors. When a franchisor has established a good credit rating with its suppliers but as a result of rapid growth requires resources faster than it is able to pay for them, trade credit may become the only way that growth can be sustained. A key supplier has a strong economic incentive for helping a growing franchisor continue to prosper and may therefore be more willing to negotiate credit terms that are acceptable to both parties.

☐ *Equipment Leasing.* Most rapidly growing franchisors are desperately in need of the *use* but not necessarily the *ownership* of certain vital resources to fuel and maintain growth. Therefore, equipment leasing offers an alternative to ownership of the asset. Monthly lease payments are made in lieu of debt service payments. The effective rate of a lease is usually much less than the comparable interest rate for a loan.

☐ *Factoring.* Under the traditional factoring arrangement, a company sells its accounts receivables (or some other income stream such as royalty payments in the case of franchising) to a third party in exchange for immediate cash. The third party, or factor, assumes the risk of collection in exchange for the ability to purchase the accounts receivable at a discount determined by the comparative level of risk. Once notice has been provided to debtors of their obligation to pay the factor directly, the seller of the accounts receivable is no longer liable to the factor in the event of a default, except for a holdback amount retained by the factor to partially offset losses.

☐ *Miscellaneous Sources of Nonbank Debt Financing.* Debt securities such as bonds, notes, and debentures may be offered to venture capitalists, private investors, friends, family, employees, insurance companies, and related financial institutions. Many smaller businesses will turn to traditional sources of consumer credit, such as home equity loans, credit cards, and commercial finance companies to finance the growth of their business. In addition to the Small Business Administration (SBA) loan programs, many state and local governments have created direct loan programs for small businesses.

Although all available alternative sources of debt financing should be actively considered, traditional bank loans from commercial lenders are the most common source of capital for franchisors. Franchisors should take the time to learn the lending policies of the institution, as well as the terms and conditions of the traditional types of loans such as term loans, operating lines of credit, real estate loans, and long-term financing.

Negotiating with Commercial Lenders

Negotiating the financing documents that will be executed by the franchisor in a typical commercial bank loan requires a delicate balancing of the requirements of the lender and the needs of the borrower. The lender will want to have all rights, remedies, and protection available to mitigate the risk of loan default. On the other hand, the franchisor, as borrower, will want to minimize both the amount of collateral given to secure the debt and the level of control exercised by the lender under the affirmative and negative covenants of the loan agreement while achieving a return on its assets that greatly exceeds its debt service payments.

Before examining each document involved in a typical debt financing, you should understand some general rules of loan negotiation:

☐ *Interest Rates.* A banker will generally calculate the rate of interest in accordance with prevailing market rates, the degree of risk inherent in the proposed transaction, the extent of any preexisting relationship with the lender, and the cost of administering the loan.

☐ *Collateral.* The commercial lender may request that certain collateral be pledged that has a value equal to or greater than the proceeds of the loan. When collateral is requested, franchisors should attempt to keep certain key assets of the business outside of the pledge agreement so that they are available to serve as security in the event that additional capital is needed at a later time. Beyond the traditional forms of tangible assets that may be offered to the lender as collateral, borrowers should also consider intangibles such as assignment of lease rights, key person insurance policies, intellectual property, and goodwill. Naturally, the loss of these assets could be very costly to the franchisor in the event of default and should be pledged only as a last resort.

☐ *Prepayment Rights.* Regardless of the actual term of the loan, the borrower should negotiate a right to prepay the principal of the loan without penalty or special repayment charges. Many commercial lenders seek to attach prepayment charges to term loans with a fixed rate of interest in order to ensure that a minimum rate of return is earned over the projected life of the loan.

❑ *Hidden Costs and Fees.* Many commercial banks attempt to charge the borrower a variety of direct and indirect costs and fees in connection with the debt financing. Included in this category are closing costs, processing fees, filing fees, late charges, attorneys' fees, out-of-pocket expense reimbursement (courier, travel, photocopying, etc.), court costs, and auditing or inspection fees.

❑ *Commitment Fees.* Many lenders also charge a fee for issuing a firm commitment to make the loan after conducting its credit review and obtaining credit committee approval to make the loan. Typically, all or some of this is reimbursable if the borrower actually draws the loan.

❑ *Restrictive Covenants.* The typical loan agreement will include a variety of affirmative and negative restrictive covenants designed to protect the interests of the lender. Franchisors should carefully review these covenants to ensure that the implementation of the company's business plan will not be unduly impeded.

Securitization of Income Streams for Established Franchisors

The concept of bringing an established revenue stream to the capital markets to raise capital at an efficient cost is not new—securitization has been around for decades—but when Arby's raised $290 million through the securitization of its royalty stream, new ground was broken in the franchising community for more established systems. Between 2000 and 2010, a number of larger systems turned to securitization transactions to raise money for system expansion, acquisitions, balance sheet restructuring, or retirement/replacement of existing debt obligations at higher borrowing costs, including Domino's Pizza ($1.7 billion), Applebee's ($1.8 billion), Sonic Corporation ($600 million), IHOP ($245 million), Dunkin' Brands ($1.6 billion), Hilton Hotels (over $20 billion) and Quizno's (unpublished size of transaction). The cost of capital over time can be significantly less in comparison to traditional commercial banking options or debt securities offerings—as much as 200 basis points per annum or more, depending on the transaction and the underwriter. The main difference is that the focus shifts away from the franchisor's *own* financial condition and onto the predictability of the royalty streams due to the franchisor from its franchisees. The conversion of your franchise company's royalty streams into marketable securities is a complex transaction; be sure to get the right legal, accounting, and underwriting support and advice.

The Use of Initial Public Offerings by Growing Franchisors

In an initial public offering (IPO), a growing enterprise opts to register its securities with the Securities and Exchange Commission (SEC) for sale to the general investing public for the first time. Many growing franchisors view the process of "going public" as the epitome of financial success and reward. And many national franchisors have successfully completed public offerings and maintained strong market capitalization values over the past decade, including Shoney's (family restaurants), Wendy's International (fast food), TCBY Enterprises (frozen yogurt), Snelling & Snelling (personnel place-ment), McDonald's Corporation (fast food), Medicine Shoppes International (pharmacy stores), Ponderosa (steak houses), Postal Instant Press (printing centers), Service Master (janitorial services), Regis Corp. (hair care), Nathan's Famous (hot dogs), Quizno's (submarine sandwiches), Yum! Brands (multi-ple food brands), Chipotle (spin-off from McDonald's, fast food), Back Yard Burgers (restaurants), 1-800-Flowers (retail and online florists), Buffalo Wild Wings (restaurants), and Amplifon (medical and dental products). However, the decision to go public requires considerable strategic planning and analy-sis from both a legal and a business perspective. The planning and analysis process involves:

❏ A weighing of the costs and benefits of being a public company.
❏ An understanding of the process and costs of becoming a public com-pany.
❏ An understanding of the obligations of the company, its advisors, and its shareholders once the franchisor has successfully completed its public offering.

Costs and Benefits of the IPO

For the rapidly expanding privately held franchisor, the process of going public presents a number of benefits, including:

❏ Significantly greater access to capital.
❏ Increased liquidity for the franchisor's shares.
❏ Greater prestige in the financial markets.
❏ Enhancement of the franchisor's public image (which may have the ef-fect of increasing franchise sales).
❏ Opportunities for employee ownership and participation.
❏ Broadened growth opportunities, including the potential for merger, ac-quisition, and further rounds of financing.
❏ An immediate increase in the wealth of the franchisor's founders.

However, the many benefits of being a public company are not without their corresponding costs, which must be seriously considered in the strate-gic planning process. Among these costs are:

❏ The dilution in the founders' control of the entity.
❏ The pressure to meet market and shareholder expectations regarding growth and dividends.
❏ Changes in management styles and employee expectations.
❏ Compliance with complex regulations such as disclosure obligations imposed by federal and state securities laws.

❏ Stock resale restrictions for company insiders.

❏ Vulnerability to shifts in the stock market.

❏ The sharing of the franchisor's financial success with hundreds, even thousands, of other shareholders.

Many franchisors have not been intimidated by the disadvantages of being publicly held, primarily because they (1) are already operating in a disclosure-oriented business, (2) are already compelled to provide audited financial statements, and (3) feel that being publicly held will increase credibility, thereby generally increasing franchise sales.

Preparing the Registration Statement

The registration statement consists of two parts: the *offering prospectus* (which is used to assist underwriters and investors in analyzing the company and the securities being offered) and the *exhibits and additional information* (which are provided directly to the SEC as part of the disclosure and registration regulations). The registration statement is part of the public record and is available for public inspection.

A variety of alternative forms are used for the registration statement. The alternative form chosen depends on the franchisor's history, size, and nature of the specific offering. The most common form used is Form S-1, which is required for all companies (unless an alternative form is available). The S-1, however, is complicated, has several requirements that must be fulfilled *before* going public, and requires the description of the franchisor's business, properties, material transactions between the company and its officers, pending legal proceedings, plans for distribution of the securities, and the intended use of the proceeds from the IPO. However, also available are Form S-3 (subject to certain requirements) for companies who are already subject to the reporting requirements of the Securities Exchange Act of 1934 (Exchange Act) and Form S-4, which is limited to corporate combinations.

S-1, S-3, and S-4 forms are filed and processed at the SEC's headquarters office in Washington, D.C., by the Division of Corporate Finance.

The SEC's Small Business Initiatives

In 1992, under what was known as Regulation S-B, the SEC implemented the Small Business Initiatives (SBIs), significantly modifying its special provisions for offerings by smaller companies, which may be of benefit to many emerging growth franchisors who are not already subject to the reporting requirements of the Exchange Act. The SBIs were designed to streamline the federal registration process in connection with IPOs to encourage investment in small businesses and disclosure requirements going forward. Regulation S-B was repealed in its entirety, effective March 15, 2009.

Currently, companies that qualify as "smaller reporting companies" may benefit from employing the recently adopted scaled disclosure requirements in Regulation S-K, which in many respects incorporate the scaled disclosure requirements found in the former Regulation S-B. Companies that have a public float of less than $75 million or that do not have a public float but have revenues of less than $50 million during the most recent fiscal year qualify as smaller reporting companies.

Regardless of which form is ultimately selected, a series of core procedural rules and disclosure items must be addressed.

The Key Elements

The key disclosure areas of the registration statement are as follows:

- ❏ *Cover Page/Forepart.* The SEC has very specific requirements as to the information that *must* be stated on the cover page and forepart of the prospectus. This includes summary information pertaining to the nature of the franchisor's business, the terms of the offering, the determination of the offering price, dilution, plan of distribution, risk factors, and selected financial information.

- ❏ *Introduction to the Company.* This is an overview of the company, its business, employees, financial performance, and principal offices.

- ❏ *Risk Factors.* This section is a description of the operating and financial risk factors affecting the franchisor's business with particular regard to the offering of the securities (such as depending on a single customer, supplier, or key personnel), the absence of operating history in the new areas of business that the franchisor wants to pursue, an unproven market for the products and services offered, or a lack of earnings history.

- ❏ *Use of Proceeds.* This section explains the anticipated use of the proceeds to be raised by the offering.

- ❏ *Capitalization.* This is a description of the capital structure of debt obligations, the company's anticipated dividend policy, and dilution of purchaser's (investor's) equity.

- ❏ *Description of Business and Property.* In this part, describe the key assets, principal lines of business, human resources, properties, marketing strategies, and competitive advantages of the company, and any of its subsidiaries, for the last five years.

- ❏ *Management and Principal Shareholders.* This section contains a discussion of the key management team and description of each member's background, education, compensation, and role in the company, as well as a table of all shareholders who hold a beneficial interest of 5 percent or more.

- ❏ *Litigation.* This is a statement of any material litigation (either past, pending, or anticipated) affecting the franchisor or any other adverse legal proceedings that would affect an investor's analysis of the securities being offered.

- ❏ *Financial Information.* This section is a summary of financial information such as sales history, net income or losses from operations, long-term debt obligations, dividend patterns, capital structure, founder's equity, and shareholder loans.

❑ *Securities Offered and Underwriting Arrangements.* Here is a description of the underwriting arrangements, distribution plan. and the key characteristics of the securities being offered.

❑ *Experts and Other Matters.* A brief statement is made about the identity of the attorneys, accountants, and other experts retained as well as the availability of additional information from the registration statement filed with the SEC (such as indemnification policies for the directors and officers, recent sales of unregistered securities, a breakdown of the expenses of the offering, and a wide variety of corporate documents and key agreements).

An Overview of the Registration Process

When the initial draft of the registration statement is ready for filing with the SEC, you have two choices: either file the document with the transmittal letter and required fees *or* schedule a prefiling conference with an SEC staff member to discuss any anticipated questions or problems regarding the disclosure document or the accompanying financial statements.

The initial registration process is generally governed by the Securities Act, which is designed to ensure full and fair disclosure of material facts to prospective investors in connection with the offer and sale of securities. The Securities Act requires the company to file a registration statement with the SEC in addition to providing a prospectus to prospective investors.

Once the registration statement is officially received by the SEC, it is then assigned to an examining group (composed usually of attorneys, accountants, and financial analysts, within a specific industry department of the Division of Corporate Finance). The length of time and depth of the review by the examining group will depend on the history of the company and on the nature of the securities offered. For example, a company that operates in a troubled or turbulent industry and that is publicly offering its securities for the first time should expect a detailed review by all members of the examining group.

Following the initial review, a deficiency or comment letter will be sent, suggesting changes to the registration statement. The modifications of the statement will focus on the quality of the disclosure (such as an adequate discussion of risk factors or the verbiage in management's discussion of the financial performance), not on the quality of the company or the securities being offered. In most cases, the company will be required to file a material amendment to address the staff's concerns. This process continues until all concerns raised by the examining group have been addressed. The final pricing amendment is filed following the pricing meeting of the underwriters and the execution of the final underwriting agreement. The SEC has developed detailed regulations and restrictions on what information may be released to the public or the media during this period (the so-called quiet period), especially communications that appear to be designed to influence the price of the shares. The registration statement then is declared effective, and the securities can be offered to the public. The registration statement is declared effective 20 days after the final amendment has been filed, unless the effective date is accelerated by the SEC. Most companies tend to seek an accelerated effective date, which is usually made available if the company has complied with the examining group's suggested modifications.

In addition to SEC regulations, a company offering its securities to the public must also meet the requirements of NASD and state securities laws. NASD will analyze all elements of the proposed corporate package for the underwriter to determine its fairness and reasonableness. The SEC will not deem a registration statement effective for public offering unless and until the NASD has approved the underwriting arrangements as being fair and reasonable.

Section 18 of the Securities Act states that federal securities laws do not supersede the jurisdiction of any state securities commission to investigate and bring enforcement actions with respect to fraud, deceit, or unlawful conduct by a broker or dealer. Although various exemptions from formal registration are often available, the state securities laws must be checked very carefully as to the filing fees, registered agent requirements, disclosure obligations, and underwriter or broker/dealer regulations for each state in which the securities will be offered.

The Closing and Beyond

Once the final underwriting agreement is signed and the final pricing amendment is filed with the SEC, the registration statement will be declared effective and the selling process begins. Throughout the selling period, the franchisor must *wait patiently* and hope that any minimum sales quotas (such as for all-or-nothing offerings) are met and that the offering is well received by the investing public.

To facilitate the mechanics of the offering process, you may want to consider retaining the services of a registrar and transfer agent who will be responsible for issuing stock certificates, maintaining stockholder ownership records, and processing the transfer of shares from one investor to another. These services are usually offered by commercial banks and trust companies (which also offer ongoing support services such as annual report and proxy mailing, disbursement of dividends, and custody of the authorized but unissued stock certificates). Once the offer and sale of the shares to the public have been completed, a closing must be scheduled to exchange documents, issue stock certificates, and disburse net proceeds.

In addition to the obligations discussed previously, you are usually required to report the company's use of the proceeds raised from the sale of the securities on the first periodic report filed under the Exchange Act through the disclosure of the application of all the offering proceeds or disclosure of the termination of the offering, whichever is later. *The information should be substantially similar to the discussion contained in the prospectus provided to prospective investors.*

Ongoing Reporting and Disclosure Requirements

The Exchange Act generally governs the ongoing disclosure and periodic reporting requirements of publicly traded companies. Section 13 grants broad powers to the SEC to develop documents and reports that must be filed. The three primary reports required by Section 15(d) are as follows:

- ❏ *Form 10-K* is the *annual* report that must be filed within 60 days after the close of the company's fiscal year covered by the report for a large accelerated filer, 75 days for an accelerated filer, or 90 days for all other companies. It must also include a report of all significant activities of the company during its fourth quarter, an analysis and discussion of the financial condition, a description of the current officers and directors, and a schedule of certain exhibits. The 10-K requires issuer's income, cash flows and changes in stockholders' equity for the prior three years, and the balance sheets for the prior two years, *provided* that a "smaller reporting company" may submit an audited balance sheet at the end of each of the most recent two fiscal years, and audited statements of income, cash flows, and changes in stockholders' equity for each of the two fiscal years preceding the date of the most recent audited balance sheet.

- ❏ *Form 10-Q* is the *quarterly* report that must be filed no later than 40 days for large accelerated filers and accelerated filers and 45 days for all other companies after the end of each of the first three fiscal quarters of each fiscal year. This quarterly filing includes copies of quarterly financial statements (accompanied by a discussion and analysis of the company's financial condition by its management) and a report as to any litigation as well as any steps taken by the company that affect shareholder rights or that may require shareholder approval. The 10-Q requires an issuer's:
  - ❏ Balance sheet from the previous year and a report of the most recent fiscal quarter.
  - ❏ Statements of income for the most recent quarter, for the period between the end of the previous year and the end of the most recent quarter, and for corresponding periods of the previous year.
  - ❏ Statements of cash flows for the period between the end of the previous year and the end of the most recent quarter, and for corresponding periods of the previous year, *provided* that a "smaller reporting company" may provide other information in accordance with Rule 8-03 of Regulation S-X.

- ❏ *Form 8-K* is a report designed to ensure that *all material information* pertaining to significant events affecting the company is disclosed to the investing public as soon as it is available, but not later than 4 days (unless otherwise specified in Form 8-K) after the occurrence of the particular event that triggers the need to file Form 8-K.

The duty to disclose *material information* (whether as part of a Form 8-K filing or otherwise) to the general public is an ongoing obligation that continues for as long as the company's securities are publicly traded. An ongoing compliance program must be established to ensure that all material corporate information is disclosed as fully and as promptly as possible. A *fact* is generally considered to be material if there is a substantial likelihood that a reasonable shareholder would consider it important in his or her investment decision (whether to buy, sell, or hold or how to vote on a particular proposed corporate action). The following kinds of information are examples of what is typically considered material for disclosure purposes:

- ❐ Acquisitions and dispositions of other companies or properties
- ❐ Public or private sales of debt or equity securities
- ❐ Bankruptcy or receivership proceedings affecting the issuer
- ❐ Significant contract awards or *terminations*
- ❐ Changes in the key management team

Pursuant to Section 12(g), certain companies of publicly traded securities are subject to additional reporting and disclosure requirements. For example, if a company either elects to register its securities under 12(g) or has issued a class of equity security (other than an exempted security) held by more than 500 shareholders and at least $1 million worth of total assets, then it will also be subject to the rules developed by the SEC for (a) proxy solicitation, (b) reporting of beneficial ownership, (c) liability for short-swing transactions, and (d) tender offer rules and regulations.

- ❐ *Proxy Solicitation.* Due to the difficulty of assembling each and every shareholder of a corporation for matters that require a shareholder vote, voting by proxy is a fact of life for most publicly held corporations. When soliciting the proxies of shareholders for voting at annual or special meetings, special statutory rules must be carefully followed. The request for the proxy must be accompanied by a detailed proxy statement that should specify the exact matters to be acted upon and any information that would be required by the shareholder in reaching its decision.

- ❐ *Reporting of Beneficial Ownership.* Section 16(a) requires that all officers, directors, and 10 percent shareholders (if any) file a statement of beneficial ownership of securities. Filed on Form 3, the statement must reflect all holdings (direct and indirect). Section 16(a) also requires that whenever the officers and directors increase or decrease their holdings by purchase, sale, gift, or otherwise, the transaction must be reported on Form 4 no later than the second business day following the day of the transaction.

- ❐ *Liability for Short-Swing Transactions.* Section 16(b) requires that officers, directors, employees, or other insiders return to the company any profit that they may have realized from any combination of sales and purchases, or from purchases and sales, of securities made by them within any six-month period. Any acquisition of securities (regardless of form of payment) is considered to be a purchase. The purpose of

Section 16(b) is to discourage even the possibility of directors and officers taking advantage of inside information by speculating in a company's stock. Liability is automatic if a sale and purchase take place within six months, even if the individual involved in the transaction did not actually take advantage of inside information.

❏ *Tender Offer Rules and Regulations.* Sections 13 and 14 generally govern the rules for parties who wish to make a tender offer to purchase the securities of a publicly traded corporation. Any person acquiring (directly or indirectly) beneficial ownership of more than 5 percent of an equity security registered under Section 12 must report the transaction by filing a Schedule 13D within 10 days from the date of acquisition. Schedule 13D requires disclosure of certain material information such as the identity and background of the purchaser, the purpose of the acquisition, the source and amount of funds used to purchase the securities, and disclosure of the company. If the purchase is in connection with a tender offer, then the provisions of Section 14(d) also apply, pursuant to which the terms of the tender offer must be disclosed (as well as the plans of the offerer if it is successful and the terms of any special agreements between the offerer and the target company). Section 14(e) imposes a broad prohibition against the use of false, misleading, or incomplete statements in connection with a tender offer.

Rule 10b-5 and Insider Trading

A great deal of attention has been devoted by the business and financial press to the SEC's Rule 10b-5 and its application in the prosecution of insider trading cases. Here's the text of the rule:

It shall be unlawful for any person, directly or indirectly, by the use of any means or instrumentality of interstate commerce, or of the mails or of any facility of any national securities exchange:

(a) to employ any device, scheme, or artifice to defraud;

(b) to make any untrue statement of a material fact or to omit to state a material fact necessary in order to make the statements made, in light of the circumstances under which they were made, not misleading; or

(c) to engage in any act, practice, or course of business which operates or would operate as a fraud or deceit upon any person,

in connection with the purchase or sale of any security.

The most frequent use of Rule 10b-5 has been in insider trading cases, typically those in which an officer, director, or other person who has a fiduciary relationship with a corporation buys or sells the company's securities while in the possession of material, nonpublic information. However, Rule 10b-5 is also used in a variety of other situations, such as when:

❏ A corporation issues *misleading* information to the public or keeps silent when it has a duty to disclose.

❐ An insider *selectively* discloses material, nonpublic information to an-other party, who then trades securities based on the information (gener-ally called "tipping").

❐ A person *mismanages* a corporation in ways that are connected with the purchase or sale of securities.

❐ A *securities* firm or another person manipulates the market for a security traded in the over-the-counter market.

❐ A securities firm or securities *professional* engages in certain other forms of conduct connected with the purchase or sale of securities.

Therefore, all officers, directors, employees, and shareholders of pub-licly traded companies (or companies considering being publicly traded) must be keenly aware of the broad scope of this antifraud rule in their trans-actions that involve the company.

Disposing of Restricted Securities

All shares of a public company held by its controlling persons [which typi-cally includes its officers, directors, and 10 percent shareholders (if any)] are deemed "restricted securities" under the Securities Act. The sale of restricted securities is generally governed by Rule 144, which generally re-quires, in the case of a public company's nondebt securities, as a condition of sale that:

❐ The company be current in its periodic reports to the SEC during the 12 months preceding the sale.

❐ The restricted securities have been beneficially owned for at least six months preceding the sale.

❐ The amount of securities that may be sold in any three-month period be limited to the greater of 1 percent of the outstanding class of securities *or* the average weekly reported volume of trading in the securities on a registered national security exchange (if the securities are listed).

❐ The securities be sold only in brokers' transactions or transactions di-rectly with a market maker, and the notice of the sale be filed with the SEC concurrently with the placing of the sale order in the case of a broker or the execution directly with a market maker.

❐ If the sale in reliance on Rule 144 during any three-month period in-volves 5,000 shares or $50,000, a report of the transaction on Form 144 must be filed.

Due to relatively recent changes in the law, the conditions may vary depending on the facts, and therefore securities counsel should be consulted to ensure compliance with Rule 144. The franchisor and the managers must understand the planning and registration process prior to pursuing a public offering of the company's securities. A substantial amount of time and ex-pense can be saved if the process of planning begins early in the development, methods of operation, and formulation of strategies for the company's growth. As with any contemplated method of capital formation, going public has its costs and benefits, all of which should be carefully weighed and understood by the franchisor's management and advisory team prior to selling the first share of stock to the public.

Understanding Financing Programs to Fuel Franchisee and Area Developer Growth

In addition to equity-driven capital formation strategies, franchisors may want to access the debt markets to finance the development of additional company-owned units and/or to fuel its own growth. Such capital formation alternatives can be made available to its franchisees and area developers, which will in turn become sources of capital for the franchisor in the form of new initial franchise fees and royalties.

When franchisees and area developers look for capital to build initial and additional units, the traditional sources of debt financing from commercial lenders are not the only choices. There are a wide range of choices:

❑ *Leasing.* A leasing company (the lessor) acquires real estate, equipment, or other fixed assets, then executes a contract with the franchisee as the user of the asset. The lessee makes fixed payments to the lessor for a specified time. Leasing provides a flexible, creative alternative to purchasing property.

❑ *Factoring.* Factors typically purchase the franchisee's receivables, usually at a significant discount. Let's say the franchisee has the opportunity to expand, but not enough cash to do so. If the franchisee has outstanding receivables from reliable customers, they might be able to find a factor who will give them a percentage of those receivables in cash right away, in exchange for 100 percent of the receivables when they are paid. Factoring is a risk-driven business; depending on the overall conditions of your industry and the relative risks in collecting from the people who owe the franchisee's business money, factors will discount the value of the receivables significantly. Factoring is an expedient option when other short-term financing, such as a working capital loan or revolving line of credit, is unavailable.

❑ *Small Business Administration (SBA) Guaranteed Loans.* These are administered by a federal agency created to provide financial assistance to businesses that lack access to capital markets (stock and bond markets) enjoyed by larger, more creditworthy corporations.

❑ *State and Local Programs.* In an effort to improve their local economies, most states, as well as many municipalities and counties, sponsor a variety of public funding sources for specialized small business concerns. At the state level, nearly all states have some form of state economic development agency or state finance authority that make loans or guarantees to small businesses. State commerce departments often have direct or participating loan programs that may be even more attractive than SBA-guaranteed loan programs. Many specialized programs are geared toward helping women and minorities at the state level. Since programs differ from state to state, it would be impractical to describe all of them here.

Leasing

Regardless of changes in tax laws and accounting regulations, leasing's greatest appeal continues to be that it permits companies to acquire assets with very little or no down payment. Most rapidly growing franchisees and area developers are in need of the use, but not necessarily the ownership, of certain resources to fuel and maintain growth. Therefore, leasing offers an alternative to ownership. Monthly lease payments are made in lieu of debt service payments.

Types of Leases

There are two types of leases: operating leases and finance leases. Most leases for small office equipment—fax machines, copiers, and the like—are operating leases, in which ownership of the machines reverts to the vendor at the end of the lease term. For tax purposes, operating lease payments are treated as an operating expense, not as a capital investment, and are deducted immediately from your operating revenues. In addition, the lease does not appear as a liability on your balance sheet, as a loan to purchase the same equipment would. That may make it easier for you to borrow money in the future.

Finance leases, also known as full-payout or closed-end leases, require you to purchase the equipment at the end of the lease period at a percentage of the original price or for a nominal amount. Because a finance lease is, in effect, a loan in which ownership eventually passes to you, the equipment is treated for tax purposes as a depreciable asset, and the lease will appear on your balance sheet as a liability.

In deciding which option is best for franchisees, the key factors are their cash position, the availability and cost of borrowing, and the potential obsolescence of equipment. Franchisees with strong cash positions and good banking relationships are often best served by buying or borrowing equipment that will have a long life. If obsolescence is a concern, a short-term operating lease will bring flexibility. But if cash flow is a problem and the equipment will remain viable for years, a long-term finance lease with a final residual payment will give you the lowest payments plus a purchase option.

Who Should Lease?

Financing new equipment—from computers to phone systems to capital equipment—is a major issue for many business owners. Franchisees might want to consider leasing even if they have the cash to purchase the assets they need to grow their business. By leasing, they might find that they can regulate their cash flow more effectively because they have predictable, regular monthly installments as opposed to a single lump-sum payment, thereby ensuring that royalty payments are made to the franchisor on a timely basis.

Advantages and Disadvantages of Leasing

❑ *Ownership.* The most obvious downside to leasing is that when the lease runs out, the leasee does not own the equipment. Of course, this may also be an advantage, particularly for equipment like computers where technology needs may change very quickly.

❑ *Total Expense.* Leasing is almost always more expensive than buying, assuming you don't need a loan to make the purchase. For example, a three-year lease for a $5,000 computer system (at a typical rate of $40 per month per $1,000) will cost you a total of $7,200 when that same computer could be *purchased* for at least half that price.

❑ *Finding Funds.* Lease arrangements are usually more liberal than loans. Although a bank might require two or three years of business records before granting a loan, many leasing companies evaluate your credit history on shorter terms (six months is fairly typical). This can be a significant advantage for a start-up business.

❑ *Cash Flow.* This is the primary advantage to leasing. It eliminates a large, single expense that may drain your cash flow, freeing funds for other day-to-day needs.

❑ *Taxes.* Leasing almost always allows the franchisee to expense its equipment costs, meaning that your lease payments can be deducted as business expenses. On the other hand, buying may allow you to deduct up to $18,000 worth of equipment in the year it is purchased (as part of first-year's accounting as an expense; anything above that amount gets depreciated over several years). With the first-year expense deduction, the "real cost" of a $5,000 computer system may be only $3,400.

❑ *Technology Needs.* Technology advances at a rapid rate. If the franchisee buys a computer or other high-tech equipment outright, it may find itself with outdated equipment in two or three years, with no discernible re-sale value. Leasing may allow the franchisee to try out new equipment and update its system regularly to stay on top of the technology curve.

The Process

An effective way to organize the process is to send a simple fill-in-the-blank bid form to several leasing companies you think might be interested in getting your business. Larger companies do that all the time, and you can do it too. Prospective lessors will still need to do thorough credit checks, but with a well-designed bid form, the rest of the process should be greatly streamlined. Figure 13-3 shows a model bid form.

Figure 13-3. Bid request form. The upper shaded area is filled in by the company requesting the bid. The lower, unshaded area is filled in by the prospective lessor.

Company name:	For the record, tell lessors the name of the entity seeking leasing information.
Product:	Supply name of equipment manufacturer and model number.
Features:	Indicate any additional features that might increase or decrease the resale value.
Cost to company:	Tell lessors the best price quoted for equipment listed.
List price:	What does it list for? This may influence the residual value at the end of the lease.
Lease start date:	When do you propose to start making payments? For comparison, you want everyone on the same schedule.
Payment frequency:	Specify how you propose to pay (for example, monthly, in advance or in arrears). Leasing companies may have other preferences; you want all bidders to use the same assumptions.
Bid due date:	To simplify the process, give everyone the same deadline. As a courtesy, tell lessors either here or elsewhere on the form when the winner will be notified.
Lease term:	Tell lessors how long you aim to use the equipment for, recognizing there are some standards. (Leases on equipment that is not so technologically sensitive tend to be longer than those on, say, computers.) If you like, you can ask lessors to price more than one lease term.
Notes:	If there are any other considerations you want lessors to be aware of (for instance, that the lease should be structured as an operating lease or full-payout lease), note them here.
Bidder:	The name of the leasing company submitting the bid.
Lease rate:	You want lessors to quote you a specific price for the term (or terms) you ask for.
Signature:	Make sure it's signed by someone with the authority to stand behind it (as opposed to a salesperson).
Date:	Even though this isn't a contract, you want it dated to provide a time frame. Most bidders will make commitments with expiration dates.

Lease Terms

Here are some issues to look for when the franchisee or area developer negotiates its lease or in the franchisor's review of the lease contract:

❐ *Length of the Lease.* This is often called the "term" of the lease and is usually between 12 and 36 months. The shorter the term of the lease is, the higher the monthly payments will be. For a computer lease, 36 months is typical, although the franchisor might want to look at a 24-month lease to keep up with changing technology.

❐ *Total Cost.* Analyze all the charges for which you will be accountable over the term of the lease. These include your initial down payment, monthly payments, a security deposit, any insurance charges, and service or repair costs.

❐ *Cancellation Clause.* This allows you to break your lease, although you will be liable for substantial penalties. This way, if you close your business, change its focus, or no longer need a piece of equipment, you will not be liable for the entire term of the lease.

❐ *Assignment.* Find out if the franchisee can assign the lease to another party, and, if so, what are the costs of the transfer? For example, if you are selling or reorganizing all or part of your company, you want to factor these costs in as part of the transaction.

❐ *Modern Equipment Substitution.* If technology changes rapidly, the franchisee might want to consider this option. This allows you to update or exchange your equipment so you don't get stuck with something that is obsolete.

❐ *Service Plans.* Find out if the franchisee's lease comes with an on-site service plan, and, if so, determine its length. If the lease includes only one year of on-site service, you may need to buy a service contract for the remainder of the lease; otherwise, you will be responsible for all repairs yourself after the first 12 months. Also, be sure the contract spells out when the service will be performed (ideally, the next business day after you've notified them of the problem).

When a Lease Is Not a Lease

Read the fine print of any lease you sign. The IRS considers some leases as capital purchases, which means you cannot deduct your monthly payments. A capital purchase has occurred if the terms of your lease agreement are constructed so that you meet one of the following criteria:

❐ The franchisee has a "bargain buyout," that is, the franchisee can purchase the machine for a token amount at the end of the lease.

❐ The franchisee is leasing the machine for 75 percent of its useful life.

❐ The total amount paid for the equipment during the period of the lease equals more than 90 percent of the fair market value of the machine. Keep in mind that payments include finance charge and sales tax. Remember to deduct these charges to find the true price you paid for the equipment.

Where Do I Find a Lessor?

For a list of lessors, contact the Equipment Leasing and Finance Association at 1825 K Street NW, Suite 900, Washington, DC 20006, 202-238-3400, www.elfaonline.org.

Factoring

The roots of factoring can be traced back 4,000 years to the time of Hammurabi when ancient merchants would sell their accounts receivables to a third-party financier at a discount. Surprisingly, modern-day factoring is very similar to the way it was back then. It is simply the process of purchasing accounts receivable, or invoices, from a business at a discount. Factoring provides the business with immediate cash and earns investors a desirable rate of return on their money. In modern times, factoring was originally used in the garment industry. Then World War II came along and created a need for the financing of war materials. Congress subsequently passed the Uniform Commercial Code (UCC), which allows business owners to file a lien on receivables of inventory. Factoring then took root in manufacturing, and it has expanded into other industries, including distribution, business-to-business services, high tech, and health care.

Factoring's swift growth can be attributed to toughened loan requirements and the difficulties start-up and growing companies have in obtaining capital. An increasing number of small and midsized companies are turning to it as a cash management tool. They have learned what big corporations have known all along: Factoring is a viable solution to a need nearly every business has, and its benefits often outweigh its costs.

If most companies have a single point of vulnerability, it is accounts receivable. Entrepreneurial companies almost invariably make the mistake—especially in their early or fast-growth stages—of paying much more attention to making sales than to collecting receivables.

Under the traditional factoring arrangement, a company sells its accounts receivables to a third party in exchange for immediate cash. The third party, or factor, assumes the risk of collection in exchange for the ability to purchase the accounts receivable at a discount, typically 50 to 95 percent, of the face value of the invoices. The amount of the discount is usually determined by the level of risk that debtors will default and by prevailing interest rates. Once the factor collects the balance, he returns the 20–40 percent discount to the company, minus a 3–5 percent fee.

Types of Factoring

There are two basic types of factoring agreements: recourse and nonrecourse. In a recourse agreement, you agree to repurchase or pay for any invoices the factor cannot collect from your customers. The factor still agrees to advance money, take on the collection responsibility, and earns a fee for it. But if the customer does not pay, the invoices are turned back to you for payment. This eliminates any financial risk for the factor. For example, assume the factoring agreement is a recourse agreement and the factor failed to collect $10,000 of the receivables. The franchisor pays the factor the $10,000, and the receivable comes back for collection from the customer.

The nonrecourse agreement has no repurchase or repayment provision. In other words, the factor owns the invoice once it has been purchased, whether it's collectible or not. In this case, if the factor fails to collect the $10,000 from the customers, the factor is out the money; the franchisor does not have to pay the factor or try to collect from the customer. To compensate for this additional risk, the factoring fee on a nonrecourse agreement is slightly higher than on a recourse agreement, typically 10 to 20 percent.

Under a nonrecourse agreement, factors are not obliged to buy every invoice the client presents. They can reject invoices from customers they deem to be uncreditworthy.

Factoring can help the following types of companies:

- ❐ *New Companies.* Early-stage companies often lack the financial track record required for bank financing.

- ❐ *High-Growth Companies.* Factoring can benefit companies that are growing so quickly that traditional loans are unavailable. Fast growth often demands cash. Cash flow may be negative as a company's receivables and payables expand faster than its cash flow allows. The bank may reject such a company because a fast-growth company presents a higher risk than a stable-growth company, especially if the receivables are not controlled properly.

- ❐ *Turnaround Situations.* Companies that have a glitch in operations can use factoring to reposition.

- ❐ *Seasonal Businesses.* Factoring can benefit seasonal businesses such as textiles, carpet, electronics, and clothing. Seasonal businesses may have a cash crunch at certain times of the year, which makes them natural candidates for factoring.

Advantages of Factoring

- ❐ *Unlimited Capital.* The only financing source that grows with your sales (that we know of) is factoring. This allows you to constantly have the ability to meet increasing demand; so as sales increase, more money becomes immediately available to you.

- ❐ *No Debt Incurred.* Factoring is not a loan, so you do not incur any debt. This can make for a very attractive balance sheet and make it easier to obtain other financing or, ultimately, to sell the company.

- ❐ *Elimination of Bad Debt.* The risk of bad debt can be fully assumed by a nonrecourse factor, thus eliminating this expense from your income statement.

- ❐ *No Loss of Business Equity.* Ownership percentages are unchanged with a factoring arrangement (unlike most venture capital arrangements).

- ❐ *Ability to Offer Credit Terms to Your Customers.* Factoring allows your business to be more competitive by offering credit terms to potential and current customers without the risk of a negative cash flow impact.

- ❐ *Leverage off Your Customers' Credit.* The franchisee does not need to be creditworthy to factor its invoices. In fact, it does not have to be in business for three years, be profitable, or meet any other conventional lender qualifications to factor. The company only needs to have a creditworthy customer, and it can qualify for a factoring arrangement.

❑ *Establish Good Credit for Your Business.* Paying the franchisee's company's bills in a timely manner (including the royalties to the franchisor) is less of a challenge with improved cash flow. Factoring makes cash immediately available to keep cash flow steady.

❑ *Invoice Processing Service.* The franchisor can greatly reduce the franchisee's cost of processing invoices because factors handle much of the work. Mailing invoices (addressing envelopes, stuffing them, paying for postage), posting invoices to a computer system, depositing checks, entering payments on the computer, and producing regular reports can all be delegated to the factor.

❑ *Professional Collections.* A good factor can handle collections more professionally and more productively than most companies can internally. This could translate into further cost savings for your business.

❑ *Factoring Is Easy and Fast.* The franchisee doesn't need tax returns, personal financial statements, business plans, or projections to process a factoring application. Usually, your account is established in about one week of the receipt of signed contracts. Thereafter, accepted invoices are converted to cash within 24 hours. Bureaucracy prohibits banks from processing loans that fast.

Disadvantages of Factoring

❑ *Risk of Fiscal Addiction.* If the franchisee is not careful, the franchisee's company can get caught in a vicious cycle. Over time, the cost of factoring may eat away at profits to the point that the company factors again, just to pay for next month's operations. A cash flow consultant can sometimes help, for example, by figuring out a way to stretch vendors out a bit further or by suggesting a line of credit. These options may eventually wean your company away from factoring.

❑ *Intrusion.* Some owners perceive factoring as intrusive because the factoring company verifies and monitors collection of receivables.

❑ *Cost.* Factored capital tends to be more expensive than loans from banks. The two basic charges are a commission for a factored agreement and interest on a bank loan. The commission varies according to the volume of invoices, the average size of the invoice, and analysis of your customer list. The bank's interest rate varies according to prevailing rates and the financial strength of your company.

What Do Factors Look For?

Companies considering factoring should have a variety of creditworthy customers and solid financial statements. Factors often judge the strength of a company by the quality and distribution of its customers. Your company's financial strength and management will be analyzed. Having professionals on your team (such as CPAs, attorneys, and financial consultants) can help maintain orderly financial statements.

Where Do I Find a Factor?

To find a factoring company, look in The *Edwards Directory of American Factors*, published by Edwards Research Group, Inc., P.O. Box 95101, Newton, MA 02195, 1-800-963-1993, mace@edwardsresearch.com, or contact the Commercial Finance Association at 370 Seventh Avenue, Suite 1801, New York, NY 10001, 212-792-9390, www.cfa.com. The Commercial Finance Association is an international and national trade association for the asset-based financial services industry, including factors.

SBA Programs

The Small Business Administration (SBA) offers a wide range of programs for all types of businesses at various stages of development and provides a significant number of loan guaranties for franchisee-related projects every year. Since 1953, the SBA has helped 20 million Americans start, gain, and expand their businesses, placing more than $170 billion in direct or guaranteed loans. In 2007, the SBA guaranteed nearly 100,000 loans for over $14 billion under its 7(a) program, with an average loan of $143,000. These include the 7(a) Loan Guaranty, Microloan, and the 504 Certified Development Company (CDC) loans. (See Figure 13-4.) These loans are increasingly made to franchising companies because they are viewed as a powerful economic development tool, particularly in communities with average incomes below the poverty line.

Although the SBA oversees the programs from the agency's Washington, D.C., headquarters, commercial lenders nationwide actually issue the loans

Figure 13-4. SBA programs.

7(a) Loan Guaranty	The 7(a) Loan Guaranty Program is SBA's primary and most flexible lending program, according to the SBA Web site. It provides loans to start-up and existing small businesses unable to secure financing on reasonable terms through normal lending channels. The program operates through private-sector lenders that provide loans that are, in turn, guaranteed by the SBA, which has no funds for direct lending or grants.
Veteran Programs	Designed to increase the capital available to veterans starting businesses seeking loans up to $500,000 at very accessible rates.
Export Loans	A loan and technical assistance program to help small businesses gain access to export financing and support.
Certified Development Company (504 Loan) Program	This program, commonly referred to as the 504 program, makes long-term fixed-rate loans available for purchasing land, buildings, and machinery and equipment, and for building, modernizing, expanding, or renovating existing facilities and sites. In 2007, the average 504 Loan was $592,000.

and handle the paperwork. To participate in the SBA programs, commercial lenders must be licensed by the SBA.

The most active and expert lenders qualify for the SBA's streamlined lending programs. Under these programs, lenders are delegated partial or full authority to approve loans, which results in faster service from the SBA.

- ❐ *Certified lenders* are those who have been heavily involved in regular SBA loan-guarantee processing and have met certain other criteria. They receive a partial delegation of authority and are given a three-day turnaround by the SBA on their applications (they may also use regular SBA loan processing). Certified lenders account for nearly a third of all SBA business loan guaranties.

- ❐ *Preferred lenders* are chosen from among the SBA's best lenders and enjoy full delegation of lending authority in exchange for a reduced amount of the SBA guarantee. This lending authority must be renewed at least every two years, and the SBA examines the lender's portfolio periodically. Preferred loans account for more than 10 percent of SBA loans.

Use of Loan Funds

An SBA loan guarantee can be used for working capital to expand an existing franchised business or to open a new unit. The capital may also be used for real estate renovation, purchase, or construction and for equipment purchases. Almost all small businesses are eligible for the SBA programs, except for those established for speculative investment, such as apartment buildings.

Eligibility

The franchisee's business generally must be operated for profit and fall within the size standards set by the SBA. According to the SBA, a small business is independently owned and operated and is not dominant in its field. Depending on the industry, size-standard eligibility is based on the average number of employees for the preceding 12 months or on sales volume averaged over a three-year period. The SBA small-business standards can be found at www.sba.gov.

7(A) Loan Guarantees

Use of Proceeds

A franchisee or area developer can use a 7(a) loan to:

- ❐ Expand or renovate facilities.
- ❐ Purchase machinery, equipment, fixtures, and leasehold improvements.

❒ Finance receivables and augment working capital.

❒ Refinance existing debt (with compelling reason).

❒ Finance seasonal lines of credit.

❒ Construct commercial buildings.

❒ Purchase land or buildings.

Terms, Interest Rates, and Fees

The length of time for repayment depends on the use of the proceeds and the franchisee's or area developer's ability to repay. However, the term is usually five to ten years for working capital and up to 25 years for the purchase or major renovation of fixed assets such as real estate or equipment. (The length of the loan cannot exceed the useful life of the equipment.)

Both fixed- and variable-interest rates are available. Rates are pegged at no more than 2.25 percent over the lowest prime rate for loans with maturities of less than seven years and up to 2.75 percent for loans with longer maturities. For loans under $50,000, rates may be slightly higher.

The SBA charges the lender a nominal fee to provide a guarantee, and the lender may pass this charge on to the franchisee. The fee is based on the maturity of the loan and the dollar amount that the SBA guarantees. On any loan with a maturity of one year or less, the fee is just 0.25 percent of the guaranteed portion of the loan. On loans with maturities of more than one year where the portion that the SBA guarantees is $80,000 or less, the guarantee fee is 2 percent of the guaranteed portion. On loans with maturities of more than one year where the SBA's portion exceeds $80,000, the guarantee fee is figured on an incremental scale, beginning at 3 percent. All references to the prime rate refer to the lowest prime rate as published in the *Wall Street Journal* on the day the SBA receives your application.

How the Application Works

The franchisee submits a loan application to a lender for initial review. Following your presentation, the lender checks with the SBA—prior to the formal application—for ballpark feasibility of the project. Then, if the SBA considers the project feasible and creditworthy, the lender submits a letter of intent to the SBA if interim financing is to be supplied prior to formal consideration of the loan request.

The actual application is then forwarded, and the lender deals directly with the SBA officers. The SBA processes can take as many as 20 working days or as few as two. If the lender approves the loan subject to an SBA guaranty, the lender forwards a copy of the application and a credit analysis to the nearest SBA office. After SBA approval, the lender closes the loan and disburses the funds; the franchisee makes monthly loan payments directly to the lender. As with any loan, the franchisee is responsible for repaying the full amount of the loan.

No balloon payments, prepayment penalties, application fees, or points are permitted with 7(a) loans. Repayment plans may be tailored to each individual business.

What the Franchisee Must Take to the Lender

Documentation requirements may vary; contact your lender for the necessary information. Common requirements include:

- ❏ Purpose of the loan.
- ❏ History of the business.
- ❏ Business plan.
- ❏ Financial statements for three years (existing business).
- ❏ Schedule of terms for any outstanding debts (existing business).
- ❏ Aging of accounts receivable and payable (existing business).
- ❏ Projected opening day balance sheet (new business).
- ❏ Lease details.
- ❏ Amount of investment in the business by the owner(s).
- ❏ Projections of income, expenses, and cash flow.
- ❏ Signed personal financial statements.
- ❏ Personal resume(s.)

What the SBA Looks for

- ❏ Good character.
- ❏ Management expertise and commitment necessary for success.
- ❏ Sufficient funds, including the SBA-guaranteed loan, to operate the business on a sound financial basis (for new businesses, this includes the resources to withstand start-up expenses and the initial operating phase).
- ❏ Feasible business plan.
- ❏ Adequate equity or investment in the business.
- ❏ Sufficient collateral.
- ❏ Ability to repay the loan on time from the projected operating cash flow.

Collateral

The franchisee must pledge readily available assets to adequately secure the loan. Personal guaranties are required from all the principal owners of the business. Liens on personal assets of the principals also may be required. However, in most cases, a loan will not be declined when insufficient collateral is the only unfavorable factor.

The SBA Franchise Registry

In 2007, the SBA established its Franchise Registry (www.franchiseregistry. com) to streamline its review of the eligibility for loans to franchisees of those franchisors that submit its documents to the SBA. Franchisors who are approved by the Registry have one or more programs that comply with the SBA loan eligibility standards. Some franchisors may register multiple programs. For example, a fast-food franchise could have one set of documents for its typical stand-alone single unit, another for a co-branded offering, and yet others for kiosk or food court formats.

504 Certified Development Company Program

This program, which was designed to enable small businesses to create and retain jobs, provides growing businesses with long-term, fixed-rate financing for the purchase of major fixed assets, such as land, buildings, and machinery.

According to SBA definitions, a certified development company (CDC) is a nonprofit corporation set up to contribute to the economic development of its community or region. CDCs work with the SBA and private sector lenders to provide financing to small businesses.

Usually, a 504 CDC project includes *either* a loan secured with a senior claim on the borrower's assets from a private sector lender covering as much as 50 percent of the project cost, *or* a loan secured with a junior position on assets through the CDC, with SBA assistance, covering as much as 40 percent of the cost and a contribution of at least 10 percent equity from the small business being helped. The maximum SBA share is generally $750,000. The CDC's portfolio must create or retain one job for every $35,000 provided by the SBA.

Contacting the SBA

The SBA has offices located throughout the United States. For the one nearest you, look under "U.S. Government" in your telephone directory, or call the SBA Answer Desk at 800-U-ASK-SBA or 800-827-5722. To send a fax to the SBA, dial 202-205-7064. The SBA can be contacted by e-mail at answerdesk @sba.gov. For the hearing impaired, the TDD number is (704) 344-6640. Or check their Web site at www.sba.gov.

CHAPTER 14

Management and Leadership Issues in Building a Successful Franchising Organization

 s already explained, franchising is all about leadership. The strategic essence of franchising is relationship management. Franchisees enter into the relationship with an expectation that the leaders of the franchise system will be committed to the success of each franchisee, work hard to continue to make improvements to the franchise system, and be a role model in communicating clearly and effectively the vision and goals of the franchise system as well as in sharing the best practices that will drive performance at the unit level. Franchisees invest their life savings on a premise of integrity, transparency, and the absence of hidden agendas. The more successful leaders of franchise companies, though styles can and will vary, typically have the following personality traits and characteristics.

❏ *Compassion.* Franchise leaders display a heartfelt commitment to the success of the system and understand the premise that, if the franchisees win, then the franchisor wins. Their attention is not just on the strongest franchisees, but also on those who are struggling.

❏ *Effective Communicators and Listeners.* Franchisor leaders are typically strong communicators and public speakers and have an ability to motivate and inspire an audience of franchisees, especially when changes to the system are being introduced. They are also great listeners and actively seek the input and constructive criticism of their franchise network and take action in response to their legitimate concerns.

❏ *Business Acumen.* Franchise leaders commit themselves to continuously learning both the fundamentals of the business as well as the art of franchising. They stay on top of new developments in the marketplace and are often respected market leaders and pioneers in their industries.

❏ *Mentors and Coaches.* Franchise leaders think like coaches and mentors; they are accessible team builders, care about each player, and genuinely enjoy the process of helping others and developing their businesses. They do not coach from their armchairs; they visit the field often

Box 14-1. Management tips for franchisor leaders.

- *Win the respect of your team and the franchisees.* Most team members and the franchisees in the system get caught up in the vision of the founder and the romantic heat of a franchisor on a rapid ascent. But that passion can be fleeting, especially in a tight labor market, if the founder or leaders do not walk the talk by continuing to share and communicate their vision and objectives and by rewarding those who help the franchisor meet their goals.

- *Be values driven and establish priorities around those values.* Take the time to make sure that everyone understands the company's values, the team at corporate headquarters as well as the franchisees in the field. Trust in your team once you are sure that they understand and embrace your core values.

- *Do not use threats, guilt, and yelling to motivate your team.* Fear will yield short-term results but is not likely to be an effective long-term motivator.

- *Do not be afraid of some degree of employee turnover, provided that your turnover rates stay below industry standards.* Aiming for a zero turnover rate may lead to complacency and mediocrity by keeping people in positions (or promoting them into positions) for which they are unqualified. A certain degree of turnover helps bring a new perspective and fresh ideas as to how things are getting done and how they *ought* to be done.

- *Take the time and effort to really ask what benefits the employees want and need in order to get the highest motivational results.* Do not force-feed an off-the-shelf menu of benefits and assume that they will be satisfactory. Offer options to reflect the diversity in your workforce and avoid a one-size-fits-all approach. Carefully monitor what your competitors are offering to ensure that your programs keep pace. Remember to focus on more than just cash; often the intangible factors make the *real* difference.

- *Technology is great, but don't forget the value of human interaction.* Many early-stage franchisor leaders are so dependent on e-mail, voicemail, cell phones, and pagers that they do not spend enough face-to-face time with their team. To really listen to feedback, new ideas, performance goals, and other things going on, you need to meet with your staff in person. *But* don't be there *too much*; nobody gets motivated by a hovering micromanager.

- *"Treat people as you want to be treated,"* and *"You get what you give."* These old adages are also very true in the workplace of the early-stage franchisor. The way to hold on to quality people is not just to pay them well but also to treat them well. Create a positive, challenging, high-energy workplace where everyone is treated with respect; that kind of workplace can be very hard to leave, even for more money. Another old adage—"Do What You Say and Say What You Do"—also works well; that is, commit to clear communication channels and keep the promises made to the workforce.

- *Recognition is in the small details.* A pat on the back, a positive gesture, a big smile, a congratulatory franchise-wide e-mail, a move to a bigger office, a small gift, and many other low-cost gestures can go a long way in motivating and rewarding employees, especially at an early-stage franchisor. Big bonuses and stock options are great, but they are not the only motivator. Be quick to celebrate and to share achievements publicly, but give consecutive criticism privately.

- *Finally, don't fool yourself into thinking that you have what it takes to motivate people.* People need to motivate themselves. Your role as an entrepreneur or leader of an early-stage franchisor is to create a *culture,* an *environment,* and *systems* that inspire and empower people to motivate themselves and that properly reward self-motivation when results are achieved.

and demonstrate their commitment to the franchise system in person and with enthusiasm. They tend to command respect and do not hesitate to give respect to others when it is earned.

❐ *Change Agents.* Franchise leaders welcome and embrace change. They understand that the franchise system must continue to evolve and do not fear being the agents and advocates to implement these changes. Change will also take place within the franchisor's organization; the management team in the early stages of the launch of the franchising program may or may not be the right team as the system grows and becomes more complex. The franchisor's leadership must be ready and willing to make the necessary changes but also manage turnover rates, which tend to be very disruptive to the franchise system and raise concerns among the franchisees. The leadership must continue to make changes and upgrades to the system's communication and computer technology to ensure maximum system performance.

Building a Management Team

Recruiting and retaining a talented management team can be one of the most difficult aspects of managing the growth of a franchise system. Early-stage franchisors are not only competing with big firms with large resources, but with each other. Let's face it: There are only so many highly qualified operations and field support personnel who will work for an unproven franchising system, let alone a sales and marketing veteran. But many early-stage franchisors have improved their ability to compete for talented staff by offering benefits that bigger franchisors may not necessarily offer, such as an opportunity to participate in ownership and critical decision making, flexible schedules, informal work environment, less red tape, and an openness to new ideas and innovation. Creativity, flexibility, and aggressive performance-based compensation are the best tools available to small and emerging franchisors.

Many recent human capital solutions and strategies are being considered and implemented by early-stage franchisors to solve recruitment and retention challenges, and there will always be something new and trendy. Current strategies include "open book management," the use of free agents, outsourcing critical functions [including closely competing service providers and application service providers (ASPs), who host and support your software systems], employee leasing, telecommuting and flexible hours, and many others to meet the needs of a changing workforce that is facilitated by technological development. Emerging growth franchisors have struggled to keep up with the rapidly changing demographic composition of the workforce, the need for highly skilled technical workers (which often leads to an increase in the need to recruit abroad and manage employer-sponsored immigration strategies), the demand for a work/life balance and quality of life in the workplace, the need to respect and support diversity in the work-

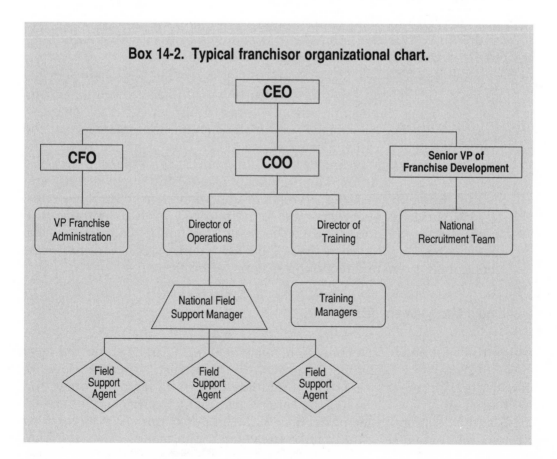

Box 14-2. Typical franchisor organizational chart.

place, and the challenge of staying competitive with larger employers competing for the same workforce. The shortage on the quality and quantity of labor can and will be one of the most significant hurdles in the way of a franchisor's growth plans.

Emerging growth franchisors must custom-tailor their recruitment programs to find employees who may be willing to be more patient from a pure compensation perspective. Perhaps prospective employees may value non-compensation-based factors in evaluating different positions (such as leadership or management practices, corporate culture, flexible hours, training opportunities, or special rewards and incentives), or they may be less skilled but have an attitude that makes them easily trainable. However, proceed carefully and create a balance. Many dot.com companies in the late 1990s hired very young workers and devoted significant portions of their overhead to chill-out rooms, pool tables, vending machines, parties, and retreats, leaving little time for any actual work to get done and misleading young workers into thinking that they could become millionaires through their stock options by playing ping-pong all day. Many of these companies are now out of business, and their employees are out of jobs.

Recruitment efforts should therefore focus on sharing the franchisor's medium-term growth objectives and career advancement opportunities, its leadership style, training opportunities, and respect for the work/life balance. Emphasize any unique or general programs that are or may soon be in place to facilitate quality-of-life issues, such as on-site child care, affiliations with nearby health clubs, casual dress policies, or a willingness to support telecommuting. In review and evaluating potential candidates, emerging growth franchisors need to look for workers who have strong communication skills, who are willing to be flexible and take responsibility, and who have a positive attitude and high energy levels. These intangible skills may need to compensate for a lack of direct experience or academic credentials. The candidates should understand and at least in part share the visions of the founder and the CEO of the franchisor, which means that the visions must be communicated early to all candidates. Subjects that should be clearly explored from the outset are the systems in place to maintain and measure the employee's performance, as well as *how these systems may very likely change as the franchisor grows and evolves.*

Recruiting practices need to be a lot more systematic. Job descriptions should be prepared, shared, and, where appropriate, modified with the input of the new employee so that expectations are clear from the outset. Also critical is that the employee understand that *early-stage franchisors are not the same as larger franchisors* and that the elements of the job description may change quickly as different growth objectives are set and subsequently achieved. Questions should be tailored to ensure that the candidate would be comfortable and productive in a culture of rapid evolution and change. Looking for candidates who are naturally curious, who enjoy problem solving, who are creative and flexible will help ensure their fit with the culture and the change that they are likely to encounter in an early-stage franchise.

The recruiting team for an early-stage franchisor must themselves be very well trained on the franchisor's objectives and strengths; they are one part cheerleader and one part salesperson. For small franchisors, the recruiters will not have the tools of big salaries and signed bonuses to work with; so they must be armed with a strong knowledge of the franchisor's objectives and intangible strengths. But they are also one part psychologist and need to have an excellent ability to evaluate a candidate's intangible skills—personality, drive, motivation, creativity, and other characteristics. This is not an easy task without some training and experience. Too much time is often spent on reviewing and asking questions about the information contained on the written resume instead of thinking outside the box. A standard interview and sloppy reference check may be sufficient for a local dry cleaning shop or for absorption into a Fortune 500 company, but for emerging growth businesses, every hire is a critical one and mistakes are costly.

The approach to recruitment must be creative and aggressive. Merely relying on classified ads and even employee referral bonuses will not cut it. Even the use of headhunters and Web-based job sites will not meet your recruitment needs and hiring objectives. Many franchisors are turning to full-time, in-house recruitment teams that are totally focused on meeting the hiring needs of the franchisor by participating in all possible hiring channels. Full-time recruiters can demonstrate their commitment and creativity by being focused on finding the best and brightest talent in nontraditional ways, always and everywhere. For example, they will upgrade to first-class, and they will check out fellow travelers' luggage tags on airplanes to see if they work for a competitor and may be interested in leaving. They will strike up conversations at sporting events and parties when fellow attendees are wearing clothes or hats that bear the trademark of a competitor. The constant networking, schmoozing, and data gathering all make for the most qualified team. As soon as the franchisor realizes that recruitment is as much about marketing as it is about human resources management, the sooner the team will be built and strengthened. The recruitment process is a 24/7 commitment and very time-consuming. Be prepared to kiss a lot of frogs before finding the right candidate for a position.

Establishing a Board of Directors and Advisory Boards

The quality of the leadership team of the franchisor is critical to the long-term success of the franchise system. But whom does the senior management team turn to for advice and guidance? Who provides the franchisor's executives with general policy and direction on which to build and execute a specific growth plan? For most early-stage and growing franchisors, the answer is twofold: (1) a formal board of directors and (2) an informal advisory board (or series of advisory boards for specific purposes).

These two boards are often confused, but they actually play very different roles and have very different responsibilities. The *board of directors* is required under virtually all applicable state corporate laws and owes very specific fiduciary duties to the shareholders of the corporation. The basic governance structure is that the shareholders elect the directors, who in turn appoint the officers. The role of the directors is to set broad goals and policy objectives for the franchisor, which will benefit and protect the interests of the shareholders. The officers' role is to develop and implement plans to meet these goals and objectives. A strong director has board-based business experience, strong industry knowledge, a useful rolodex, adequate time to devote to truly understanding the company's key challenges and weaknesses, the objectivity to challenge decisions made by the management team, good listening skills, and the ability to act as a sounding board for the team; the director has also generally been well trained at the university of hard knocks. A good director does not get easily discouraged if the company gets off course, nor does he or she view the world through rose-colored glasses. The board members should take their responsibilities very seriously and not be too casual when it comes to critical tasks, like board meeting preparation and attendance, maintaining confidentiality, or pursuing what appears to be a personal agenda. Each board member and the board as a whole must be constantly guided by what is in the best interest of the shareholders.

On the other hand, an *advisory board* is not required by state corporate laws, does not owe the same levels of fiduciary duties to the shareholders (and hence cannot generally be held as responsible for their acts or recommendations), and can be much more informal with regard to the number of meetings and agendas for meetings. The advisory board can be assembled for general purposes, or a series of advisory boards could be set up for very specific purposes, such as technical review, marketing strategy, recruitment and compensation, or research and development. An advisory board can also be an excellent way to get a second opinion on certain matters without interrupting existing relationships. For example, you may want access to a highly respected business lawyer but be reluctant to fire your current law firm; asking that lawyer if he or she is willing to serve on your advisory board can be a good compromise. The board of directors seats are usually initially set aside for cofounders and investors, and many prospective advisory board members may be reluctant to accept the responsibility that comes with a board of director seat, especially at the outset of the relationship. Of course, the showcase value of putting a long list of names of people who barely know you and who will never show up for any meetings dilutes the value of the credibility that you seek to establish when appointing advisors. Prospective investors will put varying weights on the strength and composition of the advisory board in making their final investment decisions and will often want direct access to the members as part of their due diligence process and to ascertain the depth of their commitment.

A critical difference between a board of directors and an advisory board is management's ability to accept or ignore the recommendations of any advisory board, a decision they do not have to make when a mandate comes down from the board of directors. Also, because members of the advisory board do not owe the same duties to the company and its shareholders, they can be used to mediate disputes by and among the officers or between the officers and the directors. They can also be used in identifying potential board of director candidates or as a recruiting ground for eventual seats on the board.

Since the rules governing the advisory board are not set forth in a corporate law statute, be very clear about the expectations of each advisory board member as well as about how they will be compensated for their efforts. The best way to capture these objectives and rewards is to prepare an advisory board member agreement.

Formal Responsibilities of the Board of Directors

Each act or decision of the board must be performed in good faith and for the benefit of the corporation. The legal obligations of the directors fall into three broad categories: a duty of care, a duty of loyalty, and a duty of fairness.

❐ *Duty of Care.* The directors must carry out their duties in good faith and with diligence, care, and skill in the best interests of the corporation. Each director must actively gather information to make an informed decision regarding company affairs and in formulating company strategies. In doing so, the board member is entitled to rely primarily on the data provided by officers and professional advisors, *provided that the board member has no knowledge of any irregularity or inaccuracy in the information.* In some instances, board members have been held personally responsible for misinformed or dishonest decisions made in bad faith, such as the failure to properly direct the corporation or knowingly authorizing a wrongful act.

❐ *Duty of Loyalty.* The duty of loyalty requires directors to exercise their powers in the interest of the corporation and not in their own interest or in the interest of another person (including a family member) or organization. The duty of loyalty has a number of specific applications, such as the duty to avoid any conflicts of interest in dealings with the corporation and the duty not to personally usurp what is more appropriately an opportunity or business transaction to be offered to the corporation. For example, if an officer or director of the company was in a meeting on the company's behalf and a great opportunity to obtain the licensing or distribution rights for an exciting new technology were to be offered at the meeting, trying to obtain these rights individually and not first offer them to the corporation would be a breach of loyalty.

❐ *Duty of Fairness.* The last duty a director has to the corporation is that of fairness. For example, duties of fairness questions may come up if a director is also the owner of the building in which the corporate headquarters are leased and is seeking a significant rent increase upon renewal. Allowing the director to vote on this proposal would be a breach of fairness. The central legal concern under such circumstances is usually that the director may be treating the corporation unfairly in the transaction because the director's self-interest and gain could cloud his duty of loyalty to the company. When a transaction between an officer or director and the company is challenged, the individual has the burden of demonstrating the propriety and fairness of the transaction. If any component of the transaction involves fraud, undue overreaching, or the waste of corporate assets, it is likely to be set aside by the courts.

For the director's dealings with the corporation to be upheld, the interested director must demonstrate that the transaction was approved or ratified by a disinterested majority of the company's board of directors.

To meet the duties of care, loyalty, and fairness to the corporation, each board member should follow these guidelines:[1]

❒ The directors should be furnished with all appropriate background and financial information relating to proposed board actions well in advance of a board meeting. An agenda, proper notice, and a mutually convenient time, place, and date will ensure good attendance records and compliance with applicable statutes regarding the notice of the meetings.

❒ A valid meeting of the board of directors may not be held unless a quorum is present. The number of directors needed to constitute a quorum may be fixed by the articles or bylaws, but it is generally a majority of board members.

❒ The board should work with the company attorney to develop a set of written guidelines on the basic principles of corporate law for all officers and directors. Keep the board informed about recent cases or changes in the law.

❒ If the board or an individual director is in doubt as to whether a proposed action is truly in the best interests of the corporation, they should consult the attorney immediately—*not* after the transaction is consummated.

❒ Careful minutes should be kept of all meetings and comprehensive records of the information on which board decisions are based. Be prepared to show financial data, business valuations, market research, opinion letters, and related documentation if the action is later challenged as being uninformed by a disgruntled shareholder. Well-prepared minutes will also serve a variety of other purposes, such as written proof of the director's analysis and appraisal of a given situation, proof that parent and subsidiary operations are being conducted at arm's length and as two distinct entities, or proof that an officer did or did not have authority to engage in the specific transaction being questioned.

❒ Candidates for the board of directors should be chosen carefully. Avoid the consideration or nomination of someone who seems credible but is unlikely to attend any meetings or have any real input to the management and direction of the company. Often, the most high-profile business leaders are spread too thin with other boards and activities to add any meaningful value to a company's growth objectives. Such a passive relationship will only invite claims by shareholders of corporate mismanagement. Avoid inviting a board candidate who is already serving on more than five to seven boards, depending on their other com-

---

1. Many of these guidelines, albeit in a diluted format in some cases, can be adopted to govern the selection and operation of the company's advisory boards.

mitments. Similarly, do not accept an invitation to sit on a board of directors of another company unless you're ready to accept the responsibilities that go with it.

❐ In threatened takeover situations or friendly offers to purchase the company, the board has to make decisions that will be in the best interests of *all* shareholders, not just the board and the officers. Any steps taken to defend against a takeover by protecting the economic interests of the officers and directors (such as lucrative golden parachute contracts that ensure a costly exit) must be reasonable in relation to the threat.

❐ Any board member who independently supplies goods and services to the corporation should not participate in the board discussion or vote on any resolution relating to his or her dealings with the corporation, in order to avoid self-dealing or conflict-of-interest claims. A disinterested board must approve proposed actions after the material facts of the transaction are disclosed and the nature and extent of the board member's involvement are known.

❐ Questionnaires should be issued periodically to officers and directors regarding possible self-dealings or conflicts of interest with the corporation. Incoming board members and newly appointed officers should be provided with a detailed initial questionnaire. These questionnaires should also always be circulated among the board prior to any securities issuances (such as a private placement or a public offering).

❐ Don't be afraid to get rid of ineffective or troublesome board members, even if their egos or reputations get in the way of a need to replace them. Get someone who is more committed or who can be more effective. Avoiding the choice of close friends for the board may be advisable, because they may be either difficult to terminate or lazy in the execution of their duties. Maintain the quality of the board, and measure it against the growth and maturity of the company. Emerging businesses tend to quickly outgrow the skills and experiences of their initial board of directors, who then need to be replaced with candidates with a deeper and wider range of experiences. Try to recruit and maintain board members who bring strategic benefits to the company but who are not too close for comfort in that their fiduciary duties prevent them from being effective because of the potential conflict of interests. This requirement is especially applicable to your outside team of advisors, such as attorneys and auditors, who may not be able to render objective legal and accounting advice if they wear a second hat as a board of director member. It may be easier for these professionals to sit on your advisory board, which is less likely to cause conflicts.

❐ Board members who object to a proposed action or resolution should either vote in the negative and ask that such a vote be recorded in the minutes or abstain from voting and promptly file a written dissent with the secretary of the corporation.

Following these guidelines can help ensure that your board of directors meets its legal and fiduciary objectives to the company's shareholders and also provides strong and well-founded guidance to the company's executive team to help ensure that growth objectives are met.

Corporate Governance and Reporting in the New Age of Scrutiny: Understanding the Obligations of Franchisors in a Post–Sarbanes-Oxley Environment

Since the collapse of Enron and Worldcom and more recently in light of the Madoff and Stanford scandals, *the public's trust in our corporate leaders and financial markets—as either employees, shareholders, or bond holders—has been virtually destroyed.* Franchisees go through similar experience in their selection of a franchisor; they want to see a leadership team and corporate culture that are dedicated to integrity, transparency, and good governance practices as a condition to investing their personal savings into the development of your brands and systems in their local marketplace. By law, franchisees are not afforded the same types of rights as shareholders, but under principles of effective franchise management, many of the same relationships and communications best practices can still apply.

Rebuilding the Public's Trust and Confidence

At the heart of the solution is a return to the fundamentals of what it means to serve as an executive or a board member of a publicly traded or emerging growth privately held company. Our corporate governance laws created duties of care, duties of fairness (to avoid self-dealing and conflicts of interest), duties of due diligence, duties of loyalty, and the business judgment rule to help ensure that we *all* serve on boards, advisory councils, or committees primarily for the purposes of serving others, to help, to guide, to mentor. The aim is to be a fiduciary and to look out for the best interests of the company's shareholders—not to perpetuate greed or fraud. We seem to have lost sight of our *responsibility* to those constituents whom the laws dictate that we serve.

In response, Congress acted relatively swiftly in passing the Sarbanes-Oxley Act, which President Bush signed into law on July 30, 2002. The Securities Exchange Commission, the New York Stock Exchange, the Department of Justice, NASDAQ, state attorney generals, and others had also responded quickly to create more accountability by and among corporate executives, board members, and their advisors to shareholders and employees. Central themes included:

❑ Heightened objectivity in the composition of board members.
❑ Increased independence and autonomy for auditors.
❑ Tightened control over financial reporting.
❑ Stiffened penalties for abuse of the laws and regulations pertaining to corporate governance, accounting practices, and financial reporting.
❑ New rules to ensure fair and prompt access to the information and events that affect the company's current status and future performance.

Box 14-3. Some final thoughts on effective franchisor leadership and management.

- *Be obsessed with being a great teacher and a great student every day.* Leaders love to teach others, especially as franchisors, but also embrace the daily joy of learning and growing as a person

- *Invest heavily in your human capital as your greatest strategic asset.* Make sure your team is well trained and well treated. Clearly define work flow processes, realistic goals and expectations, pathways for reward and advancement, and key performance indicators (KPIs). *We often go into painstaking detail to prepare an excellent operations manual for our franchisees but have no similar protection for the franchisor's corporate headquarters.*

- *Adapt the Tao of Curious George.* Take an investigatory mind-set to problem solving and due diligence. Ask hard questions and then ask more questions. Take nothing for granted.

- *Walk a mile in another's shoes.* Understand multiple perspectives before arriving at conclusions. Gather many data points, especially from those who will be affected by your decisions. *How many times do we make decisions that will affect the franchise systems without talking to franchisees?*

- *Haste makes waste.* We are living in a society where everyone expects decisions to be made in real time, without much thought or analysis. Step away from the situation long enough to engage in some clear and objective thinking, especially when your decision will have far-reaching consequences.

- *Have a transition and succession plan in place.* You will not be around forever. Invest in mentoring programs, identify future leaders, and teach them how to lead, how to manage, and how to govern in ways that they could not have learned in business school. Teach them to learn from their mistakes and to develop the character traits that will one day empower them to replace you.

- *Commit to excellent customer service.* Use computer and communications technologies, such as e-mail, intranets, interactive computer training, and private satellite networks to support and communicate with franchisees. What systems are in place to ensure excellence in the interactions with targeted home and business customers? Do you have a procedure for gathering feedback and reacting to problems in the field? When is the last time you spoke directly with the franchisees' customers? What are you doing to educate your targeted customers on quality and product/service differentiation issues? How can you achieve the Good Housekeeping Seal of Approval status with customers (e.g., known as setting the standards for quality)? What can you do at the community and grassroots level to promote and enhance this image (e.g., controlling and enhancing the customer's buying experience)? Do you treat franchisees as *your* customers?

- *Make sure that all key players in the organization (not just the CFO) commit to taking the time to truly understand and analyze the economics of the core business.* Does the current franchise fee and royalty structure make sense? Is it fair? How often are royalty and other financial reports closely reviewed and analyzed? Are key observations and trends shared in the field?

- *Develop a bona fide understanding of the key factors that make your franchisees successful.* What are the common characteristics of your top 20 percent franchisees in each division? What can you learn from these common characteristics? What can you do to recruit more candidates with these same characteristics and skill sets?

We have truly entered a new age of scrutiny—an era of validation and verification. The role of the board and its committees are being redefined, reexamined, and retooled. A new set of best practices, procedures, and protocols are being written as we speak, and this process will continue into 2011 and beyond. Internal controls and systems need to be designed to ensure compliance with these new rules of the game, and managers must be held accountable for enforcement and results. The CEO's new job description reads "Forget the Gravy, Where's the Beef" and includes less pay, less perks, and less power in exchange for more performance and less tolerance for error or abuse. CEOs must live in a new era that will feature more accountability and shorter tenure. Even politicians have jumped on the bandwagon, building campaigns and governance policies that are dedicated to candor, transparency, and accountability.

Yet the key question remains: Can we truly legislate and mandate trust, integrity, and leadership? Will new laws and stock exchange guidelines truly restore public confidence in the markets and get directors and officers focused on the standards of diligence, commitment, and responsibility? How far does any proposed legislation that is still on the horizon need to go to get officers and directors truly focused on their most important task—*maximizing bona fide shareholder value*?

In this new era, earning trust and building shareholder value must be done the old-fashioned way, not via exaggerated revenues, the mischaracterization of expenses, the use of special-purpose entities to disguise debt obligations, or the use of creative accounting to inflate earnings. The recapturing of shareholder trust will be a costly and time-consuming process; both institutional and individual investors must get past their disgust for the greed and negligence shown by some of our corporate leaders.

Best Practices for Effective and Ethical Decision Making

Leaders of franchisors must embrace an ethical framework for decision making, not only with respect to the management of their relationships with franchisees, but with respect to all key strategic relationships, as well as with their family, friends, and community. The ripple effect of a franchisor's conduct is significant in the impact it will have on the franchise system, the customers, the employees of each franchisee, and all of their families. Imagine the damage that a scandal involving a Ray Kroc or Fred DeLuca would have on the franchise systems of McDonald's® or Subway®. Ethical behaviors affect all aspects of the world around you, as shown in Figure 14-1.

Franchisors can apply a wide variety of tests to help guide their decision making and efforts toward an ethical result:

1. *Relevant Information Test.* Have we gathered as much information as possible to make an informed decision and an action plan for this situation?

2. *Involvement Test.* Have we involved as many as possible of those who have a right to have input to, or actual involvement in, making this decision and action plan?

3. *Consequentialist Test.* Have we attempted to allow for the consequences of this decision and action plan on any who could be significantly affected by it?

4. *Ethical Principles Test.* Do this decision and action plan uphold the relevant ethical principles in this situation?

5. *Core Values Test.* Is this proposed action, inaction, or conclusion consistent with our core values, ethical standards, and culture?

6. *Fairness Test.* If we were any one of the stakeholders in this situa-

Figure 14-1. The ripple effect of integrity.

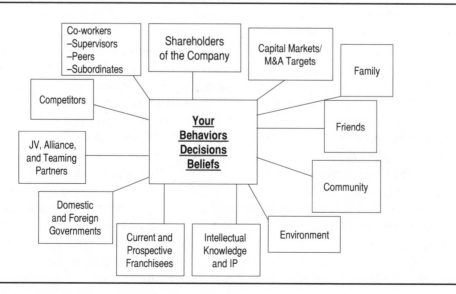

tion, would we perceive this decision and action plan to be fair, given all the circumstances? Are we treating one group of people unfairly in comparison to a similarly situated or equally deserving group?

7. *Universality Test.* Would we want this decision and action plan to become "universal law" so that it would be applicable to all—including ourselves—in similar situations?

8. *Preventive Test.* Do this decision and action plan prevent or minimize similar situations from happening again?

9. *Light-of-Day (or 60 Minutes TV Program) Test.* Can our decision and action plan—*including* how we made it—stand the test of broad-based public disclosure if everyone were to know everything about our actions?

10. *Stakeholder/Member Value Test.* Is this decision consistent with our legal and moral obligation toward *all* of our shareholders (or other stakeholders)? Does it meet the fiduciary obligations that we owe to them to protect and strengthen the company?

Here is a ten-step ethical decision-making framework that leaders of franchisors can use to help make the difficult decisions that may have competing consequences and outcomes, such as intrasystem disputes:

Step 1. Identify the key facts.
- ❒ Role-play key stakeholders to see what *they* see as facts.
- ❒ Watch out for assuming causative relationships among coincidental facts.

Step 2. Identify and analyze the major stakeholders.
- ❒ Make sure to identify both direct and indirect stakeholders.
- ❒ Genuinely walk in their shoes to see what *they* value and want as a desired outcome.

Step 3. Identify the underlying driving forces.
- ❒ Think like a doctor. Look for what may be the *cause* of the apparent or expected symptoms of the problem.

Step 4. Identify/prioritize operating values and ethical principles.
- ❒ Think of this step as determining the up-front design parameters for an effective solution.
- ❒ Don't rush this step. Gathering diverse viewpoints and building consensus here will pay off later.

Step 5. Decide who should be involved in making the decision.
- ❒ All stakeholders have a right to have *their* best interests considered.
- ❒ If you can't actually involve all stakeholders, have someone role-play their point of view.

Step 6. Determine and evaluate all viable alternatives.
- ❐ Imagine possible consequences of each alternative cascading down on each stakeholder.
- ❐ Analyze the cost-benefit aspect of these consequences—actual and as perceived.

Step 7. Test a preferred alternative with a worst-case scenario.
- ❐ This step helps prevent a rush to judgment toward a wrong solution.
- ❐ Emphasize this step when all stakeholder interests are *not* being adequately considered.

Step 8. Add a preventive component.
- ❐ "Problem-solving heroes" want to get on to the next problem and won't take time for this step.
- ❐ Only immediate-solution decisions usually come back to bite you.

Step 9. Decide and build a short- and long-term action plan.
- ❐ The devil's usually in the details. Take the time needed to be detailed and comprehensive.
- ❐ Make sure that the means used in your action steps correlate with your desired ends.

Step 10. Monitor the consequences of your concrete action plan.
- ❐ Were the desired and planned outcomes as hoped? Are adjustments necessary?
- ❐ What did we learn? What would we do differently next time?

CHAPTER 15

The Role of the Chief Financial Officer and Related Financial and Administrative Management Issues

 s discussed in the previous chapter, as a franchisor grows and matures, its management team must also evolve to meet new challenges and solve new problems. In the early stages, the franchise's management team is heavily focused on sales and marketing, which are often necessary prerequisites to building a critical mass of franchisees. But as the emphasis shifts from franchise sales to service and support, additional personnel must be recruited in the areas of operations, administration, and finance. The management teams of many rapidly growing franchisors often lack experienced financial officers who can bring economic discipline to the organization and perform ongoing analysis of the company's business model. Effective financial management, reporting systems, and analysis are the keys to the ongoing success of a growing franchise system.

When a franchisor reaches that critical stage of growth requiring a full-time financial officer, the first reaction is typically panic. First, the position must be added to the overhead; second, the founder doesn't know where to start looking. Even the well-respected and well-recognized executive recruitment firms who specialize in franchising admit that there is a lack of truly qualified and experienced financial managers. Many franchisors have unsuccessfully recruited from the accounting profession. These professionals can be very well trained in the areas of accounting or tax planning, but they may lack the operational experience to truly understand the special financial dynamics of the franchisor-franchisee relationship. The ideal candidate will have had some initial training as a certified public accountant but will also have had hands-on experience as a CFO or comptroller of a franchise company, or at least with a firm with a similar structure and method of distribution and growth, such as dealerships, retailing, or licensing.

The overall task of the CFO is to manage the cash flow and profitability of the franchisor. The three cost areas that must be managed carefully are:

❏ *Recruitment costs*, such as marketing, advertising, trade shows, marketing personnel, and the like.

❏ *Preopening costs*, such as the costs to get the franchisee up and running, including training, site selection, and other types of preopening assistance.

❏ *Maintenance costs*, such as the various ongoing training and support costs to maintain a healthy and mutually profitable relationship.

The CFO's job is to continue to study the financial model between the franchisor and the franchisee, such as the pricing of the *initial franchise fees* (which are designed to cover the first two cost areas) and the rates of *royalty fees* (which are intended to the third) to ensure that the ongoing relationship with the franchisee is financially viable for the franchisor.

The day-to-day job tasks of a well-rounded CFO typically include those shown in Figure 15-1.

One of the continuing challenges of the chief financial officer of the start-up and growing franchisor is to avoid the common financial mistakes that harm or even destroy franchisors at various critical stages in their development. If you or your company have never made the following mistakes, then try to avoid them. If it is too late, then try to learn from the mistakes and avoid making them again.

Figure 15-1. The daily tasks of the CFO.

Development of accounting and reporting systems	Development of cash flow management programs	Preparation of financial statements in satisfaction of federal and state franchise laws
Financial analysis and forecasting for proposed new products and services to be offered by franchisor	Development of capital formation strategies	Initial and ongoing analysis of franchise and royalty fee structure
Development of royalty and related fee collection and reporting systems	Management of banking relationships	Development of accounts payable and accounts receivable management programs
Federal and state tax planning	Review and critique of franchisee financial reports	Development and implementation of operating controls and internal budgeting/reporting systems
Analysis of vendor relations and cooperative buying programs	Liaison to outside accounting firms and law firms	Financial analysis of strategic plans and growth targets
Analysis of proposed mergers and acquisitions, real estate development, and international expansion	Coordination of operations, marketing, management, and other departments within the franchisor	Review of travel budgets, trade shows, and related promotional expenses
Careful and thorough financial due diligence on each prospective franchisee or area developer		

❑ *Undercapitalization.* Lack of operating capital is the kiss of death for many early-stage franchisors. Although franchising, as a method of business growth, is less capital intensive than internal growth, a sufficient working capital reserve is still required for development and implementation of the franchising program, as well as for the ongoing costs of support.

❑ *Cash Flow Mismanagement.* Any time the CFO needs to put pressure on the marketing staff to "close a deal so that we can pay the rent this month," cash flow is being mismanaged. Not only is the franchisor undercapitalized in such a scenario, but cash flow is being misdirected and mismanaged. General operating expenses and support costs should be paid for with royalty income, not with franchise sales. Robbing Peter to pay Paul will result in a compromise of franchise screening and qualification standards, as well as creating an undue financial burden on the franchisor.

❑ *Underestimation of the Costs of Ongoing Support and Service.* Ask franchisors how they arrived at their prevailing royalty rates, and they will answer "From our competitors!" Ask them how much it *actually* costs to support and service each franchisee, and you will get a blank stare. The royalty rate must be a reflection of a detailed analysis of the costs of maintaining support systems for the franchisees, not a number picked from the air!

❑ *Lack of Adequate Forecasting for the Performance of the Typical Franchisee.* Regardless of whether your company chooses to provide earnings claims, the forecasting of the performance of a typical franchisee is a critical step in building a franchising program. The *internal* analysis of a typical franchisee's performance will help the franchisor determine the viability of the franchising program from the franchisee's perspective as well as help predict its own stream of royalty income on a per-unit, per-annum basis.

❑ *Underestimation of Marketing and Promotional Expenses.* What is your cost per lead? What is your cost per award? Many early-stage franchisors are unable to predict or measure their actual costs in generating leads, screening prospects, and ultimately awarding the franchise to a qualified candidate. This may lead to an unpleasant surprise at the end of the quarter or fiscal year, when you discover that franchises are being awarded at a loss or that marketing costs are running well beyond budget.

❑ *Underbudgeting for Costs of Resolving Disputes with Franchisees.* How much do you think it will cost to resolve a genuine dispute with a disgruntled franchisee? Take that number, triple it, and you are probably getting close. Litigation is costly, drawn-out, and frustrating. Alternative dispute resolution techniques, such as arbitration and mediation, may be more cost-effective, but they still can be quite expensive. In building a franchise system, disputes with franchisees are inevitable, so it is best to begin building a war chest now so that a fight down the road does not unexpectedly cripple the franchisor.

❑ *Commingling of Advertising Resources.* Many early-stage franchisors inadvertently commingle funds received by their franchisees into a national advertising fund (which is supposed to help build brand awareness and create more customers for all franchisees) with the funds set aside to conduct marketing efforts to attract *more franchisees*. These accounting errors are not only a breach of the franchise agreement but also create franchisee resentment, tax issues, and accounting problems for the franchisor.

❒ *Miscalculation of Projected Item VII Opening Expenses.* Nobody likes unexpected financial surprises, especially not franchisees that are opening up a new business. Your prospective franchisees will naturally rely heavily on the projected start-up costs included in Item VII of the FDD in doing their own financial planning and capital formation. Yet many early-stage franchisors try to keep the total figures in Item VII as low as possible for marketing purposes on the theory that, the lower the cost to open, the more franchisees they will be able to award. Being on the conservative side in projecting Item VII costs is far wiser, allowing plenty of reserves for working capital. This will result in less disgruntled and unpleasantly surprised franchisees and serve to help marketing efforts over the long run.

The challenge of the CFO of a growing franchisor is a continuing one. The position does not require merely *collecting* financial data. It entails regularly renewing and analyzing the data collected from the franchisee and communicating observations and tips for improvement to the franchisor's management team, to the field support staff, and to the franchisees and their managers in the trenches.

The CFO must carefully study industry trends and single-unit performance to determine the most critical financial ratios or benchmarks. For many retail and food services franchise systems, these include preroyalty cash flow (PRCF) and weekly per store averages (WPSA) measurements. These benchmarks are analyzed both at the franchisor's corporate headquarters and by the franchisees on a collaborative/peer analysis basis.

For example, select groups of Kwik Kopy franchisees gather at the International Center for Entrepreneurial Development (ICED) campus outside Houston from time to time and, led by a trained moderator. analyze each other's financial statements and performance. The franchisees become financial and strategic sounding boards for one other in the areas of financial analysis, budgeting, forecasting, cash flow and profitability analysis, goal setting, and general strategic planning. The results of these meetings are used to improve overall performance as well as to provide a basis for future business and estate planning. The CFO can also use this data to develop a set of financial best practices to disseminate this information into the field as well as to update training programs and operations manuals. Franchisees generally respond well to this peer-driven process rather than feeling that the franchisor is dictating a set of standards for profit and loss statement (P&L) preparation and analysis.

Steps to Improve the Franchisee's Profitability

One of the age-old critiques of the financial structure of the franchisor-franchisee relationship is that the royalties payable to the franchisor are typically based on gross *sales*, not net *profits*. Therefore, franchisees often perceive, rightly or wrongly, that the franchisor will build a culture of support and training that overfocuses on building sales but not on improving profits. Naturally, in the long run, it is in neither party's best interest for franchisees to operate at a break-even or loss level on a sustained basis; such a course leads only to franchisee resentment and frustration, to store closings, and to litigation.

Therefore, the CFO and financial team must communicate a commitment to the profitability of the franchisee. Also, financial management training and support programs must be available to teach the franchisees how to prepare and analyze a P&L statement. In addition, field support personnel should have some financial analysis background and training. The field support personnel must be trained to detect red flags in the franchisee's P&L statements, to effectively communicate tips and traps to the franchisees, and to conduct nonadversarial strategic audits that focus on unit economic performance and profitability. The franchisor must teach the franchisee how to market, price, and deliver the underlying products and services in the system profitably. The franchisor must also take steps to negotiate volume discounts and develop cost management training for the benefit of the franchisees, recognizing that profitability is a combination of increasing sales and controlling costs. The franchise fee and royalty structure should continue to be analyzed to ensure that it is in line with current market trends and actual store performance data.

Some franchisors have offered to bring certain financial management and administrative services support functions that would otherwise be performed by the franchisees or area developers and their accountants under the franchisor's roof for a monthly fee. Franchisors may consider bringing one or more of the following functions under the responsibility of the franchisor's headquarters:

❑ Per-unit calculation of revenue and expenses by accounting category based on the franchisor's standard chart of accounts and calculation of royalty-based revenue and royalty fees (as each term is defined in the franchise agreement)

❑ Administration and maintenance of payroll, and administration of the processing of payroll and calculation of applicable tax and other withholdings relating to the franchisee or area developer's units, either through the franchisor's designated payroll service bureau or through in-house technology

❑ Administration of accounts payable (including check generation and wire transfers)

❑ Administration of recurring cash transfers between the franchisee's or area developer's applicable unit and corporate bank accounts

❑ Maintenance of lease files and compliance with related reporting and disbursement obligations

❑ Administration and maintenance of a franchisee or area developer general ledger trial balance, balance sheet, income statement, and certain

Box 15-1. Agenda for unit performance audit.

In times of economic recession and financial market turmoil, franchisees need to be armed all the more with the tools and the support they require to survive and thrive. Although the accumulation of these skills and experience is technically their own responsibility, franchisors who develop training programs and conduct periodic mandatory store operations and financial performance audits will enjoy a much healthier franchise system. Try to instill a what-gets-measured-gets-managed philosophy with each of your franchisees. Topics to be covered in this strategic audit should include at a minimum these ten items:

1. Market trends and competitive analysis
2. Store-level SWOT (strengths, weaknesses, opportunities, and threats) analysis
3. Quality and integrity/durability of sales revenues and accounts receivable analysis
4. Strategic review of all fixed and variable costs, vendor relationships, and operating expenses
5. Break-even analysis
6. Benchmarking and key metrics assessment
7. Cash flow and cash management analysis
8. Candidacy for growth/additional unit assessment
9. Taxes and estate planning, including owner(s) compensation and benefits
10. EBITDA and shareholder value drivers analysis

other corporate and unit reports by accounting category per the franchisor's standard chart of accounts and consistent with periodic reports the franchisor customarily prepares in the normal course of business to manage its financial affairs, and periodic distribution of such reports to franchisee or area developer using the franchisor's standard report distribution system

❏ Maintenance of all accounting records supporting franchisee or area developer financial statements (consistent with the franchisor's record retention program) in reasonable fashion, separately and discretely from the accounting records of the franchisor

❏ Preparation of period end reconciliations and associated period end journal entries for all franchisee and area developer balance sheet accounts

❏ Quarterly review and edit of the franchisee's or area developer's vendor masterfile for current and accurate data, including updates to the vendor masterfile as directed by the franchisee or area developer

❏ Approval and coding of invoices for disbursement

❏ Selection of accounting policies to be applied to the franchisee's or area developer's books and records, with the franchisor consistently applying the appropriate policies selected by the franchisee or area developer

❏ Negotiation of terms and conditions between the franchisee or area developer and its suppliers, vendors, and others, such as remittance due dates and discounts

❏ Final review and approval of annual financial statements

❏ Cash investment activities, with the franchisor initiating and managing repetitive and/or fixed cash management activities as directed in writing by the franchisee or area developer

❏ Preparation of budgets (except that the franchisor will develop a budget process and calendar to facilitate the preparation of annual budgets by the franchisee or area developer)

❏ Preparation, filing, or signing of any tax returns required to be filed by the franchisee or area developer, with the exception of sales and use tax returns that are prepared but not filed or signed by the franchisor

❏ Bidding, negotiating, and establishing (but not administering) health, dental, disability, life, and 401K benefit programs and accounts on behalf of the franchisee or area developer and for each covered employee

❏ Bidding, negotiating, establishing, and administering a directors and officers liability insurance program annually on behalf of the franchisee or area developer, as requested

❏ Bidding, negotiating, establishing, and administering property, liability, umbrella, and related insurance programs annually on behalf of the franchisee or area developer

❏ Bidding, negotiating, establishing, and administering a workers' compensation insurance program annually on behalf of the franchisee or area developer

❏ Performing claims reduction programs for each of the preceding insurance programs

❏ Setting up and administering option accounts, including option grant summaries, vesting, and option exercise bookkeeping and administration for optionees of the franchisee or area developer

❏ Performing year-end accrual analyses for health, dental, and FLEX plans on behalf of the franchisee or area developer.

Additional Duties of the CFO

In many early-stage and emerging growth franchisors, the chief financial officer is also responsible for administrative and human resources issues.

Many franchising executives hold the title of vice president of finance and administration, thereby requiring a knowledge and expertise not only of financial skills but also of current trends and developments in labor and employment laws. A working knowledge of these complex and constantly changing laws is important not only to manage an efficient and litigation-free workforce at the franchisor level but also to communicate the basics of these laws and requirements to the franchisees for the management of *their* staffs to avoid unnecessary claims and litigation. Franchisors should include this information in the initial training program, in the operations manual, and in periodic updates and bulletins to ensure that franchisees have access to this information. At the same time, franchisors need to be careful *not* to cross the line into what may be perceived as the interference with the day-to-day management of the franchisee's business, possibly leading to vicarious liability. In recent years, employees and other injured third parties have tried to include the franchisor as a defendant in employment-law-related claims against the franchisee, albeit with limited success thus far.

Understanding the Basics of Employment Law

This section of Chapter 15 presents a basic overview of certain key aspects of employment and labor law. Inasmuch as these laws are changing and evolving constantly, be sure to check with a qualified employment lawyer before developing employment policies, either for internal use or for dissemination to franchisees.

The employment *at-will doctrine* (which dates back to England's Statute of Labourers) allows for the termination of employment by either the employer or the employee at any time for any reason or for no reason at all. The systems and procedures implemented by a franchisor for hiring and firing personnel trigger a host of federal and state labor and employment laws, which you must understand regardless of the size of your company. Failure to understand these laws, however, can be especially damaging to the small franchisor because of the extensive litigation costs incurred as the result of an employment-related dispute. Litigation between employers and employees continues to clutter our nation's tribunals. In fact, suits under federal employment laws currently comprise the single largest group of civil filings in the federal court system. Federal and state legislatures have been equally active in designing new laws in the labor and employment arena, and small business groups have been quick to respond to the adverse impact of these laws.

The growing body of employment law encompasses topics such as employment discrimination, comparable worth, unjust dismissal, affirmative action programs, job classification, workers' compensation, performance appraisal, employee discipline and demotion, maternity policies and benefits, employee recruitment techniques and procedures, employment policy manuals and agreements, age and retirement, plant closings and layoffs, sexual harassment and discrimination, occupational health and safety standards, laws protecting the handicapped, and mandated employment practices for government contractors. The most comprehensive federal statutes and regulations affecting employment include:

- ❏ *Equal Pay Act of 1963*, prohibiting unequal pay based on gender.
- ❏ *Title VII of the Civil Rights Act of 1964*, prohibiting discrimination based on race, color, religion, sex, or national origin.
- ❏ *Age Discrimination in Employment Act of 1967 (ADEA)*, prohibiting discrimination against individuals aged 40 or older.
- ❏ *Rehabilitation Act of 1973*, prohibiting discrimination against handicapped individuals by all programs or agencies receiving federal funds and all federal agencies. The act also protects reformed or rehabilitated drug or alcohol abusers who are not currently using drugs or alcohol. In addition, this law has been interpreted to cover people with AIDS and HIV infection and those perceived as having AIDS.
- ❏ *Vietnam Era Veteran's Readjustment Assistance Act of 1974*, requiring government contractors to take affirmative action to recruit, hire, and promote qualified disabled veterans and veterans of the Vietnam era.
- ❏ *Immigration and Nationality Act*, prohibiting employers from discriminating on the basis of citizenship or national origin.
- ❏ *Pregnancy Discrimination Act of 1978*, prohibiting discrimination against pregnant women.
- ❏ *The Immigration Reform and Control Act of 1986*, making it unlawful for employers to recruit, hire, or continue to employ illegal immigrants to the United States and containing nondiscrimination provisions similar to those of the Immigration and Nationality Act.

Recent Federal Statutes and Regulations

- ❏ *Americans with Disabilities Act of 1990 (ADA).* This act prohibits discrimination against a qualified applicant or employee with a disability and covers employers with 25 or more employees. The ADA is based on the Civil Rights Act of 1964 and on Title V of the Rehabilitation Act of 1973. To fall within the ADA, a person's disability must be a physical or mental impairment that substantially limits at least one major life activity. This covers a range of physical and mental problems, from visual, speech, and hearing impairments to cancer, heart disease, arthritis, diabetes, orthopedic problems, and learning disabilities such as dyslexia. HIV infection also is considered a disability. The ADA also prohibits discrimination based on a "relationship or association" with disabled persons, makes sure the disabled have access to buildings, and ensures other accommodations; it also protects recovered substance abusers and alcoholics. As the courts begin to interpret various vaguely worded provisions of the ADA, franchisors can take comfort that in certain cases deep pockets do not automatically equal liability.

    According to two recent federal district court decisions, a fast-food franchisor could not be held liable for violations of the Americans with

Disabilities Act at franchise premises owned and operated by franchisees. In *Neff v. American Dairy Queen, Inc.* and *Young v. American
Dairy Queen, Inc.,* it was uncontroverted that the franchisor could not
be held liable under the Act as an owner, lessor, or lessee of the premises. However, the lawsuits alleged that the franchisor was liable for
violations as an "operator" of the premises because the franchise agreement gave the franchisor operating control over the franchises. However, according to the federal district court in San Antonio, the
franchisor did not operate its local franchises "under a definition of the
word."

The fact that the franchisor had the right to approve all modifications to a franchise did not permit the franchisor to require an existing
franchisee to make modifications to an existing structure. Furthermore,
there was no showing that the franchisor exercised its approval rights
in any way inconsistent with the disabilities law. A franchisor might be
subject to liability for refusing to approve plans to bring a franchise into
compliance with the law, the court held. However, merely possessing a
veto power for structural modifications did not constitute operation of
the premises for the purposes of the law. Neither decision is binding on
other federal courts.

❐ *Civil Rights Act of 1991.* This recent legislation expanded the legal
rights and remedies to individuals who have experienced employment-
related discrimination on the basis of their race, color, religion, sex, or
national origin. Employees are now able to recover consequential monetary losses, damages for future lost earnings and nonpecuniary injuries
such as pain and suffering, and emotional distress and punitive damages. The act also permits jury trials in these types of cases. Before the
1991 act, employees' remedies were essentially limited to monetary
damages for lost back pay, reinstatement or promotion, if appropriate,
and attorneys' fees.

❐ *Family and Medical Leave Act of 1993 (FMLA).* The FMLA prohibits
employers from interfering with, restraining employees from, or denying employees reasonable leave for medical reasons, for the birth or
adoption of a child, and for the care of a child, spouse, or parent who
has a serious health condition. The leave is unpaid leave, or paid leave
if it has been earned, for a period of up to 12 work-weeks in any 12
months. During the leave period, the employer must maintain any group
health plan covering the employee. At the conclusion of the leave, an
employee generally has a right to retain the same position or an equivalent position with equivalent pay, benefits, and working conditions.
Under the FMLA, an employer is defined as any person engaged in commerce or in any industry or activity affecting commerce, who employees
50 or more employees for each working day during each of 20 or more
calendar work-weeks in the current or preceding calendar year.

In addition to these federal laws, many state legislatures have enacted
antidiscrimination laws that go beyond the protection afforded at the federal

level. These state laws must also be carefully reviewed to ensure that employment practices comply at both the federal and state levels of regulation.

Preparing the Personnel Manual

A rapidly growing franchisor should develop a personnel manual and handbook for the purposes of communicating to all employees the details of its management procedures and guidelines. Some of these recommended policies and compliance tools should also be included in your operations manual for distribution to your franchisees. A well-drafted personnel manual can serve as a personnel training program, as a management tool for improving the efficiency of the franchisor, as an employee morale builder, and as a guardian against excessive litigation. The personnel manual should be sufficiently detailed so as to provide guidance to employees on all key company policies; however, overly complex manuals tend to restrict management flexibility and lead to employee confusion and uncertainty.

Also crucial is that your attorney review the manual before it is distributed to staff members, especially since some courts have recently held that the employment manual can be treated as if it were a binding contract under some circumstances. And because the manual is also a written record of the company's hiring, compensation, promotion, and termination policies, it could be offered as evidence in employment-related litigation. Courts recently seem increasingly more willing to look at statements made in the personnel manual (or every unwritten employment policy of the company) in disputes between employers and employees. Although the exact contents of the manual will vary depending on the nature and size of the franchisor, as well as on its management philosophies and objectives, all personnel manuals should contain the categories of information listed in Figure 15-2.

Preparing Key Personnel Employment Agreements

Although employment agreements are typically reserved for employees of the franchisor who are either senior management or who serve key technical functions, these documents serve as an important and cost-effective tool to safeguard confidential business information and preserve valuable human resources. When combined with a well-developed compensation plan, both provide an economic and legal foundation for long-term employee loyalty.

There are many other reasons why employment agreements with key employees of the franchisor are fundamental to a small franchisor's existence and growth. For example, venture capital investors will often insist on employment agreements between the franchisor and its founders and/or key employees in order to protect their investment. Second, individuals with special management or technical expertise may insist on one as a condition to joining the company. Finally, it serves as an important human resources management tool in terms of the description of duties, the basis for reward, and the grounds for termination.

Figure 15-2. What the personnel manual should contain.

- Key goals and objectives of the franchisor
- Background of the franchisor and its founders
- Description of the products and services offered by the franchisor
- Current organizational chart and brief position descriptions
- Compensation and benefits:
  - Hours of operation
  - Overtime policies
  - Vacation, maternity, sick leave, and holidays
  - Overview of employee benefits (health, dental, disability, etc.)
  - Performance review, raises, and promotions
  - Pension, profit-sharing, and retirement plans
  - Eligibility for fringe benefits
  - Rewards, employee discounts, and bonuses
  - Expense reimbursement policies

- Standards for employee conduct:
  - Dress code and personal hygiene
  - Courtesy to customers, vendors, and fellow employees
  - Smoking, drug use, and gum chewing
  - Jury duty and medical absences
  - Personal telephone calls and visits
  - Training and educational responsibilities
  - Employee use of company facilities and resources
  - Employee meals and breaks
  - Use of company-owned and -issued technology (laptops, PDAs, etc.)

- Safety regulations and emergency procedures
- Procedures for handling employee grievances, disputes, and conflicts
- Employee duties to protect intellectual property
- Term and termination of the employment relationship:
  - Probationary period
  - Grounds for discharge (immediate *versus* notice)
  - Employee termination and resignation
  - Severance pay
  - Exit interviews

- Maintenance of employee records:
  - Job application
  - Social Security and birth information
  - Federal and state tax, immigration, and labor/employment law documentation
  - Performance review and evaluation report
  - Benefit plan information
  - Exit interview information

- Special legal concerns:
  - Equal employment opportunity
  - Sexual harassment cases
  - Career advancement opportunities
  - Charitable and political contributions
  - Garnishment of employee wages
  - Policies regarding the award of franchises to employees or their family members

- Dealing with the news media and distribution of press releases
- Summary and reiteration of the role and purpose of the personnel manual
- Employee acknowledgment of receipt of manual (to be signed by the employee and placed in his or her permanent file)

The essential provisions of a key employee employment agreement include:

☐ *Duration.* The crucial judgment that you must make when determining the duration is whether the arrangement best suits the employer as a temporary, trial arrangement or as a long-term relationship. Other factors that should influence the decision about the duration are the nature of the job, the growth potential of the candidate, the business plans of the franchisor, the impact of illness or disability, how the estate will be treated in the event of the death of the employee, and trends in the industry. A separate section should be added addressing what effect a subsequent merger or acquisition of the franchisor would have on the agreement. The provisions should also specify the exact commencement and expiration dates of employment, the terms and procedures for employee tenure or renewal, and the grounds for early termination.

☐ *Duties and Obligations of the Employee.* The description of the nature of the employment and the employee's duties should include:

  ☐ The exact title (if any) of the employee.

  ☐ A statement of the exact tasks and responsibilities and a description of how these tasks and duties relate to the objectives of other employees, departments, and to the franchisor overall.

  ☐ A specification of the amount of time to be devoted to the position and to individual tasks.

  ☐ Where appropriate, a statement about whether the employee will serve on the franchisor's board of directors, and, if so, whether additional compensation will be paid for serving on the board. For certain employees, such as executive and managerial positions, the statement of duties should be defined as broadly as possible (e.g., "as directed by the Board" so that the employer has the right to change the employee's duties and title if human resources are needed elsewhere), with a statement merely limiting the scope of the employee's authority or ability to incur obligations on behalf of the franchisor. This statement will offer a franchisor limited protection against unauthorized acts by the employee, unless apparent or implied authority can be established by a third party.

☐ *Compensation Arrangements.* The type of compensation plan will naturally vary depending on the nature of the employee's duties, industry practice and custom, compensation offered by competitors, the stage of the franchisor's growth, market conditions, tax ramifications to both employer and employee, and the skill level of the employee. A schedule of payment, calculation of income, and a statement about the conditions for bonuses and rewards should be included.

☐ *Expense Reimbursement.* The types of business expenses for which the employee will be reimbursed should be clearly defined.

☐ *Employee Benefits.* All benefits and perquisites should be clearly defined, including:

❐ Health insurance.

❐ Cars owned by the franchisor.

❐ Education and training.

❐ Death, disability, or retirement benefits.

❐ Defined compensation plans.

❐ Pension or profit-sharing plans.

In addition, any vacation or sick leave policies should be included either in the employment agreement or in the personnel manual (or in both).

❐ *Covenants of Nondisclosure.* Trade secrets owned by a franchisor may be protected with covenants that impose obligations on the employee not to disclose (in any form and to any unauthorized party) any information that the franchisor regards as confidential and proprietary. This should include, among other things, customer lists, formulas and processes, financial and sales data, agreements with customers and suppliers, business and strategic plans, marketing strategies and advertising materials, and anything else that gives the employer an advantage over its competitors. This covenant should cover the preemployment period (interview or training period) and extend through the term of the agreement into post-termination. The scope of the covenant, the conditions it contains regarding the use and disclosure of trade secrets sources, the forms of information it describes, and the geographic limitations it covers should be broadly drafted to favor the employer. However, a nondisclosure covenant will be enforceable only to the extent necessary to reasonably protect the nature of the intellectual property at stake.

❐ *Covenants against Competition.* Any franchisor would like to be able to impose a restriction on its employees so that one who leaves the franchisor will be absolutely prohibited from working for a competitor in any way, shape, or manner. Courts, however, have not looked favorably on such attempts to rob individuals of their livelihood, and they have even set aside the entire contract agreement on the basis of such a section. The courts require that any covenants against competition be reasonable as to scope, time, territory, and remedy for noncompliance. The type of covenants against competition that will be tolerated by the courts vary from state to state and from industry to industry, but they must always be reasonable under the circumstances. An attorney with a background in this area must be consulted when drafting these provisions.

❐ *Covenants Regarding Ownership of Inventions.* Questions that might arise regarding the ownership of intellectual property developed by an employee during the term of employment should be expressly addressed in the agreement. If they are not specifically addressed, basic common law rules regarding ownership of an employee's ideas, inventions, and discoveries will govern. These rules do not necessarily favor the employer, especially if there is a question of fact as to whether the discovery was made while working outside the scope of the employment *or* if it is established that the employee did not utilize the employer's resources in connection with the invention. In the absence of a written agreement, the common law principle of shop rights generally dictates that, if an invention is made by an employee, if it does not utilize the resources of the employer, even if it is made outside of the scope of the employment, ownership is vested in the employee, subject, however, to a nonexclusive, royalty-free, irrevocable license to the employer.

❐ *Protection of Intellectual Property upon Termination.* The agreement should contain provisions regarding obligations of nondisclosure and noncompetition upon the termination of employment, and, when an employee leaves, these obligations should be reaffirmed with an exit interview with at least one witness present during the exit interview. For example, a franchisor should inform the exiting employee of the employee's continuing duty to preserve the confidentiality of trade secrets, reiterate specific information regarded as confidential, and obtain assurances and evidence (including a written acknowledgment) that all confidential and proprietary documents have been returned and no copies retained. The name of the new employer or future activity should be obtained, and, under certain circumstances, the new employer may even be notified of the prior employment relationship and its scope. These procedures put the new employer/competitor on notice of the franchisor's rights and prevent it from claiming that it was unaware that its new employee had revealed trade secrets. Finally, the franchisor should also insist that the employee not hire co-workers after the termination of employment with the franchisor.

Employers should nevertheless carefully consider the long-term implications of the terms and conditions contained in the employment agreement. Once promises are made to an employee in writing, the employee will expect special benefits to remain available throughout the term of the agreement. Your failure to meet these obligations on a continuing basis will expose you to the risk of litigation for breach of contract.

Structuring an Employee Recruitment and Selection Program

The federal employment laws seek to protect each employee's right to be hired, promoted, and terminated without regard to race or gender. The agency tasked with enforcing these laws is the Equal Employment Opportunity Commission (EEOC). Under very limited circumstances, the EEOC will tolerate "discriminatory practices" in the recruitment and termination processes, *but* only if the criteria for making the determination are based on a "bona fide occupational qualification" (BFOQ) or a requirement reasonably and rationally related to the employment activities and responsibilities of a particular employee or a particular group of employees, rather than to all employees of the employer.

The equal opportunity laws do not require a franchisor to actively recruit or maintain a designated quota of members of minority groups; however, they do prohibit companies from developing recruitment and selection
procedures that treat an applicant differently because of race, sex, age, religion, or national origin. In determining whether a franchisor's recruitment
policies have resulted in the disparate treatment of minorities, the courts and
the EEOC will be looking objectively at:

❒ The nature of the position and the education, training, and skill level
   required to fill the position.

❒ The minority composition of the current workforce and its relationship
   to local demographic statistics.

❒ Prior hiring practices.

❒ The recruitment channels (such as newspapers, agencies, industry publications, universities, etc.).

❒ The information requested of the candidate in the job application and
   in the interview.

❒ Any selection criteria or testing (or related performance) measure implemented in the decision-making process.

❒ Any differences in the terms and conditions of employment offered to
   those who apply for the same job.

Anyone alleging discrimination in the hiring process needs to demonstrate that the following key facts were present, specifically that:

❒ The applicant was a member of a minority class that is protected under
   federal law (such as an African American).

❒ The individual was qualified for the job that was open.

❒ The individual was denied the position.

❒ The advertised position remained open after the individual was rejected
   and that the company continued to interview applicants with the same
   qualifications as the rejected candidate.

If an applicant successfully demonstrates these facts, then the burden
usually shifts to the company, who must then present legitimate business
reasons for not hiring the applicant.

Preventive Measures

You can implement several preventive measures to protect against discrimination claims. Ultimately these measures will prevail when and if a disgruntled applicant files a discrimination charge. First, a well-drafted job
description that accurately reflects the duties of the position should be prepared before publicly advertising for the position: the skills, ability, and
knowledge needed to perform the position competently; the compensation

and related terms and conditions of employment; and the education, training, prior work experience, or professional certification (if any) that the position may require. A well-prepared job description will not only help you determine the qualities you are looking for in an employee and hire the right person, but will also serve as protection against a claim that the standards for the position were developed arbitrarily or in violation of applicable antidiscrimination laws.

Second, make sure your advertising and recruitment program meets EEOC standards by insisting that all job advertisements include the phrase "Equal Opportunity Employer." The context of the advertisement should not indicate any preference toward race, sex, religion, national origin, or age unless it meets the requirements of a BFOQ for the position. If employment agencies are used as a recruitment device, then inform them in writing of the company's nondiscrimination policy. If applicants are recruited from universities or trade schools, be certain that minority institutions are also visited. When selecting publications for the placement of advertisements for the positions, target all potential job applicants and advertise in minority publications where possible.

Third, develop a job application form that is limited to job-related questions and that meets all federal, state, and local legal requirements. Questions in the application regarding an individual's race or religion should not be included. In court, the company will generally bear the burden to prove that any given question on the application, especially those relating to handicap, marital status, age, height or weight, criminal record, military status, or citizenship, is genuinely related to the applicant's ability to meet the requirements of the position. Even questions regarding date of birth or whom to contact in the event of an emergency should be reserved for post-hiring information gathering.

Finally, an EEO compliance officer should be designated to monitor employment practices with the responsibility to (1) structure position descriptions, job applications, and advertisements; (2) collect and maintain applicant and employee files; (3) meet with interviewers to review employment laws that affect the questions that may be asked of the applicant; and (4) work with legal counsel to ensure that the employment policies as well as recent developments in the law are adequately communicated to all employees.

The Interview

From a *legal* perspective, the questions asked in an interview must substantially be job related and be posed uniformly to all candidates for the position. The exact types of questions that may be asked varies depending on applicable state laws, and therefore state and local employment laws within the franchisor's jurisdiction should be consulted for further guidance. As a general rule, the following types of questions should be avoided:

❐ What is your marital status and how many children do you have? How do family responsibilities affect your ability to meet work-related obligations?

❑ What is your religious affiliation? What religious holidays do you expect will interfere with work-related obligations?

❑ What is your national origin? Where are your parents from? What is your native language?

❑ Do you have any specific disabilities, or have you ever been treated for any diseases?

❑ Does your spouse object to your traveling or anticipated relocation? Will you be able to make child care arrangements given the long hours of this job?

In addition, several topic areas are not necessarily prohibited, but nevertheless should be asked carefully to avoid an indirect claim of discrimination. These questions include those concerning the applicant's prior or current drug history, social clubs and hobbies, or the career plans of a spouse.

Notwithstanding these difficult guidelines, still several types of questions are legally available for screening candidates, such as:

❑ Why are you leaving your current position, and how does this position resolve some of those problems?

❑ What was the most challenging project that you were responsible for in your last position?

❑ Do you have any physical or mental impairments that would restrict your ability to perform the responsibilities of this position?

❑ Are there any criminal indictments currently pending against you? What is the nature of these charges?

❑ What are your expectations regarding this position? How do these expectations influence your short- and long-term career goals?

Guidelines for Proper Termination of Employment

The decision to terminate an employee can be both emotional and frustrating—and it can result in expensive litigation if not handled properly. These days, wrongful termination lawsuits are not idle threats; they can be costly disputes to resolve with no real winners.

When an employee wins a lawsuit for unfair termination, the remedies for unjust dismissal have ranged from simple reinstatement to back pay and actual damages to even punitive damages for certain cases. Employers have also faced charges of discrimination or violation of federal statutes in connection with the termination of an employee. To successfully defend against these types of claims, you must be prepared to demonstrate that employee performance evaluations, policies contained in personnel manuals, and grounds for termination were implemented and enforced in a nondiscriminatory fashion, not as a result of any act contrary to applicable federal law. Specific, clear, and uniform guidelines should be developed for probation periods, opportunities to improve job performance, availability of training, and termination procedures.

Five Steps to Prevent Lawsuits

These steps can be taken prior to, during, and after the employee has been fired:

❏ *Step One.* The first step (well before the actual termination) is careful record keeping. Comprehensive records should be kept on each employee, including any formal performance appraisal or informal warnings, comments, or memos prepared by a supervisor to demonstrate the employee's poor work or misconduct. If a case ever gets to litigation, these documents and records may be the only evidence available to support that the employer had valid reasons for terminating the employee.

❏ *Step Two.* Ensure that you have a proper basis for termination. This step involves a careful review of personnel manuals, policy statements, memoranda, and related documentation to ensure that no implied representation or agreement has been made regarding the term of employment, severance pay, or grounds for termination that may be inconsistent with the company's intentions. The various grounds for termination should be clearly stated in the personnel manual, which should include, among other things: (1) discriminatory acts toward employees or hiring candidates, (2) physical or sexual abuse, (3) falsifying time records or other key documents, (4) willful or negligent violation of safety or security rules, (5) violation of company policies, (6) unauthorized disclosure of the franchisor's confidential information, (7) refusal to perform work assigned by a supervisor, (8) destroying or damaging company property, (9) misappropriation or embezzlement, or (10) drug abuse or gambling on company premises.

❏ *Step Three.* Ensure that all alternatives to termination have been considered. An employee who has been performing poorly should be provided with plenty of advance notice of management's disappointment with his or her performance through personal and written evaluations, warning notices, and published employment policies. When the cause for termination involves an act of insubordination, improper conduct, or related incidents, witness statements, accident reports, customer complaints, and related documentation should all be collected and reviewed. Even once the immediate supervisor has made a termination decision and collected the evidence supporting the cause, a member of management, at least one level above the direct supervisor of the employee, should make an independent review of the proposed dismissal. An opportunity to cure the defect in performance should be strongly considered. The reviewer should take the time to confront the employee and hear his or her side of the story prior to making the final dismissal decision. Written records of these meetings should be placed in the employee's file. The reviewer should question the supervisor and co-workers of the employee to gather additional facts and to ensure that all company policies and procedures have been followed, especially those regarding performance appraisal and employee discipline.

❐ *Step Four.* Once the decision has been reached, conduct an exit interview during which the reasons for the employee's discharge are explained. The explanation should be candid and concise, in accordance with all available evidence, and consistent with any explanation of the termination that will be provided to the employee. You should emphasize to the employee that the reasons for termination are legitimate and are consistent with the company's past practices under similar circumstances. The employee should also be advised what will be told to prospective employers and reminded of any covenants not to compete and of the employee's continuing obligation to protect the company's trade secrets.

❐ *Step Five.* The final step is to prepare a comprehensive release and termination to further protect the company against subsequent litigation. The employee should be given an opportunity to have the document reviewed by legal counsel. The release and termination agreement should (1) be supported by valid consideration (e.g., some form of severance pay or covenants); (2) be signed by the employee knowingly and voluntarily; (3) include the grounds for termination in the recitals; (4) contain covenants against competition, disclosure, and litigation; (5) include all possible defendants in an employment action (company, officers, directors, subsidiaries, etc.); (6) avoid commitments regarding references to future employers; and (7) be checked carefully against all applicable federal and state laws.

The broad scope of federal and state antidiscrimination laws make it imperative for owners (and their managers) to understand their obligations in structuring employee recruitment, selection, training, compensation, reward, employee testing, and seniority programs. Charges of discrimination may be defeated if proper documentation is maintained, such as a complete personnel file of the former employee, detailed records of complaints of supervisors and co-workers related to the cause of termination, copies of actual work produced by the employee that was unsatisfactory, a written record reflecting the race and sex of other persons dismissed or disciplined for the same or similar purposes, and the name, race, and sex of the individual replacing the discharged employee.

The welfare and motivation of the management team and of employees at all levels are clearly one of the most valuable assets of a rapidly growing franchisor. If they are treated unfairly in the hiring or termination process, however, they can become the largest liability as well as a major deterrent to franchise sales. Prospective franchisees who are perceptive will notice the culture and general satisfaction level of your staff when they come to visit your headquarters. Employees who are mistreated or confused are not likely to communicate the message to a prospect that you wish to convey. Prospective franchisees' reaction might be, "Why should I buy a franchise from a company that can't even keep its own staff motivated and productive?" Employment agreements and personnel manuals are useful tools to define the rights and obligations of the employer and employee to each other and to ensure that your workforce is informed and motivated.

CHAPTER 16

Special Issues in Mergers and Acquisitions

he wave of mergers and acquisitions (M&As) that occurred throughout the 1980s were primarily financially motivated, and in the roll-ups of the 1990s, acquirer's stock was used as acquisition currency to consolidate fragmented industries (and in many cases the expected economics of scale did not come to pass). The more recent mergers and acquisitions in 2008 and 2009, however, were motivated primarily by strategic considerations. Synergies between the acquiror and acquiree of the two or more merging companies were expected to lead to efficiencies, competitive benefits, and improved operating margins, or private equity firms got much more strategic in the assembly of their portfolios and the expected synergies between companies.

Franchisors have been the center of attention in the midst of this new and more strategic wave of M&A activity, on both a large and medium scale. The attractiveness of established consumer brands, steady cash flow, predictable and durable revenue streams, a dedicated distribution channel, value-driven menus of products and services, strategic real estate locations, strong and experienced management teams, already audited financial statements, strong internal and quality controls, and other features are *all* character traits that make franchisors attractive candidates for strategic acquisitions by other franchisors, by nonfranchisor strategic buyers, and by private equity and buyout funds for acquisition, investment, or recapitalization purposes.

In the period 2004–2009, dozens of significant transactions took place, and the pace is not expected to slow down any time soon. In fact, the characteristics of most franchisors will only make them more attractive candidates inasmuch as the overall capital markets have slowed down and become focused on quality over quantity. A wide variety of industries and transactional sizes have been represented—Hollywood Tans®, Johnny Rockets®, Serve Master®, Cartridge World®, the Dwyer Group®, Back Yard Burger®, Macaroni Grill®, and Au Bon Pain®. All these companies, as well as dozens of others, were bought either by other franchisors or by private equity funds. Some of the more significant transactions included the $2.43 billion purchase of Dunkin' Brands (which includes Dunkin' Donuts®, Baskin-Robbins ice cream, and Togo's sandwich shops) by Bain Capital; Thomas H. Lee Partners and Carlyle Group from the French conglomerate, Pernod Riccard; the Blackstone Group's purchase of Hilton Hotels for $26 billion (it had already bought the La Quinta chain for $3.4 billion); and Triarc's purchase of Wendy's® for over $2 billion.

Some franchisors turned to refranchising (e.g., turning company-owned units into franchises, which include a sale of the operating assets) in order to raise new cash and to manage operating expenses and capital expenditures. Well-heeled multiunit operator franchisees were able to add units at attractive terms in systems such as Pizza Hut®, Hardees® and Applebee's®. And some multiunit operators have themselves been targets for acquisition by private equity firms such as Sentinel Capital and Olympus Partners.

Private equity funds such as Roark Capital Group has focused on franchisors, buying a controlling stake in Carvel in 2008, whose largest competitor—Dairy Queen®—had been bought by Warren Buffett's Berkshire Hathaway just a few years earlier. Roark, in affiliation with FOCUS Brands, owns or controls a wide variety of household-name franchising, including Schlotsky's®, Cinnabon®, Moe's Southwest Grill®, Fast Signs®, and Money Mailer®. Roark now has over $1.5 billion in capital under management and controls over a dozen franchisors generating $3 billion in system-wide revenues.

Finally, many franchisors have engaged in recapitalizations and restructurings, as well as management buyouts, as a form of (or alternative to) M&A transactions. Recent transactions include Bojangles® ($25 million buyout), Comfort Keepers® ($44 million buyout), Meineke Car Care® ($128 million management-lead recap), Worldwide Express® ($15 million buyout), and Coverall® ($59 million management-lead buyout). For the sources of recapitalization funds and resources, the same characteristics that make franchisors attractive as M&A candidates (e.g., strong brands, unit diversification, market protection, predictable and durable cash flows, etc.) are also attractive to providers of transactional equity and debt capital. Older and more mature franchise concepts that may have been launched 20 or 30 years ago are looking at these types of financing transactions very carefully as they prepare to transition ownership to the next generation or to select management groups as an alternative to traditional M&A.

Because franchisors are just as susceptible as nonfranchise companies to the pressures of competition, shifts in demand and demographics, or the need to respond to changes in law or technology, mergers or acquisitions of competing or complementary franchise systems are a viable strategy for responding to these pressures. Thus, franchisors consider a merger or acquisition with another franchisor or nonfranchise companies consider franchise systems as viable acquisition targets for various reasons, some of the common ones including:

❐ The desire to add new products or services to existing lines without the expense and uncertainty of internal research and development.

❐ The desire to expand into a new geographic market or customer base without the expense of attracting new franchisees into these locations or of developing a new advertising and marketing program.

❐ The need to increase size to effectively compete with larger companies or to eliminate the threat of a smaller competitor.

❐ The desire for market efficiencies through the acquisition of suppliers (backward integration) or existing franchisees or distributors (forward integration).

❐ The need to strengthen marketing capabilities or improve the quality of management personnel.

Numerous complex issues are involved in the merger or acquisition of any company, including both legal and business considerations. This is especially true for franchisors, however, which not only must address the potential issues related to taxes, securities regulation, labor laws, employee benefits, antitrust, environmental regulation, corporate governance, bankruptcy, and antitrust compliance, but which also must understand the nature of the assets of the franchise system being acquired and the unique relationship between the franchisor and its franchisees. Franchisors who are considering their first acquisition must understand that the transaction is a *process, not an event.* (See Figure 16-1.) The management of the process, the quality of the franchisor's team of advisors, and a clear understanding of the franchisor's transactional objectives will all go a long way to ensuring that the completed deal is ultimately a success for the franchisor, its shareholders, and the overall system. A key component of the management of this process will also be an analysis of how the proposed transaction may affect the franchisor-franchisee relationship, including the potential dilution of its brands,

Figure 16-1. The franchisor's acquisition process.

The franchisor's planning and implementation of an acquisition program typically involves the following steps:
- Develop acquisition objectives.
- Analyze projected economic and financial gains to be achieved by the acquisition.
- Assemble an acquisition team (managers, attorneys, accountants, and investment bankers) and begin the search for acquisition candidates.
- Prepare due diligence analysis of prime candidates (franchise systems, vertical suppliers, systems that could be developed or converted into franchise systems, etc.).
- Begin initial negotiations and valuation of the selected target.
- Select the structure of the transaction.
- Identify sources of financing for the transaction.
- Undergo detailed bidding and negotiations.
- Obtain all shareholder and third-party consents and approvals.
- Structure the legal documents.
- Prepare for the closing.
- Hold the closing.
- Perform postclosing tasks and responsibilities.
- Implement the integration of the two entities.

the overlap of its territorial rights, and potential confusion in the product and service mixes offered to consumers.

Analysis of One or More Target Companies

Franchisees must begin the acquisition or merger process with a plan identifying the specific objectives to be accomplished by the transaction and the criteria to be applied in analyzing a potential target company operating in the targeted industry. Once acquisition objectives have been identified, the next logical step is to narrow the field of candidates. Some of the qualities that a viable acquisition target might possess are that it:

❐ Operates in an industry that demonstrates growth potential.

❐ Has taken steps necessary to protect any proprietary aspects of its products and services.

❐ Has developed a well-defined and established market position.

❐ Possesses "strong" franchise agreements with its franchisees with minimal amendments or "special exceptions."

❐ Has good relationships with its franchisees, strong customer satisfaction, and brand loyalty to its core products and services offered by its franchisees.

❐ Is involved in a minimal amount of litigation (especially if the litigation is with key customers, distributors, franchisees, or suppliers).

❐ Is in a position to readily obtain key third-party consents from lessors, bankers, creditors, suppliers, and investors (as required). (The failure to obtain necessary consents to the assignment of key contracts or to clear encumbrances on title to material assets may seriously impede the completion of the transaction.)

❐ Is in a position to sell so that negotiations focus on the terms of the sale, *not* on whether to sell in the first place.

In addition to these general business issues, the following issues should be examined when examining the potential acquisition of a franchise system:

❐ The strength and registration status of the target's trademarks and other intellectual property

❐ The quality of the target's agreements and relationships with its franchisees

❐ The status of any litigation or regulatory inquiries involving the target

❐ The quality of the target franchise sales staff

❐ The quality of the franchisee relationships, including the regularity of the franchisor's cash flow from royalty obligations

❐ The strength of the target franchisor's training, operations, and field support programs; manuals; and personnel

❐ The existence of any franchisee association and its relationship with the franchisor

❐ The strength and performance of the target's company-owned units (as applicable)

Sometimes, instead of the acquirer affirmatively seeking acquisition targets, the process is reversed, and the target, rather than the acquirer, solicits offers to be acquired. Such an acquisition candidate may offer an excellent opportunity for the acquirer, although the target's operations and financial condition should be closely inspected for any liability or potential pitfall that may be hidden behind the good intentions of the sellers.

Regardless of who approaches whom, the inspection of a potential target will be necessary (often referred to as the due diligence review). Preliminary due diligence may be undertaken before any offer is made, and more thorough due diligence certainly has to be completed by the acquirer's in-house and outside business and legal advisors before completing the deal.

The Due Diligence Review

Before conducting a thorough due diligence review of an acquisition candidate, the franchisor may want to conduct a preliminary analysis. In most cases, the principals of each of the companies will meet to discuss the possible transaction. The key areas of inquiry at this stage are:

❐ The financial performance to date and the projected performance of the target

❐ The strength of the target's management team.

❐ The target's intellectual property.

❐ The condition of the target's franchise system, including an understanding of the terms of the target's existing franchise and area development agreements.

❐ Any potential liabilities of the target that may be transferred to the franchisor as a successor company.

❐ The identification of any legal or business impediments to the transaction, such as regulatory restrictions or adverse tax consequences.

In addition to a direct response from the target's management, information also may be obtained from outside sources, such as trade associations, customers, and suppliers of the target; industry publications; franchise regulatory agencies; chambers of commerce; securities law filings if the company is publicly traded on a stock exchange or through the NASDAQ stock markets; or private data sources, such as Dun & Bradstreet, Standard & Poor's, and Moody's. Some of this information may be readily available on the Internet.

Once the two companies have agreed to move forward, a wide variety of legal documents and records, as applicable, should be carefully reviewed and analyzed by the acquiring entity and its legal counsel. The purpose of due diligence is to help answer two very basic questions: (1) Why are we doing this deal? (2) What risks will we assume if we decide to move forward?

The following is an illustrative list of some of the questions that the acquirer and its legal and accounting representatives will be trying to answer as they begin to draft the acquisition agreements that will memorialize the deal:

- ❏ What approvals will be needed to effectuate the transaction (e.g., director and stockholder approval, governmental consents, lenders' and lessors' consents, etc.)?

- ❏ Does the transaction raise any antitrust problems? Will filing be necessary under the premerger notification provisions of the Hart-Scott-Rodino Act?

- ❏ Are there any federal or state securities registration or reporting laws to comply with?

- ❏ What are the potential tax consequences to the buyer, seller, and their respective stockholders as a result of the transaction?

- ❏ What are the buyer's potential postclosing risks and obligations? To what extent should the seller be held liable for such potential liability? What steps, if any, can be taken to reduce these potential risks or liabilities? What will it cost to implement these steps?

- ❏ Are there any impediments to the transfer of key tangible and intangible assets of the target company, such as real estate and intellectual or other property?

- ❏ Are there any issues relating to environmental and hazardous waste laws, such as the Comprehensive Environmental Response Compensation and Liability Act (the Superfund law)?

- ❏ What are the obligations and responsibilities of buyer and seller under applicable federal and state labor and employment laws? For example, will the buyer be subject to successor liability under federal labor laws and as a result be obligated to recognize the presence of organized labor and therefore to negotiate existing collective bargaining agreements?

- ❏ To what extent will employment, consulting, confidentiality, or non-competition agreements need to be created or modified in connection with the proposed transaction?

- ❏ What are the terms of the target's agreements with its existing franchisees? Are these agreements assignable? Do they contain clauses giving the franchisor discretion to change the system or ownership? Could any of these terms cause problems for the acquiring franchisor at a later date?

- ❏ Is the target currently involved in litigation with franchisees, creditors, competitors, or suppliers? Is there threatened litigation or potential litigation? What is the risk of exposure to the acquiring franchisor?

- ❏ Have the target's registration and disclosure documents been properly filed and updated?

Some of the questions that will be analyzed by the acquirer's business and accounting advisors are:

❏ Does the target franchisor fit into the long-range growth plans of the acquiring franchisor?

❏ What are the target franchisor's strong points and weaknesses? How does management of the acquiring franchisor plan to eliminate those weaknesses?

❏ Has the acquiring franchisor's management team developed a comprehensive plan to integrate the resources of the target?

❏ What is the target franchisor's ratio of company-owned outlets to franchisees?

❏ Are the target's products and services competitive in terms of price, quality, style, and marketability?

❏ Does the target franchisor manufacture its own products? What proportions are purchased from outside sellers?

❏ What is the target's past and current financial condition? What about future projections? Are they realistic?

❏ What is the target franchisor's sales history? Has there been a steady flow of franchise sales and royalty payments?

❏ What is the target franchisor's attrition rate? Have there been many recent terminations or transfers? Have any of these been contested by franchisees as lacking good cause?

The Role of the Franchisee in a Proposed Merger or Acquisition

Unlike other types of growing companies involved in mergers and acquisitions, franchisors have existing contractual vertical distribution systems in place through their franchisees. The interests of these franchisees ought to be taken into account when the franchisor's counsel analyzes the legal consequences and potential costs of the proposed merger or acquisition. These franchisees are clearly interested parties whose contractual and other legal and equitable rights must be considered. There is no statutory or legal basis for disclosing the intent to engage in a merger or acquisition, nor is there typically a contractual requirement to obtain their approval. Nevertheless, good franchisee relations practice would dictate their involvement in some fashion. The cooperation level of the franchisee networks of both buyer and seller can either greatly facilitate the transaction or virtually kill the deal, depending on how this communication problem is handled.

For example, if one franchisor acquires another in a competitive or parallel line of business, careful merger planning and negotiation will be necessary to ensure a smooth integration of the target's franchise system into the buyer's existing operations (assuming that only one system will survive after the transaction) and to avoid potential litigation or costly settlement with affected franchisees of either system. In addition, if conversion or change is planned as a result of the merger or acquisition, franchisors should expect to

involve franchisees, at least to a certain extent, in the decision-making process. The acquiring franchisor should not automatically assume that franchisees in the acquired system will be willing to convert to the buyer's
existing system. When change or conversion is contemplated, some attrition
and/or franchisee resistance should be expected in both systems, and the
impact and costs of this attrition and resistance will typically be reflected in
the purchase price of the target franchisor.

On one hand, the franchisee is typically neither a shareholder, creditor,
investor, officer, nor director of the franchisor and would technically be governed only by the terms of franchise agreements, which usually gives broad
latitude to the franchisor to assign rights or modify the franchise system. Yet
to ignore the fact that the franchisee is clearly an interested and affected
party in any change in the franchisor's organizational structure or system is
unrealistic and could result in very costly litigation that might even outweigh any anticipated benefits to the proposed merger or acquisition. (See
Figure 16-2.) A game plan must be put in place and clearly communicated to
help them adapt and evolve to the impact that the transaction will have on
their operations.

Special Problems Relating to Franchisees of the Acquiring or the Acquired Franchise System

A number of potential issues for dispute between the acquiring or acquired
franchisor and its franchisees may arise as a result of a merger or acquisition.
Whether they arise will, of course, depend on a variety of factors, including
the similarity of the businesses of the merging systems, the territories in
which they operate, the terms of the contracts with existing franchisees in

Figure 16-2. Legitimate concerns of the franchisee network in a merger or acquisition.

Clearly, the franchisee will have some legitimate questions and concerns when it first learns of the
proposed transaction. The savvy franchisor will anticipate these concerns and integrate the proposed
solutions into its acquisition plan and communications with the franchisees and/or the franchisee association:

- What are the acquiring franchisor's plans for the acquired system? Consolidation and conversion? At whose cost? Liquidation? Growth?
- What is the reputation and management philosophy of the acquiring franchisor? What are its
  attitudes toward field support and ongoing training?
- Will the acquiring franchisor be sensitive to the rights and concerns of the franchisees? Or will
  the franchisees adopt a "we'd rather fight than switch" mentality toward the new buyer in anticipation of hostile negotiations?
- What is the financial strength of the acquiring franchisor? Will the acquiring franchisor open up
  new opportunities for the franchisees, such as access to new product lines, financing programs
  for growth and expansion, product purchasing, and cooperative advertising programs?
- If the target franchisor owns real property that is leased to franchisees, will the terms and
  conditions of the current leases be honored by the acquiring franchisor? What about other
  contractual obligations? Are there any special relationships with third-party vendors that will be
  affected or damaged by the transaction?

each system, the size and market power of the merging franchisors, the competitors (or lack of them) for each of the franchisors, and, most importantly, the plans of the surviving company. Because franchisors have an implied obligation to act in good faith and in a commercially reasonable manner (a covenant recognized by many state courts in their interpretation of the franchise relationship), both franchisors should pay special attention to such issues as:

❒ What is the extent of any territorial exclusivity granted to the franchisees of each system? Is exclusivity given only for a certain trademark or line of business? Is territorial exclusivity conditioned on the performance of the franchisees? Will substantially similar franchisees violate this exclusivity?

❒ Will all existing franchisees of both systems be maintained, or will a consolidated distribution system result in the termination of some franchisees?

❒ Will franchisees be required or requested to convert to a new business format? Who will pay the costs of building conversion, new training, products, and services? Will the franchisor finance all or part of the conversion costs?

❒ Will existing franchisees of each system be forced to add the products and services of the other? Will this present tying or full-line forcing problems?

❒ Does the acquiring franchisor have sufficient support staff to adequately service the new franchisees, or will the acquiring company's existing franchisees be ignored in order to develop and market the new acquisitions? What rights do the existing franchisees have to challenge this lack of attention?

❒ Will a new, third type of system, combining the products and services of the acquiring and acquired franchisors, be offered to prospective franchisees of the surviving entity? Will existing franchisees of either system be eligible to convert to the new system?

❒ Can the acquiring franchisor legitimately enforce an in-term covenant against competition when the franchisor itself has acquired and is operating what is arguably a competitive system?

❒ Do the franchisees of either franchisor have a franchisee association or franchisee advisory council? Must these groups be consulted? What duty does the franchisor have to involve these groups in merger planning? What about regional and multiple franchisees holding development rights?

❒ Does either franchisor have company-owned outlets in its distribution system? What will be the status of these outlets after the merger or acquisition?

❒ To what extent will royalty payments, renewal fees, costs of inventory, performance quotas, and advertising contributions be affected by the contemplated merger or acquisition? On what grounds could franchisees challenge these changes as unreasonable, breaches of contract, or violations of antitrust laws? How and when will these changes be phased into the system? Will the franchisees be given a chance to opt in or opt out (mandatory versus optional changes)?

❑ Will the proposed transaction result in the termination of some of the franchisees of either system due to oversaturation of the market, territorial overlap, or underperformance? What legal and statutory rights of the franchisee are triggered?

The Consequences of Inadequate Planning and Due Diligence

The consequences of inadequate pretransaction planning and investigation to both the acquirer and the target in a transaction combining two or more franchise systems can be financially devastating, often resulting in years of litigation while the franchise system suffers. An example is a recent stock purchase acquisition of a food concept by another similar concept. The seller's management intentionally concealed from the buyer material information concerning certain contractual defaults and potential litigation problems. Although the buyer escrowed some of the purchase price to cover the costs of defending franchisee litigation that was disclosed, the undisclosed litigation was costing far in excess of the amount reserved. To complicate matters, the same management who had concealed the litigation wrought indemnification from the buyer, who had agreed to limited indemnity for the sellers and their managers because of a claimant's ability, under certain franchise and trade practices statutes, to sue individual officers and directors personally. Now the buyer must address both the successor liability claim *and* the dispute with the former management.

In another example, the owners of a franchise system that was to be sold failed to inform the buyer of serious disagreements with its franchisees. The relationship between the seller and the franchisees had deteriorated to the point that they had retained a lawyer to represent them at a meeting with the franchisor. Fortunately, the buyer learned of the meeting and the problems and decided to delay the transaction pending the seller's ability to work the problem out with the franchisees.

Finally, in another case, two publicly traded franchise companies signed a letter of intent to move forward with a combination that would be paid for in the stock of the acquirer. Negotiating the basic terms of the transaction took a substantial amount of time and effort by both companies and their representatives. Finally, after agreement in principal was reached, the companies discovered serious securities law impediments. After further expense and effort on everyone's part, they simply could not satisfy the regulators at the Securities and Exchange Commission. The deal was scrapped.

Thus, the difficult legal and strategic issues that are triggered in a merger or acquisition by and among franchisors can either be resolved—and litigation avoided—with careful pretransaction planning and investigation by the acquiring and acquired franchisors, or cause the deal to fail. Among the criti-

---

Box 16-1. Common mistakes made by the franchisor buyer during the due diligence investigation.

- Mismatch between the documents provided by the seller and the skills of the buyer's review team. Perhaps the seller has particularly complex financial statements or highly technical reports that must be truly understood by the buyer's due diligence team. Make sure there is a capability fit.

- Poor communication and misunderstandings. The communications should be open and clear between the teams of the buyer and the seller. The process must be well orchestrated.

- Lack of planning and focus in the preparation of the due diligence questionnaires and in the interviews with the seller's team. The focus must be on asking the *right* questions, not just a lot of them. Seller's will resent wasteful fishing expeditions when the buyer's team is unfocused. There should be a clear fit between the questions asked and the compelling strategic rationale underlying the transaction.

- Inadequate time devoted to tax and financial matters. The buyer's (and seller's) CFO and CPA must play an integral part in the due diligence process in order to gather data on past financial performance and tax reporting, unusual financial events, or disturbing trends or inefficiencies.

- The buyer must insist that its team will be treated like welcome guests, not as spies from the enemy camp. Many times the buyer's counsel is sent to a dark room in the corner of the building to inspect documents without coffee, windows, or phones. Providing reasonable accommodations and support for the buyer's due diligence team enhances and expedites the transaction.

- Failure to closely examine the intangible factors that drive a deal's success. Many deals fail because of a lack of a shared vision or conflicting corporate cultures. The franchisor's due diligence must include a process for measuring the likelihood that the two cultures and systems will ultimately fit after the post.

---

cal steps toward a successful transaction, communication with the franchisees of both systems is of paramount importance.

Preparing the M&A Documentation

Once the due diligence has been completed, valuations and appraisals conducted, terms and price initially negotiated, and financing arranged, the acquisition team must work carefully with legal counsel to structure and begin the preparation of the definitive legal documentation to memorialize the transaction. The drafting and negotiation of these documents will usually focus on the past history of the seller, the present condition of the business, and a description of the rules of the game for the future. They also describe the nature and scope of the seller's representations and warranties, the terms of the seller's indemnification of the buyer, the conditions precedent to the closing of the transaction, the responsibilities of the parties during the time period between execution of the purchase agreement and actual closing, the terms and structure of payment, the scope of postclosing covenants of competition, the deferred or contingent compensation components, and any predetermined remedies for breach of the contract.

Virtually all key issues in the acquisition agreement fall into one of these three categories: consideration, mechanics, and allocation of risk. The chart in Figure 16-3 is designed to be a diagnostic tool to ensure that the franchisor and its team and all other parties to the transaction understand the acquisition agreement. It can also be used to ensure that the three key categories of issues have been addressed and that the definitive documents are reflective of the business points reached between the parties.

Other Key Issues in Preparing and Negotiating the Acquisition Agreement

Allocation of Risk

The acquisition agreement is, in many ways, merely a tool for *allocating risk*. The franchisor as buyer will want to hold the seller accountable for any postclosing claim or liability relating to situations that occurred while the seller owned the company *or* that occurred as a result of a misrepresentation or material omission by the seller. The seller, on the other hand, wants to bring as much finality to the transaction as possible to allow some degree of

Figure 16-3. Understanding the acquisition documents.

Consideration	Mechanics	Allocation of Risk
• Structure	• Conditions to closing	• Representations and warranties (R&W's) two-way street (due diligence driven)
• Scope of purchase	• Timetable	
• Price	• Covenants (including covenants not to compete)	
• How/when paid		• Indemnification
• Deferred consideration/ security	• Third-party and regulatory approvals	• Holdbacks and baskets
• Earn-outs and contingent payments	• Schedules (exceptions/ substantiation)	• If seller is taking buyer's stock or notes (then R&W's are a two-way street)
• Other ongoing financial relationships between buyer and seller	• Opinions	• Collars
	• Dispute resolution	• R&W insurance
• Employment/consultant agreements		• Methods for dealing with surprises
• Postclosing adjustments		

sleep at night. When both parties are represented by skilled negotiators, a middle ground is reached, both in general and on specific issues of actual or potential liability. The franchisor's counsel will want to draft changes, covenants, representations, and warranties that are strong and absolute to protect its interests as a buyer. The seller's counsel will seek to insert phrases like ". . . except insignificant defaults or losses which have not, or are not likely to, at any time before or after the closing, result in a material loss or liability to or against the buyer . . . ," leaving some wiggle room for insignificant or nonmaterial claims. The battleground will be the indemnification provisions and any exceptions, carve-outs, or baskets that are created to dilute these provisions. The weapons will be the buzzwords explained in "Playing with the Buzzwords" (see page 344).

Scope of the Assets

The typical buyer will want to specify a laundry list of categories of assets to be purchased, but the typical seller will want to modify the list by using words like "exclusively" or "primarily." The seller may want to exclude all or most of the cash on hand from the schedule of assets to be transferred. In some cases, the seller may want to license some of the technology rights in lieu of an outright sale or, at the very least, obtain a license back of what has been sold.

Security for the Seller's Takeback Note

When the seller is taking back a note from the buyer for all or part of the consideration, the issue of security for the note is always a problem. Naturally, the seller will want noncontingent personal and corporate guaranties from the buyer and from anyone else whom it can manage to get. The buyer will be reluctant to offer such broad security. Several creative compromises have been reached between parties, including partial or limited guarantees, the acceleration of the note based on postclosing performance, the right to repurchase the assets in the event of a default, the issuance of warrants or preferred stock in the event of default, commercial lender–like covenants to prevent the buyer from getting into a position where it is unable to pay the note (such as dividend restrictions, limitations on excessive salaries, etc.), or contingent consulting agreements in the event of a default.

Who's on the Line for the Financial Statements?

The financial statements provided by the seller to the buyer in connection with the due diligence and prior to closing are often a hotly contested item. The timing and scope of the financial statements, as well as the standard to which they will be held, are at issue. The buyer and its team may prefer a hot-off-the-press and recently completed audited set of financials from a Big 5 accounting firm, and the seller will want to serve up a best-efforts unaudited and uncertified guesstimate. Somewhere between the two extremes is where most deals wind up, with verbiage such as "of a nature customarily reflected," "prepared in substantial accordance with GAAP," and "fairly present the financial condition." The scope of the liabilities included on the statements, in addition to who will bear responsibility for unknown or undisclosed liabilities, will also be negotiated in the context of the financial statements.

Playing with the Buzzwords

Any veteran transactional lawyer knows that certain key buzzwords can be inserted into sections of the acquisition agreement that will detract, enhance, or even shift liability by and among the buyer and seller. Depending on which side of the fence you are on, look out for words or phrases like the following as tools for negotiation:

- ❒ "materially"
- ❒ "to the best of our knowledge"
- ❒ "could possibly"
- ❒ "without any independent investigation"
- ❒ "except for . . ."
- ❒ "subject to . . ."
- ❒ "reasonably believes . . ."
- ❒ "ordinary course of business"
- ❒ "to which we are aware . . ."
- ❒ "would not have a material adverse affect on . . ."
- ❒ "primarily relating to . . ."
- ❒ "substantially all . . ."
- ❒ "might" (instead of "would")
- ❒ "exclusively"
- ❒ "other than claims which may be less than $__"
- ❒ "have received no written notice of . . ."
- ❒ "have used our best efforts (or commercially reasonable efforts) to . . ."
- ❒ even merely "endeavor to . . ."

C H A P T E R   1 7

Managing the Transfer and Renewal Process

critical but often overlooked area of franchising management is the administration of the transfer and renewal process. Although the transfer of a franchise is a very different and usually more complex transaction than the renewal of a franchise, both situations highlight an important aspect of the relationship between franchisor and franchisee: *Franchises are awarded, not sold*. As a result, the franchisor has every right to impose certain conditions to approve either event.

The renewal of the term of the franchise agreement is like a husband and wife renewing their marriage vows, each restating their mutual desire to continue the relationship. The renewal is the ideal time for the franchisor to impose certain conditions and for franchisees to make sure that they are ready to commit to another five, ten, or twenty years of meeting its obligations under the franchise agreement and operations manual.

The transfer process, on the other hand, is more akin to a divorce. The franchisee, for a variety of reasons such as retirement, health challenges, relocation, burnout, or frustration, has decided to end its relationship with the franchisor, and a third party has been identified to assume responsibility for the operation and management of the franchised business. To protect itself against the fear of the unknown, the franchisor must impose certain conditions to the approval or authorization of a transfer or resale. Due diligence—especially in a post-Enron and post-Madoff era—is especially critical on the proposed transference and the franchisor should remain in the middle of the transfer process to ensure that the transferee is viable, qualified, and capable of operating the franchised business. The franchisor must play the role of facilitator, investigator, and traffic cop to protect itself against misrepresentations being made by the franchisee to the prospective transferee about the obligations of the franchisor, the financial performance of the franchised unit, and the overall characterization of the franchised system.

This chapter will highlight the key issues that arise in the course of these two critical transactions, with an emphasis on the types of conditions that should be imposed prior to approval by the franchisor of the proposed renewal or transfer.

The Regulatory Aspects of Transfer and Renewal

As both a matter of good business practices and the result of a string of recent cases, franchisors should assume that they will be subject to the tests of "good faith and fair dealing" when making decisions regarding the renewal of a franchise relationship and/or the approval or rejection of a request to transfer ownership of the franchised business. When refusing to review an existing franchise relationship or the approval of a proposed transfer, the franchisor must act reasonably and have a justifiable reason based on legitimate business concerns. Cases such as *Vylene Enterprises vs. Naugles* have long stood for the principle that franchisors are obligated to negotiate renewal or transfer terms in good faith, However, when unreasonable terms have been imposed as a condition for renewal or transfer, courts have varied significantly in their interpretation and enforcement of this principle. Courts and regulations will generally frown upon provisions in the franchise agreement or a set of provisions that vest unlimited, sole, or arbitrary discretion in the hands of the franchisor when it comes to transfer or renewal rights.

In addition to these legal and business principles, at least 16 states and two other U.S. jurisdictions regulate the renewal of franchise relationships: Arkansas, California, Connecticut, Delaware, Hawaii, Illinois, Indiana, Iowa, Michigan, Minnesota, Mississippi, Missouri, Nebraska, New Jersey, Washington, Wisconsin, Puerto Rico, and the Virgin Islands. In addition, many states have adopted statutes that regulate renewals of petroleum and automobile dealerships, heavy equipment dealerships, alcoholic beverage distributorships, and other specific industries. The federal Petroleum Marketing Practices Act (PMPA) also regulates the renewal of the franchise relationships that it covers.

These statutes generally impose certain conditions or procedural requirements on franchisors that do not wish to renew a franchise agreement, including that:

- ❐ A franchisor have good cause for nonrenewal.
- ❐ It give the franchisee an opportunity to cure when nonrenewal is based on a breach of the agreement.
- ❐ It give notice of nonrenewal within a specified period of time before the franchise agreement expires.
- ❐ It repurchase inventory and equipment from the franchisee or pay the franchisee for the goodwill of the franchise.
- ❐ It waive any noncompete agreements.

Such statutes often provide for damages or injunctive relief if the franchisor violates their requirements. Some states take the time to articulate in their statutes specific reasons why consent may be withheld, and others require the franchisor to set forth a material reason for denying the consent to a transfer. A few states, such as Hawaii and Michigan, deem it an "unfair or deceptive act" to refuse to permit the transfer of a franchise without good cause. See Figure 17-1 for a sample renewal and release agreement.

Figure 17-1. Renewal and release agreement.

RENEWAL AND RELEASE AGREEMENT

THIS AGREEMENT is made and entered into this _____ day of _____, 20__, by and between _____, a _____ corporation whose principal place of business is _____ ("Franchisor") and _____ whose principal place of business is _____ ("Franchisee").

WITNESSETH:

WHEREAS, on _____, Franchisor and Franchisee entered into a written Franchise Agreement by the terms of which Franchisee was granted a license to operate a _____ business in connection with the Franchisor's System and Proprietary Marks (the "Franchise") at the following location: ; and

WHEREAS, pursuant to Section _____ of that Franchise Agreement, Franchisee desires to renew the Franchise for an additional ten (10) year period and Franchisor desires to allow said renewal.

NOW, THEREFORE, in consideration of the mutual promises, covenants, and conditions contained herein and for other good and valuable consideration, the receipt of which is hereby acknowledged, the parties agree as follows:

1. *Renewal of Franchise Agreement.* Pursuant to Section _____ of the Franchise Agreement, Franchisee hereby renews the Franchise for an additional period of ten (10) years.

2. *Execution of Current Franchise Agreement.* Concurrently with the execution hereof, Franchisee shall execute Franchisor's current form of Franchise Agreement which agreement supersedes in all respects that Franchise Agreement executed by and between Franchisor and Franchisee on _____ and any other prior agreements, representations, negotiations, or understandings between the parties.

3. *Renewal Fee.* Concurrently with the execution hereof, Franchisee shall pay to Franchisor the sum of $_____ representing the renewal fee as provided in Section _____ of the Franchise Agreement.

4. *Release of Franchisor.* Franchisee, individually and on behalf of Franchisee's heirs, legal representatives, successors, and assigns, hereby forever releases and discharges Franchisor, its subsidiaries and affiliates, their respective officers, directors, agents, and employees from any and all claims, demands, controversies, actions, causes of action, obligations, liabilities, costs, expenses, attorney's fees, and damages of whatsoever character, nature, and kind, in law or in equity, claimed or alleged and which may be based upon or connected with the Franchise, the Franchise Agreement or any other agreement between the parties and executed prior to the date hereof, including but not limited to any and all claims whether presently known or unknown, suspected or unsuspected, arising under the franchise, securities, or antitrust laws of Canada, the United States, or any state, or municipality.

5. *Acknowledgment of Performance.* Except as provided herein, the parties hereto acknowledge and agree that all conditions to renewal provided in Section _____ of the Franchise Agreement have been satisfactorily complied with or performed.

6. *Execution of Documents.* The parties agree to execute any and all documents or agreements and to take all action as may be necessary or desirable to effect the terms, covenants, and conditions of this Agreement.

(continues)

Figure 17-1. (Continued).

IN WITNESS WHEREOF, the parties hereto have hereunder caused this Renewal and Release Agreement to be executed the day and year first above written.

ATTEST: FRANCHISOR

_____   By: _____, President

WITNESS: FRANCHISEE

_____   By: _____

As a general matter, courts have recognized the following grounds as being a reasonable basis for disapproving a proposed transfer:

❒ Transferee's lack of business experience

❒ Possible dilution of sales because the transferee sells a competitor's product

❒ Transferee's unrealistic sales predictions, failure to account for capital improvements, insufficient working capital, and debt load

❒ Transferee's conditioning its purchase on an application to relocate the franchise

❒ Transferee's unacceptable character

❒ Transferee's inadequate training to operate the franchise

❒ Transferee's inadequate financial and management experience to operate the franchise

❒ Transferee's failure to provide required and necessary financial information concerning a major investor

❒ Transferee's poor sales records with its current franchise

❒ Transferee's default of a franchise agreement with its current franchisor

Overall, courts have interpreted reasonability requirements not in terms of the franchisor's subjective fairness but under an objective analysis of the franchisor's business reasons for disapproving a requested transfer or assignment. The courts' focus has been on whether the reason given for disapproval or the conditions imposed on the consent are reasonably related to the likely viability of the franchise after transfer. As franchisors add conditions to the grant of consent, or base disapproval on grounds that are not legitimate business concerns, the likelihood that the court will reject that disapproval increases.

Managing the Renewal Process

Franchise rights are awarded to franchisees for a specified initial term and subject to the continuing obligation to meet certain obligations and follow certain standardized systems. As the term of the agreement draws to a close, the franchise agreement should specify the obligations of the franchisee that must be met as a condition to renewal. As a whole, most franchisees will want to renew their relationship with the franchisor if their expectations have been met, and in a 2008 study conducted by FRANdata, the annualized renewal rate of franchise agreements in most instances was 94 percent.

Certain key issues, such as royalty rates, performance standards, territorial allocations, and advertising fund contributions, may need to be revisited. For obvious reasons, franchisees will resent any significant changes to the relationship, especially if the possibility of these proposed changes is not disclosed to them in their initial offering circular. Franchisees often complain when the renewal fee structure forces them to essentially repurchase their franchise at the commencement of each new term. Although the term "repurchase" shows an obvious misunderstanding of the nature of the franchise relationship, it does highlight a legitimate concern of the franchisee: They do not want to be unduly penalized for being successful in building up local goodwill and capturing local market share. If the renewal fee structure is not viewed as fair and reasonable or if the key terms of the franchise agreement significantly change upon renewal, then the renewal process is likely to be a source of conflict and dispute.

A well-drafted franchise agreement should impose, at a minimum, the following conditions to a renewal of the term:

1. At least six (6) months prior to the expiration of the initial term of this Agreement, Franchisor shall inspect the Franchised Business and give notice of all required modifications to the nature and quality of the products and services offered at the Franchised Business, the Software, advertising, marketing and promotional programs, necessary to comply with the Franchisor's then current standards, and, if Franchisee elects to renew this Agreement, shall complete to Franchisor's satisfaction all such required modifications, as well as adopt and implement any new

---

Box 17-1. Ten criteria that courts have honored as conditions for approving a transfer.

- Work experience
- Educational background
- Aptitude and work ethic
- Financial strength
- Character
- Knowledge of the underlying industry

- Ability to devote full-time and best efforts to the operation of the business
- Residence in the locality of the franchised business
- Equity stake in the ownership of the business
- Freedom from conflicts of interest

methods, programs, Software updates and modifications and techniques required by Franchisor's notice no later than three (3) months prior to expiration of the initial term of this Agreement;

2. Franchisee shall give Franchisor written notice of such election to renew not less than three (3) months prior to the end of the initial term of this Agreement;

3. Franchisee shall not be in default of any provision of this Agreement, any amendment hereof or successor hereto, or any other agreement between Franchisee and Franchisor, or its subsidiaries, affiliates and suppliers and shall have substantially complied with all the terms and conditions of such agreements during the terms thereof;

4. Franchisee shall have satisfied all monetary obligations owed by Franchisee to Franchisor and its subsidiaries, affiliates and suppliers and shall have timely met those obligations throughout the term of this Agreement;

5. Franchisee shall execute upon renewal Franchisor's then current form of Franchise Agreement, which agreement shall supersede in all respects this Agreement, and the terms of which may differ from the terms of this Agreement, including, without limitation, by requiring a higher percentage royalty fee and/or National Advertising Fund contribution, increase in the Minimum Local Advertising Expenditure and the implementation of additional fees; provided, however, that in lieu of the then current initial franchise fee or its equivalent, for such renewal period, Franchisee shall be required to pay a renewal fee of _____ percent (___%) of the then current initial franchise fee paid by new franchisees of the Franchisor but in no event shall said renewal fee exceed _____ Dollars ($_____);

6. Franchisee shall comply with Franchisor's then current qualification and training requirements;

7. Franchisee, its shareholders, directors and officers shall execute a general release, in a form prescribed by Franchisor, of any and all claims against Franchisor and its subsidiaries and affiliates, and their respective officers, directors, agents and employees provided, however, that Franchisee shall not be required to release Franchisor for violations of federal or state franchise registration and disclosure laws; and

8. Franchisee shall present evidence satisfactory to Franchisor that it has the right to remain in possession of the premises where the Franchised Business is located for the duration of the renewal term.

In the event that any of the above conditions to renewal have not been met, no later than three (3) months prior to the expiration of the initial term of this Agreement, Franchisor shall have no obligation to renew this Agreement and shall provide to Franchisee at least sixty (60) days prior written notice of its intent not to renew this Agreement, which notice shall set forth the reasons for such refusal to renew.

If the franchise operates a retail location, it is quite common to impose a substantial (or sometimes cosmetic) remodeling or refurbishment requirement as an additional condition to renewal in order to ensure that the facility is in compliance under then current trade dress and design standards. This could impose a significant expense on the renewing franchisee, and, when remodeling costs will be extensive, as much advance notice as possible should be given, and reasonable timetables for the physical transformation should be established.

Managing the Transfer Process

A wide variety of issues and obligations are triggered when a current franchisee (the transferor) proposes to sell or transfer its rights under the franchise agreement to a third party (the transferee) because such a transfer must always be subject to approval by the franchisor. Some of the key issues in the administration and management of the transfer process include:

❑ *Franchisor's Rights of First Refusal.* Many modern-day franchise agreements provide the franchisor with a right of first refusal to essentially match the terms offered by a bona fide third party in the event of a sale or transfer by the franchisee. All of the proper notification, approval, exercise, or waiver procedures set forth in the agreement must be followed.

❑ *Data Gathering.* Assuming that the franchisor will *not* be exercising its rights of first refusal, the franchisor must begin its due diligence on the proposed transferee. The franchisee and the proposed transferee must be diligent and timely in meeting all information requests of the franchisor in the areas of business experience, financial capability, employment and educational history, and so on. The franchisor should *always* meet with the prospective transferee for a face-to-face interview.

❑ *Document Control.* The franchisor should be provided with copies of all correspondence, listings, sales contracts, bulk sales transfer notices, broker agreements, and any other paperwork related to the transaction to ensure against any misrepresentations, inaccurate earnings claims, or false statements about the franchisor being made by the transferor to the transferee in connection with the proposed transaction. The franchisor should play the role of document reviewer, not document validator. It will be tempting for the transferee to contact the franchisor directly to get its opinions on the fairness of the sales terms, the accuracy of the store's financial performance, or the credibility of the transferee's proposed business plan or pro forma financial statements. Franchisors should facilitate the process but resist the temptation of playing a role beyond the review and approval level, *unless* they serve as direct remarketers of the franchise.

❑ *Franchise Remarketing.* In recent years, some franchisors have become very active in the remarketing of their franchises, essentially serving as brokers on behalf of current franchisees who want to sell their businesses. The so-called secondary market for franchised businesses continues to flourish as franchising has matured. Many of the franchises initially awarded in the 1970s and 1980s are now operated by baby boomers nearing retirement age, and franchisees are ready to transfer ownership. Franchisors must decide what role they plan to play in this process and what their compensation will be for locating a qualified transferee.

☐ *Transfer Fees.* The franchisor must devote time and resources to the review and approval of a proposed transfer. Often the franchisor's attorneys must be brought in to review its terms. The transferee, once approved, must be trained and supported. All of the costs must be borne by someone, and it is typically *not* the franchisor. Therefore, the franchise agreement should provide for a transfer fee that is at least enough to cover all of the franchisor's training and administrative costs to be incurred in connection with the transfer.

☐ *Debt Assumption.* One of the typical conditions of the approval of the transfer is that the franchisee pay all of its outstanding financial obligations to the franchisor. In the case of a troubled franchisee, the transferee may be buying the business in exchange for a promissory note, leaving little or no cash for the transferor to pay its debts to the franchisor. If the franchisor is also taking a promissory note back from the transferee, then the terms of the repayment, the security agreements, financing statements, and personal guaranties of both transferor and transferee must be prepared. Any other defaults by the transferor that must be cured as a condition to approving the transfer should be clearly explained to the transferee, especially if any of those defaults will be cured *after* the consummation of the transfer.

☐ *Disclosure of the Transferee.* Regardless of specific legal requirements, good franchising practice dictates that the franchisor should provide the proposed transferee with a copy of its current disclosure document and clearly explain any new developments, obligations, or problems that may affect the proposed transferee's decision to buy the business and become part of the franchise system. Proposed transferees who are about to become new franchisees do not want to hear about major changes to the system, class action lawsuits against the franchisor, or the impending bankruptcy of the franchisor *just after* they invested their life savings into the purchase of the business.

☐ *Inspection and Audit.* The franchisor should always arrange for its field support staff to visit the site of the proposed transfer to conduct an inspection and audit. This will give the franchisor insight into any unreported fees owed as well as help determine whether any refurbishment is required as a condition of the approval of the transfer. This is also an opportune time for the franchisor to collect all copies of the operations manual and any other confidential information back from the transferor.

☐ *Execution of Documents.* A wide variety of legal documents may be prepared by the franchisor for execution by the transferor and transferee as a condition to approving the transfer. These documents may include mutual releases, guaranty agreements, representation and acknowledgment letters (for execution by the transferee, representing their capabilities and acknowledging their undertaking of certain responsibilities, etc.), lease agreements, or consent to sale agreement. Figure 17-2 shows

Figure 17-2. Franchise transfer agreement.

FRANCHISE TRANSFER AGREEMENT

THIS AGREEMENT is made and entered into this _____ day of 20__, _____, by and between _____, a _____ corporation, whose principal place of business is _____ (hereinafter the "Franchisor"); and _____, whose principal place of business is _____ (hereinafter the "Transferor"); and , whose principal place of business is (hereinafter the "Transferee").

W I T N E S S E T H:

WHEREAS, on _____, Franchisor and Transferor entered into a written Franchise Agreement by the terms of which Transferor was granted a license to operate a Center in connection with the Franchisor's System and Proprietary Marks (hereinafter "the Franchise") at the following location: ;

WHEREAS, Transferor desires to sell, assign, transfer, and convey all of its right, title, and interest in and to the Franchise to Transferee and Franchisor is willing to consent to said transfer, upon the terms and conditions in the said written Franchise Agreement and upon the terms and conditions herein; and

WHEREAS, Franchisor has elected not to exercise its right and option to purchase the Transferor's interest on the same terms and conditions offered to the Transferee, as provided by Section _____ of the Franchise Agreement entered into between the Franchisor and the Transferor.

NOW, THEREFORE, in consideration of the mutual promises, covenants, and conditions contained herein and for other good and valuable consideration, the receipt of which is hereby acknowledged, the parties agree as follows:

1. *Transfer.* Subject to the provisions contained herein, Transferor hereby sells, assigns, transfers, and conveys all of its right, title and interest in and to the Franchise to Transferee and Franchisor consents to said transfer, upon the terms and conditions in the said written Franchise Agreement and upon the terms and conditions herein.

2. *Release of Franchisor.* Transferor hereby releases and discharges Franchisor and its officers, directors, shareholders, and employees in their corporate and individual capacities from any and all claims, actions, causes of action, or demands of whatsoever kind or nature.

3. *Transferee's Agreement.* In lieu of an initial franchise fee customarily paid under the terms of the Franchise Agreement and upon payment of a transfer franchise fee to Franchisor by Transferee in the sum of ($____), which sum is equivalent to _____ percent (____%) of the initial franchise fee currently being charged by Franchisor to new franchisees, and concurrently with the execution hereof, Franchisor shall offer Transferee the standard form of Franchise Agreement now being offered by Franchisor to new franchisees and such other ancillary agreements as Franchisor may require for the Franchise. The term of said Franchise Agreement offered by Franchisor to Transferee shall end on the expiration date of the Franchise Agreement entered into by and between Franchisor and Transferor and with such renewal term(s) as may be provided by the Franchise Agreement entered into by and between Franchisor and Transferor. Except as provided herein, the Franchise Agreement offered by Franchisor to Transferee, if executed by Transferee, shall supersede the Franchise Agreement entered into by and between Franchisor and Transferor in all respects and the terms of the Transferee's Agreement may differ from the terms of the Transferor's Agreement, including, without limitation, a higher percentage royalty fee and advertising contribution.

(continues)

Figure 17-2. (Continued).

4. *Transfer Fee.* Concurrently with the execution hereof, Transferor shall pay to Franchisor a Transfer Fee of _____ Dollars ($_____) to cover Franchisor's administrative expenses in connection with this transfer.

5. *Training.* At the Transferee's expense the Transferee and the Transferee's manager shall attend and successfully complete any training programs currently in effect for current franchisees.

6. *Upgrades.* At the Transferee's expense the Transferee shall upgrade the premises referred to herein to conform to the design concepts now being used in other franchised locations and shall complete the upgrading and any other reasonable requirements specified by Franchisor and which relate to said upgrading on or before

7. *Receipt of Documents.* On or before _____ Transferee shall sign an Acknowledgment of Receipt acknowledging Transferee's receipt of all required legal documents including Franchisor's Franchise Offering Circular, Franchisor's current Franchise Agreement, and related agreements and documentation.

8. *Transferee's Obligations.* Transferee hereby assumes and agrees to faithfully discharge all of the Transferor's obligations under the Franchise Agreement entered into by and between Franchisor and Transferor.

9. *Guaranty by Transferee.* Transferee understands and acknowledges that the obligations of the Transferor under the Franchise Agreement entered into by and between Franchisor and Transferor were guaranteed by Transferor and Transferee hereby agrees to guaranty the full and complete performance of all such obligations and agrees to execute a written guaranty in a form satisfactory to Franchisor.

10. *Transferor's Liability.* Transferor understands, acknowledges, and agrees it shall remain liable for all obligations to Franchisor in connection with the Franchise prior to the effective date of the transfer and shall execute any and all instruments reasonably requested by Franchisor to evidence such liability.

11. *Transferor's Warranties.* Transferor warrants and represents that it is not granting any security interest in the Franchise or in any of its assets.

12. *Survivability.* Transferor acknowledges, understands, and agrees that those provisions of Section _____ and Section _____ of the Franchise Agreement entered into by and between Transferor and Franchisor, to the extent applicable, shall survive this Agreement.

13. *Transferor's Obligations.* Transferor acknowledges, and agrees that each of its obligations regarding transfer must be met by the Transferor and are reasonable and necessary.

14. *Transferor's Monetary Obligations.* Transferor understands, acknowledges, and agrees that all of its accrued monetary obligations and any other outstanding obligations due and owing to Franchisor shall be fully paid and satisfied prior to any transfer referred to herein.

15. *Waiver.* The failure of any party to enforce at any time any of the provisions hereof shall not be construed to be a waiver of such provisions or of the right of any party thereafter to enforce any such provisions.

16. *Modifications.* No renewal hereof, or modification or waiver of any of the provisions herein contained, or any future representation, promise, or condition in connection with the subject matter hereof, shall be effective unless agreed upon by the parties hereto in writing.

17. *Execution of Documents.* The parties agree to execute any and all documents or agreements and to take all action as may be necessary or desirable to effectuate the terms, covenants, and conditions of this Agreement.

18. *Binding Effect.* This Agreement shall be binding upon the parties hereto, their heirs, executors, successors, assigns, and legal representatives.

19. *Attorney's Fees.* Transferor shall pay to Franchisor all damages, costs, and expenses, including reasonable attorneys fees, incurred by Franchisor in enforcing the provisions of this Agreement.

20. *Severability.* If any provision of this Agreement or any part thereof is declared invalid by any court of competent jurisdiction, such act shall not affect the validity of this Agreement and the remainder of this Agreement shall remain in full force and effect according to the terms of the remaining provisions or part of provisions hereof.

21. *Construction.* This Agreement shall be governed by and construed in accordance with the laws of the State of _____.

IN WITNESS WHEREOF, the parties hereto have hereunder caused this Franchise Transfer Agreement to be executed the day and year first above written.

ATTEST: FRANCHISOR

_____   By _____, President

WITNESS   Transferor

_____   _____

                                                Transferee

                                                By: _____

a sample transfer agreement. Also, standard documents must be executed by the transferee, such as local cooperative advertising participation agreements, sign lease agreements, equipment leases, or inventory purchase agreements.

In addition to these key issues, a well-drafted franchise agreement should include, at a minimum, the specific contractual conditions listed in Figure 17-3, which must be met prior to the approval of a transfer.

Figure 17-3. Franchise agreement provisions.

1. All of Franchisee's accrued monetary obligations and all other outstanding obligations to Franchisor, its subsidiaries, affiliates and suppliers shall be up to date, fully paid and satisfied;

2. Franchisee shall not be in default of any provision of this Agreement, any amendment hereof or successor hereto, any other franchise agreement or other agreement between Franchisee and Franchisor, or its subsidiaries, affiliates or suppliers;

3. The Franchisee and each of its shareholders, officer and directors shall have executed a general release under seal, in a form satisfactory to Franchisor, of any and all claims against Franchisor and its officers, directors, shareholders and employees in their corporate and individual capacities, including, without limitation, claims arising under federal, state and local laws, rules and ordinances, provided, however, that Franchisee shall not be required to release Franchisor for violations of federal and state franchise registration and disclosure laws;

4. The transferee shall enter into a written assignment, under seal and in a form satisfactory to Franchisor, assuming and agreeing to discharge all of Franchisee's obligations under this Agreement; and, if the obligations of Franchisee were guaranteed by the transferor, the transferee shall guarantee the performance of all such obligations in writing in a form satisfactory to Franchisor;

5. The transferee shall demonstrate to Franchisor's satisfaction that the transferee meets Franchisor's educational, managerial and business standards; possesses a good moral character, business reputation and credit rating; has the aptitude and ability to operate the Franchised Business herein (as may be evidenced by prior related experience or otherwise); has at least the same managerial and financial criteria required of new franchisees and shall have sufficient equity capital to operate the Franchised Business.

6. At Franchisor's option, the transferee shall execute (and/or, upon Franchisor's request, shall cause all interested parties to execute) for a term ending on the expiration date of this Agreement and with such renewal term as may be provided by this Agreement, the standard form of Franchise Agreement then being offered to new franchisees and such other ancillary agreements as Franchisor may require for the Franchised Business, which agreements shall supersede this Agreement in all respects and the terms of which agreements may differ from the terms of this Agreement, including, without limitation, a higher percentage royalty fee, National Advertising Fund contribution, increase of the Minimum Local Advertising Expenditure and the implementation of additional fees;

7. The transferee shall upgrade, at the transferee's expense, the Franchised Business to conform to the current specifications then being used in new Franchised Businesses, and shall complete the upgrading and other requirements within the time specified by Franchisor;

8. Franchisee shall remain liable for all direct and indirect obligations to Franchisor in connection with the Franchised Business prior to the effective date of the transfer and shall continue to remain responsible for its obligations of nondisclosure, noncompetition and indemnification as provided elsewhere in this Agreement and shall execute any and all instruments reasonably requested by Franchisor to further evidence such liability;

9. At the transferee's expense, the transferee and its manager and employees shall complete any training programs then in effect for current franchisees upon such terms and conditions as Franchisor may reasonably require;

10. The transferee shall have signed an Acknowledgement of Receipt of all required legal documents, such as the Franchise Disclosure Document (FDD) and the then current Franchise Agreement and ancillary agreements; and

11. Transferor shall pay to Franchisor a Transfer Fee equal to _____ percent (_____%) of the then current initial franchise fee paid by new franchisees of Franchisor but in no event shall said Transfer Fee exceed _____Dollars ($____) to cover Franchisor's administrative expenses in connection with the proposed transfer.

CHAPTER 18

Strategic and Structural Alternatives
to Franchising

As discussed in Chapter 1, a wide variety of intellectual property leveraging strategies, beyond business-format franchising, can be deployed to meet growth objectives. Many successful companies for one reason or another do not necessarily meet the foundational requirements needed to develop a business-format franchising program or simply choose to leverage their intellectual capital in a different strategic manner. They pursue these alternatives for various reasons:

❐ Some companies want to avoid the perceived obligations of being a franchisor

❐ Some companies want to avoid the disclosure requirements of federal and state law for a number of reasons

❐ Some companies are afraid of the perceived liability risk of being a franchisor

❐ Some companies can achieve greater distribution efficiencies or *do not need (or want) the control*

❐ Some companies do not need or want their trademarks licensed

❐ Some companies are not prepared to be a franchisor or lack the proprietary foundation to truly have a system

❐ International companies who are not franchisors in their home country do not want to be in the United States

From a strategic and structural perspective, if you have determined to structure a program that will be exempt from one or more of the definitions of a franchise discussed in Chapter 5, on what basis will the exemption be made? Which element of the test are you prepared to discard or sacrifice?

❐ Will you choose not to include a license of your trademark at the cost of the value of your goodwill?

❐ Will you choose not to provide significant support to your distribution channels at the cost of losing them to a more supportive competitor?

❏ Will you loosen the grip over the distribution channel at the risk of sacrificing quality control?

❏ Will you waive the initial fee at the risk of the program becoming a loss leader or worse?

These are difficult decisions, and the solutions are not clear-cut from either a business or a legal perspective. There is always the risk that a regulator or a disgruntled franchisee or distributor will disagree with you. You must work with qualified counsel to identify an alternative that will have a reasonable basis for an exemption and still make sense from a strategic perspective. The balance of this chapter will look at the many alternatives currently being tested by many U.S. and overseas companies. As you can see, the lines of demarcation are not always clear. The differences among many of these alternatives may in fact be in name only. Some of these concepts are truly innovative and have not been tested by the courts or the regulators. In these borderline cases, a regulatory no-action letter procedure is strongly recommended. Other concepts are not very innovative at all and merely borrow from long recognized and analogous legal relationships, such as chapter affiliation agreements in the nonprofit arena or network affiliation agreements in radio and television broadcasting. Still others are genuine alternatives to franchising such as licensing and distributorships, our first two major topics in this area.

Chapter 19 provides an overview of the two most common forms of licensing arrangements: merchandise licensing and technology transfer and licensing. Chapter 20 will look at joint ventures and strategic alliances. Other major alternatives to franchising are considered in this chapter.

Because franchising can be incorporated in varying degrees, what follows is a comparison of franchising with other strategic alliances: trademark licensing, product distributorship, employment relationship, partnerships and joint ventures, and agency relationships.

Franchising Compared with Trademark Licensing

Franchise rights can be characterized as active rights in contrast to the passive rights normally attendant to licensing. The licensor's interest is normally limited to supervising the proper use of the license and collecting royalties. The franchisor, however, exerts significant active control over the franchisee's operations.

In licensing to others to use one's trademark, licensors generally want to limit the licensee's ability to modify the trademark or to reduce its value through use in connection with symbols or products that will lessen the mark's goodwill. Franchisors who license the use of a trademark similarly impose limits on the franchisees, but also, as part of the franchise relationship, franchisors normally insist that franchisees agree to a variety of other limitations and requirements as to the conduct of the franchised business. Thus, unlike the mere license to another of the right to use a trademark, the franchisor seeks not only to protect the goodwill already associated with the trademark but also, by franchising, to enhance the mark's goodwill.

Franchising Compared with Product Distributorship

Distributors are often selected for some of the same reasons that lead to decisions to franchise. A centrally located company that manufactures enough of a product to sell on a regional or national basis is often not equipped to deal with the variety of personalities, peculiarities, or other phenomena of localities.

Generally little control is exercised over the distributor's manner of conducting business. Although geographical or business-line restrictions may be imposed on distributors as a means to keep them from competing with each other, fewer restrictions are placed on a distributor's operations. The distributor is not granted a license to "use" anything. Rather than do business under one particular company's marks, distributors often handle the products of many manufacturers.

The main difference between a franchise and a distributorship are that:

❐ The franchisor assumes a larger obligation to teach the franchisee how to deal in the product (though this kind of activity occurs with distributorships too).

❐ The franchisee deals with just one company, whereas a distributor will often, though not always, distribute goods or services of many different producers.

❐ The franchise relationship often involves a greater community of interest (though, again, not always, because a distributor of an extremely successful product may very well find its own success inextricably tied to his supplier's success or failure).

❐ The basis on which a franchisor is paid normally differs from that on which a distributor's supplier is paid.

In each of these areas, however, the parties may arrange their affairs so that a product distributorship looks like a franchise or vice versa. For example, a franchisee with a large amount of leeway in how to run its business may look like an independent distributor. An independent distributor of an extremely successful product may be subject to many controls by the producer and may begin to resemble a franchisee.

Franchising Compared with the Employment Relationship

In many respects, the franchise relationships may resemble that between an employer and an employee. Both kinds of relationships are characterized by the control that one party exercises over the other's activities. Almost any kind of control that an employer might exert over an employee can appear in the typical franchise agreement. Examples include working hours, services to be performed by patrons, behavior, appearance, and a variety of other work details.

The franchise diverges from the employer/employee relationship in several respects. The most significant difference is that, unlike the franchisee, an employee does not normally make a payment to the employer for the right to enter into or continue the relationship. In addition, the franchisee normally makes a significant investment or promises to do so in order to establish the relationship. Perhaps more importantly, the franchisee seeks a significant profit potential; although employee participation in the employer's revenues or profits is not uncommon, it is still not the norm.

Franchising Compared with Partnerships and Joint Ventures

The franchisor-franchisee relationship has been compared to that between partners or joint venturers. The parties enter into an agreement establishing a relationship in which the parties conduct business for profit. Both parties' property and skills are in some sense contributed to the venture. However, even though a franchisor normally exacts a periodic royalty, the element of profit sharing is missing from the franchise relationship. Moreover, the normal franchise agreement does not authorize either party to act on the other's behalf, even though either may be affected, favorably or otherwise, by actions taken by the other. Furthermore, a joint venture is a partnership with reference to a specific venture or single transaction, whereas the franchise relationship is usually expected to have a longer duration and to involve regular and frequent transactions between the parties and with others.

Franchising Compared with Agency Relationships

Franchise relationships also manifest some of the characteristics of agency relationships. An agent conducts some business or manages some affair on behalf of and for the account of the principal. A franchisee, however, merely publicizes its relationship with another while conducting business on its own behalf. Furthermore, unlike an agent, a franchisee has no authority to act on behalf of the franchisor.

Distributorships, Dealerships, and Sales Representatives

Many growing product-oriented companies choose to bring their wares to the marketplace through independent third-party distributors and dealerships. These dealers are generally more difficult to control than is a licensee or franchisee, and as a result the agreement between the manufacturer and the distributor is much more informal than that of a franchise or license agreement. This type of arrangement is commonly used by manufacturers of electronic and stereo equipment, computer hardware and software, sporting goods, medical equipment, and automobile parts and accessories.

In developing distributor and dealership agreements, growing companies must be careful to avoid being included within the broad definition of a franchise under FTC Rule 436, which requires the preparation of a disclosure document. To avoid such a classification, the agreement should impose minimal controls over the dealer, and the sale of products must be at bona fide wholesale prices. In addition, the manufacturer must offer no more than minimal assistance in the marketing or management of the dealer's business. A well-drafted distributorship agreement should address the key issues, as outlined in Figure 18-1.

Distributors are often confused with sales representatives, but there are many critical differences between the two. Typically, a distributor buys the product from the manufacturer, at wholesale prices, with title passing to the distributor when payment is received. The distributor usually pays no actual fee for the grant of the distributorship, and the distributor will typically be permitted to carry competitive products. The distributor is expected to maintain some retail location or showroom where the manufacturer's products are displayed. The distributor must maintain its own inventory storage and warehousing capabilities. The distributor looks to the manufacturer for technical support; advertising contributions; supportive repair, maintenance, and service policies; new product training; volume discounts; favorable payment and return policies; and brand name recognition. The manufacturer looks to the distributor for in-store and local promotion, adequate inventory controls, financial stability, preferred display and stocking, prompt payment, and qualified sales personnel. Although the distributorship network offers a

Figure 18-1. Elements of distributorship agreement.

---

1. What is the scope of the appointment? Which products is the dealer authorized to distribute and under what conditions? What is the scope, if any, of the exclusive territory to be granted to the distributor? To what extent will product, vendor, customer, or geographic restrictions be applicable?

2. What activities will the distributor be expected to perform in terms of manufacturing, sales, marketing, display, billing, market research, maintenance of books and records, storage, training, installation, support, and servicing?

3. What obligations will the distributor have to preserve and protect the intellectual property of the manufacturer?

4. What right, if any, will the distributor have to modify or enhance the manufacturer's warranties, terms of sale, credit policies, or refund procedures?

5. What advertising literature, technical and marketing support, training seminars, or special promotions will be provided by the manufacturer to enhance the performance of the distributor?

6. What sales or performance quotas will be imposed on the dealer as a condition to its right to continue to distribute the manufacturer's products or services? What are the rights and remedies of the manufacturer if the dealer fails to meet these performance standards?

7. What is the term of the agreement and under what conditions can it be terminated? How will post-termination transactions be handled?

---

viable alternative to franchising, it is not a panacea. The management and control of the distributors may be even more difficult than that involved in franchising (especially without the benefit of a comprehensive franchise agreement), and the termination of these relationships is regulated by many state antitermination statutes.

The sales representative or sales agent is an independent marketing resource for the manufacturer. The sales representative, unlike the distributor, does not typically take title to the merchandise, maintain inventories or retail locations, or engage in any special price promotions unless these are instigated by the manufacturer.

Cooperatives

Cooperatives (co-ops) have been formed as associations of member companies in the same or similar industries in order to achieve operating, advertising, and purchasing efficiencies and economies of scale. Typically the co-op is owned and controlled by its members. Commonly known retail co-ops (which are often confused with franchise systems) include Ace Hardware and NAPA Auto Parts, and an example of a well-known agricultural co-op is the Sunkist brand of citrus fruits and juices. Co-ops have been especially effective in certain inventory-intense industries, such as hardware, automobile parts and accessories, pharmacies, and grocery stores. Typically, each independent business may use a common trade identity in its advertising and promotion; however, ownership of the actual trademarks rests with the cooperative itself. Retail co-ops, if properly structured, are exempt from FTC Rule 436 and from some state franchise laws. The organization and ongoing operation of the co-op should be periodically reviewed by counsel to ensure that certain federal and state antitrust and unfair competition laws are not violated.

A co-op is a business owned and controlled by the people who use its services. They finance and operate the business for their mutual benefit. By working together, they can reach an objective unattainable by acting alone. These mutually beneficial services can include obtaining production supplies, processing and marketing member products, or providing functions related to purchasing, marketing, or providing a service. The co-op may be the vehicle to obtain services otherwise unavailable or that are more beneficial to members. The underlying function of the co-op is to increase member income or in other ways enhance their way of living. A co-op may or may not be incorporated and may or may not have its own staff or operate independently from its constituent members.

The four most basic operating characteristics of a co-op are:

1. *Service at Cost.* The purpose of a co-op is to provide a service to its user/owners at the lowest possible cost, rather than generate a profit for investors. However, the co-op must generate income sufficient to cover all administrative costs and meet continuing capital needs. Because many costs cannot be absolutely determined before year

end, a co-op must charge competitive market prices, or fees for services, and then determine its at-cost basis at year end.

2. *Financial Obligation and Benefits Proportional to Use.* Benefits are tied to use rather than to the amount of investment. Likewise, members are obligated to provide financing in proportion to the use that produces those benefits. Most co-ops' bylaws provide a system of returning capital contributions to maintain proportionality on a current basis. The bylaws should also include a provision that establishes the co-op's obligation to return net margins (total income from all sources minus expenses) to patrons. The return of net margin to members based on their use of the co-op is called a patronage refund.

3. *Democratic Control.* Voting control is vested with the membership, either on an equal basis or according to use, rather than based on the amount of stock each member holds. Democratic control is usually expressed as one-member/one-vote. A few cooperatives have limited proportional voting based on use.

4. *Limited Return on Equity Capital.* This feature means that payments for use of members' equity capital (primarily in the form of stock dividends) are limited. It does not mean that benefits realized from the co-op, monetary or otherwise, are limited. The overriding value of the co-op to its owners is in the range of services or economies of scale that it provides. Limiting the return on equity capital is a mechanism to support distribution of benefits according to use. It helps to keep management decisions focused on providing services attuned to members' need. Limiting the payment for the use of equity capital is recognized by both federal and state laws. Some state laws require that co-ops either limit the dividends on stock or member capital to 8 percent per year or follow one-member/one-vote control.

Co-ops usually perform any one or a combination of four kinds of service functions, but with varying strategic emphasis:

1. *Purchasing.* Co-ops provide members with consumer goods, products for resale through their members, or equipment and supplies for their business operation. Individual co-ops may form federations of cooperatives to obtain further benefits of group purchasing.

2. *Marketing.* Co-ops market the products their members produce—crafts, agricultural products, and the like. Marketing includes assembling, processing, and selling products or services in retail or wholesale markets for members.

3. *Service.* Co-ops provide services related to the production of a product or service for business or the home. These services may include credit, electricity, telephones, insurance, research, telecommunications, common management, or other shared services.

4. *Production.* Co-ops pool production and distribution resources in large-scale industries, such as agricultural products or electrical utilities.

Regulatory Issues

As under the FTC's trade regulation rule, a co-op that licenses marks to its members or that purchases and resells private label merchandise may be a franchisor under certain state law definitions. State definitions of a *franchise* commonly incorporate the following: (1) granting the right to sell goods or services using a mark or advertising owned by or designating the grantor; (2) payment, directly or indirectly, of a fee for the privilege of entering into or maintaining the relationship; and (3) either a grantor-prescribed marketing plan (under California's model of state franchise law) or a community of interest in marketing the subject goods or services (under Minnesota's model). Some states, such as New York and Michigan, have even more inclusive exclusions for partnerships or cooperative associations. Most state administrators, however, have authority under their respective statutes to establish exemptions by rule, although such exemptions are only from the formal registration process, not from the disclosure requirements or anti-fraud provisions of the statutes. No state has exempted buying co-ops to date. In fact, the North Dakota commissioner of securities held that the Best Western motel system, organized as a retailer cooperative, was clearly a franchisor under the North Dakota Franchise Act and subject to the registration and disclosure obligations of the act, notwithstanding the apparent exemption for such organizations under the FTC rule.[1]

Multilevel Marketing Plans

Multilevel marketing (MLM) is a method of direct selling of products or services according to which distributors or sales representatives sell products to the consumer outside of a retail store context and often in a one-to-one setting. In some cases, the distributors purchase the manufacturer's products at wholesale and profit by selling the product to the consumer at retail price. In other instances, distributors sponsor other sales representatives or distributors and receive commissions on the sales made by the sponsored representative or any further representative sponsored in a continuous down-line sales organization. Leading merchandisers who use this form of marketing are Shaklee Corporation, Amway Corporation, and Mary Kay Cosmetics.

MLM companies are regulated by numerous overlapping laws that vary from state to state. These programs are affected by a combination of pyramid statutes, business opportunity statutes, multilevel distribution laws, franchise and securities laws, various state lottery laws, referral sales laws, the federal postal laws, and Section 5 of the Federal Trade Commission Act.

Recently, many MLM plans have been targeted for prosecution and litigation based on these laws. To date, the enforcement of statutes and regulations has been selective and arbitrary, and many regulatory officials have developed negative attitudes toward the legality of any one MLM program.

---

1. Cooperative Lodgings Group's Franchise System, State Official Rules, Bus. Fran. Guide (CCH) ¶ 7708.

Therefore, from a legal standpoint, MLM is an uncertain and speculative activity, and there is no assurance that even the most legitimate MLM program will be immune from regulatory inquiry.

Multilevel Marketing Statutes

Six states have laws specifically regulating companies that adopt multilevel marketing programs: Georgia, Louisiana, Maryland, Massachusetts, New Mexico, and Wyoming. Any MLM company operating in any of these states typically must file an annual registration statement giving notice of its operations in that state and must appoint that state's secretary of state as its agent for service of process.

A *multilevel marketing company* is typically defined by these states as an entity that "sells, distributes, or supplies, for valuable consideration, goods or services, through independent agents or distributors at different levels and in which participants may recruit other participants in which commissions or bonuses are paid as a result of the sale of the goods or services or the recruitment of additional participants."

In addition to imposing the annual registration requirement, several states have placed additional regulations governing the activities of the MLM companies, such as:

❏ Requiring that MLM companies allow their independent representatives or distributors to cancel their agreements with the company, and upon such cancellation the company must repurchase unsold products at a price not less than 90 percent of the distributor's original net cost.

❏ Prohibiting MLM companies from representing that distributors have or will earn stated dollar amounts.

❏ Prohibiting MLM companies from requiring distributors to purchase certain minimum initial inventories (except in reasonable quantities).

❏ Prohibiting that compensation be paid solely for recruiting other participants.

Business Opportunity Laws

A *business opportunity* is typically defined as the sale or lease of products or services to a purchaser for the purpose of enabling the purchaser to start a business and in which the seller represents that it:

❏ Will provide locations or assist the purchaser in finding locations for the use of vending machines.

❏ Will purchase products made by the purchaser using the supplies or services sold to the purchaser.

❏ Guarantees the purchaser will derive income from the business opportunity that exceeds the price paid for the business opportunity or that the seller will refund all or part of the price paid for the business opportunity if the purchaser is unsatisfied with the business opportunity.

❐ Will, upon the payment by the purchaser of a certain sum of money (usually between $25 and $500), provide a sales program or marketing program that will enable the purchaser to derive income from the business opportunity that exceeds the price paid for the business opportunity.

This definition (or some variation of it) can be found in the statutes of over 20 states nationwide. Although the first two elements do not apply to MLM companies, the third and fourth elements would in all probability relate to MLM companies that offer to repurchase sales kits and unsold inventory if a distributor discontinues selling and its sales kits exceed the amounts specified in the various state statutes. Interestingly, the very requirement imposed on MLM companies by many of the relevant statutes (e.g., requiring the company to buy back unused products) is an element of a business opportunity.

Business opportunity offerers are required to file a registration statement with the appropriate state agency (usually the Securities Division or Consumer Protection Agency) and a disclosure statement (similar to that required of franchisors) that would then be provided to each prospective offeree.

MLM companies are, however, often exempt from the coverage of the business opportunity laws by virtue of so-called sales kit exemptions in the statutes. This type of exemption excludes from the calculation of required payment monies paid for sales demonstration equipment or materials sold to the purchaser at the company's cost.

Of additional interest to MLM companies is the typical exemption in the business opportunity laws for the sale of an ongoing business. This allows the sale of a distributorship or business opportunity to another without triggering the business opportunity laws. The following states have adopted business opportunity statutes: California, Connecticut, Florida, Georgia, Iowa, Kentucky, Louisiana, Maine, Maryland, Minnesota, Nebraska, New Hampshire, North Carolina, Ohio, South Carolina, Texas, Utah, Virginia, and Washington.

Pyramid Laws

Consumers often confuse legitimate *multilevel marketing programs* (which are generally valid methods for distributing products and services to the public) with *pyramid schemes* (which are generally unlawful schemes subject to criminal prosecution in many states).

Numerous laws and regulations have been enacted in the United States to prohibit pyramid schemes. Some the state laws declare unlawful are what they call "pyramid sales schemes," "chain distributions," "referral selling," "endless chains," and the like. Pyramid distribution plans have also been declared unlawful as lotteries, unregistered securities, violations of mail fraud laws, or violations of the Federal Trade Commission Act.

Broadly speaking, a pyramid distribution plan is a means of distributing a company's products or services to consumers. Pyramid schemes generally consist of several distribution levels through which the products or services are resold until they reach the ultimate consumer. A pyramid differs from a valid multilevel marketing company in that, in its elemental form, a pyramid is merely a variation on a chain letter and almost always involves large numbers of people at the lowest level who pay money to a few people at the utmost level. New participants pay a sum of money merely for the chance to join the program and advance to the top level, where they will profit from the initial payments made by later participants.

One of the most common elements of pyramid schemes is an intensive campaign to attract new participants, who serve to fund the program by providing the payoff to earlier participants. Some schemes use high-pressure sales techniques such as go-go chants and money hums to increase crowd enthusiasm. Often meetings are held in distant locations with everyone traveling to them by bus as a captive audience. These bus rides and meetings may include an emotional pep rally type of recruiting approach. In one New Jersey case, prospective recruits who did not sign up at the initial meeting were taken on a charter plane trip to the company's home office, during which flight, known as a "go tour," they were subjected to intense pressure to sign contracts before the plane landed. On the plane, references were made to the success of others, large amounts of money were displayed amid talk of success, and at times piles of cash and contracts were dropped into the laps of prospects. The format of the meetings is often completely scripted and prepared strictly in accordance with the company's guidelines and policies. These scripts invariably make reference to the financial success awaiting those who participate. In the New Jersey case, recruits were told that they could easily become millionaires.

A pyramid scheme *always* involves a certain degree of failure by its participants. A pyramid plan can work only with unlimited supplies of new participants. At some point the pyramid will fail to attract new participants, and the individuals who joined later will not receive any money because there will be no new bottom level of participants to support the plan.

To avoid prosecution, the promoters of pyramid schemes often attempt to make their plans resemble multilevel marketing companies. Pyramid schemes therefore often claim to be in the business of selling products or services to consumers. The products or services, however, are often of little or no value, and there is no true effort to sell them because emphasis remains almost solely on signing up new participants who are needed to feed the machine.

There are several ways to distinguish a legitimate multilevel marketing program from unlawful pyramid schemes:

❑ *Initial Payment.* Typically the initial payment required of a distributor of products and services of a multilevel marketing program is minimal; often the distributor is required to buy only a sales kit that is sold at cost. Because pyramid plans are supported by the payments made by the new recruits, participants in a pyramid plan are often required to pay substantial sums of money just to participate.

❏ *Inventory Loading.* Pyramid schemes typically require participants to purchase large amounts of nonrefundable inventory to participate in the program. Legitimate multilevel marketing companies usually re-purchase any such inventory if the distributor decides to leave the business. Many state laws require the company to repurchase any resalable goods for at least 90 percent of the original cost.

❏ *Headhunting.* Pyramid plans generally make more money by recruiting new prospects (head-hunting) than by actually selling the products. Multilevel marketing programs, on the other hand, make money by the sale of legitimate and bona fide products to consumers.

More than 25 states have laws prohibiting pyramid schemes, whether as "endless chains," "chain distribution schemes," or "pyramids." Programs with the following three elements are prohibited:

1. An entry fee or investment that must be paid by the participant in order to join
2. Ongoing recruitment of new prospects
3. The payment of bonuses, commissions, or some other valuable to participants who recruit new participants

Generally, the purchase by a participant of a sales kit (at cost) is not deemed to be an entry fee or investment.

The following is a summary of other laws used to prosecute pyramid plans (the same laws are often used to regulate multilevel marketing companies):

❏ *Referral Sales Statutes.* More than ten states prohibit referral sales programs, which are generally defined to include the payment of some compensation to a buyer in return for furnishing to the seller the names of prospective recruits. Thus, any scheme in which buyers are told that they can receive a return of the money paid if they provide a list of names to the seller is an unlawful referral sale.

❏ *Lottery Statutes.* Many states prohibit pyramid programs as lotteries on the basis that financial success in the program is not based on skill and judgment but on the element of chance, such as the chance that an endless stream of new participants will join the program, causing the original participant to receive a return higher than the initial entry fee paid to join.

❏ *Securities Laws.* The sale of a security that is not registered is a violation of state and federal law. The Securities and Exchange Commission (SEC) has taken the position that the money paid by a prospect to participate in a scheme (with the expectation of profit based primarily on the activities of other parties) will be considered to be an investment contract or security that must be registered with the SEC.

❑ *Mail Fraud Laws.* Pyramid programs have been prosecuted under mail fraud laws that prohibit endless chain schemes involving the exchange of money or other things of value through use of the U.S. mail.

❑ *Federal Trade Commission Act.* Section 5 of the FTC Act prohibits unfair methods of competition in commerce and unfair or deceptive practices. This broad provision has been used to justify action by the FTC against pyramid programs. In one of its most famous cases, the FTC argued that Amway Corporation was an illegal pyramid program. The FTC ultimately determined that Amway is *not* a pyramid scheme because the only so-called investment was a sales kit sold to distributors at cost, Amway guaranteed it would repurchase unsold inventory, and the *sponsoring distributor received nothing from the mere act of sponsoring* but rather began to earn money only when the newly recruited distributor sold products to consumers.

Multilevel marketing is a method of distributing goods or services not through retail stores but rather through the efforts of independent distributors or sales agents. These distributors have a great deal of flexibility in training their own salespeople and will earn money arising out of products sold by them (i.e., the down-line sales organization) as well as from sales resulting from their own efforts. Because the initial cost is often minimal, multilevel marketing is increasing in popularity and is attractive to individuals interested in starting a business without a substantial capital investment.

Consulting and Training Services

Many veterans of a particular industry choose to share their expertise with others by charging fixed or hourly fees for consulting or training services. Instead of being licensed, this information is essentially sold to the client or seminar attendee at a fixed price. If support is needed by the client, then additional time may be purchased. This alternative creates competitors without the benefit of an ongoing royalty fee and should be considered only if the expertise to be conveyed falls short of what would be needed in a business-format franchise or even in a licensing situation.

Employee Ownership and Profit Sharing

Many growth companies initially turn to franchising as an expansion alternative because of the need to develop so-called motivated managers at each site. The theory is that this owner/operator has a better feel for the local market and as an owner will be more motivated to promote the franchisor's products and services. This is the model that has helped propel the growth of Kinko's over the years. But managers can be motivated and made to feel like owners in many ways, such as employee stock ownership plans, executive stock option arrangements, and profit-sharing plans. As an alternative to franchising, each unit could be separately incorporated, with a minority stock interest granted to the key individuals responsible for the operations of that unit. Such an arrangement could be done on a per-store or regional basis. Although this results in some dilution of the ownership and control of the store or region, the managers are expected to execute a shareholders' agreement that places certain stock transfer restrictions as well as predetermined buyout arrangements on the ownership of the stock. Naturally, the terms of these stock ownership and profit-sharing arrangements should be structured with the assistance of a tax accountant and securities law counsel.

CHAPTER 19

Structuring Licensing Programs and Agreements

icensing is a contractual method of developing and exploiting intellectual property by transferring rights of use to third parties *without* the transfer of ownership. Virtually any proprietary product or service may be the subject of a license agreement, ranging from the licensing of the Mickey Mouse character by Walt Disney Studios in the 1930s to modern-day licensing of computer software and high technology.

From a legal perspective, licensing involves complex issues of contract, tax, antitrust, international, tort, and intellectual property law. From a business perspective, licensing entails a weighing of the advantages of licensing against the disadvantages in comparison to alternative types of vertical distribution systems. From a strategic perspective, licensing is the process of maximizing shareholder value by creating new income streams and market opportunities by uncovering the hidden or underutilized value in your portfolio of intellectual assets and finding licensees who will pay for the privilege of having access to and use of this intellectual capital.

Many of the economic and strategic benefits of licensing to be enjoyed by a growing company closely parallel the advantages of franchising:

❏ Spreading the risk and cost of development and distribution
❏ Achieving more rapid market penetration
❏ Earning initial license fees and ongoing royalty income
❏ Enhancing consumer loyalty and goodwill
❏ Preserving the capital that would otherwise be required for internal growth and expansion
❏ Testing new applications for existing and proven technology
❏ Avoiding or settling litigation regarding a dispute over ownership of the technology

The disadvantages of licensing are also similar to the risks inherent in franchising:

❏ A somewhat diminished ability to enforce quality control standards and specifications

❏ A greater risk of another party infringing on the licensor's intellectual property

❏ A dependence on the skills, abilities, and resources of the licensee as a source of revenue

❏ Difficulty in recruiting, motivating, and retaining qualified and competent licensees

❏ The risk that the licensor's entire reputation and goodwill may be damaged or destroyed by the act or omission of a single licensee

❏ The administrative burden of monitoring and supporting the operations of the network of licensees

The usage and application of intellectual assets inside large, medium-size, and small companies range from being actively exploited to benign neglect to everything in between. Research and development efforts may yield new product and service opportunities that are not critical to the company's core business lines, technologies, and that become orphaned (e.g., lacking internal support or resources) due to political reasons or changes in leadership. Or perhaps the company simply lacks the expertise or the resources to bring the products or services to the marketplace. In other cases, the underlying technology may have multiple applications and usages, but the company does not have the time or resources to develop the technology beyond its core business. The better managed intellectual capital–driven companies will recognize these assets as still having significant value and develop licensing programs. For example, IBM reported well over $2 billion in licensing revenues in its 2009 annual report, and much of this revenue represented high-margin cash flow streams that also helped offset its research and development costs. Other industry leaders such as GE, Texas Instruments, Dow Chemical, and DuPont are building organizational infrastructure, strategies, and systems to do a better job of managing and licensing their intellectual capital assets.

Value extraction through licensing is a key theme running throughout the boardrooms of corporate America and is not limited to Fortune 500 companies. Businesses of all sizes and with relatively small intellectual property portfolios can still apply these same strategic principles and approaches to the management of their intellectual capital. Even sectors outside private industries—universities, government laboratories and agencies, trade associations, and professional societies—are understanding the value drivers and economic benefits of licensing.

Companies of all sizes are realizing that invention for the sake of the inventor *or* innovation without revenue streams can be very harmful to shareholder value. In a post-Enron world, where boards of directors are governed by the pressures of Sarbanes-Oxley and an unforgiving capital market, no company can afford to allow valuable assets to be ignored or to go to waste. Without the desire or resources available to *directly* transform innovation into new products and services, licensing (as well as joint ventures, as discussed in the next chapter) offers an excellent way to *indirectly* bring these innovations to the marketplace, particularly in rapidly moving industries where the windows of opportunity may open and close quickly.

Also critical is developing an overall set of intellectual capital licensing policies, strategies, and objectives. The goals of the licensing program should be aligned with the overall strategic goals and business plans of the company. The licensing process should help determine which technologies or brands will be made available for licensing, which will not be, and why. The process should also define how licenses will be selected, how their performance will be monitored and measured, and under what circumstances licensees will be terminated.

Failure to consider all of the costs and benefits of licensing could easily result in a regretful strategic decision or in an unprofitable license agreement due to either an underestimation of the licensee's need for technical assistance and support or an overestimation of the market demand for the licensor's products and services. To avoid such problems, a certain amount of due diligence should be conducted by the licensor prior to any serious negotiations with a prospective licensee. This preliminary investigation generally includes market research, legal steps to fully protect intellectual property, and an internal financial analysis of the technology with respect to pricing, profit margins, and costs of production and distribution. It will also include a more specific analysis of the prospective licensee with respect to its financial strength, research and manufacturing capabilities, and reputation in the industry.

Licensing programs offer many of the same benefits of franchising, such as more rapid market penetration through shifting the capital costs of expansion. They also share many of the same risks inherent in franchising, such as the possible loss of quality control and a dependence on the skills and resources of the licensee. In addition, the recent emphasis has been on brand-extension licensing, which is discussed later in this chapter.

The two principal types of licensing occur at different levels in the marketplace: (1) technology licensing, where the strategy is to find a licensee for exploitation of industrial and technological developments; and (2) merchandise and character licensing, where the strategy is to license a recognized trademark or copyright to a manufacturer of consumer goods in markets not currently served by the licensor.

Technology Transfer and Licensing Agreements

The principal purpose behind technology transfer and licensing agreements is to join the technology proprietor, as licensor, with the organization that possesses the resources to properly develop and market the technology, as licensee. This marriage, made between companies and inventors of all shapes and sizes, occurs often between an entrepreneur with the technology but without the resources to adequately penetrate the marketplace, as licensor, and the larger company, which has sufficient research and development, production, human resources, and marketing capability to make the best use of the technology. The industrial and technological revolution has witnessed a long line of very successful entrepreneurs who have relied on the resources of larger organizations to bring their products to market, such as Chester Carlson (xerography), Edwin Land (Polaroid cameras), Robert Goddard (rockets), and Willis Carrier (air conditioning). As the base for technological development becomes broader, large companies look not only to entrepreneurs and small businesses for new ideas and technologies, but also to each other, foreign countries, universities, and federal and state governments to serve as licensors of technology. (See Figure 19-1.)

In the typical licensing arrangement, the proprietor of intellectual property rights (patents, trade secrets, trademarks, and know-how) permits a third party to make use of these rights according to a set of specified conditions and circumstances set forth in a license agreement. Licensing agreements can be limited to a very narrow component of the proprietor's intellectual property rights, such as one specific application of a single patent. It can also be much broader in context, such as in a classic technology transfer agreement, where an entire bundle of intellectual property rights are transferred to the licensee, typically in exchange for initial fees and royalties. The classic technology transfer arrangement is actually more akin to a sale of the intellectual

Figure 19-1. Why growing companies develop technology licensing programs.

- To match promising technology with the resources necessary to bring it to the marketplace

- To raise capital and earn royalty income (Many entrepreneurs have had doors slammed in their face by commercial banks and venture capitalists, who have ultimately obtained growth capital and cash flow from licensees.)

- As a defensive strategy

  - The licensor may want to have its competitors as licensees instead of watching as they eventually develop their own technology.

  - Or the licensee may want to preempt a competitor or gain access to its confidential information by approaching the competitor to obtain a license. (*Warning:* Some competitors will acquire an exclusive license to technology merely to "sit on it" so that it never enters the marketplace. Be prepared to negotiate certain performance standards or limits to exclusivity in the agreement to avoid such a trap.)

- To shift (or share) the product liability risk inherent in the production or marketing of hazardous or dangerous products with the licensee

- To reach new geographic markets unfamiliar to the technology proprietor, such as overseas, where the technology may need to be adapted or otherwise modified to meet local market conditions

- To make the widest possible use of the technology by licensing other applications or by-products of the technology that may be outside the licensor's expertise or targeted markets

- To avoid or settle actual or pending litigation (Many litigants in intellectual property infringement or misappropriation cases wind up settling the case using some form of a cross-license in lieu of costly attorney's fees and litigation expenses.)

property rights, with a right by the licensor to get the intellectual property back if the licensee fails to meet its obligations under the agreement.

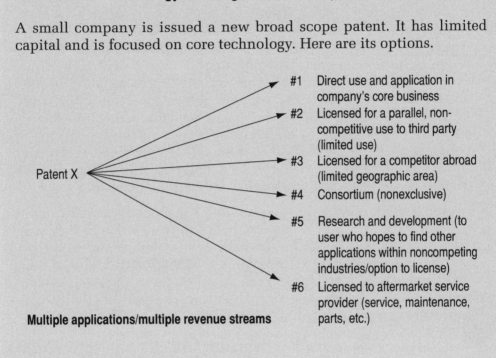

Box 19-1. Technology licensing to create multiple revenue streams.

A small company is issued a new broad scope patent. It has limited capital and is focused on core technology. Here are its options.

Patent X

#1   Direct use and application in company's core business

#2   Licensed for a parallel, non-competitive use to third party (limited use)

#3   Licensed for a competitor abroad (limited geographic area)

#4   Consortium (nonexclusive)

#5   Research and development (to user who hopes to find other applications within noncompeting industries/option to license)

#6   Licensed to aftermarket service provider (service, maintenance, parts, etc.)

Multiple applications/multiple revenue streams

Key Elements of a Technology Licensing Agreement

Once the decision to enter into more formal negotiations has been made, the terms and conditions of the license agreement should be discussed. Naturally these provisions vary, depending on whether the license is for merchandising an entertainment property, exploiting a given technology, or distributing a particular product to an original equipment manufacturer (OEM) or value-added reseller (VAR). As a general rule, any well-drafted license agreement should address the following topics:

❐ *Scope of the Grant.* Clearly set forth in this section are the exact scope, extent of exclusivity, and subject matter of the license must be initially addressed in the license agreement. Any restrictions on the geographic scope, rights and fields of use, permissible channels of trade, restrictions on sublicensing (including the formula for sharing sublicensing fees, if provided), limitations on assignability, or exclusion of enhancements or improvements to the technology (or expansion of the product line) are covered by the agreement.

❐ *Term and Renewal.* This section contains the commencement date, duration, renewals and extensions, conditions to renewal, procedures for

Box 19-2. Tips for the prospective licensor.

- *Finding the Right Dance Partner.* The quest for the appropriate licensee should be approached with the same zeal and diligence that one would adopt in the search for a marriage partner. No stone should remain unturned, either in narrowing the field of prospective licensees or in the due diligence process applied to a particular proposed licensee. The goals and objectives of each party, the financial strength of the licensee, the licensee's past licensing practices, the qualifications of the licensee's jurisdiction (other states, other countries), and the skills of the licensee's sales and marketing team *should all be examined prior to the commencement of the negotiation of the license agreement.* Access to the licensor's intellectual property should be severely restricted unless and until these criteria have been examined and met to the satisfaction of the licensor.

- *Avoiding the Inferiority Complex.* Although a small company or entrepreneur, looking to license its technology to a larger business, often faces an uphill battle, this is not sufficient reason to merely roll over in the licensing negotiations. In too many horror stories, entrepreneurs were too impressed and intimidated by the larger company's resources and lawyers, and as a result sold their soul at far below the current or eventual market value of the technology.

- *Don't Go in Naked, and Don't Be a Motor Mouth.* Many prospective licensors make the mistake of telling too little or saying way too much in the initial meetings and negotiations with the prospective licensee. Finding the right balance of disclosure to pique the interest of the licensee without giving away the farm is never easy; however, a commonly accepted solution is the licensing memorandum. The licensing memorandum, when used in tandem with confidentiality agreements, can provide the prospective licensee with the information it needs to conduct the preliminary analysis without jeopardizing the rights of the licensor. The memorandum should contain a discussion of the technology and the portfolio of intellectual property rights that protect the technology, the background of the proprietor, the projected markets and applications of the technology, the proposed terms and financial issues between licensor and licensee, and a discussion of existing competitive technology and technological trends that could affect the future value of the license.

- *Things Can and Will Change—Be Prepared.* Like marriages, most licensing agreements are intended to continue over a long period of time. As a result, predicting technological, social, economic, and political trends that will affect the rights and obligations of the licensor and licensee during the term of the agreement is difficult. Licensing agreements, like all legal documents, require a certain degree of precision to be enforceable and workable for the parties; however, the inevitability of change should result in a framework of trust and flexibility. Not every detail will be addressed nor every change in the external environment anticipated. Technologies become obsolete, governments get overthrown, rock stars lose popularity, movie sequels flop, and a corporation's personnel may be restructured, but the licensing agreement must be flexible enough to handle all unforeseen changes.

providing notice of intent to renew, grounds for termination, obligations upon termination, and licensor's reversionary rights in the technology.

❏ *Performance Standards and Quotas.* To the extent that the licensor's consideration will depend on royalty income that will be calculated from the licensee's gross or net revenues, the licensor may want to impose certain minimum levels of performance in terms of sales, advertising, and promotional expenditures and human resources to be devoted to the exploitation of the technology. Milestone payments might also be tied to the achievement of certain key events, such as regulatory approvals of the core technology. Naturally, the licensee will argue for a best efforts provision that is free from performance standards and quotas. In such cases, the licensor may want to insist on a minimum royalty level that will be paid regardless of the licensee's actual performance.

❏ *Payments to the Licensor.* Virtually every type of license agreement includes some form of initial payment and ongoing royalty to the licensor. Royalty formulas vary widely, however, and may be based on gross sales, net sales, net profits, fixed sum per product sold, or a minimum payment to be made to the licensor over a given period of time. Or they may include a sliding scale to provide some incentive to the licensee as a reward for performance. Royalty rates may vary from industry to industry and in some cases will vary depending on the licensed product's stage of development. For example, in a typical merchandise licensing agreement, royalty rates range from 7 to 12 percent of net sales depending on the strength of the licensor's brands whereas manufacturing royalty rates may be lower when the licensee will need to make significant capital expenditures to bring the product to the marketplace. In the biotechnology and medical device industries, the royalty rates may vary based on the stage of development of the product and its progression through the FDA approval process. A biotech or pharmaceutical treatment or compound that has already cleared Phase III approval may command royalties as high as 20 percent of sales, whereas a preclinical trial product or compound may command a royalty rate of only 2 percent, depending on the likelihood of ultimate commercialization.

❑ *Quality Control Assurance and Protection.* Quality control standards and specifications for the production, marketing, and distribution of the products and services covered by the license must be set forth by the licensor. In addition, procedures should be included in the agreement that allow the licensor an opportunity to *enforce* these standards and specifications, such as a right to inspect the licensee's premises; a right to review, approve, or reject samples produced by the licensee; and a right to review and approve any packaging, labeling, or advertising materials to be used in connection with the exploitation of the products and services that are within the scope of the license. Certain types of licensors may also want to consider placing a ceiling on the allowances for returned merchandise, perhaps in the 3 to 5 percent range of total goods sold. This helps prevent the licensee from producing a significant amount of substandard product, which could dilute the brand, damage the technology, or otherwise expose the licensor to harm or potential liability.

❑ *Insurance and Indemnification.* The licensor should take all necessary and reasonable steps to ensure that the licensee has an obligation to protect and indemnify the licensor against any claims or liabilities resulting from the licensee's exploitation of the products and services covered by the license. These provisions should address any minimum insurance coverages (naming the licensor as an additional insured), as well as an exclusion from liability or ceilings on the responsibilities of the licensee.

❑ *Accounting, Reports, and Audits.* The licensor must impose certain reporting and record-keeping procedures on the licensee to ensure an accurate accounting for periodic royalty payments. Further, the licensor should reserve the right to audit the records of the licensor in the event of a dispute or discrepancy, along with provisions as to who will be responsible for the cost of the audit in the event of an understatement.

❑ *Duties to Preserve and Protect Intellectual Property.* The obligations of the licensee, its agents, and employees to preserve and protect the confidential nature and acknowledge the ownership of the intellectual property being disclosed in connection with the license agreement must be carefully defined. Any required notices or legends that must be included on products or materials distributed in connection with the license agreement (such as the status of the relationship between licensee and licensor or the identification of actual owner of the intellectual property) are also described in this section. The agreement should also be clear as to which party and at whose expense and control will any disputes regarding the ownership of the intellectual property be handled.

❑ *Technical Assistance, Training, and Support.* Any obligation of the licensor to assist the licensee in the development or exploitation of the subject matter being licensed is included in this section of the agreement. The assistance may take the form of personal services or documents and records. Either way, any fees due to the licensor for such support services that are over and above the initial license and ongoing royalty fee must also be addressed.

❑ *Warranties of the Licensor.* A prospective licensee may demand that the licensor provide certain representations and warranties in the license agreement. These may include warranties regarding the ownership of the intellectual property, such as absence of any known infringements of the intellectual property or restrictions on the ability to license the intellectual property, or warranties pledging that the technology has the features, capabilities, and characteristics previously represented in the negotiations.

❑ *Infringements.* The license agreement should contain procedures under which the licensee must notify the licensor of any known or suspected direct or indirect infringements of the subject matter being licensed. The responsibilities for the cost of protecting and defending the technology should also be specified in this section.

❑ *Termination.* The license agreement should provide some guidance on the licensor's ability to terminate the rights granted in the event of material breach (such as nonpayment of royalties), change in control, insolvency, or other default of the licensee. The notice and procedures for termination should be discussed as well as the wind-down or phase-out periods following termination.

Understanding the Benefits of Licensing In

Not all licensing strategies involve the leveraging of *your* intellectual capital. In some cases, the growth can be driven by the licensing of stale, ignored, or underdeveloped technology or brands of another company. Licensing in can be used to:

❑ Add value or fill in missing strategic puzzle pieces.

❑ Enhance consumer recognition and loyalty.

In licensing, the following strategic questions are critical:

❑ Do large competitors or players in parallel industries have technology that you could use (either in its current form or where you would have a license to explore new opportunities)?

❑ Could a missing puzzle piece or a core technology be an accelerant for growth in your product lines or services?

❑ Would special training, certificates, distribution rights, or clearances enhance growth, opportunities, or market share?

❑ Is a competitor's technology, for which you have a channel or application, dormant or ignored?

❐ Do you have a product/service that is (or is destined soon to be) com-
moditized where the license or access to an existing brand would add
significant value?

❐ Is a recognized brand in the marketplace that has been uncreative or
unaggressive, and have you spotted an opportunity?

❐ Have you been the licensee or franchisee of another company and developed enough of your own systems to become a licensor or franchisor?

Special Issues in Negotiating and Drafting Technology Licensing Agreements

A wide variety of special contractual issues must be addressed in the preparation of a technology license agreement:

❐ *Defined Terms.* What many entrepreneurs may initially view as legal
boilerplate is often the most hotly contested component of the license
agreement. This initial section of the license agreement is intended to
do much more than make the document easier to read. It defines some
of the key aspects of the relationship with respect to the specific field of
the technology licensed, the territory to be covered, the milestones and
objectives that must be met, the specific patents or trademarks that will
be included within the scope of the license, and the nature of the compensation to be paid to the licensor.

❐ *Reports to the Licensor, Record Keeping by the Licensee.* In all licensing
agreements, adequate reporting and record keeping by the licensee are
critical to ensure that the licensor receives all royalty payments when
due. In a technology licensing agreement, additional reports should be
prepared monthly or quarterly that disclose the licensee's actual use of
the technology; research studies or market tests that have directly or
indirectly used the technology; the marketing, advertising, or public relations strategies planned or implemented that involve the technology;
progress reports regarding the meeting of established performance objectives and timetables; reports of any threatened or actual infringement
or misappropriation of the licensor's technology; and any requests for
sublicenses or cross-licenses that have been made by third parties to the
licensee.

❐ *Exclusivity of the License Granted.* The term "exclusive" in the context
of a licensing agreement negotiation is often misunderstood. Exclusivity
could apply to a territory, an application of the technology, or a method
of production of the products that results from the technology. Exclusivity may or may not include the licensor itself and may or may not permit
the granting of sublicenses or cross-licenses to future third parties who
are not bound by the original license agreement. Exclusivity may or may
not be conditioned on the licensee meeting certain predetermined performance standards. Exclusivity may be conditional for a limited time
period on the continued employment of certain key technical staff of

the licensee. All of these issues, surrounding what on its face appears to be a simple term, must be discussed in the negotiations and ultimately addressed in the license agreement.

❐ *Technical Support and Assistance, Dependence on Key Personnel.* The proper development and exploitation of the technology often depend on the availability of the proprietor and the licensor's technical team to provide support and assistance to the licensee. The conditions under which this team will be available to the licensee should be included in the technology license agreement. Provisions should be drafted to deal with scheduling conflicts, the payment of travel expenses, the impact of disability or death of the inventor, the availability of written or video-taped data in lieu of the inventor's physical attendance, the regularity and length of periodic technical support meetings, and the protection of confidential information.

❐ *Merchandise and Character Licensing Agreements.* The use of commonly recognized trademarks, brand names, sports teams, athletes, universities, television and film characters, musicians, and designers to foster the sale of specific products and services is at the heart of today's merchandise and character licensing environment. Manufacturers and distributors of products and services license these words, images, and symbols for products that range from clothing to housewares to toys and posters. Certain brand names and characters withstand the test of time, and others fall prey to fads, consumer shifts, and stiff competition.

The trademark and copyright owners of these properties and character images are motivated to license for a variety of reasons. Aside from the obvious desire to earn royalty fees and profits, many manufacturers view this licensing strategy as a form of merchandising *to promote the underlying product or service.* The licensing of a trademark for application on a line of clothing helps to establish and reinforce brand awareness at the consumer level. For example, when Hurley® licenses a leisure apparel manufacturer to produce a line of Hurley® apparel, the hope is to sell more skateboards, appeal to the lifestyle of its targeted consumers, maintain consumer awareness, *and* enjoy the royalty income from the sale of the clothing line. Similar strategies have been adopted by manufacturers to revive a mature brand or failing product. In certain instances, the spin-off product that has been licensed was almost as financially successful as the underlying product it was intended to promote.

Brand name owners, celebrities, and academic institutions must be very careful not to grant too many licenses too quickly. The financial rewards of a flow of royalty income from hundreds of different manufacturers can be quite seductive but must be weighed against the possible loss of quality control and dilution of the name, logo, or character. The loyalty of the licensee network is also threatened when too many licenses are granted in closely competing products. Retailers also become cautious when purchasing licensed goods from a licensee if they fear

Box 19-3. Tips for successful brand licensing.

- *Choose your partners wisely.* Brand licensing typically requires a closer working relationship between licensor and licensee than does technology or software licensing, to make sure that consistent brand image is maintained in all relevant market segments. Be clear in your articulation and enforcement of brand promise, positioning, and brand values. The core of the brand must have values that transcend and add value to products and services in new categories and segments. It must mean something to the consumer and have enough loyalty to carry over into other industries and applications.

- *Build in checks and balances, both operationally and contractually.* All brand licensing, co-branding, and brand-extension licensing should add to the value of the core brand of the owner/licensor, not dilute or harm that value. Build in quality control provisions, inspection and performance standards, and marketing and usage guidelines to protect the integrity of your brands.

- *Be proactive in developing new potential applications, market segments, and licensed categories into which your brands could be licensed.* Do not rely solely on your licensees for new ideas or new product development. Licensing is a proactive, not a reactive way to build shareholder value when it is implemented properly. Keep pushing your licensees to produce goods and services bearing your name that will be innovative and product leaders in the segments, not just more of the same under a different name.

- *Get involved in product design, packaging, product features (materials, shapes, etc.), promotional plans, and other variations of your licensees.* Do not let brand licensing be a part-time commitment of the marketing department of the company. Make sure that proper resources are committed to building a brand licensing department that will review quarterly and annual business plans of licensees, enforce performance milestones and quality control guidelines, and coordinate joint marketing efforts, such as trade shows, promotional campaigns, and sales meetings.

that quality control has suffered or that the popularity of the licensed character, celebrity, or image will be short-lived. Their fears may result in smaller orders and an overall unwillingness to carry inventory, especially in the toy industry, where purchasing decisions are being made by (or at least influenced by) the whims of a five-year-old child who may strongly identify with a character image one week and then turn away to a totally different character image the next week. Manufacturers and licensees have to develop advertising and media campaigns to hold the consumer's attention for an extended period of time. Only then will the retailer be convinced of the potential longevity of the product line. This type of media support requires a balancing of the risks and rewards between licensor and licensee in the character-licensing agreement in the areas of compensation to the licensor, advertising expenditures by the licensee, scope of the exclusivity, and quality control standards and specifications.

In the merchandise licensing community, the name, logo, symbol, or character is typically referred to as the "property," and the specific product or product line (e.g., T-shirts, mugs, posters, etc.) is referred to as the "licensed product." This area of licensing offers opportunities and benefits to both the owners of the properties and the manufacturers of the licensed products. For the owner of the property, brand recognition, goodwill, and royalty income are strengthened and expanded. The manufacturer of the licensed products has an opportunity to leverage the goodwill of the property to improve sales of the licensed products. The manufacturer has an opportunity to hit the ground running in the sale of merchandise by gaining access to and use of an already established brand name or character image.

Naturally, each party should conduct due diligence on the other. From the perspective of the property owner, the manufacturer of the licensed product should demonstrate an ability to meet and maintain quality control standards, possess financial stability, and offer an aggressive and well-planned marketing and promotional strategy. From the perspective of the manufacturer of the licensed property, the owner of the property should display a certain level of integrity and commitment to quality, disclose its future plans for the promotion of the property, and be willing to participate and assist in the overall marketing of the licensed products. For example, the unwillingness of a star basketball player to appear for promotional events designed to sell his own specially licensed line of basketball shoes would present a major problem and would likely lead to a premature termination of the licensing relationship.

Special Issues in Negotiating and Preparing Merchandise and Character Licensing Agreements

Several key areas must be addressed in the preparation and negotiation of a merchandise licensing agreement:

- ❏ Scope of the territorial and product exclusivity
- ❏ Assignability and sublicensing rights
- ❏ Definition of the property and the licensed products
- ❏ Quality control and approval
- ❏ Ownership of artwork and designs
- ❏ Term renewal rights and termination of the relationship

Box 19-4. Sample agenda for a branding strategy meeting.

- Management's vision and strategy for the brands—leadership and communication of the branding vision. What are the strategic, financial, and marketing goals for the brands?

- Applications and uses of the brands

- Consistency or inconsistency in the application and usage of the brands. For example, will the brands be licensed in connection with all technology licenses? Vice versa? Stand-alone?
  - At the customer level?
  - At the corporate cultural level?

- What value propositions do the brands represent? What role does brand play in the decision making of the current and targeted customers or channel partners? What tools are being used to convey and maintain the branding messages?

- Promotion and marketing strategies for the brands

- Brand merchandising opportunities (clothing, etc.)

- Co-branding and brand-extension licensing

- How does branding strategy fit into other programs in place to increase customer loyalty and drive new revenue streams?

- In what forms will the brands manifest themselves (e.g., words, symbols, slogans, shapes, spokesperson, sounds, jingles, etc. versus the underlying product or service)?

❏ Initial license and ongoing royalty fees

❏ Performance criteria for the licensee

❏ Liability insurance

❏ Indemnification

❏ Duty to pursue trademark and copyright infringement

❏ Minimum advertising and promotional requirements

❏ Accounting and record keeping of the licensee

❏ Inspection and audit rights of the licensor

❏ Rights of first refusal for expanded or revised characters and images

❏ Limitations on licensee's distribution to related or affiliated entities

❏ Representations and warranties of the licensor with respect to its rights to the property

Four Critical Steps:

1. Building a brand-driven organization.

2. Develop a comprehensive brand architecture that provides strategic direction.

3. Develop a brand strategy. (This should include a compelling value proposition and a differentiating message that resonates with target sets of customers.)

4. Build effective and efficient brand-building systems (with a system to track results).

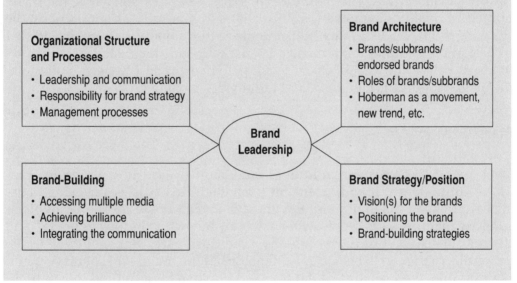

❐ The availability of the licensor for technical and promotional assistance

❐ Miscellaneous provisions, such as law to govern, inurement of good-will, nature of the relationship, notice, and force majeure.

The definition of the scope of permitted use is usually accomplished with the use of schedules, illustrations, and exhibits. For example, suppose a manufacturer of children's sportswear wanted to license the likeness of former NBA great Michael Jordan for a new line of clothing. Will the property consist of unlimited use of the name and likeness of Mr. Jordan, or will it be only for a specific drawing or caricature of his face? Similarly, will the licensed products be defined as virtually any style or size of children's sportswear, or will they be limited to "children's short-sleeved T-shirts up to size 20 and matching children's short pants"? And when engaged in celebrity licensing, preserving the right to terminate or modify agreements based on the conduct, reputation, and public perception of the celebrity is critical, as was necessary in character licensing arrangements with Martha Stewart, Michael Vick, and Tiger Woods. Naturally, there is room for much variation and negotiation in these defined terms and in dictating standards of conduct

when humans act like humans. To avoid claims and litigation over the unauthorized use of the property, the licensor and licensee should clearly communicate their intent to counsel before preparation of the merchandise licensing
agreement.

The key economic issue in the agreement is the section dealing with
royalty payments that the licensee must pay the licensor in exchange for the
use of the property over a period of time. The royalty obligation is usually
stated as a fixed percentage of the licensee's sales of the licensed products or
as a lump sum per unit of the licensed product. Royalty rates are based
purely on market forces and on the negotiation skills of the parties and their
counsel. This section must also address the basis for the calculation of the
royalty payment (e.g., the definition of gross revenues, net sales, etc.), any
minimum royalty payments that must be paid quarterly or annually by the
licensee to the licensor, any adjustments to the royalty rate (which is tied
to performance, inflation, a change in market conditions, etc.), royalties on
noncash sales, and the licensee's obligation to prepare reports and statements to support the calculation of the royalty payment.

Brand-Extension Licensing

Over the past few years, one form of merchandise licensing has grown rapidly in importance: brand-extension licensing. This type of licensing is designed to widen the depth and the breadth of the market for the products or
services identified with the owner's brand, but with the development and
distribution costs at the cost of the licensed third party. Some of these transactions have proven to be natural extensions of the brand and some were not.
For example, the licensing of the Starbucks® name for a limited line of high-
quality ice creams, Sunkist® for orange soda, or Hershey's® for chocolate milk
were brand-extension licensing projects that have all been very successful
and allowed the owners of the trademarks to enjoy instant entry into a new
industry with minimal capital investment or market research. The ability to
penetrate new markets, generate new income streams, build the value of the
company's brand name, and increase overall brand awareness has made
brand-extension licensing a very viable and profitable strategy for companies
like Gerber®, which had a successful launch into the electronic nursery monitor business and related baby products through brand-extension licensing.
It seems unlikely that a company like Gerber would have launched into the
electronics industry without the strategic benefits of a brand-extension licensee.

In the United States alone, retail sales of *licensed* branded products are
estimated to have surpassed $100 billion in 2008 and will reach $150 billion
by the year 2012. Products born of brand-extension licensing have become
staples for quality and value-driven consumers who regularly look for successful brand-licensed items. This marriage between a product and a well-
recognized brand name allows trademark owners to enter into new industries without the capital investment required to actually manufacture and
distribute the licensed product. Subject to strict quality control guidelines,

companies with registered trademarks can penetrate new markets, build new profit centers, increase brand awareness and recognition, facilitate international expansion, and even modernize a brand's image with the appropriate brand-extension licensing strategic partners. Of course, there is a limit on what the consumer will accept. The image or brand recognition of Ben & Jerry's® would be barely enhanced if it were to license its name to an automobile parts manufacturer in order to produce a new line of tires; nor would their implied endorsement be likely to enhance the sale of the tires. Yet the recent move by Starbucks to license their name for a limited line of new, prepackaged ice cream seems to have been a big hit with quality-conscious consumers who knew the Starbucks name as a symbol of quality and a natural jump to a related product like ice cream.

The temptation to extend the equity and value of your brand into other areas is not without its risks. There are quality control issues, the risk of overbranding or misbranding from a consumer perspective, and product liability issues. The key to successful brand extension is that the brand itself must stand for something greater than the original product *and* that the consumer's perception of the extended brand is a natural one. The brand on a stand-alone basis must represent an attitude, a feeling, or a cachet that holds water when it is applied to another product. It worked well when the Gap® brand-extended a license for perfume and when Calvin Klein® brand-extended a license for eyewear, but backfired for Harley-Davidson® when it awarded a license for a line of cigarettes. Although the extension seemed natural, consumers were not convinced that the motorcycle manufacturers had a brand that would lend quality and value to a pack of smokes. Even nonlicensed extensions of brands that would seem to be a home run have failed due to inadequate market research. For example, when our society started eating more chicken than beef, A-1® steak sauce launched a poultry sauce that did very poorly notwithstanding a multimillion-dollar advertising budget. Researchers missed the fact that the A-1® brand had been associated in their minds with *steak*, not necessarily with *sauce*. Yet other brand-extension licensing deals have succeeded in spite of basic logic. One might think that the last thing anyone wants to smell like is a sweaty basketball player; yet the Michael Jordan line of men's cologne has sold reasonably well. This superstar's cachet is transcendental.

The development of an effective brand-extension licensing program involves the following components (see also Figure 19-2):

❑ *Discipline.* Avoid the temptation to overbrand. A key part of brand management is determining your zone of appropriateness and figuring out what your brand *does not* represent. This determination can be even more important than understanding what it *does* represent.

❑ *Market Research. Really* understanding your customers and their reasons for being loyal to your brand is critical. Understanding the *source* of that loyalty will lead to natural zones of expansion into other products and services—if you listen carefully.

❑ *Due Diligence.* The selection of the right brand-extension licensees who have a strong reputation in their underlying industry and the resources to execute a well-written market development plan is critical.

(text continues on page 394)

Figure 19-2. Form of license agreement.

LICENSE AND DISTRIBUTION AGREEMENT

THIS LICENSE AND DISTRIBUTION AGREEMENT (the "Agreement") is made this _____ day of 20____ by and between LICENSOR (the "Licensor"), whose address is _____, and LICENSEE (the "Licensee"), whose address is _____ .

WITNESSETH:

WHEREAS, Licensor has developed and currently manufacturers, markets and sells food vacuum sealers and related accessories, which are primarily marketed to preparers (the "Products") and, in connection therewith, is the owner of U.S. Patent Nos. _____ and _____, patent applications, if any (the "Licensed Patents"), and certain valuable technical information, know-how and data relating to the Products (collectively with the Licensed Patents, the "Product Technology");

WHEREAS, Licensor uses the [unregistered] trademark and such related mark or other marks in marketing the Products, [a portion/all] of which are shown on Exhibit A, attached hereto and incorporated herein by reference (the "Licensed Marks");

WHEREAS, Licensee desires to obtain the exclusive right to use the Product Technology and Licensed Marks in connection with the manufacturing, marketing and selling of food vacuum sealers or any product to which any application of Product Technology may be made by Licensee, which products may be sold for _____ Dollars or less at retail, and related accessories (the "Accessories") primarily for home use (collectively, the "Home Products");

WHEREAS, Licensor desires to license the Product Technology and Licensed Marks to Licensee and allow Licensee to manufacture, market and sell Home Products pursuant to the terms hereof; and

WHEREAS, Licensee desires to license the Product Technology and Licensed Marks from Licensor and manufacture, market and sell Home Products pursuant to the terms hereof.

NOW THEREFORE, in consideration for the foregoing and the mutual covenants and agreements contained herein, the parties hereto agree as follows:

1. *Grant and Acceptance of License.* Subject to the terms and conditions in this Agreement, Licensor hereby grants to Licensee, and Licensee hereby accepts, the exclusive worldwide right and license to use the Product Technology to enable Licensee to manufacture, market and sell Home Products in the Licensed Territory during the Term (defined in Section 10 below). Licensor agrees that he shall not use the Product Technology in the manufacture, marketing and sale of Home Products or any competitive product line within the Licensed Territory during the Term nor shall he grant to any other person or entity a license or other right to so use the Product Technology. Nothing herein shall be construed to limit or prohibit Licensor from manufacturing, marketing and selling Products in the Licensed Territory during the Term. The "Licensed Territory" shall mean the entire world for purposes of this Agreement.

2. *Term of License.* Unless sooner terminated by the terms of Section 10 hereof, the license granted herein shall continue until the expiration of the Term.

3. *Trademark License.* Subject to the terms and conditions of this Agreement, and for so long as Licensee shall have the exclusive right and license to use the Product Technology (as provided in Section 1), Licensor licenses and grants to Licensee the exclusive right and license to use any or all of the Licensed Marks in connection with the marketing of Home Products in the Licensed Territory; provided that Licensor retains the right to use the Licensed Marks in connection with the sale of Products (including promotional materials used to promote the Products). Licensee shall have the right to use any trade names or trademarks it deems appropriate in marketing the Home Products and may register in the name of Licensee such trademarks (other than the Licensed Marks) with the U.S. Patent and Trademark Office or any state agency without the approval of Licensor.

4. *Distribution Arrangements.* Licensor hereby grants to Licensee the exclusive right to manufacture, market and sell Home Products in the Licensed Territory. In connection therewith, Licensee shall have the right to use the Product Technology and Licensed Marks in accordance with the terms of this Agreement. Licensee agrees to use its reasonable efforts to establish a designated manufacturing facility to manufacture Home Products in commercial quantities, and to promote the sale of the Home Products within the Licensed Territory. In that regard, Licensee shall at its expense and within a reasonable time after the date hereof, begin to develop and carry out a marketing and sales program (which includes the use of direct mail, catalogs, promotional material and television commercials/infomercials) designed to promote sales of Home Products, and exert its reasonable efforts to create, supply and service in the Licensed Territory as many Home Products as is commercially practical; provided, however, nothing contained in this Agreement shall effect or limit Licensee's right to develop, manufacture, distribute, advertise, market and sell any other products and/or services. Licensee shall be solely responsible with regard to establishing a designated manufacturing facility and marketing and sales program and Licensor shall have such responsibility financial or otherwise. Subject to the quality control standards set forth in Section 6 hereof, Licensee shall have complete control with respect to the manufacturing, marketing and selling of Home Products in the Licensed Territory, including without limitation, the wholesale and retail prices at which Home Products are sold. Licensor agrees to name Licensee as an "Additional Insured" on all policies of insurance having coverage for product liability.

5. *Royalty Payments.* Licensee agrees to pay Licensor an annual royalty equal to _____ percent (_____%) [Parties to Discuss] of Net Sales generated from the sale of the Home Products exclusive of Accessories. Licensee agrees to pay Licensor an annual royalty payment equal to _____ percent (_____%) [Parties to Discuss] of Net Sales generated from the sale of Accessories. Such royalty shall be paid within sixty (60) days after the end of each calendar year. During the Term of this Agreement, royalty payments shall accrue on a monthly basis. For purposes of this Agreement, Net Sales shall be defined as _____ [Parties to Discuss].

6. *Quality Control.*

(a) *Standards.* Licensee shall ensure that all Home Products it distributes (by sale, transfer or otherwise) are manufactured consistent with the reasonable and necessary quality control standards, if any, established and delivered in writing to Licensee by Licensor.

(b) *Inspection.* From time to time and upon reasonable prior notice by Licensor, Licensor may request Licensee to submit samples of Home Products manufactured by Licensee or its designee for Licensor's approval, which approval shall not be unreasonably withheld. Unless otherwise approved by Licensor, the quality of all Home Products manufactured, marketed and sold by Licensee pursuant to this Agreement shall be of a quality at least equal to such samples. Licensee agrees to provide Licensor with requested samples of Home Products within thirty (30) days after Licensor requests such samples.

(continues)

Figure 19-2. (Continued).

7. *Technical Assistance.* Licensor shall, at his sole expense and at the request of Licensee, provide technical assistance to Licensee or any of its designees during the Term of the Agreement in connection with the use of Product Technology (including, but not by way of limitation, technical assistance relating to the manufacture, design and promotion of Home Products). Licensor further agrees to fully assist and cooperate with Licensee in procuring acceptance and listing of Home Products by Underwriters Laboratories Inc. and the Canadian Standards Association. Licensor hereby agrees to provide such technical assistance initially for a minimum of four (4) hours per day until such time as Home Products can be manufactured by Licensee or its designee in commercially reasonable quantities, as determined by Licensee in its sole discretion. Once Home Products are being manufactured in commercially reasonable quantities, Licensor agrees to provide technical assistance as requested by Licensee, including that which is necessary to manufacture, market and sell new products and accessories, and implement developments and improvements relating to the Products, as provided in Section 8(a) below.

8. *New Technology.*

(a) *Licensor's New Products, Accessories, etc.* Licensor shall promptly provide and make available to Licensee any information about new products, accessories, developments or improvements relating to the Products. Licensee shall have the right to review and research such information on a confidential basis to determine whether it is reasonably adaptable for use with or application on Home Products for such time as it deems appropriate. Further, Licensee shall have the first right of refusal to license such information from Licensor. Any such information licensed by Licensee shall, for purposes hereof, be included within the meaning of "Product Technology" and thereby subject to the terms of this Agreement.

(b) *Licensee's New Products, Accessories, etc.* Any new products, accessories, developments or improvements relating to the Home Products are developed by Licensee or any party with whom Licensee has entered in a contract, agreement or other similar arrangement during the term of this Agreement (the "New Technology") shall remain the property of Licensee. Licensee may determine whether and to what extent it desires to seek trademarks, patents or take other necessary legal steps to protect the New Technology without any interference by Licensor. In the event Licensee shall not seek trademarks, patents or take other necessary legal steps to protect any or all elements of the New Technology, Licensor shall have the right, in his discretion and at his expense, to seek trademarks or patents, or take other legal steps to protect any and all elements of the New Technology. Licensee shall reasonably assist Licensor in seeking such trademarks, patents, or such protection if requested, including securing and execution of trademark or patent applications and other appropriate documents and papers, and Licensor shall pay or reimburse Licensee for all expenses incurred by Licensee in connection with providing such assistance.

9. *Claims; Infringement.* Licensor represents and warrants that he has full power and authority to grant the license to Licensee as provided herein, the Product Technology and Licensed Marks are free and clear of all liens, claims and encumbrances of any nature whatsoever, and there are no governmental or regulatory proceedings, investigations or other actions pending or concluded that adversely affect the Product Technology or Licensed Marks. Licensor represents and warrants to Licensee that there are no patent, trademark or copyright infringements with respect to the Product Technology or the Licensed Marks nor are there any threatened, pending or contemplated actions, suits or proceedings against Licensor or otherwise with respect to the same. No such infringement actions, suits or proceedings would result by reason of the transactions contemplated by this Agreement. Licensor shall promptly notify Licensor of any allegation or claim that the use of the Product Technology or the Licensed Marks infringes upon the rights of any other person or entity. Licensor agrees to defend Licensee and its directors and officers against any infringement, unfair competition or other claim respecting Licensee's use of the Product Technology or the Licensed Marks. Further, Licensor hereby agrees to indemnify, defend, hold

harmless, Licensee and its directors and officers from and against any and all claims or actions, suits, proceedings, damages, liabilities, costs and expenses (including, without limitation, reasonable attorneys' fees) arising out of (a) any patent, trademark or copyright infringement by Licensor, (b) Licensor's unfair competition, misappropriation of confidential information, technology, know-how or trade secrets, and resulting from Licensor's use of the Product Technology or Licensed Marks, or (c) otherwise arising by reason of Licensee's legitimate use of the foregoing in compliance with this Agreement.

10. *Termination of Agreement.*

(a) *Duration.* Unless sooner terminated as otherwise herein provided, the term of this Agreement shall commence upon the date hereof and shall expire on the [_____ (____)] anniversary of that date (the "Initial Term"). Licensee shall have the right and option to renew this Agreement for term commencing on the day following the Initial Term and expiring on the [_____(____)] anniversary of the day following the Initial Term by giving Licensor notice of the exercise of such option at least ten (10) days prior to the end of the Initial Term. The Initial Term, along with such renewal term, if any, shall be referred to herein as the "Term."

(b) *Termination by Licensor.* In addition to any other right of Licensor contained herein to terminate this Agreement, Licensor shall have the right to terminate this Agreement by written notice to Licensee upon the occurrence of any one or more of the following events:

(i) failure of Licensee to make any payment required pursuant by this Agreement when due; or

(ii) intentional, persistent and material failure of Licensee to comply in any material respect with the quality control standards required pursuant to Section 6.

(c) *Termination by Licensee.*

(i) In addition to any other right of Licensee contained herein to terminate this Agreement, Licensee shall have the right to terminate this Agreement by written notice to Licensor upon the occurrence of any one or more of the following events:

(A) the insolvency of Licensor;

(B) the institution of any proceeding by Licensor, voluntarily or involuntarily, under any bankruptcy, insolvency or moratorium law;

(C) any assignment by Licensor of substantially all of his assets for the benefit of creditors;

(D) placement of Licensor's assets in the hands of a trustee or receiver unless the receivership or trust is dissolved within thirty (30) days thereafter; or

(E) any breach by Licensor of any representation, warranty or covenant contained in this Agreement that, if curable, is not cured by Licensor within thirty (30) days after its receipt of written notice thereof from Licensee. If such breach is not cured within such thirty (30) days period, or is not curable, then termination shall be deemed effective on the date of such notice.

(ii) If at any time following the first _____(____) months of the Term, Licensee determines in good faith that its continued use of Licensor's Product Technology in the manufacture, marketing and sale of Home Products is commercially impracticable by reason of (A) a continued failure (after Licensee has exerted its best efforts to overcome such failure) in the performance of Home Products, or (B) Licensee's inability, after exerting its best efforts, to produce Home Products at its designated manufacturing facility, Licensee may, at its option, terminate this Agreement without further obligation to Licensor (other than payment for accrued royalties, if any) upon thirty (30) days prior written notice to Licensor.

(continues)

Figure 19-2. (Continued).

(d) *Exercise.* Licensor or Licensee, as the case may be, may exercise the right of termination granted hereunder by giving the other party ten (10) days prior written notice of that party's election to terminate and the reason(s) for such termination. After the expiration of such period, this Agreement shall automatically terminate unless the other party has previously cured the breach or condition permitting termination, in which case this Agreement shall not terminate. Such notice and termination shall not prejudice either party's rights to any sums due hereunder and shall not prejudice any cause of action or claim of such party accrued or to accrue on account of any breach or default by the other party.

(e) *Failure to Enforce.* The failure of either party at any time, or for any period of time, to enforce any of the provisions of this Agreement shall not be construed as a waiver of such provision or of the right of such party thereafter to enforce each and every such provision.

(f) *Effect of Termination.* Subject to the terms of Section 8 hereof, in the event this Agreement is terminated for any reason whatsoever: (i) Licensee shall return any plans, drawings, papers, notes, writings and other documents, samples and models pertaining to the Product Technology, retaining no copies, and shall refrain from using or publishing any portion of the Product Technology; and (ii) Licensor shall return any plans, drawings, papers, notes, writings and other documents, samples and models, retaining no copies, pertaining to New Technology. Upon termination of this Agreement, Licensee shall cease manufacturing, processing, producing, using, selling or distributing Home Products and shall retain no right of any kind to use anywhere in the world the Product Technology or the Licensed Marks; provided, however, that Licensee may continue to sell in the ordinary course of business for a period of one-hundred eighty (180) days after the date of termination reasonable quantities of Home Products which are fully manufactured and in Licensee's normal inventory at the date of termination and Licensee may fulfill all outstanding purchase orders received by Licensee through the date of termination (irrespective of the one-hundred eighty (180) day period) if all monetary obligations of Licensee to Licensor have been satisfied.

11. *Independent Contractor.* Licensee's relationship to Licensor hereunder shall be that of a licensee and licensor only. Licensee shall not be the agent of Licensor and shall have no authority to act for or on behalf of Licensor in any matter. Persons retained by Licensee as employees or agents shall not by reason thereof be deemed to be employees or agents of Licensor.

12. *Compliance.* Licensee agrees that it will comply in all material respects with all material laws and regulations relating to its manufacture, marketing, selling or distributing of Home Products and its use of Product Technology and the Licensed Marks. Licensor agrees that he will comply in all respects with all federal, state and local laws and regulations relating to the manufacture and distribution of Products and his use of Product Technology and the Licensed Marks. Licensor will not at any time take any action which would cause Licensee or Licensor to be in violation of any such applicable laws and regulations. Licensor represents and warrants that the Products comply and shall continue to comply with the requirements necessary for acceptance and listing by Underwriters Laboratories Inc. and the Canadian Standards Association.

13. *Definitions.* The following terms, whenever used in this Agreement, shall have the respective meanings set forth below.

(a) *Accessories* means accessory products related to the Home Products including, without limitation, bags, canisters, trays, valves and containers.

(b) *Products* means food vacuum sealers and related accessories currently manufactured, marketed and sold by Licensor which are marketed primarily to gourmet food preparers.

(c) *Home Products* means food vacuum sealers or any product to which any application of Product Technology may be made by Licensee, which sealers or products may each be sold for _____ Dollars or less at retail, and the Accessories.

(d) *Licensed Patents* means U.S. Patent Nos. _____ and _____, and patent applications related to the Products, if any, owned by Licensor.

(e) *Licensed Marks* means the [unregistered] trademark and such related mark or other marks used by Licensor in marketing the Products, [a portion/all] of which are shown on Exhibit A, attached hereto and incorporated herein by reference.

(f) *Product Technology* means, subject to Section 8(a) hereof, the Licensed Patents and certain valuable technical information, know-how and data of Licensor relating to the Products.

14. *General and Miscellaneous.*

(a) *Governing Law.* This Agreement and all amendments, modifications, alterations, or supplements hereto, and the rights of the parties hereunder, shall be construed under and governed by the laws of the State of New York and the United States of America.

(b) *Interpretation.* The parties are equally responsible for the preparation of this Agreement and in any judicial proceeding the terms hereof shall not be more strictly construed against one party than the other.

(c) *Place of Execution.* This Agreement and any subsequent modifications or amendments hereto shall be deemed to have been executed in the State of New York.

(d) *Notices.* Any notice herein required or permitted to be given, or waiver of any provision hereof, shall be effective only if given or made in writing. Notices shall be deemed to have been given on the date of delivery if delivered by hand, or upon the expiration of five (5) days after deposit in the United States mail, registered or certified, postage prepaid, and addressed to the respective parties at the addresses specified in the preamble of this Agreement. Any party hereto may change the address to which notices to such party are to be sent by giving notice to the other party at the address and in the manner provided above. Any notice herein required or permitted to be given may be given, in addition to the manner set forth above, by telecopier, telex, TWX or cable, provided that the party giving such notice obtains acknowledgment by telecopier, telex, TWX or cable that such notice has been received by the party to be notified. Notice made in this manner shall be deemed to have been given when such acknowledgment has been transmitted.

(e) *Assignments.* Licensor shall not grant, transfer, convey, sublicense, or otherwise assign any of his rights or delegate any of his obligations under this Agreement without the prior written consent of Licensor. Licensee shall have the right to freely grant, transfer, convey, sublicense, or otherwise assign any of its rights or delegate any of its obligations under this Agreement.

(f) *Entire Agreement.* This Agreement constitutes the entire agreement between Licensor and Licensee with respect to the subject matter hereof and shall not be modified, amended or terminated except as herein provided or except by another agreement in writing executed by the parties hereto.

(g) *Headings.* The Section headings are for convenience only and are not a part of this Agreement.

(h) *Severability.* All rights and restrictions contained herein may be exercised and shall be applicable and binding only to the extent that they do not violate any applicable laws and are intended to be limited to the extent necessary so that they will not render this Agreement illegal, invalid or unenforceable. If any provision or portion of any provision of this Agreement not essential to the commercial purpose of this Agreement shall be held to be illegal, invalid or unenforceable by a court of competent jurisdiction, it is the intention of the parties that the remaining provisions or portions thereof shall constitute their agreement with respect to the subject matter hereof, and all such remaining provisions or portions thereof shall remain in full force and effect.

(continues)

Figure 19-2. (Continued).

(i) *Survival of Representations and Warranties.* The parties hereto agree that all representations and warranties of Licensor contained herein shall survive the expiration or termination of this Agreement, and shall continue to be binding on the parties without limitation.

(j) *Attorneys' Fees, etc.* In the event either party brings any action, suit or proceeding against the other party to enforce any right or entitlement which it may have under this Agreement, either party shall, to the extent it is successful in pursuing or defending the action, and in addition to all other rights or remedies available to it in law or in equity, be entitled to recover its reasonable attorneys' fees and court costs incurred in such action.

IN WITNESS WHEREOF, the parties hereto have executed this License and Distribution Agreement as of the day and year set forth above.

Witness: "Licensor"

_____   _____

                                                    "Licensee"

                                            _____

Exhibit A

Licensed Marks

[This is a list of the brands covered by the scope of the license agreement.]

❐ *Quality Control.* The brand owner must take a proactive role in maintaining and enforcing quality control standards in the manufacturing and distribution of the branded products or services. This requirement includes not only direct quality issues but also indirect issues, such as the distribution channels selected, the nature of the advertising and marketing campaigns, etc.

An effectively managed brand-extension licensing program can build brand awareness and brand equity if the company understands why consumers have an affinity for the brand if the trust is not violated or misinterpreted. To the extent that brands can influence consumer behavior and gain consumer behavior, they can be a very powerful marketing tool and an intangible income-producing asset.

CHAPTER 20

Joint Ventures and Strategic Alliances

nother key intellectual property leveraging strategy is the establishing of partnering relationships whereby two or more companies work together to achieve a specific purpose or work toward the attainment of common business objectives. Joint ventures, strategic partnering, cross-licensing, co-branding, and technology transfer agreements are all strategies designed to obtain one or more of the following: (1) direct capital infusion in exchange for equity and/or intellectual property or distribution rights; (2) a so-called capital substitute by which the resources that would otherwise be obtained with capital are obtained through joint venturing; or (3) a shift of the burden and cost of development (through licensing) in exchange for a potentially more limited upside.

These various types of partnering arrangements have been used for a wide variety of business purposes and to meet intellectual capital leveraging objectives, including joint research and copromotion; distribution and commercialization (particularly between defense and government contractors looking for new applications and markets for products initially developed for the military and governmental sectors); and cross-licensing and sublicensing of new technologies. The participants in these agreements could be at various points in the value chain or distribution channel. They can be agreements among direct or potential competitors (e.g., to cooperate rather than compete as a precursor to a merger and/or to join forces to fend off an even larger competitor). Or they can be agreements among parallel producers (e.g., to widen or integrate product lines) or among parties linked at different points in the vertical distribution channel (e.g., to achieve distribution efficiencies).

One of the key factors to analyze when structuring these relationships is the respective *position* of each party that will influence the structure, economies, and key objectives. The basic positions can be illustrated in matrix format, as follows:

Goliath/Goliath	David/David
David/Goliath	Value webs/federations

In *Goliath/Goliath* partnering transactions, two very large companies get together to comarket or cross-promote each other's brands, either to capture more customers or to achieve certain efficiencies. An easy-to-understand example is that of two major airlines serving different primary geographic routes but honoring each other's frequent flyer programs or McDonald's promoting a new Disney film by offering licensed toys when a consumer buys a kid's meal.

In *David/David* partnering relationships, two smaller companies, both with limited resources, join forces to leverage off each other's strengths on a peer-to-peer basis in order to achieve a defined business purpose or set of objectives. An example is that of two small government contractors with complementary skills entering into a teaming agreement in order to jointly bid on a new request for proposal (RFP) that neither could qualify for on a stand-alone basis. In these relationships, many of the principles discussed in this chapter should be carefully reviewed to make sure each gets the intended benefit of the agreement. The key to peer-to-peer partnering relationships is to avoid greed. To work well, *both* party's objectives must be met, and the sharing of the rewards must be parallel with the level of effort and the sharing of risks.

In *David/Goliath* partnering relationships, a smaller company is partnering with a much larger strategic ally, which may be a large domestic corporation, a foreign conglomerate, or even a university or government agency looking to commercialize a technology. In these transactions, David and its counsel must work hard to negotiate and protect the benefits and objectives of the relationship, because it will be subject to the red tape, bureaucracy, and potential shifts in strategic focus that are typical of many Goliaths.

In *value webs/federations*, there are multiple participants to the joint venture, strategic alliance, cooperative, or consortium, each maintaining its operational and ownership autonomy but coming together to share resources, distribution channels, or costs in some way to increase revenues or reduce expenses. The alignment of shared interests may be very broad or may be more limited, such as cooperative advertising or a shared Web site or toll-free phone number to generate new business. In emerging technology industries, value webs may be created by five or six companies that are bringing technical components or solutions to the table to meet a customer's (or series of customers) real or perceived needs.

With technology developing rapidly, competition becoming more intense, business operations becoming more global in nature, and industry convergence taking place on a number of different fronts, the number and the pace of deal making in the joint venture and strategic alliances areas are very likely to quicken and increase over the next few years. A key component in any fast growing company's business strategy is the need to combine and share core competencies and resource capabilities in a manner and within a structure where autonomy can be preserved.

Understanding the Differences between Joint Ventures and Strategic Alliances

Joint ventures are typically structured as a partnership or as a newly formed and co-owned corporation (or limited liability company) in which two or more parties are brought together to achieve a series of strategic and financial objectives on a short-term or a long-term basis. Companies considering a joint venture as a growth strategy should give careful thought to the type of partner they are looking for and what resources each party will be contributing to the newly formed entity. Like the raising of a child, each parent will be making their respective contribution of skills, abilities, and resources.

Strategic alliances can be any number of collaborative working relationships in which no formal joint venture entity is formed but rather two independent companies become interdependent by entering into a formal or informal agreement built on a platform of:

❒ Mutual objectives
❒ Mutual strategy
❒ Mutual risk
❒ Mutual reward

The relationships are commonly referred to as: (1) teaming, (2) strategic partnering, (3) alliances, (4) cross-licensing, and (5) co-branding.

Box 20-1. Key terms differences between joint ventures and strategic alliances.

	Joint Ventures	*Strategic Alliances*
Term	Usually medium to long term	Short term
Strategic objective	Often serves as precursor to a merger	More flexible and noncommittal
Legal agreements and structure	Actual legal entity formed	Contractual driven
Extent of commitment	Shared equity	Shared objectives
Capital resources	Each party making a capital contribution of cash or intangible assets	No specific capital contributions (may be shared budgeting on even cross-investment)
Tax ramifications	Possible double taxation unless pass-through entities are utilized	No direct tax ramifications

Regardless of the specific structure, the underlying industry, or even the actual purpose of the strategic relationship, all successful joint venture and strategic alliance relationships share a common set of essential success factors:

❏ A complementary, unified force or purpose that bonds the two or more companies together

❏ A management team committed at levels to the success of the venture, free from politics or personal agendas

❏ A genuine strategy synergy where the sum of the whole truly exceeds its individual parts (e.g., $2 + 2 + 2 = 7$)

❏ A cooperative culture and spirit among the strategic partners that lend themselves to trust, resource sharing, and a friendly chemistry among the parties

❏ A degree of flexibility in the objectives of the joint venture to allow for changes in the marketplace and an evolution of technology

❏ An actual alignment of management styles and operational methods, at least to the extent that it affects the underlying project (as in the case of a strategic alliance) or the management of the new company created (as in the case of a formal joint venture)

❏ The general levels of focus and leadership from all key parties that are necessary to the success of any new venture or business enterprise

The strategic benefits of these relationships are to:

❏ Develop a new market (domestic/international).
❏ Develop a new product (research and development).
❏ Develop/share technology.
❏ Combine complementary technology.
❏ Pool resources to develop a production or distribution facility.
❏ Acquire capital.
❏ Execute a government contract.
❏ Gain access to a new distribution channel or network or sales/marketing capability.

Due Diligence before Selecting Joint Venture or Strategic Alliance Partners

Conduct a thorough review of prospective candidates and extensive due diligence on the final candidates. Develop a list of key objectives and goals to be achieved by the joint venture or licensing relationship, and compare this list with those of your final candidates. Take the time to understand the strategic fit (or potential tension) with the corporate culture and decision-making process in each company. Consider some of the following issues: (1) How does this fit with your own processes? (2) What about each prospective partner's previous experiences and track record with other joint venture relationships? (3) Why did these previous relationships succeed or fail?

In many cases, smaller companies looking for joint venture partners wind up selecting a much larger Goliath, which offers a wide range of financial and nonfinancial resources that will allow the smaller company to achieve its growth plans. The motivating factor under these circumstances for the larger company is to get access and distribution rights to new technologies, products, and services. In turn, the larger company offers access to pools of capital, research and development, personnel, distribution channels, and general contacts that the small company desperately needs.

But proceed carefully. Be sensitive to the politics, red tape, and different management practices that may be in place at a larger company and that will be foreign to many smaller firms. Try to distinguish between what is promised and what will actually be delivered. If the primary motivating force for the small firm is really only capital, then consider whether alternative (and perhaps less costly) sources of money have been thoroughly explored. Ideally, the large joint venture partner will offer a lot more than just money. If the primary motivating force is access to technical personnel, then consider whether purchasing these resources separately might be a better strategy than entering into a partnership in which you give up a certain measure of control. Also, consider whether strategic relationships or extended payments terms with vendors and consultants can be arranged in lieu of the joint venture.

Drafting a Memorandum of Understanding Prior to Structuring the Agreement

Prior to drafting the definitive joint venture or alliance agreements, hammering out a memorandum of understanding to reflect a business handshake on all critical points of the relationship is beneficial. The lawyers can use this document as a starting point in the preparation of the formal agreements. The memorandum of understanding should address the following topics:

❑ *Spirit and Purpose of the Agreement.* Outline why the partnering arrangement is being considered and its perceived mission and objectives. Describe operating principles that will foster communication and trust. What are the strategic and financial desires of the participants?

❑ *Scope of Activity.* Address what products, services, buildings, or other specific projects will be included and excluded from the venture. Identify target markets (i.e., regions, user groups, etc.) for the venture and any markets excluded from the venture that will remain the domain of the partners. If the venture has purchase and supply provisions, state that the newly formed entity or arrangement will purchase or supply specific products, services, or resources from or to the owners.

❑ *Key Objectives and Responsibilities.* Clarify and specify objectives and targets to be achieved by the relationship, when to expect achieving these objectives, any major obstacles anticipated, and the point at which the alliance will be self-supporting, brought out, or terminated. Participants should designate a project manager who will be responsible for

Box 20-2. The strategic alliance acid test.

- *Start with the end in mind.* These relationships are not necessarily intended to last forever. Have an exit plan in mind.

- *Don't be left out of the game.* If everyone in your industry is teaming up with others, don't be the only player to fly solo.

- *Align alliance goals with your overall corporate goals.* Do not allow for big strategic gaps or inconsistencies between the clearly stated goals of the alliance and your own strategic objectives.

- *Don't be afraid to fail.* Not all relationships in life or in business will be successful. and alliances may not work out as intended. You cannot win or lose if you don't run the race. Put mechanisms in place to manage risk if things do not work out. Hope for the best, but assume the worst in advance of consummating the transaction.

- *Put governance and decision making at the top of the priority list.* Be crystal clear with alliance partners as to *how* decisions will be made and *how* disputes will be handled. Discussing it later is a recipe for disaster.

their company's day-to-day involvement in the alliance. If a separate detached organization will be created, the key persons assigned to the venture should be designated, if doing so is practical. Responsibilities should be outlined to make it clear to other partners who will be doing what.

❏ *Method for Decision Making.* Each partnering relationship will have its own unique decision-making process. Describe who is expected to have the authority to make which types of decisions in what circumstances, who reports to whom, etc. If one company will have operating control, it should be designated at this point.

❏ *Resource Commitments.* Most partnering relationships involve the commitment of specific financial resources, such as cash, equity, staged payments, loan guarantees, etc., to achieve the ultimate goals. Other soft resources may be in the form of licenses, knowledge, research and development, a sales force, contracts, production, facilities, inventory, raw materials, engineering drawings, management staff, access to capital, the devotion of specific personnel for a certain percentage of their time, and the like. If possible, these soft resources should be assigned a financial figure so that a monetary value can be affixed and valued along with the cash commitments to the internal commitment. In some circumstances, the purchase of buildings, materials, consultants, advertising, and other services will require capital. These external costs should be itemized and allocated between the partners in whatever formula is agreed. If any borrowing, entry into equity markets (public offerings, private placements, etc.), or purchase of stock in one of the partners is anticipated, this should be noted. In anticipation of additional equity infusions, the partners should agree on their own ability to fund the overruns or enable the venture to seek other outside sources. The manner of handling cost overruns should be addressed. Pricing and costing procedures should be mentioned, if applicable.

❏ *Assumption of Risks and Division of Rewards.* What are the perceived risks? How will they be handled and who will be responsible for problem solving and risk assumption? What are the expected rewards (new product, new market, cash flow, technology, etc.)? How will the profits be divided?

❏ *Rights and Exclusions.* Who has rights to products and inventions? Who has rights to distribute the products, services, technologies, and so on? Who gets the licensing rights? If the confidentiality and noncompetition agreements have not yet been drafted in final form at this point, they should be addressed in basic form; if the other agreements have been signed, simply make reference to them.

❏ *Anticipated Structure.* This section should describe the intended structure (written contract, corporation, partnership, or equity investment). Regardless of the legal form, the terms, percentages, and formulas for exchange of stock should be spelled out, if possible at this stage. Default provisions and procedures should be addressed, at least at the preliminary level.

Structuring the Joint Venture or Strategic Alliance

Unlike franchising, distributorships, and licensing, which are almost always vertical in nature, joint ventures, alliances, and even consortiums are structured as *either* horizontal *or* vertical levels of distribution. At the horizontal level, the joint venture is often the first step or precursor to an actual merger, in which two or more companies operating at the same level in the distribution channel join together (either in a partnership or by joint ownership of a specially created corporation) to achieve certain synergies or operating efficiencies. Fast-growth companies should answer the following key strategic questions before and during joint venture or strategic alliance negotiations:

❏ Exactly what types of tangible and intangible assets will each party contribute to the joint venture? Who will have ownership rights in the property contributed during the term of the joint venture and thereafter? Who will own property developed as a result of joint development efforts?

❏ What covenants of nondisclosure or noncompetition will be expected of each joint venturer during the term of the agreement and thereafter?

❏ What timetables or performance quotas for completion of the projects contemplated by the joint venture will be included in the agreement?

**Box 20-3. Tips for structuring strategic relationships and
avoiding the classic pitfalls and mistakes.**

- *Negotiating Ostrich Deals.* Senior-level executives cannot have their
heads in the sand when defining key objectives. You must include
in the goal-making process middle-level management and technical
personnel who will ultimately be responsible for the success or failure of the relationship.

- *Planning Is Critical.* Disregard the impact on other potential alliance
partners or the foreclosure of other opportunities. Think through
how a deal with this particular alliance partner will impact your ability to do other deals.

- *Impact Analysis.* Watch the details and avoid taking shortcuts toward
alliance objectives. The planning process before signing the definitive documents is critical; when it gets skipped, the relationship is
much more likely to fail.

- *Perceptions Can Be Reality.* Understand the impact of the deal on customers and vendors. How will customers and vendors perceive and
interact with this alliance or joint venture? Will they be forced to shift
relationships? Will they be willing to do so? What is in it for them?

- *Trust and Respect Must Be Mutual.* Mutual trust, respect, and balanced sharing of risks and rewards must be key themes of the relationship, particularly in David/Goliath scenarios where the parties
cannot rely on peer-to-peer dynamics to create balance. Being sensitive to the needs and attitudes of your partner is the key to all types
of relationships.

- *Impatience Is the Kiss of Death.* Do not be overly aggressive in setting
up the timetable for meeting objectives. Doing so only puts unrealistic pressures on the parties to perform, and that leads only to frustration and disappointment.

- *Clear Articulation of Responsibilities.* The responsibilities and contributions of each party should be clearly addressed, with systems
and procedures to create accountability and consequences for failure
to meet responsibilities.

- *Dealing with Disputes.* The agreement must include provisions for
resolving conflicts as and when they occur. Ignoring the problem or
letting conflicts fester will not solve anything, nor will dragging the
relationship beyond the term of its useful or practical life achieve
anything. If the relationship is no longer working, bring it to a prompt
end. The agreement should also include enough flexibility to allow
the relationship to evolve and adapt to new challenges and shifts in
market conditions.

- *Clarity of Focus Is Very Important.* An ambiguous charter, scope, or purpose results in uncoordinated activities and confusion among the employees who are on the front line trying to make the venture succeed.

- *Leadership, Leadership, Leadership.* Management, leadership, good chemistry, and an ability to communicate on tough issues are all hallmarks of an effective partnering arrangement. The senior executives of both companies must be committed to making the relationship work and take visible steps in that direction. The management and operational styles and methods must be compatible or adjusted to be so, at least with respect to this venture.

- *Form Must Follow Function.* The fit between the legal structure selected and the operational objectives of the partnering arrangement should be clear. Being overly rigid would be a poor choice for a preliminary dip-our-toes-in-the-water type of partnering relationship and vice versa.

- *Do Them Often, Do Them Right.* The more experience that a fast-track growing company can gather by seeking out partnering relationships, the greater the chances are of success. These alliances and partnering relationships need to be a core port of the business growth strategy, not just ad hoc or random events.

- *NIH Syndrome.* Make sure each alliance partner avoids a not-invented-here mentality. If each alliance partner assumes that their ideas and work product are superior than those of their partners, then it is blocking itself from an ability to learn and truly profit from the working relationship.

What are the rights and remedies of each party if these performance standards are not met?

❐ How will issues of management and control be addressed in the agreement? What will be the respective voting rights of each party? What are the procedures in the event of a major disagreement or deadlock? What is the fallback plan?

Once the joint venturer has discussed all the preliminary issues, a formal joint venture agreement or corporate shareholders' agreement should be prepared with the assistance of counsel. The precise terms of the agreement between the parties depend on the nature and the structure of the arrangement.

At a minimum, however, the following topics should be addressed in as much detail as possible:

❐ *Nature, Purpose, and Trade Name for the Joint Venture.* The parties should set forth the legal nature of the relationship between themselves along with a clear statement of purpose to prevent future disputes as to the scope of the arrangement. If a new trade name is established for the venture, provisions should be made as to the use of the name and any other trade or service marks registered by the venture upon termination of the entity or project.

❏ *Status of the Respective Joint Venturers.* The agreement should clearly indicate whether each party is a partner, shareholder, agent, independent contractor, or any combination of these. Agent status, whether actual or imputed, can greatly affect liability between the venturers and with regard to third parties.

❏ *Representations and Warranties of Each Joint Venturer.* Standard representations and warranties will include ability and authority to enter into the joint venture arrangement, ownership of key IP assets to be used by the joint venture, and related issues.

❏ *Capital and Property Contributions of Each Joint Venturer.* A clear schedule should be established of all contributions, whether in the form of cash, shares, real estate, or intellectual property. Detailed descriptions will be particularly important if the distribution of profits and losses is to be based on overall contribution. The specifics of allocation and distribution of profits and losses among the venturers should also be clearly defined.

❏ *Scope of the Joint Venture Commitment.* The agreement should carefully define the scope and degree of exclusivity of the commitment to one another. Any restrictions on one or more of the joint venturers' ability to enter into other transactions that could be viewed as directly or indirectly competitive to the core business of the joint venture should be clearly defined. Any noncompete covenants, confidentiality provisions, noncircumvention privileges, rights of first refusal, and related issues should all be included in this section, including a mechanism for dealing with potential conflicts of interest and usurpation of corporate opportunity issues.

❏ *Management, Governance, Control, and Voting Rights of Each Joint Venturer.* If the proposed venture envisions joint management, it will be necessary to specifically address the appointment and control of officers and directors, as well as the keeping of books, records, and bank accounts; the nature and frequency of inspections and audits; insurance and cross-indemnification obligations; annual budgeting and business planning processes; pension and employee benefits matters; and responsibility for administrative and overhead expenses.

❏ *Rights in Joint Venture Property.* Joint venture partners should be especially mindful of intellectual property rights and should clearly address the issues of ownership use and licensing entitlements, not only for the venturers' presently existing property rights, but also for future use of rights (or products or services) developed in the name of the venture itself.

❏ *Restrictions on Transferability of Ownership Interest in the Joint Venture.* Stringent conditions should be placed on the ability of the venturers to transfer or grant liens or encumbrances on their ownership interests in the joint venture entity to third parties. This section should probably vest a right of first refusal to purchase the equity interests either in the entity or the other joint venture partners.

❏ *Default, Dissolution, and Termination of the Joint Venture.* This section could include the events that constitute a default, the opportunity to cure, the obligations of the venturers, and the distribution of assets should be clearly defined, along with procedures in the event of bankruptcy and/or insolvency of either the joint venture entity on one of its partners.

❏ *Dispute Resolution Procedures.* The parties may wish to consider arbitration or mediation as an alternative dispute resolution mechanism. The mechanics, venue, and prescribed processes to be followed in the event of a dispute should also be included.

❏ *Miscellaneous.* Provisions should also be made indicating (1) the governing law, (2) remedies under force majeure situations, (3) procedures for notice and consent, and (4) the ability to modify or waive certain provisions.

In addition to the core joint venture documents, a wide variety of ancillary agreements may be necessary to reflect all of the terms of the business arrangements between the two parties. It may also be necessary to obtain third-party consents from lenders, landlords, venture investors, and others who may have the authority to block the proposed arrangement or where the proposed transaction would be deemed to have triggered a change-in-control clause in a set of loan or investment documents.

The ancillary documents will vary based on the objectives, complexity, and nature of the transaction and may include:

❏ *Asset purchase agreements* to the extent that the newly formed joint venture entity may be purchasing assets from one or more of the partners beyond the capital contributions.

❏ *Equipment and real property lessees/sublessees* to the extent that the newly formed entity may be leasing or subleasing office space or equipment from one or more of its owners.

❏ *License agreements* to the extent that technology and/or brands will be licensed by the joint venture partners (and not assigned) to the newly formed entity.

❏ *Technical assistance and services agreements* to the extent that one or more of the joint venture partners will be providing support or assistance to the newly formed entity, either on a monthly-fee or pay-as-you-go hourly basis.

❏ *Management and support agreements* in that one of the joint venture partners might provide certain management or administrative support services to the newly formed entity, both increasing the productivity of underutilized capacity and keeping the overhead and fixed expenses of the new entity to a minimum, especially in the early days of its operations.

❏ *Distribution and marketing agreements* in that one or more of the joint venture partners might have certain distribution and marketing rights or obligations relating to the new products or services that the entity will produce or offer.

❏ *Employment agreements*

❏ *Supply agreements*

Co-branding as a Type of Strategic Alliance

Co-branding is a type of partnership relationship whereby two established brand names combine to bring added value, economies of scale, and customer recognition to each product. Businesses of all sizes, including many fast-track growth companies, are realizing the significant cost and importance of establishing brand awareness and the economies of scale that can be achieved when these expenses are shared. Campaigns and strategies to build brand recognition, brand loyalty, and brand equity have been launched by thousands of companies that recognize that a well-established brand can be the single most valuable asset on the balance sheet. This new focus on *brand equity* has set the stage for a wide variety of co-branding and brand-extension licensing transactions. Companies with strong quality-oriented brands (as well as professional sports teams, athletes, and celebrities) have sought to create new sources of revenues and to leverage their largest intangible asset—their reputation—to add to the strength of their income statements. To build brand awareness, companies are spending more money on media advertising and promotional campaigns and less on store displays and coupons.

Co-branding has emerged recently as a very popular type of strategic alliance. At the heart of the relationship, two or more established brands are paired and positioned in the marketplace to bring added value, economies of scale, and synergistic customer recognition and loyalty to increase sales and create a point of differentiation. Co-branding has appeared in many different forms, including:

❏ *Financial Services Co-branding.* In the early 1990s, credit card companies pioneered co-branding with airlines or telecommunications companies for mutual branding and shared rewards.

❏ *Consumer-Product Ingredient Co-branding.* The strength of one brand appears as an ingredient to another as an enhancement for sales and cross-consumer loyalty (e.g., Post Raisin Bran using Sun-Maid raisins in its cereal, Archways' use of Kellogg's All-Bran in its cookies, Ben & Jerry's ice cream in Heath Bar® Crunch, PopTarts with Smuckers® fruit fillings, etc.).

❏ *Implied Endorsement Co-branding.* The co-branded name or logo is used to build consumer recognition even if there is no actual ingredient used in the product (e.g., John Deere on the back of a Florsheim boot, the Doritos® Pizza Craver tortilla chips logo featured on Pizza Hut's packaging, or its Taco Supreme chips featuring Taco Bell's logo on the packaging).

❏ *Actual Composite Co-branding.* The co-branded product actually uses a branded pairing of popular manufacturing techniques or processes (e.g., Timberland boots with Gore-Tex fabric, furniture with Scotchguard® protectants, Dell or Gateway computers with Intel® inside, etc.).

❏ *Designer-Driver Co-branded Products.* Certain manufacturers have co-branded with well-known designers to increase consumer loyalty and brand awareness. For example, the Eddie Bauer edition of the Ford Explorer has been a very strong seller and product differentiator.

❏ *Retail Business Format Co-branding.* This type of co-branding is growing rapidly in the retailing, hospitality, and franchising communities. Retail co-branding is being used to attract additional customers; to create complementary product lines to offset different consumer tastes (such as Baskin Robbins and Dunkin' Donuts) or consuming patterns (e.g., combining a traditional breakfast-only consumer traffic pattern

---

Box 20-4. Advantages and disadvantages of using co-branding as a growth strategy.

Strategic Advantages of Co-branding

- Sharing costs

- Sharing marketing and packaging costs

- Sharing rent, utilities, and other overhead if in same location

- Expansion into international markets

- Facilitating brand recognition for your brand if it is tied to a well-known domestic brand in a foreign market (Many foreign markets enjoy U.S. products; so the co-branding works to their advantage.)

- Creating conveniences for customers, which can increase business for both companies (The additional traffic creates impulse buys.)

Potential Risks of Co-branding

- Difficulty building consensus between co-branding partners

- Difficulty agreeing on marketing by both parties—loss of time-to-market and loss of flexibility

- Effect of bad publicity for one company on the other

- Effect on brand if other brand fails to live up to its promises

- Effect on both brands if co-branding flops (Consumers may become confused about new products, diminishing the value of both.)

with a lunch-only traffic pattern); or to sell additional products or services to "captured customers."

Companies considering co-branding initially focus on the viability of the strategic fit between the brands. For example, a hypothetical Godiva/Slim Fast line of chocolate snack bars would benefit Slim Fast brand by its association with superior chocolates produced by Godiva. However, this co-branding would detract from Godiva's upscale brand image. In this scenario, the fit between the brands is unlikely. Also, consumer perceptions of each product and its attributes have to be understood in order to better determine whether the two brands have a common set of attributes. It may be helpful first to rate the favorableness of each brand separately, then to rate them as co-branded products, and then to explore the relative contribution of each brand to the effectiveness of the co-brand product.

The ability to penetrate new markets, generate new income streams, build the value of the company's brand name, and increase overall brand awareness has made co-branding a very viable and profitable strategy for companies. However, the temptation to extend the equity and value of your brand into other areas poses certain risks. There are quality control issues, the risk of overbranding or misbranding from a consumer perspective, and product liability issues. The key to successful co-branding is that the brand itself must stand for something greater than the original product and that the consumers' perception of the extended brand is a natural one.

Resource Directory

List of State Administrators and Agents for Service of Process

State	Address / Contact Person
California	Department of Corporations 320 West 4th Street, Suite 750 Los Angeles, CA 90013-2344 Toll-free: 866 ASK CORP www.corp.ca.gov Agent for service of process: 1515 K Street, Suite 200 Sacramento, CA 95814-4052 866 ASK CORP
Connecticut	Securities and Business Investment Division Connecticut Department of Banking 260 Constitution Plaza Hartford, CT 06103 Att: Ralph A. Lambiase, Division Director (860) 240-8230 www.state.ct.us/dob Agent for service of process: Connecticut Banking Commissioner Same as above
Florida	Department of Agriculture & Consumer Services Division of Consumer Services 407 South Calhoun Street Mayo Building, Room 121 Tallahassee, FL 32399-0800 (850) 410-3754 http://doacs.state.fl.us Agent for service of process: Same as above

Georgia	Legal and Consumer Affairs Division Department of Banking and Finance 2990 Brandywine Road, Suite 200 Atlanta, GA 30341 1-888-986-1633 www.dbf.georgia.gov Agent for service of process: Same as above
Hawaii	State of Hawaii Department of Commerce and Consumer Affairs Business Registration Division King Kalakaua Building 335 Merchant Street, Room 201 Honolulu, HI 96813 (808) 586-2744 www.hawaii.gov/dcca Agent for service of process: Director Department of Commerce and Consumer Affairs Same as above
Illinois	Franchise Division Office of the Attorney General 500 South Second Street Springfield, IL 62706 (217) 782-4465 www.ag.state.il.us Agent for service of process: Illinois Attorney General Same as above
Indiana	Securities Commissioner Secretary of State Indiana Securities Division 302 West Washington Street, Room E-111 Indianapolis, IN 46204 (317) 232-6681 www.in.gov/sos Agent for service of process: Business Services—Service of Process Attention: Service of Process Clerk 302 West Washington Street Room E-018 Indianapolis, IN 46204. (317) 232-6536
Iowa	Iowa Securities Bureau 330 Maple Street

Des Moines, IA 50319
(515) 281-5705
www.iid.state.ia.us

Agent for service of process: Same as above

Kentucky
Attorney General's Office
Consumer Protection Division
Capitol Suite 118
700 Capitol Avenue
Frankfort, KY 40601
(502) 696-5389
www.ag.ky.gov

Agent for service of process: Same as above

Louisiana
Louisiana Secretary of State
Commercial Division
P.O. Box 94125
Baton Rouge, LA 70804
(225) 925-4704
www.sos.louisiana.gov

Agent for service of process: Louisiana Secretary of State
Commercial Division
8585 Archives Avenue
Baton Rouge, LA 70804

Maine
Department of Professional & Financial Regulation
Corporation Division
35 State House Station
August, ME 04333
(207) 624-8500
www.maine.gov/pfr

Agent for service of process: Same as above

Maryland
Office of the Attorney General Securities Division
200 Street Paul Place, 25th Floor
Baltimore, MD 21202
Att: Dale Cantone, Deputy Securities Commissioner
(410) 576-7042
www.oag.state.md.us

Agent for service of process: Maryland Securities
Commissioner
200 Street Paul Place, 20th Floor
Baltimore, MD 21202-2020

Michigan
Michigan Department of Attorney General
Consumer Protection Division

Franchise Unit
P.O. Box 30213
Lansing, MI 48933
(517) 373-7117
www.michigan.gov/ag

Agent for service of process: Michigan Department of
Attorney General
Consumer Protection Division
G Mennen Williams Building, 7th Floor
525 W. Ottawa Street
Lansing, MI 48909

Minnesota   Minnesota Department of Commerce
Securities Registration
85 7th Place East, Suite 500
St. Paul, MN 55101
Attn: Dan Sexton
(651) 296-4520
http://www.commerce.state.mn.us

Agent for service of process: Minnesota Commissioner of
Commerce
Same as above

Nebraska   Department of Banking and Finance
1230 O Street, Suite 400
(P.O. Box 95006)
Lincoln, NE 68509-5006
Attn: Sheila Cahill, Legal Counsel, Bureau of Securities
(402) 471-3445
www.ndbf.ne.gov

Agent for service of process: Same as above

New Hampshire   Attorney General
Consumer Protection and Antitrust Bureau
33 Capitol Street
Concord, NH 03301-6397
Attn: Terry Robertson
(603) 271-3641
http://www.state.nh.us/nhdoj

Agent for service of process: Same as Above

New York   New York State Department of Law
120 Broadway, 23rd Floor
New York, NY 10271
Attn: Barbara Lasoff
(212) 416-8222

http://www.ag.ny.gov/bureaus/investor_protection/
franchise/fran chise.html

Agent for service of process: Department of State
One Commerce Plaza
99 Washington Avenue
Albany, New York 12231

North Carolina	The Securities Division Department of the Secretary of State 2 South Salisbury Street Raleigh, NC 27601 Attn: Mary Kelly (919) 733-3924 www.secretary.state.nc.us/sec Agent for service of process: Secretary of State Same as above
North Dakota	North Dakota Securities Dept. State Capitol, Fifth Floor 600 East Boulevard Avenue Bismarck, ND 58505-0510 Attn: Diane Lillis, Franchise Examiner (701) 328-4712 www.ndsecurities.com Agent for service of process: North Dakota Securities Commissioner Same as above
Ohio	Secretary of State 1-877-767-3453 (call for specific address) www.sos.state.oh.us Agent for service of process: Same as above
Oklahoma	Oklahoma Department of Securities Suite 860, First National Center 120 N. Robinson Oklahoma City, OK 73102 (405) 280-7700 www.securities.ok.gov Agent for service of process: Same as above
Oregon	Department of Finance and Corporate Securities Division of Finance and Corporate Securities P.O. Box 14480

Salem, OR 97309
Attn: Caroline Smith
(503) 378-4387
egov.oregon.gov/DCBS/

Agent for service of process: Director
Department of Finance and Corporate Securities
350 Winter Street NE, Room 410
Salem, OR 97301

Rhode Island   Secretary of State
                    Business Services
                    148 West River Street
                    Providence, RI 02904
                    (401) 222-3040
                    sos.ri.gov/

                    Agent for service of process: Director of the Dept. of
                    Business Regulation
                    Same as above

South Carolina   Secretary of State
                    P.O. Box 11350
                    Columbia, SC 29211
                    (803) 734-2158

                    Agent for service of process: Secretary of State
                    1205 Pendleton Street
                    Suite 525
                    Columbia, SC 29201

South Dakota   Securities Division
                    445 East Capitol Avenue
                    Pierre, SD 57501
                    Attn: Melita Hauge
                    Leonore Frieze
                    (605) 773-4823
                    http://www.state.sd.us/drr2/reg/securities/

                    Agent for service of process: South Dakota Division of
                    Securities
                    Same as above

Texas   Secretary of State
                    Corporations Section
                    P.O. Box 13697
                    Austin, TX 78711
                    (512) 463-5582
                    www.sos.state.tx.us/corp/

Agent for service of process: Office of the Attorney General
Consumer Protection Division
300 W. 15th Street
Austin, TX 78701
(512) 463-2100
www.oag.state.tx.us

Utah

Utah Division of Corporations and Commercial Code
P.O. Box 146705
Salt Lake City, UT 84114-6705
(801) 530-4849
www.corporations.utah.gov

Agent for service of process: Utah Division of Corporations and Commercial Code
160 East 300 South, 2nd Floor
Salt Lake City, UT 84111

Virginia

State Corporation Commission
Division of Securities and Retail Franchising
P.O. Box 1197
1300 E. Main Street, 9th Floor
Richmond, VA 23219
Attn: Stephen W. Goolsby, Chief Examiner
(804) 371-9051
(804) 371-9911 (fax)
www.scc.virginia.gov

Agent for service of process: Clerk of the State Corporation Commission
State Corporation Commission
1300 E. Main Street
Richmond, VA 23219

Washington

Department of Financial Institutions
Securities Division
P.O. Box 41200
Olympia, WA 98507-1200
Attn: Cheryl Pearson
(360) 902-8762
(Courier delivery address: 150th Israel Road SW, Tumwater, WA 98501)
www.dfi.wa.gov

Agent for service of process: Same as above

Wisconsin

Department of Financial Institutions
Division of Securities

P.O. Box 1768
Madison, WI 53701-1768
345 W. Washington Avenue, 4th Floor
Madison, WI 53703
Attn: Patricia Struck, Franchise Administrator
(608) 266-1064
www.wdfi.org

Agent for service of process: Wisconsin Commissioner of
Securities
Same as above

International Franchise Organizations

Argentine Franchise Association
Mr. Lucas Secades, General Manager
Av. Libertador 222, 7°—A
Buenos Aires (1001ABP), Argentina
(54) 11-4394-3318
(54) 11-4326-5499 (fax)
www.aafranchising.com

Association de Franchising de Chile (AFICH)
Hernando de Aguirre 128, of. 704
Providencia, Santiago, Chile
Attn: Carlos Fabia, President-Elect
(56) 2-234-4189
(56) 2-232-7759 (fax)

Franchisors Association of Australia
Mr. Richard Evans, Chief Executive
P.O. Box 2195
Malvern East Vic 3145
(61) 03-9508-0888
(61) 03-9508-0899 (fax)
www.franchise.org.au

Austrian Franchise Association
Mag. Susanne Seifert
Campus 21,
Liebermannstrabe A01 503
A -2345 Brunn am Gebirge, Austria
(43) 2236-31 11 88
(43) 2236-31-13-43 (fax)
www.franchise.at

Belgische Franchise Federatie
Mr. Pierre Jeanmart, Chairman

Boulevard de L'Humanite, 116/2,
B-1070 Brussels, Belgium
(32) 2-523-9707
(32) 2-523-3510 (fax)
www.fbf-bff.be
info@fbf-bff.be

Brazil Franchise Association
Ricardo Figueiredo Bomeny, Director Presidente
Av. das Nações Unidas, 10989—11 andar,
Conj. 112 Vl. Olímpia
Sao Paulo Brasil, CEP 04578-000
(55) 11-3020-8800
www.portaldofranchising.com.br

British Franchise Association
A2 Danebrook Court
Oxford Office Village
Langford Lane
Oxford, OX5 1LQ United Kingdom
01865 379 892
01865 379 946 (fax)
www.thebfa.org

Bulgarian Franchise Association
25 A Ochrid Street
9000-Varna, Bulgaria
Attn: Ms. Lubka Kolarova, President
(359) 52-256-891
(359) 52-256-891 (fax)
www.bulfra.hit.bg/

Canadian Franchise Association
Ms. Lorraine McLachlan, President & CEO
5399 Eglinton Avenue West, Suite 116
Toronto, Ontario, Canada M9C 5K6
(416) 695-2896
(416) 695-1950 (fax)
www.cfa.ca

Ceska Asociace Franchisingu
Hana Jurášková, Association Manager
Opletalova 6—budova Agropolu
11000 Praha 1, Czechoslovakia
(42) 2-242-444-509
(42) 2-242-444-935 (fax)
http://www.czech-franchise.cz/

Association Colombiana De Franquicias
Mr. Jorge Barragan, President

Cra. 100 11-90 Torre Lili, Of. 606
Santiago de Cali, Colombia
(57) 2339-2163
(57) 2339-2166 (fax)
www.centercourt.com/acolfran/

Danish Franchise Association
Mr. Finn Birkegaard, Executive Director
Lyngbyvej 20
DK-2100 Copenhagen, Denmark
(45) 3678-5822
(45) 3649-9898 (fax)
www.franchiseforeningen.dk

European Franchise Federation
179 Avenue Louise
B 1050 Brussels, Belgium
(32) 2520-1607
(32) 2520-1735 (fax)
www.eff-franchise.com

Finnish Franchising Association
Suomen Franchising-Yhdistys ry
Lonnrotinkatu 22 A 2
00120 Helsinki, Finland
358-9-5865847
www.franchising.fi

French Franchise Federation
Ms. Chantal Zimmer, Executive Director
60, rue La Boetie
Paris 75008, France
(33) 1-5375-2225
(33) 1-5375-2220 (fax)
www.franchise-fff.com

German Franchise Association
Mr. Torben Leif Brodersen, Manager
Deutscher Franchsine-Verband e.V.
Luisenstr, 41
10117 Berlin, Germany
(49) 30-278 902-0
(49) 30-278 902-15 (fax)
www.dfv-franchise.de

Handelen Hovedorganisasjon
Postboks 2483, Solli

Oslo 2 0202, Norway
Attn: Mr. Per Reidarson, President
(47) 22-558220
(47) 22-558225 (fax)

Hong Kong Franchise Association
Ms. Charlotte Chow, Senior Manager
22/F Unit A United Centre
95 Queensway, Hong Kong
(852) 2529-9229
(852) 2527-9843 (fax)
www.franchise.org.hk

Hungarian Franchise Association
1121 Budapest, Kútvölgyi út 68
Hungary
(361) 391-7313
(361) 274-4643 (fax)
www.franchise.hu

Indonesia Franchise Association (AFI)
Sekretariat AFI
J1. Darmawangsa X/A
19 Kebayoran Baru
Jakarta 12150, Indonesia
(62) 21-739-5577
(62) 21-723-4761 (fax)

Irish Franchise Association
Kandoy House
2 Fairview Strand
Dublin 3, Ireland
(353) 1-8134555
(353) 1-8134575 (fax)
http://www.irishfranchiseassociation.com/http://www.franchiseindo
nesia.org/

Israel Franchise & Distribution Association
P.O. Box 3093
Herzeliya 46590, Israel
Attn: Michael Emery, Chairman of the Board
(972) 9-576-631
(972) 9-576-631 (fax)

Italian Franchise Association
Via Melchiorre Gioia, 70
20125 Milan, Italy
Italo Bussoli, General Secretary

(39) 2-29003779
(39) 2-6555919 (fax)
http://www.assofranchising.it

Japan Franchise Association
3-6-2 Toranomon, Minato-ku,
Tokyo 105-0001, Japan
(81) 303-5777-8701
(81) 303-5777-8711 (fax)
http://jfa.jfa-fc.or.jp/

Kazakhstan Franchise Association
Andrey Zahrov Kazaf @mail.ru

Malaysian Franchise Association
1st Floor Wisma Motor, 339 Jalan Tuanku Abdul Rahman
50100 Kuala Lumpur, Malaysia
(60) 3-2697-1557
(60) 3-2697-1559 (fax)
http://www.mfa.org.my/

Mexican Franchise Association
Insurgentes Sur 1783, Desp. 101 1er. Piso
Col. Guadalupe Inn, Del. Alvaro Obregon
C.P. 01020, DF 01020, Mexico
(52) 5-661-2040
(52) 5-661-2800 (fax)
http://www.franquiciasdemexico.org/

Middle East Franchise & Distribution Association
P.O. Box 3093
Herzeliya 46590, Israel
Attn: Michael Emery, Chairman of the Board
(972) 9-576-631
(972) 9-576-631 (fax)

Netherlands Franchise Association
Mr. Andre W.M. Brouwer, Managing Director
Boomberglaan 12
1217 RR Hilversum
The Netherlands
(31) 35-624-2300
(31) 35-624-9194 (fax)
http://www.nfv.nl

Franchise Association of New Zealand Inc.
Level 1, 399 Khyber Pass Road
Newmarket, Auckland, 1023

New Zealand
64-9-523-4452
64-9-523-4446 (fax)
http://www.franchiseassociation.org.nz/

Polish Franchise Association
16 Brazownicza St
01-381 WarsawPoland
(48) 22-5608020
(48) 22-5608021 (fax)
http://franchise.org.pl/

Associacao Portuguesa Da Franchise
Sintra Business Park Edificio 1, 2D
2710-089 SintraPortugal
(35) 121-319-2938
(35) 121-319-2939 (fax)
http://www.apf.org.pt/

Romanian Franchise Association
Calea Victorieri Nr. 95, Et. 4, Ap. 16, Sect. 1
Bucharest, Romania
Attn: Violeta Popovici, Chief Executive
(401) 3126889/6180186
(401) 3126890 (fax)

Russian Franchise Association
2nd Proezd Perova Poly
Russia, Moscow 11114
(095) 305-5877, 306 2526
(095) 305-5850 (fax)
franch@matrix.rperkovrarf@mtu-net.ru

Franchising and Licensing Association (Singapore)
230 Victoria Street
#07-03 Burgis Junction Office Tower
Singapore 188024
(65) 6333-0292
(65) 6333-0962 (fax)
www.flasingapore.org

Franchise Association of South Africa
Postnet 256
Private Bag X4
Bedfordview 2008
South Africa
(27) 11-615-0359
(27) 11-615-3679 (fax)

Swedish Franchise Association
Anders Svensson, Executive Director
Sofierogatan 3A
SE-412 54 Gothenburg
Sweden
(46) 31-40-55-10
(46) 31-811-072 (fax)
www.franchiseforeningen.se

Swiss Franchise Association
Stockerstrasse 38
CH-8002 Zurich
Switzerland
(41) 44-208-25-55
(41) 44-208-25-26 (fax)
www.franchiseverband.ch

*UFRAD—Turkish Franchising
Association*
5 yol Mahallesi I[uf53]nönü Caddesi No:40 Sefaköy
Küçükçekmece
Istanbul, Turkey
(90) 212-599-17-84
(90) 212-425-57-59 (fax)
http://www.franchisedunyasi.com

Ukrainian Franchise Association
Mark G. Zarkhin, President and Founder
info@franchising.org.ua
http://www.franchising.org.ua

United States International Franchise Association
1501 K Street N.W.
Suite 350
Washington, D.C. 20005
(202) 628-8000
(202) 628-0812 (fax)
http:/www.franchise.org

Yugoslav Franchise Association—YUFA
21000 Novi Sad
Mokranjceva 28, Yugoslavia
Attn: Dr. Zdravko Glusica, President
(381) 21-614-232
(381) 21-614-232 (fax)

Federal Agencies

Federal Trade Commission, Washington, DC 20852

In addition to the preceding agencies, all major federal departments and agencies have an Office of Small and Disadvantaged Business Utilization (OSDBU), which is responsible for ensuring that an equitable share of government contracts are awarded to small and minority businesses. Sample OSDBU office phone numbers within selected agencies are:

OSDBU Directors

Cabinet Agencies

Department of Defense
Office of Small Business Programs
Crystal Gateway North
Suite 406—West Tower
201 12th Street South
Arlington, VA 22202
(703) 604-0157
(703) 604-0025 (fax)
http://www.acq.osd.mil/osbp/

Ron Poussard, Director, OSDBU
Department of the Air Force
The Pentagon
SASSB 1060 Air Force
Washington, DC 20330-1060
(703) 696-1103
(703) 696-1170 (fax)
www.selltoairforce.org

Tracey L. Pinson, Director, OSDBU
Department of the Army
The Pentagon
Room 3B514
Washington, DC 20310-0106
(703) 697-2868
(703) 693-3898 (fax)
www.sellingtoarmy.info
tracey.pinson@hqda.army.mil

Thomas D. Ray, Director, OSDBU
Defense Logistics Agency
8725 John J. Kingman Road

DB Room 1127
Fort Belvoir, VA 22060-6221
(703) 767-1652
(703) 767-1670 (fax)

Tim Foreman, Director, OSDBU
Department of the Navy
720 Kennon Street SE
Washington Navy Yard
Washington, DC 20374-5015
(202) 685-6485
(202) 685-6865 (fax)
www.donhq.navy.mil/OSBP/

James House, Director, OSDBU
Department of Agriculture
14th & Independence Avenue SW
1566 South Building
Washington, DC 20250-9501
(202) 720-7117
(202) 720-3001 (fax)
USDA Web site: www.usda.gov
OSDBU Web site: www.usda.gov/osdbu
JamesE.House@usda.gov

La Juene Desmukes, Director, OSDBU
Department of Commerce
14th & Constitution Avenue NW
Room H-6411
Washington, DC 20230
(202) 482-1472
(202) 482-0501 (fax)
www.osec.doc.gov/osdbu/
ldesmukes@doc.gov

Kristi Wilson, PhD, Director, OSDBU
Department of Education
400 Maryland Avenue SW
Room 7050, PCP
Washington, DC 20202-0521
(202) 245-6300
(202) 245-6304 (fax)
www.ed.gov/about/offices/list/ods/osdbu.html
small.business@ed.gov

Mr. Joseph Garcia, Director, OSDBU
Department of Energy
1000 Independence Avenue SW, Room 5B-148

Washington, DC 20585
(202) 586-7377
(202) 586-5488 (fax)
http://smallbusiness.doe.gov/

Debbie Ridgely, Director, OSDBU
Department of Health and Human Services
200 Independence Avenue SW
Room 360G—Hubert H. Humphrey Building
Washington, DC 20201
(202) 690-7235
(202) 260-4872 (fax)
www.hhs.gov/osdbu
Debbie.Ridgely@hhs.gov

Lans Field, Director, OSDBU
Department of Housing and
Urban Development
451 7th Street SW, Room 10156
Washington, DC 20410
(202) 708-1428
(202) 708-7642 (fax)
http://www.hud.gov/offices/osdbu/index.cfm

Mark Oliver, Director, OSDBU
Department of the Interior
1849 C Street NW, MS 2252 MIB
Washington, DC 20240
(202) 208-3493
(202) 208-7444 (fax)
www.doi.gov/osdbu

David Sutton, Director, OSDBU
Department of Justice
1331 Pennsylvania Avenue NW
National Place Bldg., Room 1010
Washington, DC 20530
(202) 616-0523
(202) 616-1717 (fax)
www.usdoj.gov/jmd/osdbu/

Jose Lira, Director, OSDBU
Department of Labor
200 Constitution Avenue NW
Room C 2318
Washington, DC 20210
(202) 693-6460
(202) 693-6485 (fax)
http://www.dol.gov/osbp/index.htm

Shapleigh Driscoll, Director, OSDBU
Department of State
Bldg. SA6, Room L-500
Washington, DC 20522-0602
(703) 875-6822
(703) 875-6825 (fax)
http://www.state.gov/m/a/sdbu/

Teresa L.G. Lewis, Director, OSDBU
Department of the Treasury
1500 Pennsylvania Avenue NW
Mail Code: 655 15th/6099
Washington, DC 20220
(202) 622-0530
(202) 927-4963 (fax)
http://www.treasury.gov/offices/management/dcfo/osdbu/

Brandon Neal, Director, OSDBU
Department of Transportation
1200 New Jersey Avenue SE
Washington, DC 20590
(202) 366-1930
(202) 366-7228 (fax)
osdbuweb.dot.gov

Gail Wegner, Acting Director, OSDBU
Department of Veterans Affairs
810 Vermont Avenue NW
Washington, DC 20420
(202) 461-4300
(202) 461-4301 (fax)
www.va.gov/osdbu

Other Independent Agencies

Mauricio Vera, Director, OSDBU
Agency for International Development
Ronald Reagan Building, USAID/OSDBU/MRC
1300 Penn Avenue NW
Room 5.8C
Washington, DC 20523
(202) 712-1500
(202) 216-3056 (fax)
http://www.usaid.gov/business/small_business/

Jeanette Brown, Director, OSDBU
Environmental Protection Agency
1200 Penn Avenue NW
Mail Code 1230T

Washington, DC 20460
(202) 566-2075
(202) 566-0266 (fax)
www.epa.gov/osdbu

Joe McAllibaugh, Director
Federal Emergency Management Agency
500 C Street SW, Room 350
Washington, DC 20472
(202) 646-2500
(202) 646-3846 (fax)

Jean Sefchick, Chief, Procurement
Federal Trade Commission
6th & Pennsylvania Avenue NW
Room H-700
Washington, DC 20580
(202) 326-2258
(202) 326-3529 (fax)
www.ftc.gov

Glenn Delgado, Assistant Administrator, OSDBU
*National Aeronautics and Space
Administration*
NASA Office of Small Business Programs
300 E Street SW
Washington, DC 20546
(202) 358-2088
(202) 358-3261 (fax)
http://www.osbp.nasa.gov/

George Leininger, OSDBU
Office of Personnel Management
1900 E Street NW
Room 1330D
Washington, DC 20415
(202) 606-2083
(202) 606-1464 (fax)
www.opm.gov

U.S. Small Business Administration (SBA)
409 Third Street SW
Washington, D.C. 20416
(800) 827-5722
www.sba.gov

Miscellaneous Agencies

Ritchie Vinson, Director, OSDBU
Corporation for National and Community Service

1201 N.Y. Avenue NW, Room 8409
Washington, DC 20525
(202) 606-6988
(202) 606-3488 (fax)

Mark Pitra, Director, OSDBU
Export-Import Bank of the U.S.
811 Vermont Avenue NW, Room 1023
Washington, DC 20571
(202) 565-3338
(202) 565-3528 (fax)

Althea A. Kireilis, Director, OSDBU
Executive Office of the President
725 17th Street NW, Room 5001
Washington, DC 20503
(202) 395-7669
(202) 395-1155 (fax)

Dennis Dorsey, Procurement Director
Federal Communications Commission
445 12th Street SW, Room 1-A-524
Washington, DC 20554
(202) 418-0992

Ronald H. Langston, Director, OSDBU, National Director Minority Business
Development
Minority Business Development
Agency
Department of Commerce
Room 5065
14th & Constitution Avenue NW
Washington, DC 20230
(202) 482-1712
(202) 482-2696 (fax)

Corenthis Kelley, Director, OSDBU
Office of Small Business and Civil Rights
Nuclear Regulatory Commission
11545 Rockville Pike, MS T2 F-18
Rockville, MD 20852
(301) 415-7380
(301) 415-5953 (fax)
http://www.nrc.gov/about-nrc/overview.html

Michael Gerich, Deputy Associate Administrator
Office of Federal Procurement Policy
725 17th Street NW, Room 9013

Washington, DC 20503
(202) 395-6811
(202) 395-3242 (fax)
www.financenet.gov

James D. Regan, Director, OSDBU
Procurement Technical Assistance
Center Program
George Mason University
4031 University Drive, Suite 200
Fairfax, VA 22030
(703) 277-7700
(703) 352-8195 (fax)
www.gmu.edu/gmu/PTAP

Rudy D. Watley, Manager, Supplier Diversity Program
Smithsonian Institute
P.O. Box 37012
VB RM 8100 MRC 921
Washington, DC 20013
(202) 633-6430
watleyr@si.edu

Steven R. Ayers, Sr. Manager, OSDBU
Tennessee Valley Authority
1101 Market Street
WR3J-C
Chattanooga, TN 37402-2801
(423) 751-7203
(423) 751-7613 (fax)

Janice Williams-Hopkins, Supplier Diversity Manager
U.S. Postal Service
475 L'Enfant Plaza West SW
Room 4430
Washington, DC 20260-5616
(202) 268-4633
(202) 268-4012 (fax)
http://www.usps.com/purchasing/supplierdiversity/diversitymenu.htm

Henry Valiulis, Director, OSDBU
R. R. Retirement Board
844 N. Rush Street
Chicago, IL 60611
(312) 751-4565
(312) 751-4923 (fax)
www.rrb.gov

Other Agencies

Export-Import Bank (Eximbank)
811 Vermont Avenue NW
Washington, D.C. 20571
(800) 565-3946

Offers financing assistance for potential exporters and companies of all sizes interested in doing business abroad.

U.S. Department of Commerce (DOC)
1401 Constitution Avenue NW
Washington, D.C. 20230
(202) 482-2000

Offers a wide variety of programs and services relating to economic development, international trade, and minority business. The U.S. Patent and Trademark Office (800-786-9199) is a division of the DOC that processes federal patent and trademark applications and publishes various resources on the protection of intellectual property.

State Agencies

Although a comprehensive state-by-state directory is beyond the scope of this chapter, virtually every state has at least one office or agency that is responsible for coordinating programs and assistance for small and minority-owned businesses. These various state programs offer a wide range of services, from technical assistance to advocacy to financial support. Each state houses the small business division in a slightly different place, but a safe place to start is with a call to the state's Department of Commerce or Department of Economic Development. A few states, such as California (916-324-1295), Connecticut (860-258-4200), Illinois (217-524-5856), and Minnesota (800-657-3858), have a stand-alone Office of Small Business. Many states offer training programs, seminars, publications, and even tax breaks to foster and encourage the growth of small businesses. The Chambers of Commerce in each state are also an excellent starting point for determining the availability and extent of small business development programs in a given region.

Trade Associations

Literally thousands of trade associations, networking groups, venture clubs, and other organizations directly or indirectly focus on the needs of small business owners, entrepreneurs, growing companies, women-owned businesses, minority-owned businesses, importers and exporters, and virtually every other group that shares common interests. Some of the more established groups with a genuine nationwide presence and solid track record are:

Alliance of Independent Store Owners and Professionals (AISOP)
3725 Multifoods Tower
Minneapolis, MN 55401
(612) 340-1568

AISOP was organized to protect and promote fair postal and legislative policies for small business advertisers. Most of its 4,000 + members are independent small businesses that rely on reasonable third-class mail rates to
promote their businesses and contact customers in their trade areas.

American Association for Entrepreneurs
http://www.aabpe.com/

The American Entrepreneurs Association was established to provide small
business owners with benefits and discounts that are generally reserved for
big businesses, such as express shipping, health insurance, and long-dis-
tance telephone rates).

International Franchise Association (IFA)
1501 K Street NW, Suite 350
Washington, D.C. 20005
(202) 628-8000
www.franchise.org

The IFA serves as a resource center for current and prospective franchisees
and franchisors, the media, and the government. The IFA has promoted programs that expand opportunities for women and minorities in franchising.

National Association of Development Companies (NADCO)
6764 Old McLean Village Dr.
McLean, VA 22101-3906
(703) 748-2575
chris@nadco.org
www.nadco.org
Executive Director: Christopher L. Crawford

NADCO is the trade group of community-based, non-profit organizations that
promote small business expansion and job creation through the SBA's 504
loan program, known as Certified Development Companies (CDC).

National Association for Female Executives (NAFE)
135 W. 50th Street, 16th Floor
New York, NY 10020
(212) 445-6235
www.nafe.com

Through education and networking programs, NAFE helps women share the
resources and techniques needed to succeed in the competitive business
world.

National Association of Investment Companies (NAIC)
1300 Pennsylvania Avenue NW
Suite 700
Washington, D.C. 20004
(202) 204-3001
www.naicvc.com

NAIC is the industry association for venture capital firms, which dedicate their financial resources to investment in minority businesses.

National Association of Manufacturers (NAM)
1331 Pennsylvania Avenue NW
Suite 1500 North
Washington, D.C. 20004
(202) 637-3000
www.nam.org

NAM serves as the voice of the manufacturing community and is active on all issues concerning manufacturing, including legal system reform, regulatory restraint, and tax reform.

National Association for the Self-Employed (NASE)
2121 Precinct Line Road
Hurst, TX 76054
(800) 232-6273
www.nase.org

NASE helps its members become more competitive by providing over 100 benefits that save money on services and equipment. NASE's members consist primarily of small business owners with few or no employees.

National Association of Small Business Investment Companies (NASBIC)
1100 H St NW
Suite 610
Washington, DC 20005
(202) 628-5055
(202) 628-5080 (fax)
bpalmer@nasbic.org
www.nasbic.org

NASBIC assists its members with attaining beneficial regulations, policies, and low-cost capital.

National Association of Women Business Owners (NAWBO)
601 Pennsylvania Ave NW
South Building, Suite 900
Washington, DC 20004
1-800-556-2926
(202) 403-3788 (fax)
national@nawbo.org
Web Site: www.nawbo.org

NAWBO uses its collective influence to broaden opportunities for women in business, and it is the only dues-based national organization representing the interests of all women entrepreneurs in all types of business.

National Business League (NBL)
1629 K Street NW, Suite 605
Washington, DC 20006
(202) 466-5483
http://www.eaglenews.com/NBL/NBLHome.html

NBL is primarily involved in business development among African Americans and serves as a voice for black business on Capitol Hill and in the federal government.

National Federation of Independent Business (NFIB)
1201 F Street NW, Suite 200
Washington, DC 20004
(202) 554-9000
(202) 554-0496 (fax)
Toll-Free: (800) 552-6342
www.nfib.com

NFIB disseminates educational information about free enterprise, entrepreneurship, and small business. NFIB represents more than 60,000 small and independent businesses before legislatures and government agencies at the federal and state level.

National Small Business United (NSBU)
1156 15th Street NW, Suite 1100
Washington, D.C. 20005
(202) 293-8830

The NSBU is a membership-based association of business owners that presents small business's point of view to all levels of government and the Congress.

National Venture Capital Association
1655 N Fort Myer Drive, Suite 850
Arlington, VA 22209
(703) 524-2549
www.nvca.org

The mission is to define, serve, and promote the interests of the venture capital industry, to increase the understanding of the importance of venture capital to the U.S. economy, and to stimulate the flow of equity capital to emerging growth and developing companies.

U.S. Chamber of Commerce
1615 H Street NW
Washington, D.C. 20062

(202) 659-6000
www.uschamber.com

The U.S. Chamber of Commerce represents 215,000 businesses, 3,000 state and local chambers of commerce, 1,200 trade and professional associations, and 72 American Chambers of Commerce abroad. It works with these groups to support national business interests and includes a Small Business Center (202-463-5503).

U.S. Hispanic Chamber of Commerce
1424 K Street NW, Suite 40
Washington, D.C. 20005
(202) 842-1212
www.ushcc.com

The Hispanic Chamber advocates the business interests of Hispanics and develops minority business opportunities with major corporations and at all levels of government.

In addition, there are a wide variety of special-purpose or industry-specific trade associations or foundations:

American Farm Bureau Federation
600 Maryland Avenue SW
Suite 1000W
Washington, DC 20024
(202) 406-3600
www.fb.com

American Financial Services Association
919 18th Street NW, Suite 300
Washington, D.C. 20006
(202) 296-5544
www.afsaonline.org/

American Society of Association Executives (ASAE)
1575 Eye Street NW
Washington, D.C. 20005
(202) 626-2723
www.asaecenter.org

Association of American Publishers
50 F Street NW, 4th Floor
Washington, D.C. 20001
(202) 347-3375
www.publishers.org

Council of Growing Companies
4903 Auburn Avenue
Bethesda, MD 20814
(800) 929-3165

Entrepreneurs' Organization (EO)
500 Montgomery Street, Suite 500
Alexandria, VA 22314
(703) 519-6700
(703) 519-1864 (fax)
info@eonetwork.org
www.eonetwork.org

National Association of Convenience Stores
1600 Duke Street
Alexandria, VA 22314
(703) 684-3600
www.nacsonline.com

National Association of Wholesaler-Distributors
1325 G Street NW, Suite 1000
Washington, D.C. 20005
(202) 872-0885
www.naw.org

National Foundation for Teaching Entrepreneurship to Handicapped and Disadvantaged Youth, Inc. (NFTE)
120 Wall Street, 29th Floor
New York, NY 10005
(212) 232-3333
www.nfte.com

National Restaurant Association
1200 17th Street NW
Washington, D.C. 20036
(202) 331-5900
www.restaurant.org

National Retail Federation
325 Seventh Street NW, Suite 1100
Washington, D.C. 20004
(202) 783-7971
www.nrf.com

Opportunity International
2122 York Road
Suite 150
Oak Brook, IL 60523

(630) 242-4100
www.opportunity.org

Software and Information Industry Association
1090 Vermont Avenue NW, 6th Floor
Washington, D.C. 20005
(202) 289-7442
www.siia.net

TechAmerica
601 Pennsylvania Ave NW
Suite 600, North Building
Washington, D.C. 20004
(202) 682-9110
www.aeanet.org

Other Miscellaneous Resources in Cyberspace

Over the past few years, hundreds of Web sites have been developed to provide resourceful support to franchisors and entrepreneurs. Web sites come
and go quickly and change often, so it's probably best to use one of the popular search engines and enter key words to narrow the scope of your search or
resource need. Next time you are surfing the Net, here are some Web sites
worth visiting:

Name	Internet Address	Features
American Society of Association Executives	http://www.asaenet.org	Represents approximately 10,000 associations serving more than 287 million people and companies worldwide and vendors that offer products and services to the association community, and also is an advocate for the non-profit sector
Ask the Lawyer	http://www.fairmeasures.com	A Web site that offers practical advice for complying with employee law and preventing lawsuits
Business Journal	http://www.amcity.com (home page)	Small Business Handbook section features expert advice for small businesses on topics such as sales and marketing, technical, business financing, and tips on shop-

		ping for business products and services
BusinessLink On-Line	http://www.buslink.com	Provider of technology hardware
CareerBuilder	http:///www.careerbuilder.com	A database of national job offerings
E-Span	http://www.espan.com	Used by human resource professionals to post jobs worldwide;' provides reference materials for human resource practitioners
IFX International	http://www.centercourt.com	Articles and information on franchising
Inc. Online	http://www.inc.com	Allows users to (1) read the current issue or browse through *Inc.* magazine's extensive archives; (2) interact with other entrepreneurs, experts, and *Inc.* editors
Info Franchise News, Inc.	http://www.infonews.com	Provides information about franchising, franchisors, and being a franchisee.
Interbiznet	http://www.interbiznet.com	
Legaldocs	http://legaldocs.com	Low-cost legal forms
Monster Board	http://www.monster.com	A variety of issues, from hiring to staffing to other related topics for human resource executives
Red Herring Magazine	http://www.redherring.com/	An integrated media company that provides a link for connecting people, companies, and industries and offers unique blend of commentary, financial analysis, and access to the leaders of emerging technologies and markets
SBA Women in Business	http://www.sba.gov/aboutsba/sbaprograms/onlinewbc/index.html	Promotes the growth of women-owned businesses through programs that address business training and technical assistance, and provides access to credit and

		capital, federal contracts, and international trade opportunities
SHRM (Society for Human Resource Management)	http://www.shrm.org	A variety of services and products for human resource professionals
Income Opportunities Magazine	http://www.incomeops.com	Dedicated to helping those interested in making money with their own business to find the best work, from home business opportunity or part-time Internet business, and also provides free tools, resources, and articles to help small businesses
Span Link Communications	http://www.spanlink.com	Provides systems integration products and services ranging from consulting to custom development to integration to support
Switchboard	http://www.switchboard.com	Electronic telephone white and yellow pages, maps, and city guides
Venture Capital Institute	http://vcinstitute.org	Wide range of venture capital resources

Franchise Law Internet Resources

American Association of Franchisees and Dealers
www.aafd.org

CCH Business Franchise Guide
http:/business.cch.com

Federal Trade Commission—Franchise and Business Opportunities
http://www.ftc.gov/bcp/franchise/netfran.shtm

Franchise Law Journal
http://new.abanet.org/Forums/franchising

Franchise Times
www.franchisetimes.com

INDEX